Family, Socialization and Interaction Process

FAMILY,

Socialization and Interaction Process

By Talcott Parsons

AND Robert F. Bales

IN COLLABORATION WITH

James Olds, Morris Zelditch, Jr., AND Philip E. Slater

THE FREE PRESS, GLENCOE, ILLINOIS

Preface

The collection of papers brought together in this volume is at first sight somewhat heterogeneous. It is true that in the social sciences, the sociology of the family in our own society, the comparative study of kinship, the experimental study of small groups, and the psychology of personality have tended to be traditionally treated as distinct problem areas, as fields of study by different groups of specialists. Indeed they have tended to be distributed among three separate disciplines; the first has traditionally been a field of sociology, the second of anthropology, and the last of psychology, whereas the study of small groups is at present shared between sociologists and psychologists.

This division of labor has had its justification during the phases of scientific development of the past and to a limited extent, we believe, still does. But at the same time the developments which have recently been taking place in all of these areas have opened up opportunities to explore intimate interrelations between the different fields of interest in a way which could not be done if each of the classes of specialists we have spoken of simply continued like the cobbler to stick to his last.

In the first instance, our interest is in the functioning of the modern American family and its place in the structure of our society. A discussion of some of the leading facts and problems of this empirical area will be presented in the first part of the book. It will be evident not only from these considerations but even on a more common-sense level, that perhaps the most important function of the family lies in its contribution to the socialization of children. In view of this fact an analysis of the family with special reference to its functions as a socializing agency should contribute importantly to our understanding, both of the family itself and of its relations to the rest of the social structure in which it exists. But one cannot effectively study the family as a socializing agency without an understanding of the process of socialization itself in its psychological

[*v*]

aspects, i. e., the process of development of the personality of the child. This accounts for our paying so much attention to psychological problems. It seems to us that a clear understanding of this aspect of the total problem-complex cannot fail to contribute to our understanding of the sociological aspects of the family.

Indeed, it is our experience, as documented in the material which follows, that the relations of interdependence and interpenetration of these problems are so close, that any depth of exploration on the one side must lead directly into deeper preoccupation with the other. Thus, from consideration of the problems of socialization in the family in our society we have been led, not only into analysis of the psychological aspects of the developmental process, but of certain problems of the organization of the personality as a system and of the mechanisms by which processes within it operate. In all this we have, of course, attempted to make the best possible use of established psychological knowledge. But we have also found that at many points a sociological perspective could throw further light on problems which are important from a psychological point of view, so that the contribution of both phases of the subject has been mutual, and not all in one direction.

We have, we think, learned much about the sociology of the family through studying the process of socialization and the organization of personality in the closest interrelations with the psychology of personality. But we feel that other sources of sociological understanding should not be neglected. One of these, the study of the articulation of the family with the other parts of the structure of the society in which it functions, is not made a subject of separate study in the present volume, though it will concern us at a number of points, particularly at the beginning of our discussion and in the analysis of the later phases of the socialization process. But two of these other sources are also of great importance and are dealt with specifically in two of the chapters of this book. The family is, among differentiated sub-systems of societies, in many respects a unique type of group or social system. Indeed, emphasis on its uniqueness has tended so to dominate sociological study of the family, that it has inhibited the attempt to find elements which are common to it and to other types of group.

In this connection we had, in previous work, however, been struck by the possible importance of the fact that the family—the "nuclear" family, that is—is everywhere a *small* group. The tendency has been to take this for granted as a simple result of the biological composition of the family, since a human couple does not typically have very many children, and hence not bother to analyze it further. But in the course of Bales's early studies of the structure of small task-oriented groups certain striking analogies to the structure of the nuclear family emerged.[1] This gave us the idea that the parents tend to constitute a "leadership coalition" in the family, and that the members of this coalition perform roles differentiated from each other in the same fundamental way as in the dual leadership of the small group; namely, in terms of the greater "instrumental" specialization of the "idea" man, analogous to the husband-father, and the greater "expressive" specialization of the "best liked" man, analogous to the wife-mother. It, therefore, seemed worth while further to explore this relationship between the structure of the family and that of the experimental small group, in the hope of its throwing more light on the structure of the family and its functioning. Chapter V by Bales and Slater presents and analyzes new data on the development of differentiated role structures in the small group and attempts to evaluate the significance of these findings for the family.

In a broad way there seems to be a good fit between the leadership structure of the small experimental group and the nuclear family in our society. But a second question immediately arises, that of how far this is a "culture-bound" phenomenon, the relevance of which is limited to our own society, or at best it and those which are structurally very similar to it. We have long been aware that kinship systems vary over a wide range, and that the American kinship system is of a distinctive and rather rare type.[2] But the nuclear family is only part of the kinship system, and there is no inherent reason why it should not turn out to be less variable than is the larger system of which it is a part.

---

1. Reported by R. F. Bales, "The Equilibrium Problem in Small Groups," in *Working Papers in the Theory of Action*, by T. Parsons, R. F. Bales, and E. A. Shils, (Glencoe, Ill.: The Free Press, 1953), Chapter IV, pp. 149-50.

2. Cf. G. P. Murdock, *Social Structure* (New York: Macmillan Co., 1949), pp. 226-7.

With particular reference to the problem of the relevance of the instrumental-expressive axis for the differentiation of the roles of the parents of each sex in the nuclear family, Zelditch has hence attempted, in Chapter VI, a preliminary study of cross-cultural materials. Broadly we may say that he finds a high level of constancy in this particular respect, which is consistent with the attribution of a substantial part in the phenomenon to the exigencies of effective functioning of the family as a small group, rather than exclusively to the biologically constitutional "nature" of the sexes.

The above considerations give the rationale for including treatments of diverse subjects such as we have in a book which is empirically focussed on the understanding of the place of the family in American society. We recognize that in bringing all these things together in one study we are following an unorthodox path. We hope that the results of our attempt will persuade the reader of the fruitfulness of sometimes breaking over the traditional lines of specialization.

In its empirical aspect we regard this volume, more than anything else, as a study in the sociology of the American family. But this empirical interest is closely interwoven with an interest in the development of theory, which we feel flows directly from our previous theoretical preoccupations. Broadly speaking, these theoretical interests center on two principal points which are intimately related to one another. The first of these concerns the interrelations of the three fundamental reference points of the general theory of action: social system, personality and culture. With special reference to the relations of social systems and personalities, we feel that the study of the process of socialization in the family constitutes a particularly strategic case. This is because we are here dealing with the relations of the two classes of system on the simplest possible level. By virtue of being a small group, the nuclear family is relatively a very simple social system, and we believe this fact to be of the greatest importance for its functioning as an agency of socialization and of personality stabilization. At the same time we believe that an essential aspect of the development of personality is a process of structural differentiation; hence, this system also will, in its earlier stages of development, be a relatively simple system in a structural sense. We are, therefore, in early socialization in the family, dealing with a situation where both the systems concerned are relatively simple. We feel that in these circumstances it should be easier to discern certain fundamental relationships between them than it is on the more complex levels where for example problems of "national character" arise. There is also an essential "cultural" aspect of this problem area which we feel can advantageously be studied in this empirical setting.

The second major theoretical problem focus concerns the nature of the processes of structural differentiation in systems of action, both personalities and social systems. Our material on socialization will provide us with an intensive view of some aspects of this process in the personality system, and the ways in which it is linked with the structure of the social situation in which it occurs. It will be of crucial importance to our analysis that the process of personality differentiation occurs in a social situation which has a certain special type of differentiated structure of its own. With respect to the process of differentiation itself, our most closely analogous material for the social system will come from the small group, which has advantages similar to the family as a field of observation. But we hope that bringing material from these sources together with our analysis of the more macroscopic aspects of social structure, will make it possible to make some important generalizations about developmental process with special reference to its structural aspects.

The work which has gone into the production of this volume involves not only the association of the authors with each other, but with other persons in a variety of research projects which have been in part independent, and in part interdependent. Hence we are indebted not only to each other, but to a good many of the people and sources of support involved in the various projects concerned.

Chapters II and III have grown, in considerable measure, out of Parsons' contribution to a study of the social mobility of high school boys in which he has collaborated with Samuel A. Stouffer and Florence Kluckhohn. The attempt in this part of the larger study has been to develop a theoretical basis for the formulation of hypotheses which would make it possible to predict, from knowledge of the microscopic variations of the structure of his family of orientation, the probable role a boy would assume in the occupational system as an adult. For this to be possible a great deal of clarification of the theoretical bases of the relations between family structure and personality development proved to be necessary. This task of clarification was undertaken largely through an informal "work group" seminar, which was in part a subseminar of the general seminar around which the larger study of mobility was organized, but which was also attended by some members of the staff of the Department of Social Relations. Besides the author of the chapters, particularly important contributors through this channel and through individual discussion have been Joseph Berger, William Caudill, Frank E. Jones, Kaspar D. Naegele, Theodore M. Mills, and Bengt G. Rundblad. The author is particularly indebted to all of the members of this group for their contribution and to several for criticism of the manuscript. His debt to Professor Stouffer and Dr. Florence Kluckhohn is also of course great. In addition, Professor Albert J. Reiss of Vanderbilt University made some particularly valuable criticisms of the manuscript.

This part of the book would not have been possible but for the financial support which has been given to the larger study of social mobility by the Harvard Laboratory of Social Relations, the Russell Sage Foundation and the Harvard Graduate School of Education. This help is gratefully acknowledged.

Chapter IV has also grown out of a larger project. Through a grant from the Laboratory of Social Relations the services of James Olds during the year 1952-53 were made available to collaborate with Parsons in exploring the possibilities of codification of the relevant parts of the developing "general theory of action" with some parts of current psychological theory. As a trained social psychologist who also, through his editorship of Part II of *Toward a General Theory of Action*,[3] was thoroughly conversant with that conceptual scheme, Olds was uniquely qualified to undertake such a task. The main results of his work on this project are being published separately in his book, *The Growth and Structure of Motives*.[4] The connections of this work with that which was going on in relation to the study of social mobility was, however, very close, so it was natural to seize the opportunity to draw on Olds's psychological knowledge, and

---

3. *Op. cit.*

4. Glencoe, Illinois: The Free Press, 1955.

his familiarity with the problem area, to work through the problem of the relation of psychological mechanisms to the process of socialization.

Chapter V has grown directly out of, and is an integral part of the results flowing from, the larger program for the study of small group interaction which Robert Bales and his associates have been carrying on for several years in the Harvard Laboratory of Social Relations. This work, at many points, has had affiliations with other programs of work contributing to this volume. On the theoretical side of course it (and Chapter VII) may be regarded as a continuation of the collaboration, the first published documentation of which was the contribution of two of us to the volume *Working Papers in the Theory of Action*.[5] It has benefitted from the financial support and facilities of the Laboratory, and support from the Rand Corporation and from the Rockefeller Foundation, as well as from the contributions of many of Bales' associates other than Slater to the general development of this program of research.

Chapter VI, finally, has grown out of Morris Zelditch, Jr.'s interests in the bearings of the General Theory of Action on some of the traditional interests of social anthropology. It has not, however, been directly the result of an organized project of research. The criticism of Professor David M. Schneider, with his wide knowledge of comparative kinship, has been particularly helpful in revision of the earlier draft of this chapter. We are indebted to Mr. Neil J. Smelser for assistance in compiling the statistical material in Chapter I, and to Miss Dorinthe Burkholder who efficiently processed the manuscript. The index and bibliography have been compiled by Morris Zelditch, Jr.

The Authors

---

5. *Op. cit.*

Contents

Figures and Tables

Family, Socialization and Interaction Process

The American Family: Its Relations to Personality and to the Social Structure

BY TALCOTT PARSONS

The American family has, in the past generation or more, been undergoing a profound process of change. There has been much difference of opinion among social scientists, as well as among others concerned, as to the interpretation of these changes. Some have cited facts such as the very high rates of divorce, the changes in the older sex morality, and until fairly recently, the decline in birth rates, as evidence of a trend to disorganization in an absolute sense. Such considerations as these have in turn often been linked with what has sometimes been called the "loss of function" of the family.[1] This refers to the fact that so many needs, for example as for clothing, which formerly were met by family members working in the home, are now met by outside agencies. Thus clothing is now usually bought ready-made; there is much less food-processing in the household, there is a great deal of commercial recreation outside the home, etc.

That changes of a major character have been going on seems to be beyond doubt. That some of them have involved disorgan-

---

1. Emphasized particularly by W. F. Ogburn. See, for instance, Chapter XIII, "The Family and its Functions," *Recent Social Trends in the U. S.*, Report of President's Research Committee on Social Trends, 1933.

ization of a serious character is clear. But we know that major structural changes in social systems always involve strain and disorganization, so the question of evaluating symptoms of disorganization, of which we can regard the high divorce rates as one, involves the question of how much is a general trend to disorganization as such, how much is what may be called the "disorganization of transition."

Certain facts about the most recent phases of development seem to us to throw doubt on the thesis of general disorganization. First, after the post-war peak, the upward trend of divorce rates has been checked, though it is too early to judge what the longer run trend is likely to be.[2] To judge the impact of the instability of marriages, also the distribution of divorces by duration of marriage and by relations to children is just as important as the absolute numbers. As the figures show, by and large divorces are, and continue to be concentrated in the early periods of marriage and in childless couples. Even though married before and divorced, once people settle down to having children there is a relatively high probability that they will stay together.[3]

---

2. *Trends of marriage and divorce rates in U.S.*—1920-1951

(RATES PER 1,000 POPULATION)

Year	Marriage rate	Divorce rate
1920	12.0	1.6
1925	10.3	1.5
1930	9.2	1.6
1935	10.4	1.7
1940	12.1	2.0
1945	12.2	3.5
1950	11.1	2.6

The divorce rate dipped a little lower to 1.3 at the depth of the depression and its high point was 4.3 in 1946. Every year since has shown a drop. The marriage rate reached its peak of 16.4 in 1946 reflecting demobilization but has remained consistently above 10 since.

Source: National Office of Vital Statistics, "Summary of Marriage and Divorce Statistics, United States, 1951," *Vital Statistics—Special Reports, National Summaries,* Vol. 38, No. 5, April 30, 1954.

3. ". . . two-thirds of those couples obtaining divorce are childless; one-fifth have only one child. In fact, there seems to be a definite relationship between childless marriages and divorce. That a relatively small number of children in the United States have divorced parents—may be owing, in part, to the fact that many couples do not stay married long enough to have a large family. Over 35 per cent of those divorced in 1940 had been married less than four years. The average length of marriages ending in divorce is less than six years."

H. E. Barnes and O. M. Ruedi, *The American Way of Life* (New York: Prentice Hall, Inc., 1951) pp. 652-53.

Second, divorce certainly has not led to a general disillusionment with marriage, so that people prefer to stay single or not to try again. In spite of a situation where it has become economically easier for single women to support themselves independently than ever before, the proportion of the population married and living with their spouses is the highest that it has ever been in the history of the census and has risen perceptibly within the recent period.[4]

Third, though down until the mid-thirties there had been a progressive decline in birth rates until on a long-run basis the population was for a time no longer fully reproducing itself, by now it has become clear that the revival of the birth rate which began in the early forties has not been only a matter of catching up the deficit of war-time, but has reached a new plateau on what appears to be a relatively stable basis.[5] This is certainly suggestive of a process of readjustment rather than of a continuous trend of disorganization.

In this connection it should be remembered that the immense increase in the expectancy of life since about the turn of the cen-

---

4. See footnote 2.

5. *Crude Birth Rates, 1915-50, United States*

RATES PER THOUSAND POPULATION

Year	Rate	Year	Rate
1915	29.5	1945	20.4
1920	27.7	1946	24.1
1925	25.1	1947	26.6
1930	21.3	1948	24.9
1935	18.7	1949	24.5
1940	19.4	1950	24.1
1941	20.3	1951	24.5
1942	22.2	1952*	24.6
1943	22.7	1953*	24.7
1944	21.2	*Provisional	

It will be noted that a consistent rise started in 1940. Even the lowest war year was only down to 20.4 (1945) and the rate has remained substantially above the level of the thirties since.

Source: National Office of Vital Statistics, "Summary of Natality Statistics, United States, 1950," *Vital Statistics—Special Reports, National Summaries,* Vol. 37, No. 7, May 19, 1953.

Note: The national office estimates that the slight drop from the 1947 boom (itself caused by demobilization) is accountable by the following: drop in first children because of lowered marriage rates, 1946-49; but rise in births of second, third and fourth children during 1946-49.

Last three years, source: Office of Population Research, Princeton University, and Population Association of America, Inc., *Population Index* (July, 1954).

tury[6] has meant that continuance of the birth rates of that time would have led to a rate of population increase which few could contemplate with equanimity. The transition from a high birth rate-high death rate population economy of most of history to one where low death rates have to be balanced by substantially lower birth rates than before is one of the profoundest adjustments human societies have ever had to make, going as it does to the deepest roots of motivation. In processes of such magnitude it is not unusual for there to be swings of great amplitude to levels which are incompatible with longer-run stability. There is at least a good case for the view that the low birth rates of the nineteen-thirties—not of course confined to the United States—constituted the extreme point of such a swing, and that extrapolating the trend up to that point simply failed to take account of adjustive processes already at work. At any rate, the recent facts have shifted the burden of proof to him who argues that the

---

6. *Estimated average length of life in years:*

ALL RACES, BOTH SEXES, UNITED STATES

1900	47.3
1910	50.0
1920	54.1
1930	59.7
1940	62.7
1950	68.4

Source: National Office of Vital Statistics, "Abridged Life Tables, United States, 1951," *Vital Statistics—Special Reports, National Summaries,* Vol. 38, No. 5, April 30, 1954.

The way birth and death rates have balanced out can be better seen from the following estimates of the net reproduction rate for the United States. It will be seen that during the 1930's the population was not quite reproducing itself but that at present rates a substantial, perhaps indeed an excessive, rate of increase is being maintained.

NET REPRODUCTION RATES FOR U.S.A.

1930-35	0.98
1935-40	0.98
1940	1.03
1941	1.08
1942	1.20
1943	1.25
1944	1.18
1945	1.15
1946	1.37
1947	1.53
1948	1.45
1949	1.45
1950	1.44

Source: Office of Population Research, Princeton University, and Population Association of America, Inc., *Population Index* (April, 1954).

disorganization of the family is bringing imminent race suicide in its wake.

There is a further bit of evidence which may be of significance. The family after all is a residential unit in our society. If the family were breaking up, one would think that this would be associated with a decline of the importance of the "family home" as the preferred place to live of the population. Recent trends of development seem to indicate that far from family homes being "on their way out" there has, in recent years, been an impressive confirmation that even more than before this is the preferred residential pattern. The end of World War II left us with a large deficit of housing facilities. Since then, once the shortages of materials were overcome, there has been an enormouse amount of residential building. In this building, as is indicated by the figures, the single family house occupies an extraordinarily prominent place.[7] It seems that the added mobility given our population by modern means of transportation, especially in making possible a considerable geographical distance between place of residence and place of work, has led to a strengthening of the predilection to have a "home of our own." In the face particularly of a level of geographical and occupational mobility which makes permanence of tenure of a residen-

---

7. *Total new construction value,* 1937-51, *corrected* 1947-49 *values*

(IN MILLIONS)

1937	$13,714
1940	16,873
1943	12,841
1945	8,439
1946	15,546
1947	17,795
1948	20,759
1949	22,180
1950	26,852
1951	26,650

% OF VALUE OF TOTAL NEW CONSTRUCTION OF RESIDENTIAL BUILDING, 1937-51

Type of construction	37	38	39	40	41	42	43	44	45	46	47	48	49	50	51
Private, residential, nonfarm*	21	23	28	29	25	10	9	11	13	28	33	35	32	40	32
Operators' dwellings, farm	1	1	1	2	2	1	1	2	2	3	4	3	3	3	3
TOTAL % for new private residential construction**	22	24	29	31	27	11	10	13	15	31	37	38	35	43	35

*Does not include hotels, dormitories, clubhouses, tourist courts and cabins.
**Does not include new public residential construction, which averages 1-3% during peacetime years, and includes barracks, officers quarters, etc.

It is not possible to find figures which exclude private multiple-family units, but the general evidence is that the proportion of these has decreased, not increased.

Source: Bureau of Labor Statistics, *New Construction, Expenditures 1915-51, Labor Requirements, 1939-51,* 1953.

tial location highly problematical, this is a most impressive phenomenon.

The situation with which we are concerned may be summed up by noting again that, in spite of divorces and related phenomena, Americans recently have been marrying on an unprecedented scale. They have been having children, not on an unprecedented scale, but on one which by contrast with somewhat earlier trends is unlikely to be without significance and, third, they have been establishing homes for themselves as family units on a very large scale. Since the bulk of home-provision has been on the financial responsibility of the couples concerned, it seems unlikely that the having of children is a simple index of irresponsibility, that we have, as Professor Carver used to put it, produced a generation of "spawners" as contrasted with "family-builders."[8]

At various later points in this volume we are going to argue both that there are certain very important elements of constancy in the structure and in the functional significance of the family on a human cultural level, and that these elements of constancy are by no means wholly or even mainly a reflection of its biological composition. But this view is, in our opinion, by no means incompatible with an emphasis, in other respects, on certain important elements of variation in the family. The set of these latter elements on which we wish now to focus attention is that concerned with the level of structural differentiation in the society.

It is a striking fact of sociological discussion that there has been no settled agreement on either of two fundamental problems. One is the problem of the structural and functional relations between the nuclear family on the one hand, and the other elements of the kinship complex in the same society. Structural analysis of kinship is, we feel, just reaching a point where the importance of clear discriminations in this field is coming to be appreciated. Second, there has been no clear conception of what are the important "functions of the family." Procreation and child care are always included, as is some reference to sexual relations, but in addition there are frequent references to "economic" functions, religious functions and various others.

8. T. N. Carver, *Essays in Social Justice* (Cambridge, Mass.: Harvard University Press, 1915).

There has been little attempt to work out the implications of the suggestion that there are certain "root functions" which must be found wherever there is a family or kinship system at all, while other functions may be present or not according to the *kind* of family or kinship system under consideration, and its place in the structure of the rest of the society.

The aspect of this problem in which we are particularly interested concerns its relations to the problem of structural differentiation in societies. It is well known that in many "primitive" societies there is a sense in which kinship "dominates" the social structure; there are few concrete structures in which participation is independent of kinship status. In comparative perspective it is clear that in the more "advanced" societies a far greater part is played by non-kinship structures. States, churches, the larger business firms, universities and professional associations cannot be treated as mere "extensions" of the kinship system.

The process by which non-kinship units become of prime importance in a social structure, inevitably entails "loss of function" on the part of some or even all of the kinship units. In the processes of social evolution there have been many stages by which this process has gone on, and many different directions in which it has worked out.

Our suggestion is, in this perspective, that what has recently been happening to the American family constitutes part of one of these stages of a process of differentiation. This process has involved a further step in the reduction of the importance in our society of kinship units other than the nuclear family. It has also resulted in the transfer of a variety of functions from the nuclear family to other structures of the society, notably the occupationally organized sectors of it. This means that the family has become *a more specialized agency than before,* probably more specialized than it has been in any previously known society. This represents a decline of *certain* features which traditionally have been associated with families; but whether it represents a "decline of the family" in a more general sense is another matter; we think not. We think the trend of the evidence points to the beginning of the relative stabilization of a *new* type of family structure in a new relation to a general social structure, one in which the family is more specialized than before, but not in any general sense less important, because the society is dependent *more* exclusively on it for the performance of *certain* of its vital functions.

We further think that this new situation presents a particularly favorable opportunity to the social scientist. Because we are dealing with a more highly differentiated and specialized agency, it is easier to identify clearly the features of it which are essential on the most general level of cross-cultural significance. The situation is methodologically comparable to the relation between the emergence of the modern type of industrial economy and the problems of economic theory. The high level of differentiation of economic from non-economic processes under modern conditions, has made possible a kind of natural experimental situation which has been crucial to the development of modern economic theory.

The American Family in the Total Society

From this perspective, then, let us review some of the most essential features of the structure of the American family-kinship system in its relation to the rest of the society.

The first feature to be noted is on the level of kinship organization as anthropologists ordinarily treat this; namely the "isolation" of the nuclear family and its relation to "bilaterality" with respect to the lines of descent. This "isolation" is manifested in the fact that the members of the nuclear family, consisting of parents and their still dependent children, ordinarily occupy a separate dwelling not shared with members of the family of orientation of either spouse, and that this household is in the typical case economically independent, subsisting in the first instance from the occupational earnings of the husband-father.[9] It is of course not uncommon to find a surviving parent of one or the other spouse, or even a sibling or cousin of one of them residing with the family, but this is both statistically secondary, and it is clearly not felt to be the "normal" arrangement.[10]

---

9. Cf. R. M. Williams, *American Society*, Chapter IV (New York: Alfred A. Knopf, Inc., 1951). Also T. Parsons, "The Kinship System of the Contemporary United States," *Essays in Sociological Theory* (rev. ed., Glencoe, Ill.: The Free Press, 1954).

10. "Sixty-four per cent of husband and wife families in 1940 had no adult relatives eighteen years old and over living in the home. Very few, about one-eighth,

Of course with the independence, particularly the marriage, of children, relations to the family of orientation are by no means broken. But separate residence, very often in a different geographical community, and separate economic support, attenuate these relations. Furthermore, there is a strong presumption that relations to one family of orientation will not be markedly closer than to the other (though there is a certain tendency for the mother-married daughter relation to be particularly close). This bilaterality is further strongly reinforced by our patterns of inheritance. In the first place the presumption is that a newly married couple will "stand on their own feet," supporting themselves from their own earnings. But so far as property is inherited the pattern calls for equal division between children regardless of birth order or sex, so that the fact or expectation of inheritance does not typically bind certain children to their families of orientation more closely than others. Furthermore, though it is not uncommon for sons to work in their fathers' businesses—almost certainly much less common than it was fifty years ago—this tendency is at least partially matched by the phenomenon of "marrying the boss's daughter," so that no clear unilateral structure can be derived from this fact.

It has been noted that the primary source of family income lies in occupational earnings. It is above all the presence of the modern occupational system and its mode of articulation with the family which accounts for the difference between the modern, especially American, kinship system and *any* found in nonliterate or even peasant societies. The family household is a solidary unit where, once formed, membership and status are ascribed, and the communalistic principle of "to each according to his needs" prevails. In the occupational world, status is achieved by the individual and is contingent on his continuing

---

of the families in which the husband was under thirty-five years of age contained any of these additional adults. . . . Nearly three-fifths of these (adult relatives) were single sons or daughters of the couple who had not left home, of whom most were between eighteen and thirty-four years old. . . . About one-eighth of the adult relatives were married, widowed or divorced parents of the husband or his wife. . . . Thus, all but one-fifth of the adult relatives were children or parents (own or in-law) of the family head and his wife."

Source: P. C. Glick, "The Family Cycle," *American Sociological Review*, Vol. 12, No. 2, April, 1947.

performance. Though of course this is modified in varying respects, there is a high premium on mobility and equality of opportunity according to individual capacity to perform. Over much of the world and of history a very large proportion of the world's ordinary work is and has been performed in the context of kinship units. Occupational organization in the modern sense is the sociological antithesis of this.

This means essentially, that as the occupational system develops and absorbs functions in the society, it *must* be at the expense of the relative prominence of kinship organization as a structural component in one sense, and must also be at the expense of many of what previously have been *functions* of the kinship unit. The double consequence is that the same people, who are members of kinship units, perform economic, political, religious and cultural functions outside the kinship context in occupational roles and otherwise in a variety of other types of organization. But conversely, the members of kinship units must meet many of their needs, which formerly were met in the processes of interaction within the kinship unit, through other channels. This of course includes meeting the need for income with which to purchase the goods and services necessary for family functioning itself.

In this type of society the basic mode of articulation between family and the occupational world lies in the fact that the *same* adults are both members of nuclear families and incumbents of occupational roles, the holders of "jobs." The individual's job and not the products of the coöperative activities of the family as a unit is of course the primary source of income for the family.

Next it is important to remember that the *primary* responsibility for this support rests on the one adult male member of the nuclear family. It is clearly the exceptional "normal" adult male who can occupy a respected place in our society without having a regular "job," though he may of course be "independent" as a professional practitioner or some kind of a "free lance" and not be employed by an organization, or he may be the proprietor of one. That at the bottom of the scale the "hobo" and the sick and disabled are deviants scarcely needs mentioning, while at the other end, among the relatively few who are in a position to "live on their money" there is a notable reluctance to do so. The "playboy" is not a highly respected type and there is no real American equivalent of the older European type of "gentleman" who did not "work" unless he had to.

The occupational role is of course, in the first instance, part of the "occupational system" but it is not only that. It is an example of the phenomenon of "interpenetration" which will be extensively analyzed below. In this connection it is both a role in the occupational system, *and* in the family; it is a "boundary-role" between them. The husband-father, in holding an acceptable job and earning an income from it is performing an essential function or set of functions for his family (which of course includes himself in one set of roles) as a system. The status of the family in the community is determined probably more by the "level" of job he holds than by any other single factor, and the income he earns is usually the most important basis of the family's standard of living and hence "style of life." Of course, as we shall see, he has other very important functions in relation both to wife and to children, but it is fundamentally by virtue of the importance of his occupational role *as a component of his familial role* that in our society we can unequivocally designate the husband-father as the "instrumental leader" of the family as a system.[11]

The membership of large numbers of women in the American labor force must not be overlooked. Nevertheless there can be

---

11. Comparative data confirm this interpretation. We now have a good deal of evidence about social situations where there is neither a strong "lineage" structure in the kinship field nor a developed "industrial" type of occupational structure. One of the first perceptive studies of this type was made by E. F. Frazier in his *Negro Family in the United States* (Chicago: University of Chicago Press, 1939). This has more recently been supplemented and refined by studies of kinship in the British West Indies. See F. Henriques, *Family and Color in Jamaica,* 1953; Lloyd Braithwaite, "Social Stratification in Trinidad," *Social and Economic Studies,* October, 1953; and especially the as yet unpublished study by R. T. Smith, *The Rural Negro Family in British Guiana* (Doctoral dissertation, University of Cambridge, 1954). Dr. Smith shows very clearly the connection between the "mother-centered" character of the lower-class rural negro family in the West Indies (his study deals with British Guiana) and the "casual" character of most of the available employment and income-earning opportunities. This is a sharp modification of the typical American pattern, but must not be interpreted to mean that the husband-father has, at the critical periods of the family cycle, altogether lost the role of instrumental leader. Dr. Smith shows that this is not the case, and that the impression to the contrary (which might for instance be inferred from Henriques' discussion) arises from failure to consider the development of the particular family over a full cycle from the first sexual relations to complete "emancipation" of the children from their family of orientation.

no question of symmetry between the sexes in this respect, and we argue, there is no serious tendency in this direction. In the first place a large proportion of gainfully employed women are single, widowed or divorced, and thus cannot be said to be either taking the place of a husband as breadwinner of the family, or competing with him. A second large contingent are women who either do not yet have children (some of course never will) or whose children are grown up and independent. The number in the labor force who have small children is still quite small and has not shown a marked tendency to increase. The role of "housewife" is still the overwhelmingly predominant one for the married woman with small children.[12]

But even where this type does have a job, as is also true of those who are married but do not have dependent children, above the lowest occupational levels it is quite clear that in general the woman's job tends to be of a qualitatively different type and not of a status which seriously competes with that of her husband as the primary status-giver or income-earner.

It seems quite safe in general to say that the adult feminine role has not ceased to be anchored primarily in the internal affairs of the family, as wife, mother and manager of the household, while the role of the adult male is primarily anchored in

12. *Population and labor force, by age and sex,* December 1950

(IN THOUSANDS)[1]

Age-sex group	Population	In Labor Force[2]	Keeping House	Not in Labor Force In School	Other[3]
Total U. S.	112,610	64,670	32,950	7,570	7,420
Total Males 14 and over	55,420	45,640	120	2,930	5,740
14-24	12,360	8,230	—	2,670	450
25-34	11,660	11,090	—	240	310
35-44	10,370	9,980	—	—	370
45-54	8,680	8,180	—	—	480
55-64	6,810	5,800	—	—	990
65 and over	5,550	2,360	—	—	3,130
Total Females 14 and over	57,180	19,030	32,830	3,640	1,680
14-24	12,150	4,780	3,580	3,600	180
25-34	12,170	4,160	7,870	—	110
35-44	10,800	4,240	6,430	—	130
45-54	8,910	3,420	5,340	—	140
55-64	6,940	1,840	4,900	—	200
65 and over	6,230	600	4,720	—	910

1. Figures under 100,000 are not included.
2. Including armed forces.
3. Including persons in institutions, disabled and retired, etc.
Source: U.S. Bureau of Labor Statistics, *Fact Book on Manpower,* January 31, 1951.

the occupational world, in his job and through it by his status-giving and income-earning functions for the family. Even if, as seems possible, it should come about that the average married woman had some kind of job, it seems most unlikely that this relative balance would be upset; that either the roles would be reversed, or their qualitative differentiation in these respects completely erased.[13]

The following table shows the status of women in the labor force by marital status. It will be noted that the percentage of married women living with their husbands who were in the labor force increased over the nine-year period from 14.7% to 22.5%.

Labor force status of women by marital status, April 1949 and April 1940

(IN THOUSANDS)

Year and marital status	Population	In labor force	
		Number	% of population
1949			
Total over 14	56,001	17,167	30.7
Single	11,174	5,682	50.9
Married, husband present	35,323	7,959	22.5
Other marital status (separated, widowed, divorced)	9,505	3,526	37.1
1940			
Total over 14	50,549	13,840	27.4
Single	13,936	6,710	48.1
Married, husband present	28,517	4,200	14.7
Other marital status	8,096	2,930	36.2

Source: U. S. Bureau of Labor Statistics, *Fact Book on Manpower*, Jan. 31, 1951.

The concentration of women without children under 5 in the labor force is shown clearly in the following table.

Comparison of labor force status of married women, with and without children under 5, April, 1949

(IN THOUSANDS)

Presence of children under 5	Population	Married women—Husband present	
		In labor force	
		Number	% of population
Total, ages 15-49	26,204	6,758	25.8
Without children under 5	15,499	5,637	36.4
With children under 5	10,705	1,121	10.5

Source: U. S. Bureau of Labor Statistics, *Fact Book on Manpower*, Jan. 31, 1951.

13. The distribution of women in the labor force clearly confirms this general view of the balance of the sex roles. Thus, on higher levels typical feminine occupations are those of teacher, social worker, nurse, private secretary and entertainer. Such roles tend to have a prominent expressive component, and often to be "supportive" to masculine roles. Within the occupational organization they are analogous to the wife-mother role in the family. It is much less common to find women in the "top executive" roles and the more specialized and "impersonal" technical roles. Even within professions we find comparable differentiations, e.g., in medicine women are heavily concentrated in the two branches of pediatrics and psychiatry, while there are few women surgeons.

The Principal Functions
of the Nuclear Family

Within this broad setting of the structure of the society, what can we say about the functions of the family, that is, the isolated nuclear family? There are, we think, two main types of considerations. The first is that the "loss of function," both in our own recent history and as seen in broader comparative perspective, means that the family has become, on the "macroscopic" levels, almost completely functionless. It does not itself, except here and there, engage in much economic production; it is not a significant unit in the political power system; it is not a major direct agency of integration of the larger society. Its individual members participate in all these functions, but they do so "as individuals" not in their roles as family members.[14]

The most important implication of this view is that the functions of the family in a highly differentiated society are not to be interpreted as functions directly on behalf of the society, but on behalf of personality. If, as some psychologists seem to assume, the essentials of human personality were determined biologically, independently of involvement in social systems, there would be no need for families, since reproduction as such does not require family organization. It is because the *human* personality is not "born" but must be "made" through the socialization process that in the first instance families are necessary. They are "factories" which produce human personalities. But at the same time even once produced, it cannot be assumed that the human personality would remain stable in the respects which are vital to social functioning, if there were not mechanisms of stabilization which were organically integrated with the socialization process. We therefore suggest that the basic and irreducible functions of the family are two: first, the primary socialization of children so that they can truly become members of the society into which they have been born; second, the stabilization of the adult personalities of the population of the

14. In terms of our technical analytical scheme we interpret this to mean that the family belongs in the "latency" or "pattern-maintenance—tension-management" subsystem as seen in functional terms. We so interpreted it in *Working Papers*, Chapter V, Sec. viii. (T. Parsons, R. F. Bales, and E. A. Shils, *Working Papers in Theory of Action* [Glencoe, Ill.: The Free Press, 1953], hereinafter referred to as *Working Papers.)*

society. It is the combination of these two functional imperatives, which explains why, in the "normal" case it is both true that *every adult* is a member of a nuclear family and that every child must begin his process of socialization in a nuclear family. It will be one of the most important theses of our subsequent analysis that these two circumstances are most intimately interconnected. Their connection goes back to the fact that it is control of the residua of the process of socialization which constitutes the primary focus of the problem of stabilization of the adult personality.

In subsequent chapters we shall develop, in a variety of applications and ramifications, the view that the central focus of the process of socialization lies in the internalization of the culture of the society into which the child is born. The most important part of this culture from this focal point consists in the patterns of value which in another aspect constitute the institutionalized patterns of the society. The conditions under which effective socialization can take place then will include being placed in a social situation where the more powerful and responsible persons are themselves integrated in the cultural value system in question, both in that they constitute with the children an *institutionalized* social system, and that the patterns have previously been internalized in the relevant ways in their own personalities. The family is clearly in all societies, and no less in our own, in this sense an institutionalized system.[15]

But it is not enough to place the child in any institutionalized system of social relationships. He must be placed in one of a special type which fulfills the necessary psychological conditions of successful completion of the process we call socialization, over

---

15. It is important not to confuse this sense of institutionalization with the usage of Burgess and his associates when they distinguish the "institutional family" from the "companionship" family. To contrast the institutional and companionship family, Burgess and Locke characterize the institutional as a family with "family behavior controlled by the mores, public opinion and law." It is a family "in which its unity would be determined entirely by the social pressure impinging on family members." The companionship form of the family has "family behavior arising from the mutual affection and consensus of its members . . . and intimate association of husband and wife and parents and children." E. W. Burgess and H. J. Locke, *The Family* (New York: American Book Co., 1950), pp. 26-27.

From the present point of view *both* types of family are institutionalized. The statuses of marriage and parenthood are most definitely linked to expectations and obligations, both legal and informal, which are not simply discretionary with the individuals concerned.

a succession of stages starting with earliest infancy. One of the principal tasks of the subsequent discussion is to explore some of these conditions. A few of them may, however, be noted here, while the reasons for their importance will be discussed as we go along. In the first place, we feel that for the earlier stages of socialization, at least, the socialization system must be a *small* group. Furthermore, it must be differentiated into subsystems so the child need not have an equal level of participation with all members at the same time in the earlier stages of the process. We will show that it is particularly important that in the earliest stage he tends to have a special relation to one other member of the family, his mother.

In this connection a certain importance may well attach to the biological fact that, except for the relatively rare plural births, it is unusual for human births to the same mother to follow each other at intervals of less than a year with any regularity. It is, we feel, broadly in the first year of life that a critical phase of the socialization process, which requires the most exclusive attention of a certain sort from the mother, takes place. Furthermore, it is probably significant that in our type of society the family typically no longer has what by other standards may be considered to be large numbers of children. Partly, in earlier times the effects of higher rates of birth have been cancelled by infant mortality. But partly, we feel the large family—say over five or six children—is a different *type* of social system with different effects on the children in it. We will not try to analyze these differences carefully here.

Another very important range of problems in the larger setting concerns the impact for the outcome of the socialization process of the role of relatives other than members of the nuclear family. Particularly important cross-culturally are siblings of the parents, the role of whom varies with the type of kinship structure. Some of the setting for consideration of these problems will be given by Zelditch in Chapter VI. In the conclusion there will be a brief discussion of their general character, but it will not be possible to deal at all adequately with them in this volume.

We should like to suggest only that what we have called the "isolation of the nuclear family" for the contemporary American scene, may, along with reduction in the average size of fam-

ily, have considerable significance for the character of the contemporary socialization process. This significance would, we
think, have something to do with the greater sharpness of the
difference in status, from the point of view of the child, between
members of the family and nonmembers. It will be our general
thesis that in certain respects the modern child has "farther to
go" in his socialization than his predecessors. There seem to be
certain reasons why the number of fundamental steps of a certain type is restricted. If this is true, each step has to be "longer"
and it is important that the "landmarks" along the way, the
"cues" presented to the child, should involve extremely clear
discriminations.

A primary function and characteristic of the family is that it
should be a social group in which in the earliest stages the child
can "invest" *all* of his emotional resources, to which he can become overwhelmingly "committed" or on which he can become
fully "dependent." But, at the same time, in the nature of the
socialization process, this dependency must be temporary rather
than permanent. Therefore, it is very important that the socializing agents should not themselves be *too* completely immersed
in their family ties. It is a condition equally important with facilitating dependency that a family should, in due course, help in
emancipating the child from his dependency on the family.
*Hence the family must be a differentiated subsystem of a society,
not itself a "little society" or anything too closely approaching it.*
More specifically this means that the adult members must have
roles other than their familial roles which occupy strategically
important places in their own personalities. In our own society
the most important of these other roles, though by no means the
only one, is the occupational role of the father.

The second primary function of the family, along with socialization of children, concerns regulation of balances in the personalities of the adult members of both sexes. It is clear that this
function is concentrated on the marriage relation as such. From
this point of view a particularly significant aspect of the isolation
of the nuclear family in our society is again the sharp discrimination in status which it emphasizes between family members
and nonmembers. In particular, then, spouses are thrown upon
each other, and their ties with members of their own families of
orientation, notably parents and adult siblings, are correspond-

ingly weakened. In its negative aspect as a source of strain, the consequence of this may be stated as the fact that the family of procreation, and in particular the marriage pair, are in a "structurally unsupported" situation. Neither party has any other adult kin on whom they have a right to "lean for support" in a sense closely comparable to the position of the spouse.

The marriage relation is then placed in a far more strategic position in this respect than is the case in kinship systems where solidarity with "extended" kin categories is more pronounced. But for the functional context we are discussing, the marriage relationship is by no means alone in its importance. Parenthood acquires, it may be said, an enhanced significance for the emotional balance of the parents themselves, as well as for the socialization of their children. The two generations are, by virtue of the isolation of the nuclear family, thrown more closely on each other.

The main basis of the importance of children to their parents derives, we think, from the implications of problems which psychoanalytic theory has immensely illuminated but which also, we think, need to be understood in their relation to the family as a social system, and the conditions of its functional effectiveness and stability. The most general consideration is that the principal stages in the development of personality, particularly on its affective or "emotional" side, leave certain "residua" which constitute a stratification (in the geological sense) of the structure of the personality itself with reference to its own developmental history. Partly these residua of earlier experience can constitute threats to effective functioning on adult levels, the more so the more "abnormal" that history and its consequences for the individual have been. But partly, also, they have important positive functions for the adult personality. To express and in certain ways and contexts "act out," motivational systems and complexes which are primarily "infantile" or "regressive" in their meaning is, in our view, by no means always undesirable, but on the contrary necessary to a healthy balance of the adult personality. At the same time the dangers are very real and regulation of context, manner and occasion of expression is very important.

We shall attempt later to mobilize evidence that a particularly important role in this situation is played by the erotic elements of the personality constitution, because of the great importance of eroticism in the developmental process.

We suggest then that children are important to adults because it is important to the latter to express what are essentially the "childish" elements of their own personalities. There can be no better way of doing this than living with and interacting on their own level with *real* children. But at the same time it is essential that this should not be an unregulated acting out, a mere opportunity for regressive indulgence. The fact that it takes place in the parental role, with all its responsibilities, not least of which is the necessity to renounce earlier modes of indulgence as the child grows older, is, as seen in this connection, of the first importance. The circumstantially detailed analysis which alone can substantiate such a set of statements, will be presented in the subsequent chapters. The general thesis, however, is that the family and, in a particularly visible and trenchant way, the modern isolated family, incorporates an intricate set of interactive mechanisms whereby these two essential functions for personality are interlocked and interwoven. By and large a "good" marriage from the point of view of the personality of the participants, is likely to be one with children; the functions as parents reinforce the functions in relation to each other as spouses.

If this be true, it would be surprising if the marital relation itself were, even in the more direct interaction of the spouses with each other, altogether dissociated from those aspects of the personality which benefit from the role of parent. It will be suggested later[16] that genital sexuality, which in a sense may be regarded as the primary "ritual" of marital solidarity, is in its symbolic significance, for *both* parties in the first instance a reënactment of the preoedipal mother-child relationship, when the love-relationship to the mother was the most important thing in the child's life. Thus it also may be regarded as "regressive" in an important sense. But like the parental relationship, it takes place in a context where its expressive or indulgent aspect is balanced by a regulatory aspect. The most important part of this is the contingency of sexual love on the assumption of fully adult responsibilities in roles other than that of marriage

---

16. Cf. Chapter III following, pp. 150-151.

directly. Put very schematically, a mature woman can love, sexually, only a man who takes his full place in the masculine world, above all its occupational aspect, and who takes responsibility for a family; conversely, the mature man can only love a woman who is really an adult, a full wife to him and mother to his children, and an adequate "person" in her extrafamilial roles. It is this "building in" to a more differentiated personality system on both sides, and to a more differentiated role system than the child possesses or could tolerate, which constitutes the essential *difference* between preoedipal child-mother love and adult heterosexual love.

Sex Role and Family Structure

It goes without saying that the differentiation of the sex roles within the family constitutes not merely a major axis of its structure, but is deeply involved in both of these two central function-complexes of the family and in their articulation with each other. Indeed we argue that probably the importance of the family and its functions for society constitutes the primary set of reasons why there is a *social* as distinguished from purely reproductive, differentiation of sex roles.

We will maintain that in its most essential structure the nuclear family consists of four main role-types, which are differentiated from each other by the criteria of generation and sex. Of these two, generation is, in its social role-significance, biologically given, since the helplessness of the small child, particularly of course the infant, precludes anything approaching equality of "power" between the generations in the early stages of socialization. This biological "intrinsicness" does not, however, we feel apply in at all the same way to sex; both parents are adults and children of both sexes are equally powerless. We will argue that the differentiation of sex role in the family is, in its sociological character and significance, primarily an example of a basic qualitative mode of differentiation which tends to appear in *all* systems of social interaction regardless of their composition. In particular this type of differentiation, that on "instrumental-expressive" lines, is conspicuous in small groups of about the same membership-size as the nuclear family, as Bales had already shown,[17] and he and Slater develop further in Chapter V.

We suggest that this order of differentiation is generic to the "leadership element" of small groups everywhere and that the problem with respect to the family is not *why* it appears there, given the fact that families as groups exist, but why the man takes the more instrumental role, the woman the more expressive, and why in detailed ways these roles take particular forms. In our opinion the fundamental explanation of the allocation of the roles between the biological sexes lies in the fact that the bearing and early nursing of children establish a strong presumptive primacy of the relation of mother to the small child and this in turn establishes a presumption that the man, who is exempted from these biological functions, should specialize in the alternative instrumental direction.

However the allocation may have come about in the course of bio-social evolution, there can be little doubt about the ways in which differentiation plays into the structure and functioning of the family as we know it. It is our suggestion that the recent change in the American family itself and in its relation to the rest of the society which we have taken as our point of departure, is far from implying an erasure of the differentiation of sex roles; in many respects it reinforces and clarifies it. In the first place, the articulation between family and occupational system in our society focuses the instrumental responsibility for a family very sharply on its one adult male member, and prevents its diffusion through the ramifications of an extended kinship system. Secondly, the isolation of the nuclear family in a complementary way focuses the responsibility of the mother role more sharply on the one adult woman, to a relatively high degree cutting her off from the help of adult sisters and other kinswomen; furthermore, the fact of the absence of the husband-father from the home premises so much of the time means that she has to take the primary responsibility for the children. This responsibility is partly mitigated by reduction in the number of children and by aids to household management, but by no means to the

---

17. "The Equilibrium Problem in Small Groups," *Working Papers*, Chap. IV.

point of emancipating the mother from it. Along with this goes, from the child's point of view, a probable intensification of the emotional significance of his parents as individuals, particularly and in the early stages, his mother, which, there is reason to believe, is important for our type of socialization.

Hence, it is suggested that, if anything, in certain respects the *differentiation* between the roles of the parents becomes more rather than less significant for the socialization process under modern American conditions. It may also be suggested that in subtle ways the same is true of the roles of spouses vis-à-vis each other. The enhanced significance of the marriage relationship, both for the structure of the family itself and for the personalities of the spouses, means that the *complementarity* of roles within it tends to be accentuated. The romantic love complex and our current strong preoccupation with the emotional importance of the "significant person" of opposite sex strongly suggests this. Indeed there has been, we think, a greatly increased emphasis on the importance of good heterosexual relations, which overwhelmingly means *within* marriage. Such disorganization within this field as there is, apart from premarital experimenting, takes primarily the form of difficulties with the current marriage relationship and, if its dissolution is sought, the establishment of a *new* one. It does not mainly take the form of centering erotic interests outside the marriage relation.

All of this seems to us to indicate that the increased emphasis, manifested in all sorts of ways, on overt, specifically feminine attractiveness, with strong erotic overtones, is related to this situation within the family. The content of the conceptions of masculinity and femininity has undoubtedly changed. But it seems clear that the accent of their differentiation has not lessened.

It seems to us legitimate to interpret the recent and, to what extent we do not know, continuing, high level of the divorce rate in this light. It is not an index that the nuclear family and the marriage relationship are rapidly disintegrating and losing their importance. The truth is rather that, on the one hand, the two roles have been changing their character; on the other, their specific importance, particularly that of marriage, has actually been *increasing*. Both these aspects of the process of change impose additional strain on family and marriage as systems, and on their members as personalities. We suggest that the high rates of divorce are primarily indices of this additional strain. When the difficulty of a task is increased it is not unreasonable to expect that a larger proportion of failures should result until the necessary adjustments have been better worked out. In this case we feel that the adjustments are extremely complex and far-reaching.

In this context two other conspicuous and related features of our modern society, which are closely related to marriage and the family, may be called to mind. The first of these is the enormous vogue of treating "human" problems from the point of view of "mental health" and in various respects of psychology. There has been and there is much faddism in these fields, but in the perspective of a couple of generations there can be no doubt of the magnitude of this movement. The United States is a society in which technological-organizational developments closely related to science have taken hold over a very wide front. It is, one might suggest, the "American method," to attempt to solve problems in foci of strain by calling in scientifically expert aid. In industry we take this for granted. In human relations it is just coming to the fore. The immense vogue of psychiatry, of clinical psychology and such phenomena are, we suggest, an index of the importance of strain in the area of the personality and the human relations in which persons are placed. In the nature of our society much of this strain relates to family and marriage relations.[18]

The second, and related, phenomenon, is what is sometimes called, with reference to child training, the "professionalization" of the mother role. It is, starting with the elementary matters of early feeding and other aspects of physical care, the attempt to rationalize, on the basis of scientific— though often pseudo-scientific—authority, the technical aspects

---

18. It has been suggested in other connections that illness should in certain respects be treated as a form of "deviant behavior" and medical practice, even if not explicitly psychotherapy, as a "mechanism of social control." This viewpoint will be very important in the subsequent analysis in this volume. See Parsons, "Illness and the Role of the Physician" in Kluckhohn, Murray and Schneider, eds., *Personality in Nature, Society and Culture,* New York: Alfred A. Knopf, Inc., 1953. For certain relations to the family, see T. Parsons and Renée Fox, "Illness, Therapy and the Modern American Urban Family," *Journal of Social Issues,* Vol. 8, pp. 31-44.

of the care of children. The breakdown of traditionalism which has long since been taken for granted in many other areas, has now penetrated far into this one. It is not surprsing in these circumstances that psychology plays a prominent part.

This involvement of applied science in so many aspects of the intimate life of personalities, as in the mother's care of her children and in the marriage relationship, suggests an important aspect of the developing American feminine role which should not be overlooked. This is that, though the tendency in certain respects is probably increasing, to specialize in the expressive direction, the American woman is not thereby sacrificing the values of rationality. On the contrary, she is heavily involved in the attempt to rationalize these areas of human relations themselves. Women do not act only in the role of patient of the psychiatrist, but often the psychiatrist also is a woman. The mother not only "loves" her children, but she attempts to understand rationally the nature, conditions and limitations of that love, and the ways in which its deviant forms can injure rather than benefit her child. In this, as in other respects, the development we have been outlining is an integral part of the more general development of American society.

Some Theoretical Problems

In conclusion of this introductory discussion we may call the attention of the reader to two major theoretical themes which we hope he will be able to follow through the different subject-matters discussed in the chapters which follow. In the concluding chapter we shall then attempt to evaluate the evidence we have presented for the question of their more general significance.

The first of these concerns the nature of the processes of differentiation in systems of action. In the sense of process, as distinguished from structural type, this is explicitly a major theme at three main points in the book. It has already been introduced with reference to the problem of assessing the significance of recent changes in the American family. It has been suggested earlier in the present chapter that these changes are to be regarded as largely consequences of a major process of structural differentiation in American society generally, through which the family has become distinctly a more specialized agency in the society as a whole than it had been. This process has not only entailed shifts of function from one agency to another, as well as structural changes, but also the kinds of emotional disturbance which we associate with processes of differentiation and reintegration.

The theme will next be brought up on the level of analysis of the personality as a system. In Chapter II, the thesis will be put forward that the main outline of the process of personality development, so far as it is legitimate to regard it as a process of socialization, can be regarded as a process of structural differentiation. We will maintain that first there occurs the establishment of a very simple personality structure through the internalization of a *single* social object, the mother on the relevant level. Then there occurs the differentiation of this system through a series of stages, into a progressively more complex system. Throughout, this process occurs in direct relation to a series of systems of social interaction, also of a progressively increasing order of structural complexity. In this chapter the main concern will be with the grosser pattern of the process from infancy to beyond adolescence.

In Chapter IV, however, Parsons and Olds will take up the same theme again with reference to personality, but this time on a much more detailed and intensive level, attempting to trace in detail the mechanisms involved in a single step of differentiation and their articulation with the more detailed structure of the situation.

Then in Chapter V, Bales and Slater will return to the same theme, of differentiation, but this time in relation to the small group as a social system. They will show that functional differentiation, as evaluated from the point of view of the system, can be shown to appear at the most microscopic level of analysis of the processes of interaction, in the differences between the distributions of "proactive" and "reactive" acts. It is then followed to the level of the differentiation of the stabler roles of the members of the small group. The process is analyzed over time, and different types of outcome of the process of differentiation are studied.

Finally, though Zelditch's material in Chapter VI does not

follow out a process of differentiation over time, it does show that structural patterns which are cognate with a fundamental pattern of such differentiation, can be identified as relatively uniform in nuclear families when these are studied cross-culturally. He shows that the nuclear family has operated, within his sample, under a considerable range of different conditions with respect to its articulation with other elements of the social structure, kinship and otherwise without altering this fundamental pattern.

We should like to suggest to the reader two main respects in which we think there is an essential uniformity in the process of differentiation in systems of action, whether they be social systems or personality systems, and whether the level be macroscopic or microscopic. The first of these concerns the relation of differentiation to the concept commonly paired with it, that of *integration.* The by no means original observation that differentiating processes always go hand in hand with integrating processes [19] seems to us to be strongly confirmed by our material. We incline to interpret this as a consequence of the organization of action in *systems.* A process of differentiation is a process of *reorganization of the system* which disturbs whatever approximation to a stable state may have existed before it began. This disturbance sets up repercussions, not only at the foci of differentiation, but throughout the other parts of the system. Thus what we mean by integration is, from one perspective, the set of adjustments in the rest of the system which are necessitated by fulfilling the conditions necessary to maintain the newly differentiated state *and at the same time* those necessary to the continuance of the whole as an ongoing system.

We feel that these circumstances underlie two conspicuous features of the differentiating process as we will portray it in the chapters which follow. The first is the fact that it takes place in some kind of a pattern of phases which is related to that of task-oriented groups, as Bales was the first to demonstrate, but with reference to which the task group presents only one type of case. In any case differentiation is not a "linear" process of continuous increase in the value of a variable which

---

19. Suggested by G. W. Allport: *Personality, A Psychological Interpretation* (New York: Henry Holt & Co., 1937).

might be called "differentiatedness." The second is the fact that the process seems to occur by relatively *discontinuous* stages, which again we interpret provisionally to mean that the "integrative" processes must have a chance to "catch up" with the consequences of a given step in differentiation before the latter process can go farther without destroying the system.

The second broad common feature of processes of differentiation in the system we are studying, concerns the role of the pattern which we will variously call "binary choice" and "fission" in the process of differentiation. This is first introduced in Chapter II in the conception that, after the first internalized social object has been established, the process of differentiation of the personality system proceeds by the "splitting" of each of these internalized objects into two. The situational focus of the process then is the exposure of the child to a system of social interaction in which there are double the number of crucially significant roles from that significant at the previous stage. Essentially the same theme is followed out in Chapter IV at the more microscopic level in the conception that, in a given specific cycle of the socialization process, the process of differentiation involving both cognitive discrimination and "relative deprivation," serves essentially to establish, by learning processes, the difference between *two* situational objects or object-categories, and that this differentiation is the focus of internalization of the new object-system.

On the small-group level, then, Bales and Slater in Chapter V introduce the same theme by their discussion of the most elementary beginnings of the qualitative differentiation of action types in the process of interaction. Essentially the pattern seems to be that when a choice or a discrimination must be made, its most primitive form is always, "either A or not-A," then if not-A is B, for the next choice the alternative is either B or not-B. It may be suggested that in the role-structure of the small group, a particularly crucial choice of this character is that between "either task-leader or not task-leader."

What we interpret to be an important cultural aspect of the process of system-differentiation, opens up on both the personality-socialization and the small-group levels. It becomes particularly clear in Chapter IV, though foreshadowed in Chapter II, that the differentiation of the child's system of cognitive orientation involves a logical elaboration which includes the establishment of hierarchically ordered categories of lesser and greater orders of generality. Thus, in first differentiating self from mother, the child must discriminate "I" from "you." But in so far as both self and mother, and the system they constitute, do not exhaust the whole world (and it is hard to see how they can constitute objects if they do—there can be no "figure" without a "ground"), then there must, on a higher order of generality, also be a discrimination between "we" who comprise the "I-you" system, and a residual "they" —the rest of the world. Thus, there is a hierarchy of at least three levels of generality—"I" and "you" as "specific" social objects; "we" as a category comprising both; and a "world" or "universe" comprising both "we" and "they" who at first are residually simply "non-we."

In the process of "culture-building" in the course of interaction, Bales has shown that a cognate structure of categories of increasing inclusiveness is progressively built up.[20] A given item of information fed into the system, must be subsumed under at least one more general category before it can be given "significance," i.e., evaluated. Then if another item of information is to be evaluated, in the simplest case it must be classified relative to the first, as belonging to the same class, or not. But, in turn, in order for this to be possible there must be at least two potential *classes*—not merely items—each capable of comprising more than one item. Finally, there must be a category comprising both of these classes, if it is only that of "things that happen."

We shall attempt to show in the final chapter that this hierarchical aspect of the cultural organization of systems of action is not only essential to them in the general sense, but is particularly crucial to the process of differentiation. On the cognitive side the discrimination of the non-A from the A is essential, if higher-order categories which comprise them both are to be defined in the culture or internalized in the personality.

The reader familiar with our previous theoretical work will not fail to observe that this binary pattern is in one sense

---

20. See Robert F. Bales, "How People Interact in Conferences," *Scientific American*, March, 1955.

implicit in the whole conceptual scheme with which we start. Thus Bales's discussion of his scoring procedure for interaction and its relation to the categories of interaction process shows that a pattern of successive dichotomous choices is implicit in it.[21] Similarly Parsons' "pattern variables" obviously have a dichotomous structure which has been the subject of considerable comment and a good deal of objection.

All this is quite true. But whether or not the pattern is implicit in previous conceptual schemes is not the point. The point is whether, when confronted with the facts of the relevant area of actual action and interaction, the scheme *works*. This is the problem we wish to call to the reader's attention. We shall return to it in the concluding chapter.

The second major theoretical theme which should be followed through our substantive analysis is that of certain structural relations between culture, personality and social systems *as systems*. This will be treated primarily in terms of the interrelations of the latter two perspectives, though that of culture is by no means absent. In Chapters II-IV the major theme will be the ways in which the developing structure of personality systems can only be understood in terms of their involvement in a successive series of systems of social interaction. Only by internalizing the culture of each of these systems in turn can its own internal structure take shape. But Bales and Slater then show in Chapter V some of the ways in which preëxistent personality structures and their cultural values "play into" the interaction process and thus to some extent determine the role structure of the group after it has had time to "settle down."

Thus our position is that from one point of view this is a typical "chicken and egg" problem. But to say this is clearly only in one rather crude way to state the problem of their relations, not to solve it. We do not feel that in any definitive sense we have "solved" it, but we do feel that we have made considerable progress.

The most important starting point of our approach lies in the conception that both personality systems and social systems are systems of action, and culture is a generalized aspect of the organization of such systems. So long as the personality system is,

---

21. Cf. *Working Papers,* Chap. V, Sec. iv.

as is the case in so much current psychological thinking, conceived simply as a set of properties of the organism, and not as an analytically independent system, we feel that the way to a solution is blocked. Then even social systems tend to lose their distinctiveness and be treated as "properties of aggregates of personalities which are properties or organisms."

Underlying the contention that it is fruitful to treat personality as a system of action, is the view that all systems of action, including both personality systems and social systems, *consist* as structures, of the "crystallization" of symbolically generalized meaningful orientations of actors to objects in their situations and the organization of the systems in these terms. Furthermore the *interactive* reference to the cases where the same entity is *both* actor and object is fundamental. The level of generalization of orientation which can legitimately be called "cultural" is, we feel, bound to the phenomenon of interaction and could not arise or be long sustained without it.

If this is the case, then personalities as systems of action and social systems on the cultural level are empirically inseparable from each other and from their culture. As we so often put it, they are not only interdependent, they interpenetrate. Specifically, personalities and social systems interpenetrate with respect to cultural pattern-content which again, as we have stated often, comes to be internalized in the personality system and institutionalized in the social system. But this common culture is in fact constitutive of the structural framework of *both* orders of system, particularly in the form of patterns of value-orientation.

Does this then mean that there is no difference, that social systems are simply resultants of a plurality of personalities, or a society is simply the "personality writ large" as has so often been contended ever since Plato? Or is the personality simply a "microcosm" of the society? We think not, quite definitely not. Such views overlook some very fundamental considerations. To us the most important is that *both* orders of system are products of processes of differentiation. But the starting points, the points at which the "trunk" of a differentiated system articulates with the "roots" and the "soil," are not and cannot be the same for the two processes of differentiation. We hope to contribute further evidence to the common view that the human personality must undergo its early development in a social system something like the human family. But looked at as part of the society, the family is, even in primitive societies, a *specialized*, i.e., differentiated, part of the larger system; it is quite erroneous to regard it as a "microcosm" of the whole. We will maintain that at one stage the evolving personality is a kind of "mirror-image" microcosm of the nuclear family, but it is crucial that it *cannot* be such an image of the whole society, since this is inevitably a more complex system than any family, and the family is specialized in relation to it. It is a corollary of the proposition that a society is a highly differentiated system, further, that it must comprise not one but at least several *types* of personality.

On the other hand, the points of reference for the differentiation of a social system are not specialized *parts* of the relevant system but *historical antecedents*, i.e., other social systems which were simpler, i.e., less differentiated than their successors. These always involve not only many personalities but a plurality of types of personalities.

We shall, in the following pages, probably go farther than almost any previous contributors to the literature in developing the thesis that neither personalities nor social systems can be adequately understood without reference to culture, to each other and to the relations of these three to each other. Or, if you will, sociology presupposes psychology *but equally,* psychology presupposes sociology, and both presuppose knowledge and analytical understanding of culture.

But strongly as we will adhere to this position, it must not be understood as leading to the erasure of the distinctions between social systems, personalities and culture. Quite the contrary, the farther we go in the exploration of their interpenetration, the more essential and the more clearly defined the distinctions become. These reference points constitute in our opinion, one of the major axes of the theory of action. As in the case of differentiation, we shall return to this theme in the final chapter.

CHAPTER II

Family Structure
and the Socialization of the Child

BY TALCOTT PARSONS

We now utilize the sketch of the American family and its functions presented in Chapter I, to approach a more intensive analysis of the relations between its structure and the processes of socialization of the child. Our primary attention will be focussed on this relationship. But we must not forget that the nuclear family is *never,* most certainly not in the American case, an independent society, but a small and highly differentiated subsystem of a society. This fact is crucially relevant to our interests at two points. First the parents, as socializing agents, occupy not merely their familial roles, but these articulate, i.e. interpenetrate, with their roles in other structures of the society, and this fact is a necessary condition, as we hope to show, of their functioning effectively as socializing agents, i.e. as parents, at all. Secondly, the child is never socialized only for and into his family of orientation, but into structures which extend beyond this family, though interpenetrating with it. These include the school and peer group in later childhood and the family of procreation which the child will help to form by his marriage, as well as occupational roles in adulthood.

Our attention will be focussed on the contemporary American

family. We do not, however, believe that the essential theoretical outline of our analysis is narrowly "culture-bound." The material brought forward later, in Chapter VI, will throw some light on this problem and we will come back to it in the conclusion.

Theoretically we will take our tools from a number of different sources. The analysis of family structure will come most directly from observation and analysis of the American family and from the relevant sociological theory. This is of course buttressed by considerable attention to the data of comparative kinship, and by consideration of small group structure and interaction process, taken particularly, though not exclusively, from the work of Bales and his associates.

On the more psychological side a most important set of reference points is derived from Freud's account of the stages of psycho-sexual development, as this has been developed and refined in subsequent work in psychoanalytic theory. In addition to that there has been extensive use made of psychological knowledge of the processes and mechanisms in the field of general and child psychology, and in personality theory. Finally, in the analysis of the processes which link family structure with the development of personality, an essential set of keys has been found in the analysis of therapy as a process of social control, and it relation to theories of the directions of deviant behavior, and of the mechanisms of social control.[1]

With increasing emphasis recent analytical work has borne in upon us the extreme importance of the fact that any large-scale social system (a society) should be considered not in a "monolithic" way, but as an intricate network of interdependent and interpenetrating subsystems. This has been one of the most important contributions of the concept of role, to throw into relief the fact that the same individual participates in *many* social systems, not merely one; he has multiple roles. Systematic application of this generalization will be one of the central themes of our analysis of the process of socialization. The child may be likened to a pebble "thrown" by the fact of birth into the social "pond." The effect of this event is at first concentrated

---

1. On this last aspect see, especially, T. Parsons, *The Social System,* Chapters VII and X (Glencoe, Ill.: Free Press, 1951). Hereinafter referred to as *The Social System.* Chapter VI of that book dealt with the process of socialization, but on a much less advanced level than the present study attempts to do.

at the particular point of entrance, but as he grows up, his changing place in the society resembles the successively widening waves which radiate from his initial position in his family of orientation. The process is inherently time-bound. He cannot participate in wider circles until he has fulfilled certain of the conditions of full participation in the narrower ones. But the metaphor breaks down in that not only his relationships outside the family but within its innermost core are transformed in a kind of "spiral" process.

From this point of view the nuclear family must be placed relative to other subsystems in a series. That it is itself a subsystem of a larger system is of course a sociological commonplace. But to break it in turn down into subsystems is a less familiar way of looking at it. Yet we will treat the family in this way and say that, in certain crucially important respects, the very young child does not participate in, is not fully a "member," of his whole family, but only of a subsystem of it, the mother-child subsystem. The marriage pair constitute another subsystem as may, for certain purposes, also the child with all his siblings, all the males in the family, all the females, etc. In fact *any* combination of two or more members as differentiated from one or more other members *may* be treated as a *social* system which is a subsystem of the family as a whole. The smaller the family of course the smaller the number of possible subsystems, and this is a very important fact about our own small family type.[2]

There are, of course, many different aspects of the organization of the relations of subsystems of the family or any other social system to each other. One set of relations is, however, particularly crucial for our purposes. This is a certain relation between different modes and levels of specialization and differentiation of role. The family is significant as a type that in its internal structure represents a very elementary level of differentiation of roles so far as social systems go and, as we shall see, this is even more the case with its mother-child subsystem.[3] At

---

2. We will see that particular importance attaches to *four* familial role-types and the subsystems generated by their relations to each other. An important field of study would be that of the effect of absence of any of these main types, *e.g.*, of father or sister for a boy.

3. Above all in this respect it is important that the family is a *small* group.

the same time the family must be sufficiently "diffuse" in function in the larger system of which it is a part to meet all the essential needs of a highly undifferentiated class of members, its small children. Hence, though families are very numerous, they are very much more alike in basic structure than are most other types of subsystem of a larger society.

The structures articulating with the family, however, must be more differentiated than is the family itself. The family offers a wide enough range of role-participations only for the young child. He must learn, by actual participation, progressively more roles than his family of orientation can offer him. It is at this point that peer group and school assume paramount importance.

Participation in a wider society, the more so the more complex its structure, thus involves participation in an ever-widening circle of subsystems of the society. The role-repertoire of the normal adult may be regarded as a point at which the increasing complexity of differentiation from the mother-child starting point, and differentiation of the society as a system into specialized subsystems, attain some sort of meeting point which is compatible with the functional needs of adult personalities.

The Pattern of Developmental Process

We will leave further strictly structural analysis of the family as a social system and of its subsystems to the points where they become directly relevant to the analysis of socialization, and now turn to the outline, in certain respects, of the process of socialization itself. We feel there is an important relationship between the phases, i.e. changes in pattern of action over time, of a task-oriented group, the phases of the psychotherapeutic (more generally, social control) process, and those of the process of socialization.[4] The essential principle of the relationship is that both therapy and socialization involve the same basic phases as task-performance, but *in reverse order*. Let us take up this general problem.

Bales and his associates have established that a group which

4. This relationship was developed in outline in *Working Papers,* Chap. V, Sec. vii. (T. Parsons, R. F. Bales, and E. A. Shils, *Working Papers in the Theory of Action* [Glencoe, Ill.: Free Press, 1953]. Hereinafter referred to as *Working Papers.*) The pattern of socialization was barely sketched at that point, but will be considerably elaborated below.

is mainly instrumentally oriented to the performance of a group task assigned by the investigator, will tend to go through three main phases of development which have been called the "adaptive-instrumental," the goal-gratificatory or "consummatory" phase and the "integrative" phase. It has also seemed useful to treat what happens to the members of a group in their roles as group members during the interval between meetings as a group as a phase of "latency." [5]

FIGURE 1

*Phase Patterns of Task-Performance
and Social Control Processes*

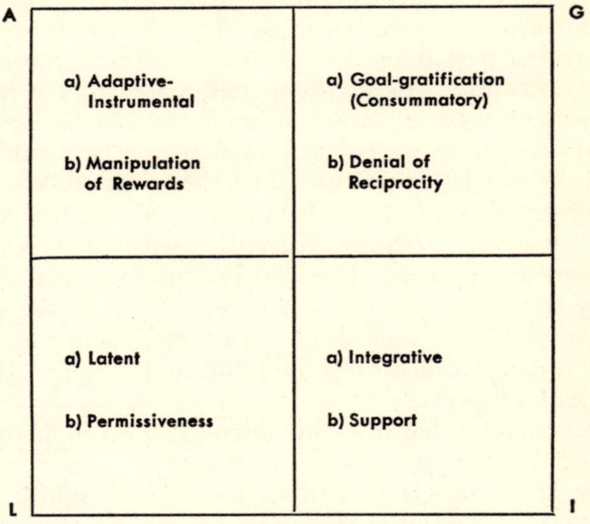

A	G
a) Adaptive- Instrumental b) Manipulation of Rewards	a) Goal-gratification (Consummatory) b) Denial of Reciprocity
a) Latent b) Permissiveness	a) Integrative b) Support
L	I

Key:
a) Task-performance phases (clockwise order) A-G-I-L
b) Learning-social control phases (counterclockwise order) L-I-G-A

When this pattern had been established and theoretically interpreted it turned out that the four components—stated in terms of the therapist's attitudes—of a paradigm of social control with special reference to psychotherapy which we had worked

5. *Working Papers,* Chap. IV. This usage of the term latency is not to be confused with that of Freud—which for convenience we will follow here—as designating the period between the oedipal resolution and adolescence. In neither case, furthermore, is it legitimate to infer that "nothing happens" in such a phase.

out previously,[6] followed by a broad temporal order of predominance, and that this order; namely (1) "permissiveness"; (2)
"support"; (3) "denial of reciprocity"; and (4) "manipulation
of rewards"; could be identified with the phases of Bales' process
in reverse. Using the dimensional diagram we have previously
found convenient[7], the broad relations of these two phase patterns are represented in Figure 1. We will not attempt to enter
into them further here but will refer the reader to the *Working
Papers* for a fuller discussion.[8]

In describing the phase-pattern of the process of socialization
we adopt, as shown in Figure 2, Freud's terminology descriptive
of the phases of psychosexual development. In fitting them in
we find it necessary to distinguish sharply between two types of
phase. One type we may call those of relative stability or integration (those designated as "a" in Fig. 2) and the other the
phases of transition between them (designated as "c"). We therefore, conceive the basic pattern as involving first the disturbance
of a relatively stable state—the very first one being that of the
foetus in the womb. The disturbance, then, is both "coped with"
in the sense of forestalling its radically disorganizing consequences (in analogy to therapy) and is "used creatively" to facilitate a learning process. The process finally leads over to a
relatively stable new "plateau" where, as it were, the gains are
consolidated. Then a new set of disturbances is introduced, and
the same order of process repeated, but at a "higher" level, at a
next turn of a "spiral."

We will contend that this fundamental aspect of *discontinuity*
of the socialization process, which we must regard as a basic
discovery of Freud, is related to the crucial significance for
socialization of the internalization of objects through interaction in a system of social relationships. The discontinuity
derives from the fact that each phase requires, as we see it, a
specific and extensive *reorganization* of the structure of the
personality as a system. The main framework of this structure,
we will attempt to show, consists of internalized social objects
systematically related to each other. The process of differentia-

6. Cf. *The Social System*, Chap. VII.

7. *Working Papers*, Chap. V, Fig. 2, p. 182.

8. Further elucidation of the problem of the meaning of this reversal of phase-
order will be found in Chapter IV, pp. 200-202 ff.

FIGURE 2

*Phase Patterns of Task-Performance
and Social Control*

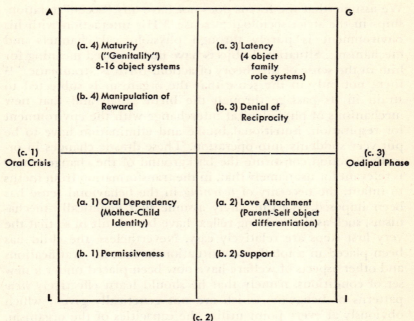

**(c. 4)
Adolescence**

A   G

(a. 4) Maturity
("Genitality")
8-16 object systems

(a. 3) Latency
(4 object
family
role systems)

(b. 4) Manipulation of
Reward

(b. 3) Denial of
Reciprocity

**(c. 1)
Oral Crisis**

**(c. 3)
Oedipal Phase**

(a. 1) Oral Dependency
(Mother-Child
Identity)

(a. 2) Love Attachment
(Parent-Self object
differentiation)

(b. 1) Permissiveness

(b. 2) Support

L   I

**(c. 2)
Anal Phase**

Key:
a(1-4) Phases of psycho-sexual development.
b(1-4) Phases of learning-social-control process.
c(1-4) Crises of transition.

tion of these objects, as subsystems of the personality, makes it necessary to establish new subsystem boundaries and new relations as of relative strength and of integration. From many sources we know that such reorganization of systems of action cannot take place by a simple linear process, but involves a more or less self-enclosed phase-pattern, which can then be repeated for a new reorganization phase of the "spiral."[9]

9. Cf. Chapter V for further evidence on this problem from small group studies.

Socialization as a Series of Phases

With this general orientation in mind, we may now proceed to outline briefly our conception of the broad content of the four pairs of phases, first, that of disturbance of a previous stable state; second, that of integration into a new "plateau" state. We assume that the foetus does not have any "social" relationships in the strict sociological sense.[10] His interaction with his environment is purely through physiological channels and mechanisms. Situational objects have not acquired meaning for him in the sense of the theory of action. Birth is "traumatic," [11] then, not only in the sense that the organism is subjected to strain in its passage through the birth canal, and that new mechanisms of physiological interchange with the environment for respiration, nutritional intake and elimination have to be put very suddenly into operation. These drastic changes in organic function constitute the background of the change which is relevant for us; namely that, in the transformation from foetus to infant, the necessity of *learning* in the behavioral sense has been imposed. We can safely assume that genetically mechanisms, such as the suckling reflex, have been built in so that the very first steps are relatively easy. Nevertheless, the child has been placed in a totally new situation in that his gratifications and other aspects of welfare have now been placed under a new set of conditions, namely that he should learn effectively *new* patterns of behavior, which are not genetically given, which obviously at every point utilize the capacities of the organism, including their maturational changes, but which can never consist *only* in "triggering off" hereditary patterns by the appropriate stimuli. The transition from being "pure organism" to the establishment of oral dependency is the "oral crisis."

We presume that these elementary learning mechanisms, about which something will have to be said later in this chapter, but more detailed treatment of which is reserved for Chapter IV, lead up under "normal" conditions to a type of state which many psychoanalysts have come to characterize as that of "oral de-

10. The mother, however, in pregnancy, develops expectations which immediately impinge on the child at birth. Pregnancy is a kind of "anticipatory" mother role. In this sense the foetus may well be a "person" to her. Perhaps this is a case of what Merton and Kitt call "anticipatory socialization."

11. Perhaps not in a strictly technical sense. This is to us an open question.

pendency." Just how we are to conceive this state will become more clearly evident as our analysis proceeds. It is the least accessible to common-sense interpretation of the four "plateau" states, so it is necessary to rely on technical observation and inference. But the most essential feature of it, we may presume, is "attachment" to one or a class of "social objects" of which the mother is the prototype, in such a way that ego's paramount gratification interests are "fused" in their relation to this object. The stability of the relation to the object then becomes for practical purposes the primary condition of the stability of the "personality," of ego himself as a system.[12] He has internalized this pattern of relationship, but nothing else on a comparable level of organization and generality. This and, so far, only this, can be said to constitute the "structure of personality" for the child. Judgments of exact timing involve technical considerations we cannot go into here, but it seems highly probable that the major completion of this stage is pre-verbal, and that the successful attainment of oral dependency is a condition of the successful learning of language.

Freud's term for the process by which this relatively stable state is upset is the "anal" phase.[13] The essential feature of it is the imposition of a new level of autonomous self-control on the child, of which sphincter-control apparently often, if not always, becomes a symbolic prototype. This phase of the process, we presume, leads up to a new relatively stable plateau in which the child comes to play a more autonomous role in interaction with the mother. This we have called "love-dependency" which comes to involve what Freud called the first "true object-attachment," as distinguished from his original meaning of "identification" which characterizes the stage of oral dependency. The essential difference lies in the autonomous component of his role. He not only *is loved,* but he actively *loves.* The prototypical object of attachment, however, is still the mother.[14]

---

12. This does not, we feel, imply complete "passivity" on the infant's part. In internalizing the mother object he acquires, we infer, not only an "image" of her as an agent of care but of her conception of *him* as the recipient of care. "He" already acts in a positive sense, at least by wanting, asking and protesting.

13. It will be noted that we have found it necessary, following much psychoanalytic opinion, to break down Freud's original "oral phase" into two, *viz.,* a) the "oral crisis"—in which oral aggression is prominent—and b) the relatively stable state of "oral dependency."

The next pair of phases are the oedipal phase and latency in Freud's sense.[15] The oedipal crisis, for both sexes, may be interpreted primarily as centering about disturbance of the love-attachment to the mother, and its resolution in the latency period, as the assumption of a new level of integration in the family of orientation as a system, in which an independent and autonomous role is played not only toward mother, but toward father and siblings. The significance of latency, i.e., of the repression of overt eroticism, at this stage will have to be taken up below when a firmer groundwork for its interpretation has been laid.

Finally, the latency period still presumes that the child's primary security rests on his integration in his family of orientation. He does not yet have a capacity for primary attachments outside this system. The critical nature of adolescence involves pressure to abandon this familial dependency and to form independent attachments outside the family. What in its psychosexual reference Freudians call maturity or "genitality" may be considered the "normal" outcome of this phase of the process. Difficult problems of the relations between familial and extra-familial participations and attachments arise in the latency period and even before. We will not attempt to go into these now, but will reserve them for treatment when a more elaborate analysis is possible.[16]

The main object of this outline has been, not to prove anything, but simply to sketch out a temporal reference scheme as a set of pegs on which to hang more detailed analysis. All that it seems useful to say about problems of validity at this point is that the correspondence between patterns of phase-process developed altogether independently of the problems of socialization, and this interpretation of the Freudian pattern, is surely remarkable.

---

14. Who does *not*, however, remain the same object. It is furthermore *most* important not to confuse the mother-object at either of these phases with the concrete woman as seen in common-sense terms by an adult who "knows" her.

15. Again we may point out that this must clearly be distinguished from our use of the term to designate one of the dimensions (and phases) of our system process of action, *e.g.,* "latent pattern-maintenance."

16. As will appear later, it has proved necessary for us to subdivide this phase in a special way which will be explained in due course.

The Social Structures Impinging on the Child

Let us now turn to the problems of the structure of the systems of social interaction which are relevant to this paradigm of socialization. Though it stands, in its most critical significance, in the middle of a series, the nuclear family may conveniently be used as the point of reference for our analysis, because of the general clarity of relationships here.

The suggestion was made in Chapter I that the main outlines of the structure of the nuclear family can be treated as a consequence of differentiation on two axes, that of hierarchy or power and that of instrumental vs. expressive function. If this is correct and relevant, it follows that so far as this aspect of its differentiation is concerned the family contains four fundamental *types* of status-role. This basic four-role pattern can be modified by a variety of factors such as stage of the family cycle, age-differential of husband and wife, interval between their ages and those of children, number, assortment by sex, and interval between children. All these and others may prove significant for more refined analyses, but there seems little doubt that these two axes of differentiation as symbolized by the two great differentiations of generation (during the pre-adult period of children) and sex, overshadow other bases of differentiation within what in any sense may be considered a "typical" nuclear family.

This role structure may then be roughly represented by the four-fold table of Figure 3. The father role is, *relative to the others* high both on power and on "instrumentality"—hence low on "expressiveness." The mother role is high on power and on "expressiveness," thus low in instrumentality. The son role is low on power but high on instrumentality, the daughter role low on power but high on expressiveness—hence low on instrumentality.[17]

17. It is probably correct to say that cross-culturally these four roles are the only ones within the nuclear family which are consistently and always symbolically differentiated, usually but not always through kinship terminology. Thus dress, personal names, etc., may supplement this. I know of no case where both parents are called exclusively by the same term. Siblings of both sexes are to be sure sometimes terminologically identified, but in such cases the discrimination will be made by other symbolic devices. There may of course be collective terms like "parents" and "children." In many "classificatory" systems of course family members may be classified with other kin (e.g., father and father's brothers), and finally distinctions may be made within such a category as between older and younger

FIGURE 3

Basic Role-Structure of the Nuclear Family

	Instrumental Priority	Expressive Priority
Superior +	Instrumental superior Father (husband)	Expressive superior Mother (wife)
Inferior −	Instrumental inferior Son (brother)	Expressive inferior Daughter (sister)

(Power)

As has already been pointed out, these distinctions are of course relative. They are defined in terms of amount and mode of influence on the functioning of the family as a social system. The power axis of this differentiation is, as we interpret it, simply the quantitative degree of such influence. This makes its interpretation relative to the generation difference almost obvious; surely the adult can affect the affairs of the family as a system more than can a small child. Of course with maturation of the child his power grows, and the inequality vis-à-vis his parents is lessened. But the basic point is clear.[18] The instru-

brother. But no known symbolic system *fails* to distinguish these four categories from each other.

18. Professor Albert J. Reiss (in private correspondence) raises the question of whether "dependency" does not confer power which is sometimes equal to or superior to that of the person on whom dependency exists. He suggests that in these terms the child may be as powerful as the parent. We think that this problem involves the discrimination between two phenomena both of which are sometimes referred to as power. We have used the term as meaning "relative importance in carrying out the functional performance of the system." If we accept socialization of the child into the values and roles of the society as the relevant family function,

mental-expressive distinction we interpret[19] as essentially the differentiation of function, and hence of relative influence, in terms of "external" vs. "internal" functions of the system. The area of instrumental function concerns relations of the system to its situation outside the system, to meeting the adaptive conditions of its maintenance of equilibrium, and "instrumentally" establishing the desired relations to *external* goal-objects. The expressive area concerns the "internal" affairs of the system, the maintenance of integrative relations between the members, and regulation of the patterns and tension levels of its component units.

We must remember that the four paramount familial roles of father, mother, son and daughter are interpreted here to be differentiated on a generically significant basis. Therefore, particularly in relating them to extrafamilial roles it will be important to think in these more generic terms. For these purposes we may refer to them as the roles of instrumental superiority, expressive superiority, instrumental inferiority and expressive inferiority respectively. The latter two mean of course instrumentally specialized *but* inferior to father, similarly with expressively specialized but inferior to mother.

We spoke above of the social systems in which the child was involved as constituting some kind of a series, of which increasing structural differentiation must be one primary aspect. Can we now suggest a more precise idea of the nature of this series and hence of what kind of transition is involved in passage from one point in the series to another? In this connection the fact that there are *four* role types which have a "primary" order of structural differentiation from each other in the nuclear family is extraordinarily suggestive. For one major aspect of differentiation is increasing complexity and one aspect of increasing complexity in turn is increasing *number* of differentiated parts of a system. The obvious series of which the number four is a step in increasing complexity is one of binary division. By

----

there can be no question that the child—so long as he is a child—cannot be the equal of his parents. The other meaning is "ability to cause trouble by threatening to disrupt the system." In this sense the child, and other persons or groups in dependent positions have considerable "power." We are not primarily concerned here with definitions but only with preventing confusion caused by possible misunderstanding of our usage.

19. Cf. *Working Papers*, Chap. V, pp. 189 ff.

binary division a four-unit system can be derived from one of two units, and two in turn can be derived from one by dividing the one. Moving in the other direction by the same principle, four divide into eight, eight into sixteen, etc. We wish to use this principle as our working assumption in analyzing the series of social structures in which the child comes to be progressively integrated in the course of the socialization process.[20]

On the assumption, then, that the four-role family structure is a stage in a series of structures whose complexity increases progressively on the binary principle, what concrete meaning can be given to the terms of the series in both directions from four as the point of reference? Moving toward decreasing complexity the subsystem mother-child comes immediately to mind. Leaning on very widespread views in the field of child development, we have above suggested that the oedipal crisis constitutes the transition from primary integration of the child with the mother as a love-object to integration in the family in such a way that, vis-à-vis ego father and siblings acquire much greater and more independent significance for his interaction. We, therefore, postulate that the two-member unit of the series is the mother-child system (in the mother's role as mother of *this particular* child, of course). This is to be considered as a social system in the strictest sense.[21]

What then could be the one-member system which is the end of the series? It clearly cannot be either the mother or the child as "individuals," since we are talking about systems of *social* interaction. Psychoanalytic theory gives us a very important clue

---

20. Anyone familiar with the recent work of the author and his associates (Shils, Bales, etc.) in the theory of action will recognize that such an assumption is a very natural one within our frame of reference. Thus the duality of formulation of the pattern variables as "alternatives of choice" suggests the significance of pairs of alternatives, choice between which can yield *two* types of consequence. Similarly, in describing the logic of classification of acts in the process of scoring interaction, Bales (*Working Papers,* Ch. V, Sec. iv) shows that the scoring process can be reduced to a series of binary choices—which can be stated in pattern variable terms. The present idea is an extension of this to the analysis of a genetic process of system-differentiation. It has been briefly discussed in Chapter I and will be analyzed in relation to interaction process in Chapter V.

21. It might be useful to compare it with the therapist-patient system, since the latter is a two-member system which has been subjected to relatively intensive sociological analysis. (Also, as we will see later, it has certain important resemblances to the marriage relation.)

here, in speaking of the "mother-child *identity*"[22] which is the referent of Freud's discussion of "primary identification." Essentially, we interpret this to mean a system of interaction on an authentically socio-cultural—i.e., meaningfully symbolic—level in which one member of the system has so little autonomy that his independent influence on the behavior of the *system*—as *actor,* note, not as a "condition" which influences the mother—may be treated as secondary. This is not, however, to say that it is not a social system in the sense that his "responsiveness" or lack of it is indifferent to the mother. Then for theoretical purposes it may be assumed that mother and child "act as one" not in the special meaning of "action in concert" which is characteristic of differentiated social collectivities, but in a special and more radical sense. It is, however, a true social system in that there is "double contingency" and the points of view of both parties must be taken into account.[23]

What in turn may lie back of this "identity" at the stage of oral dependency, we will treat as pre- or proto-social. Until the oral dependency stage is reached, the child cannot be said to have become integrated in any social system. He is more or less only an "organism" in the sense of not being *socialized,* i.e., as seen from the point of view of an observer. To his mother he is a person in process of becoming. Furthermore, we must not be understood as holding that this "identity" with the mother is given at birth and is an expression of constitutional factors. On the contrary, we conceive it in its essentials as a product of *learning.* It is the end-product of the first major phase of the socialization process. Mother and child by this time—we have suggested on the eve of language-learning—constitute an authentic social system, but one of a very special sort, a kind of limiting case of the concept social system. We will have to take up various problems connected with it later. It may be suggested that it above all could not exist independently as a "society," but only in so far as the mother plays a representative role relative to larger and more complex systems, notably in this instance the nuclear family.

---

22. Cf. especially E. H. Erikson, *Childhood and Society* (New York: W. W. Norton and Co., 1950).

23. Thus the child can fulfill the mother's expectations or withhold his compliance, and he can both ask and protest.

Next arises the question of following the binary series from the four-member case in the direction of increasing complexity in such a way as to give concrete sociological meaning to the cases of the eight- and sixteen-unit systems. This involves certain difficulties, since it means categorization which cuts across much current classification of types of social groups. However, we may suggest that the step from four to eight consists in a bifurcation of the instrumental-expressive category by a cross-cutting differentiation of universalistic and particularistic aspects. The bifurcation on the instrumental side produces a distinction which has sometimes been referred to as the difference between technical and "executive" roles.

The parallel differentiation on the expressive side is that between integrative functions which are primarily particularistic, and pattern-maintenance-tension-management functions which are primarily universalistic in focus.

These distinctions are shown in tabular form in Figure 4. The fact that it has proved necessary to resort to terms in several boxes which are not in familiar sociological usage shows that this analysis involves cutting the cake of the classification of role-types in unfamiliar ways. The justification of making these particular distinctions—these rather than others—will thus have to rest on their utility for our particular theoretical purposes. At any rate the principles on which the distinctions are made should be quite clear.[24]

A word should be said at this point as to why the universalistic-particularistic distinction has been chosen as the *principium divisionis* at this point. For theoretical reasons the selection seems to rest between that and quality-performance. The reason for the choice is that the principle of construction of our structural series concerns successive stages of integration of the developing child in progressively more complex social systems. We assume that he must approach integration in this next grade of differentiated system from a "base" of integration primarily in the nuclear family. His status in the family system is funda-

---

24. The formal character of this classification should be clear. It does not, for example, allow for the multiple functions of concrete roles. Thus, on the simpler level the concrete father has both functions in adapting the family to its external situation, *e.g.*, by earning an income, and participating in socialization functions internal to the family.

FIGURE 4

8-Fold Differentiation of Role-Types

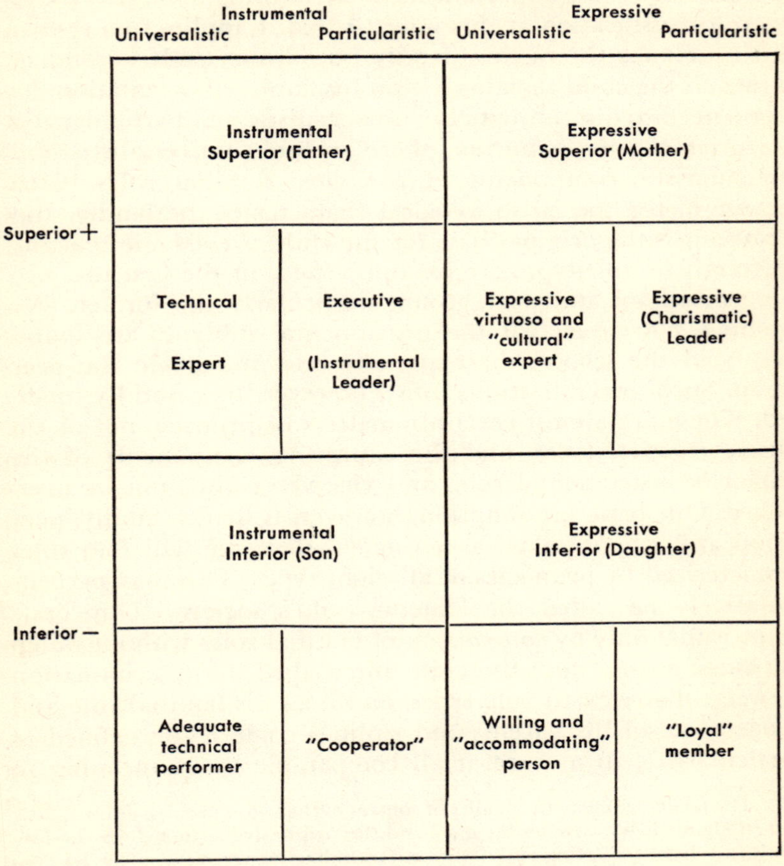

	Instrumental		Expressive	
	Universalistic	Particularistic	Universalistic	Particularistic
Superior +	Instrumental Superior (Father)		Expressive Superior (Mother)	
	Technical Expert	Executive (Instrumental Leader)	Expressive virtuoso and "cultural" expert	Expressive (Charismatic) Leader
	Instrumental Inferior (Son)		Expressive Inferior (Daughter)	
Inferior −	Adequate technical performer	"Cooperator"	Willing and "accommodating" person	"Loyal" member

mentally ascribed, as are all the other roles in the system. We presume that he cannot learn to assume primarily achieved roles until he has achieved a meaningful orientation to the *relation* between familial and extra-familial roles and objects. The universalistic-particularistic basis of discrimination seems to us to be the primary one by which the member of a subsystem becomes oriented to the larger world of which it is a part, in making clear distinctions between membership and non-membership and between qualities which cut across system-memberships and those which inhere in them.[25]

Perhaps the most important substantive thing to be said about this role-classification at this point is that it applies to a system which *includes* the nuclear family but also extends beyond it. So long as the child remains within his family of orientation, he has no need to discriminate the universalistic and particularistic categories of *role definition;* there are only universalistic and particularistic components of *the same* familial roles. Both because of the special sociological character of the family, and because it is the original base for the child, we assume that the universalistic role-types are for our society in the first instance those of school and peer group, particularly the former. We presume, moreover that the instrumental subtypes are found mainly in the school, the expressive ones mainly in the peer group. Such generalizations must, however, be carefully qualified. These are almost certainly matters of primacy, not of exclusive characteristics, and the expressive components of the primarily instrumental roles and vice versa must not be overlooked. Our basic presumption, however, is that in family, peer group and school, taken as a *single system,* we will find roles characterized by primacies of all eight types. This may perhaps tentatively be called the "latency-child's society." Our basic point is that only by *comparison* of familial roles with meaningful outside roles does the child internalize the discrimination between the relevant role types, and does his familial role and hence those of his parents and siblings come to be defined as particularistic in a sense at all comparable to its meaning to

---

25. The reader will note the duality of content of the two expressive-universalistic cells in Figure 4. We have on the one hand the "expressive virtuoso," i.e., he who excels in expressive "acting out" functions, including management of the tensions of others, and on the other hand the "cultural expert," he who excels in symbolization of normative patterns. This derives from the distinction between "tension management" and "pattern maintenance," which we have seen before is characteristic of the "latency" cell of our fundamental classificatory scheme (cf. *Working Papers*, Chap. V). We feel that this duality has fundamentally to do with problems of system-reference, with the placing of the system in question in a hierarchy of system and subsystem relationships. Looking "upward" in the series the problem is that of pattern-maintenance, i.e., the integration of a unit in the superordinate system. Looking "downward," on the other hand, is a problem of tension management, of meeting the "needs" of the system unit. We hope in the analysis of personality development which follows, to throw further light on the significance of this duality.

the adult sociologist.

The next step of differentiation we presume to be that which introduces the quality-performance distinction as a basis of role-type discrimination. It should be kept clear just what this means in the present context, which is that of categorization of components of *social structure*. It means that types of role are differentiated according to whether qualities of the incumbent, possessed independently of specific performances, or rather such performances, are the decisive criteria of allocating the *role—* not necessarily the individual incumbent as a person—to a given category. In this sense clearly the role of son is quality-oriented or ascriptive, while that of "class valedictorian" is clearly a performance-oriented or achieved-role category. Again, the relativity of these discriminations must be kept clearly in mind. There is always an ascriptive base from which relevant performances are evaluated, and similarly, there are always performances expected and differentially sanctioned in ascriptive roles. It is a question of what, within the relevant system-reference, are the critical criteria of classification. The social structure which embodies *both* the universalism-particularism and the quality-performance discriminations we interpret as the "adult" community structure.

This represents the main structural framework—structural, i.e., in terms of social systems—in which we will attempt to interpret certain crucial features of the process of socialization. It is quite clear that this framework has not been arrived at purely by induction. It has taken empirical suggestions from several sources, notably the psychoanalytic account of psychosexual development and the study of small group interaction, and attempted to put them together in terms of their relation to the main framework of pattern-variable analysis. It is felt that differentiation in terms of what we have previously treated as the basic categories of object-categorization which has been successfully used in the analysis of social structures, provided a stable theoretical point of reference. This is linked, both systematically and genetically, with the bases of elementary differentiation of the small group which, in turn, have been related to the structure of the nuclear family, and then this four-fold scheme of differentiation "projected" by the binary principle back to a one-role stage. It is thus clearly a piece of theoretical construction. The test of its usefulness and hence validity will be whether it proves capable of serving as a framework to order a range of facts about the socialization process which have heretofore not been treated in a sufficiently orderly way.

The Central Problem

It may be reiterated once more that so far we have attempted a sort of systemization only for a series of successively more highly differentiated *social* systems. We have not yet attempted to say anything very specific about personality development or its specific relations to social structure. We had best begin this next phase of exposition by stating what are to us the two most fundamental theorems of our general treatment. The first of these is that the primary structure of the human personality *as a system of action* is organized about the internalization of *systems* of social objects which originated as the role-units of the successive series of social systems in which the individual has come to be integrated in the course of his life history. His personality structure is thus in some sense a kind of "mirror-image" of the social structures he has experienced (though not of the momentary and not so much the presented as the perceived social system). He has perceived a whole series, *organized in depth*. These, then, are organized relative to functional foci which are in certain respects independent of any particular social system, or all of them put together; namely, the functional "needs" or "problems" first of the organism, later of the developing personality, *as systems*.

The second theorem is that *this* structure of personality develops, not *primarily* by a process of the modification of "primary drives" or "instincts," but by a process of differentiation of a very simple internalized object-system—we feel it legitimate to postulate a *single* such object at the beginning—into progressively more complex systems. A hypothesis which is secondary to this theorem, but none the less important, is that the principle of differentiation is that of binary fission. It will be clear that this view runs contrary to that dominant in most of current psychology, which may be stated as the view that the fundamental units of personality structure are the "primary drives" which are given in the constitution of the organism.

These then are held to become the centers of clusters of "secondary drives," all of which somehow "learn to get along together" in that the personality somehow functions as a system, without disintegrating in more than a certain proportion of cases. The "orthodox" view of this developmental problem thus revolves about the question of how originally disparate units or parts are put together to form a system. Our view is that the crucial question is that of how the originally undifferentiated system differentiates to form a more complex differentiated and of course also integrated system to be capable of the types of behavior as a system which we associate with the mature human personality.

It should be clear that our view makes the process of personality development much more closely analogous to the embryological development of the individual organism,[26] and also to the development of social systems than does the orthodox view. The case of social development may be briefly discussed. It is true that through conquest and "culture contact" and the like, disparate social elements are sometimes juxtaposed with one another and "fuse" into a single social structure which preserves elements from both. But these are clearly the exceptional cases. No serious student of comparative social institutions today would subscribe to the view that the great processes of elaboration of social structures—such as those involved in the development of modern industrial societies, took place mainly by any process other than that of differentiation within the same social systems from simpler antecedents. "External influence," such as Western influence on Japan has played a part, but surely the big thing is the process of internal system-differentiation.

The conception of the internalization of social objects is of course not new; it has above all been worked out independently and with different emphasis by Freud in his conceptions of identification and of the superego, by George Herbert Mead in his analysis of "taking the role of the other," and by Durkheim—we will draw heavily on these sources in our analysis below. It is, however, new to think in terms of the internalization of a *system* of objects and identify that with integrated participation in a specifically and technically delimited system of social inter-

---

26. For a brief discussion of the biological analogy see Appendix A.

action, and further, of course, to arrange these social systems in a continuously articulated series.[27]

Now it is necessary to review a minimum series of highlights on the psychological problem of internalization.[28] Our starting point is the consideration that, in order to account for the stability of a long term system of interaction, let us say for simplicity between two persons, there must be in the personality structure of each, *some form of organization of components* which regulates his pattern of action in relation to the other. For example, in the case of a stable marriage there must, to use Murray's term, be a personality "establishment" in the husband which serves to "orient" him to his wife, and which maintains a certain stability of that orientation throughout a range of varying stimulus-situations. This establishment must be in some sense a relatively stable subsystem of the personality which can survive, for instance, considerable variations in the wife's behavior, considerable periods of separation from her, etc. It clearly cannot be understood as only a function of the immediate stimulus situation. Such a personality establishment is what we mean by an internalized object. It is that structure in the personality which regulates the orientation of the individual to an object (or class of objects) in the situation, by defining for ego the *meanings* in the relevant respects of that object, and which has stability over time and a range of adaptability to changing conditions.

We have attempted to show elsewhere[29] that the internalized object must involve an organized pattern of the *meanings* which the external object has acquired. The accent here is both on *pattern,* i.e., *generalization* relative to any one specific percept of the object, and on *organization,* i.e., a structure of a plurality of different pattern components which have an orderly relation to each other. The significant external object, we assume, is *an actor in a role* vis-à-vis ego, an alter, conceived as a social object, or a collectivity. The organization of the internalized object then is an arrangement of patterns of meaning, with priorities and differentiation of aspects. A recent publication by

---

27. The relation between Freud and Mead in this field has been carefully and illuminatingly analyzed by Louisa P. Holt, *Psychoanalysis and Social Process* (Doctoral dissertation, Radcliffe College, 1949).

28. We will discuss this subject more in detail in Chapter IV.

29. *Working Papers,* Chap. II.

Olds[30] brings out further that the internalized object must be conceived as a system of action in the fullest sense. It is not only a "cognitive" entity but it is motivated, it involves a system of "dispositions" to respond and of functional significances for the personality as a system, i.e., of "needs." It is *both* object in the cognitive sense and need-disposition in the motivational sense. Furthermore, it has phase patterns of process or state of its own, can be latent or activated, has its particular specified goals, instrumental patterns, and integrative necessities, both within itself and relative to others in a larger system.

When the object is looked at in this way a further aspect of it becomes evident. The internalized object, that is to say, is the role-complement of the corresponding situational object. Alter is perceived in a role in relation to ego. He is perceived as an *action* system, as acting in relation to ego, and ego learns a patterned system of complementary actions toward alter. The pattern aspect which is internalized, then, is the *reciprocal interaction pattern,* the matched or complementary expectations in the form "if alter this, then ego that," and vice versa, "if ego that, then alter this." Alter as object then becomes "he who" in relation to ego under given circumstances does so and so. This is easy to see in relation to *alter.* But extension of the same principles shows that, by learning in the process of socialization *ego* comes to be *he who* in relation to alter does so and so under given conditions. *There is no other meaningful answer to the question what ego is, if ego as personality is conceived to be a system of action.* It is only that this basic pattern must be generalized to conceive ego's personality as a complex *system* of patterned action subsystems relative to *n* alters, and not only, of course, to specific and particular alters as "individuals" but to categories, collectivities, etc. This complementarity of role pattern, of course, is the aspect of the matter which Mead first clearly saw.[31]

Now the question can be raised, what is the process by which an internalized object in the above sense becomes established in the personality, and how can *systems* of such objects become

---

30. James Olds, *The Growth and Structure of Motives,* Chapter IV (Glencoe, Ill.: The Free Press, 1955).

31. Cf. G. H. Mead, *Mind, Self, and Society* (Chicago: University of Chicago Press, 1936).

established? We have already suggested that systems of social objects develop through differentiation of previously established internalizations, that it is not possible, as it were, arbitrarily to "insert" a new internalized object into a personality without reference to the previously existing object-system.[32]

With respect to the process then, it is quite clear that we interpret it *always* to have two aspects, a social interaction aspect and an "internal" personality aspect. We conceive the most important contribution of the present analysis to lie in its attempt *systematically* to articulate these two aspects, and to refuse to deal with either of them in isolation from the other. Looked at in socialization terms, there is always one, or a team of "socializing agents," the alters who, at the end of the process under consideration become players of the critical roles complementary to that of ego in the system of social interaction *into* which he is being socialized. But he will be functioning as a full member of that system, in a stable state, only at the end of the process in question. Not only ego himself, but the relevant alters must therefore play a different role at the beginning of the process, with some sort of modification of it in course until this end state is reached.

Analysis of processes of social control has shown that those who play a strategic part in such processes as agents of control must play at least a dual role. They must, to some important degree, participate with the "deviant" (e.g., the sick person) in at least a limited way "on his own terms." They must, that is to say, be authentically parts of a deviant subsystem of interaction. But at the same time they must also play an authentic role in the wider system relative to which the subsystem is defined as deviant; the physician is not himself "sick" but "represents" the society of the non-sick in his interaction with his patients. A primary aspect of the process of social control then, and similarly of socialization, consists in the transformation of this key object from predominance of the "deviant" role to that of the "conforming" one.

In an analogous way a mother, who interacts much more intensively and directly with a small child than does the father, may act as spokesman of the mother-child system in "explain-

---

32. A much more detailed analysis of the process of differentiation than can be attempted here will be presented in Chapter IV.

ing" to the father how "little" the child still is and hence what consideration she must therefore give him.

Realizing that to be a child is not to be "deviant" we can still take this paradigm as applying also to socialization.[33] The socializing agent always as a total person plays at least a dual role in relation to the "socializee." From the point of view of the larger, more complex system[34] in which he participates, one of these roles is analogous to the role of the deviant, in that it is only conditionally legitimized. Very generally we may say that the socializing agent uses his interaction in the subordinate subsystem role to motivate the child by forming an attachment to him. He then uses his other role as in some sense defining a "model" for the child to emulate and as a basis of "leverage."

Motivation of the initial effort to learn to conform with the model, however, derives from the "lower order" attachment, and the expectation that the child will attempt to follow a model not belonging to this system constitutes a violation of the expectations of the initial system, hence is frustrating. The system must, in the process, be able to cope with the products of this frustration, as well as impose the techniques of learning the new role.

The paradigm of social control referred to above, is formulated from the points of view both of the superordinate, and the subordinate system. Permissiveness is allowance of expression of need and dispositions which result from frustration and which are in conflict even with the norms of the lower level system. Support similarly is given "in spite of" failure, in some respects, to live up to the norms even of that same lower level system. "Denial of reciprocity" on the other hand is justified in terms of the norms of the wider system; to reciprocate would bring the socializing agent wholly into the lower level subsystem and undermine his other role. Similarly manipulation of rewards takes place in terms of the superordinate system role; only behavior which is in accord with the norms of the superordinate system, appropriate of course to the learner's newly acquired role within it, is positively rewarded.[35]

---

33. We can speak of deviance only if the child remains too long in a given phase of development or is prematurely pushed out of it.

34. Which, of course, is always one in the series we have sketched.

35. These relationships will be more fully analyzed in Chapter IV.

We presume, then, that each phase of the socialization process is analogous to a therapeutic process, in that the socializing agent (s) plays a dual role, and his attitudes are compounded of the four components distinguished in the social control paradigm, in the proper proportions and sequence. Let us now turn to a few highlights of the psychological aspect of the process. In a very broad way we may say that it has a cognitive facet and a motivational facet. In its cognitive aspect it is the building up of the "concepts" of the relevant objects, i.e. the appropriate internalized structures in the relevant cognitive respects. After the first social object concept has been built up we presume that the production of new concepts involves fission of previously internalized objects. This in turn involves apparently a minimum of four different "categorizations" at every step. First there must be a discrimination between those "aspects" of the previously undifferentiated object which are now treated as distinct objects. Thus as we will argue below, if the original "unicellular" personality is conceived as a "mother-child identity", the first differentiation involves the discrimination, from the point of view of the child as ego, of "you" from "me." The child becomes an object to himself *as distinguished from* the mother. But the original "identity" object does not simply disappear, it changes its character and becomes what sociologically we call a collectivity, it is the "we" which comprises both you and me. There has occurred, concomitantly with the discrimination of the you and the me, a generalization in that "weness" is a characteristic common to both objects which have had to be discriminated. Finally, in order for the category of "weness" to make sense, there is the further at least implied discrimination between "we" and "non-we" or "they," i.e., the recognition of the existence of objects which do not belong to this collectivity or category. We may treat this non-we as, in the logical-theoretical sense, a "residual category." We presume that with every step in the differentiation and organization of the object world for the child, there remains at least one such residual category, that namely of objects known to exist but not yet positively brought within the specific categorization system. However, this discrimination further implies the concept of a "world" in which both "we" and "they" are comprised.

It is further essential to note that in discriminating between the you-me categories and the we category, the child has made a distinction of *levels*. In logical, i.e., categorization, terms this is a matter of levels of generalization. But it is concomitant with actual organization of an action system. You and I act independently, but also interdependently in relation to each other. But we are also units in a system, designated as "we." There must be some conceptualization of the system as well as of its units, i.e. the system is an object just as truly as is the unit. As we put it sociologically, in some situations its members "act in concert."

There is also, however, the motivational side of the psychological process. Here we presume that much of current learning theory can be adapted to our purposes. In an exceedingly schematic way we may attempt to fit this into our social control or therapy paradigm. The patient comes to the physician with a "complaint," an unsatisfactory state of affairs which motivates him to ask for and accept "help." Then in the early stages of the process a positive transference is established. We may presume that the counterpart of these two crucial aspects of the therapeutic process is given in what we call the "dependency" of the child. This state is compounded out of three crucial elements. First there is *frustration* in that in some crucial respects the child is dissatisfied; he doesn't like what he has, he wants things he does not have and he doesn't fully understand the demands made on him. Second there is *attachment* to or dependency on the person who serves both as an agent of significant present gratifications and potentially of relief of the frustrations. Third, there is, in the relevant respects, a difference of power, in that the socializing agent controls sources of gratification and frustration which are beyond the reach of ego's control.

Within the framework of these conditions, we presume that the process of learning involves a combination of the processes of instrumental and classical conditioning, and further than this, of discrimination and generalization, by virtue of which the newly learned elements are organized within the personality system.[36] Rather than attempt to elaborate these considerations

36. The general view of the learning process we are assuming is the one sketched in *Working Papers*, Chap. V, Sec. vi. As argued there, we believe that both the broad relations between instrumental and classical conditioning, and the basic patterns of integration of a system of action, thus of new elements into it, can

in general terms here, it seems better to deal with them more specifically in connection with each of the main phases of the socialization process. We do, however, assume that the basic paradigm of a learning-control process which we have applied to socialization as a whole, also applies to *each* of the main phases of it as a subordinate phase cycle. We will, therefore attempt to repeat the application to each of the paradigms that we have outlined above as the main phases of the socialization process.

Before entering upon this, however, one further general problem needs to be taken up briefly. It seems to be an implication of the conception of a developmental process as one of differentiation by fission, that there is something of the order of a "genealogical tree" of the differentiated units of the system at any given stage of its development. Once, that is to say, a division has taken place, there is a presumption that the further "descendants" of each of the parts will remain distinct from then on. Thus in the organism, once the differentiation of ectoplasm and endoplasm has taken place, some structures are derived from one, some from the other, but none from mixtures of both. Thus there is not one part of the brain derived from endoplasm whereas the rest is ectoplasmic, nor is the liver derived from ectoplasm whereas the spleen comes from endoplasm.

We are aware that there are many empirical problems connected with such a conception. The integrative imperatives of a system make quite clear that such independently derived elements cannot subsequently be uninfluenced by each other. Nevertheless if this proposition turns out to be true even in a broad sense it can provide a most powerful tool of analysis. It can, that is to say, enable us to locate in a temporal sequence, the points at which certain crucial structural decisions for the subsequent system took place. With due caution, we hope to make considerable use of this tool in the analysis which follows.

The Establishment of Oral Dependency

Within this framework, the first broad problem of tracing the process of personality development concerns how, from the situation of the neonate, what we have called the mother-child

---

be analyzed in terms of the general paradigm of process in systems of action. Cf. also Olds, *op. cit.*

identity comes to be built up.[37] Even at this stage we will treat the problem first in social interaction terms, attempting to interweave with this the appropriate consideration of psychological processes in both adult and infant. For simplicity we will refer to mother and child, but recognizing that "agent of care" is the essential concept and that it need not be confined to one specific person; it is the function which is essential.

The neonate, we assume, is not in any technical sense a *member* of any social system. Then what is he? The answer seems to be, an object of *possession,* of the family and specifically of the mother. As an object of possession he is valued, and *taken care of.* He is an object of pride, and must be "kept in good condition." This means of course that his organic needs must be adequately met, but also as an object of pride he is attractively dressed, encouraged, when he can, to smile in order to please people, etc. He is "shown off."

At the same time, of course, parents even of the newborn, do not see the child exclusively in terms of his present state but also of his potentialities for the future. From their point of view his status as a possession is inherently temporary. They also tend, in orienting themselves to him, to recapitulate their own developmental histories.

When this process goes on for a while, two important things tend to happen. First the child develops a set of *expectations,* not only about being cared for as such but with respect to specific agency. He establishes, that is, a dependency on the specific agent of care. He receives, not merely segmental gratifications, but "care." The specific acts of care then acquire a new and more extended meaning for him, they not only in fact gratify the particular need, but they come to *symbolize* the mother's attitude of wanting to take good care of him and his own right to be taken care of. Furthermore, the qualitatively different acts of care come to be associated with the same object, the same agent, so that he acquires a diffuse attachment to *her,* a *dependency on her.* There is generalization across the lines of differentiation between segmental needs, so that being taken care of becomes a single *system* of expectations which can function as a system.[38]

37. Cf. Figure 5 for a rough outline of the process.
38. This process is classically analyzed in Freud, *The Problem of Anxiety,* trans.

But secondly this state of being taken care of is never a state of pure and unadulterated gratification. There are of course

FIGURE 5

*Establishment of Oral Dependency
and Primary Identification*

A		G
Establishment of regulated oral dependency— Primary identification Care no longer organic gratification but symbolic (oral-erotic)	Gratification of dependency needs Denial of continual and exclusive attention Oral aggression	
Child as organism, i.e. physical object of possession Mother as possessor "taking care of him." Motivation: C—organic needs M—pride of possession— "good care"	Establishment of organic dependency Expectation of "right to be cared for"	
L		I

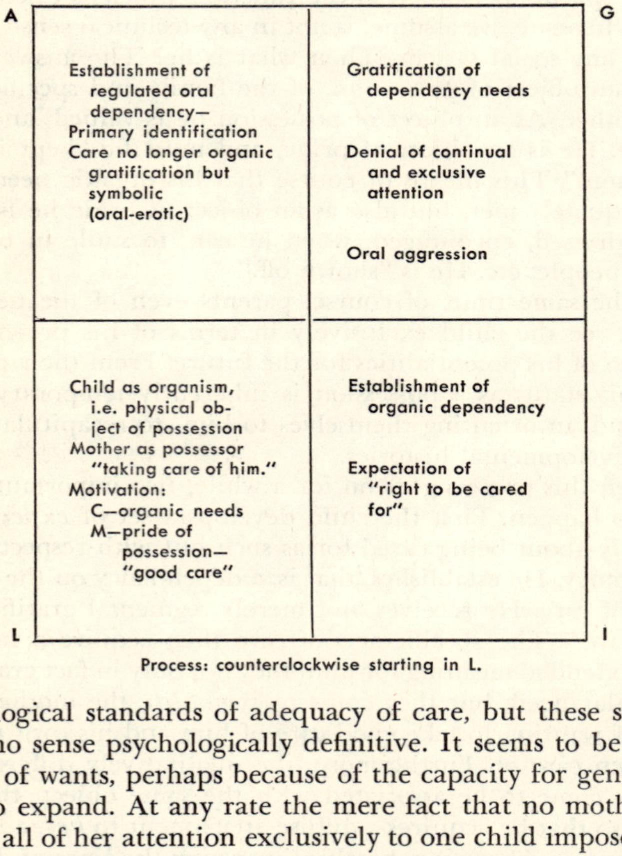

Process: counterclockwise starting in L.

physiological standards of adequacy of care, but these seem to be in no sense psychologically definitive. It seems to be in the nature of wants, perhaps because of the capacity for generalization, to expand. At any rate the mere fact that no mother can devote all of her attention exclusively to one child imposes limitations which mean that there must be elements of frustration in the situation. There has to be some sort of scheduling of gratifications, above all perhaps of attention. The rhythms of

by H. A. Bunker (New York: The Psychoanalytic Quarterly Press and W. W. Norton & Co., 1936).

care, that is, never exactly match organic rhythms, so a process of learning to adapt must take place. This means that a *conditional* element enters into the relationship. The child is not only gratified. Nor is he gratified and frustrated according to some pattern altogether independent of what he does. He soon learns to signal his needs. He learns to "ask," however primitively, or to protest, and he may or may not receive, according to the mother's reaction to his signal. The mother's care then gradually acquires the meaning of a set of *responses* to his own actions and "intentions."

We may presume that once dependency in this sense has come to be well established, the demand for attention, and for specific acts of care expands. The child manifests what, from the point of view of the mother's standards of child care, are illegitimate positive wishes. He is waked up at certain times though he would rather be allowed to sleep, he is given only so much to eat, less than he wants, he is put down when he would like her to continue to fondle him, etc. Whereas his dependency in general is welcomed and rewarded, excessive manifestations are pruned off by denial of reciprocity. Similarly, we assume that the inevitable frustrations produce aggression. Again though aggression may be treated more or less permissively, it presumably cannot, within the framework of good care, be consistently and positively rewarded at all times. In this respect, as in that of excessive demands, there is again denial of reciprocity. The balance between denial of reciprocity and positive reward gradually leads to the establishment of a stable "orientation" or expectation system in the child, the organization of his behavior both around the relation to the mother as an object, and involving certain *standards* of what are and are not legitimate expectations of his own gratification and of her behavior. When this process has reached a certain stage we can speak of the internalization of the mother as an object as having taken place, *in her role as the source of care.* It is not mother as a total personality as seen by adults which has been internalized, but that aspect of her with which ego has stood in a meaningful relationship of interaction. This internalization is what Freud meant by ego's primary identification.[39] In

---

39. Cf. S. Freud, *The Ego and the Id* (London: The Hogarth Press, 1927).

the action sense at this stage ego *is* as a personality primarily the pattern of expected reciprocal behavior in relation to this one object, his mother. But this he has had to *learn* to be, from a specific mother in a specific set of ways.

This is the sense in which it was meaningful to contend, as we did above, that his personality at this stage consists of only one internalized object. He has organized his personality over-whelmingly about a *single* role relationship, and he has in that relationship been mainly passive. The conditional element, which we believe to be of the first importance even here, has lain wholly on the mother's side. He has learned to ask and to protest, even to withhold, but *she* gratifies or frustrates. The power differential is at a maximum and ego's own role is over-whelmingly passive. The next stage, as we shall see, involves the step beyond asking and receiving or not receiving to that of *giving* and receiving *in return*.

Before leaving this stage a word may be said about oral eroticism. There seems no reason to doubt that erotic pleasure has a certain organic specificity. But we believe that the primary significance of eroticism for the socialization process is not that it is one more specific source of gratification like most of the organic needs, but that it has a special significance as a vehicle of generalization. The mouth as the locus of food-intake nat-urally is of vital significance to the child. But the fact that it is a specific source of pleasure associated with, but still partially independent of, hunger-gratification, makes it possible for oral stimulation to facilitate the stimulation of what in terms of organic function are a *variety* of different sources of gratifica-tion. This facilitates the process of symbolization on expressive levels because this specific pleasure generalizes into a diffuse feeling of well-being. Oral gratification, which is necessarily associated with the agent of care by virtue of the critical sig-nificance of feeding, can thus come to symbolize the positive aspect of dependency and hence of identification. The fact that it is originally specific but is also associated with diffuse sensa-tions of comfort and well-being is the key to its importance for this function.[40]

---

40. Cf. T. Parsons "The Incest Taboo in Relation to Social Structure and the Socialization of the Child," *British Journal of Sociology*, June, 1954.

The fact that the mouth acquires such a critical symbolic significance in a positive context seems to underlie its corresponding negative signficance, namely in connection with oral aggression. The fact is that the infant's capacity to "strike back," except by protest, is extremely limited. The mouth is, however, the primary organ of protest through crying and in course of time teeth can serve as weapons. But it seems likely that it is the fact that the mouth becomes a symbol-focus which is primarily responsible for its central place in both the eroticism and the aggression of infancy.[41]

The Transition from Oral to Love-Dependency

We may now take up the second main phase of the socialization process, that leading from oral dependency and primary identification to the establishment of what we have called the mother-child love relationship, and the differentiation of self as object from the mother-child identity.[42]

As a starting point it is essential to make clear that we assume that the child's "dependency need" has assumed priority as a regulator of his interactive behavior over any specific organic need. This of course does not mean that with extreme organic frustration, such as near starvation, there would not be "regression" to the primacy of the hunger drive. But it does mean that speaking of his behavior in relation to his mother as consisting primarily of instrumental means-acts toward gratifying his hunger drive, his comfort needs, etc. would not be an adequate way of looking at the situation. A certain level and rhythm of gratification of all these specific needs is of course a necessary condition of the stability of the dependency need as an action system. But it is this object-need-disposition system *as a system* which is the focus of the organization of the process. The specific needs are significant in so far as their gratification or frustration influences the functioning of this system as a system.

The child is, thus, no longer merely a "possession." He has become "incorporated" into a genuine social system (the sym-

---

41. It seems probable that the phantasy of the vagina dentata is associated with this context. Mouth and vagina are both cavities and identification makes it easy to attribute the teeth of one's own mouth to the other cavity symbolizing mother.

42. Cf. Figure 6.

bolism of oral incorporation is undoubtedly significant here). But he is in a limiting role in which dependency is maximized

FIGURE 6

*Establishment of Love Dependency
and the Autonomy of the Self*

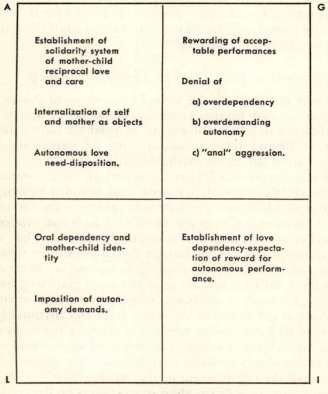

A ─────────────────────────────────── G

Establishment of
solidarity system
of mother-child
reciprocal love
and care

Internalization of self
and mother as objects

Autonomous love
need-disposition.

Rewarding of accep-
table performances

Denial of

a) overdependency

b) overdemanding
autonomy

c) "anal" aggression.

Oral dependency and
mother-child iden-
tity

Imposition of auton-
omy demands.

Establishment of love
dependency-expecta-
tion of reward for
autonomous perform-
ance.

L ─────────────────────────────────── I

Process: Counterclockwise starting in L.

and autonomy minimized, so that the autonomous component is not sufficiently important to constitute an independent boundary-maintaining action system. It is this development of an autonomy component of his personality and its differentiation from the dependency component which constitutes the next major step in socialization.

Let us look at the situation with respect to our two major elementary axes of system differentiation. Quite clearly, though we are dealing with a child much more active physically than an infant, perhaps beginning to walk and to talk, or about ready to, the power differential is still enormous. If mother and child be considered as a system, process in the system is overwhelmingly controlled by the mother. Furthermore, mediation of relations of the system to the external situation, notably the social situation, is controlled largely by the mother. Precisely because of his inferior power position the child, if he is to develop an autonomous role, must specialize in the expressive rather than the instrumental direction. We presume therefore that the structure of the two-member social system involves a relative "fusion" of these two axes of differentiation, mother is superior both in power and in instrumentality. Though presumably she is also superior in expressiveness, *relatively* this is the most readily available path for the development of an autonomous role on the child's part. How then, do we conceive the process to take place?

In the earlier stage we may say that, broadly speaking, the child's only available type of performance was to manifest a legitimate or an illegitimate need or wish, to "ask," or to protest or refuse to respond. The mother's only available sanction in turn was to gratify the wish or not to gratify it, i.e. in our technical sense to "respond" or not to. Now, increasingly, she expects the child to "do things for himself," which in view of identification we may assume is originally equivalent to "doing them for mother." This demand for autonomy is the focal source of the new type of frustration imposed. Doing things himself, then is rewarded, not only with specific segmental gratifications but with diffuse acceptance, e.g., "that's a good boy." More specific rewarding acts are defined as symbolizing this accepting attitude. The lower level of it, the floor or base line, is acceptance in the oral dependency status. But gradually, we assume, there is differentiation out from this willingness to give good care, of an activity of rewarding which is specifically a rewarding of the child's autonomous activity, his own manifestation of his "love" for his mother. On the base then of the giving and receiving of care, there develops a reciprocity of another order, an autonomous activity on the child's part and its reward by the mother. The child then is to her no longer alone "the object of her care," but also the object of her *love* which is the reaction or sanction for his autonomous actions which are directed both to himself and to her. Many specific acts of care presumably acquire meaning as symbols of this love attitude, but the primary criterion of differentiation seems to be the distinction between those rewards which are and those which are not *contingent on his autonomous initiative*. If this interpretation be correct then the apparently ironical conclusion follows that originally a mother's *love* as distinguished from care is always "conditional." We believe that this is a sensible conclusion; the conditionality of love becomes problematical not at this stage but at the next. We should, however, also remember that there is also a contingency element on the child's part—he too can refuse to love or show his love—e.g. by not eating what is offered.

Thus we have the development of a two-role system of social interaction, in which one role, that of the mother, involves first giving care, but also giving love, the other, that of the child, first giving love, but inevitably to balance the system, to some extent also giving care (both to himself and to mother)—which is a function in the system and can be defined instrumentally. The fact that he gives care to himself thus does not disturb things, though he may also "take care of" mother in small ways. Implicated in this interactive system there must, then, be two personality systems of *two* need-disposition units each, corresponding to two internalized objects. The mother, as now differentiated from the autonomous self, is primarily "she who takes care of me" which is to say she who performs the primarily instrumental role. Secondarily she is "she who loves me." In the case of the child's personality as object, on the other hand he is primarily "he who loves mother" and secondarily he who performs an instrumental function, i.e. takes care of self and mother.

As contrasted with the earlier stage, then, the primary sources of frustration are no longer negative, being forced to go ungratified for a time, but positive, the "demands"[43] for autonomous performance. Permissiveness at this stage then means a certain

43. A term used in *Patterns of Child Rearing*, a manuscript in preparation by R. R. Sears, J. W. M. Whiting *et al.*

tolerance of otherwise unacceptable activities and attitudes which appear when these new expectations are imposed. These include both regressive tendencies to remain in the old oral passivity, and actively excessive and inappropriate tendencies to autonomy and aggression. Support means steadiness of "acceptance" in spite of the "spottiness" of conformity with expectations. This means that the mother takes the attitude of a "loving" mother. She is ready and eager to reward fulfillment of expectations of autonomous performance, but there is an unconditional "floor" under her attitude in her acceptance of the child's oral dependency. The rejecting mother is not the one who has expectations and rewards conditionally but is the one who does not accept the supportive aspect of her own role as complementary to the child's love-*dependency*.

Because of the development of a more complex personality system on the part of the child, the possibilities of behavior which call for denial of reciprocity are more numerous. One obvious one of course is the regressive one, the passive expecting to be taken care of without autonomously doing his part in one or both of the two above senses. Here the mother's refusal to perform the gratifying acts of care is the primary means of enforcing her autonomy demands. But we may also expect the development of excessive, i.e. inappropriate autonomy, of which one prototype is attempting to do things beyond the child's capacity. Here he must be restrained and controlled. Finally frustration in either direction can be expected to produce aggression which in turn should not be reciprocated, either in the form of "giving in" to the child's demands, or of "fighting back."

This analysis gives us a good basis on which to interpret the significance of the anal complex at this period. It may be presumed that uniformly in all societies, though of course there is ambivalence, the predominant attitude toward human feces is one of disgust. "Cleaning up" after a child's defecation may be held always to be an onerous and unpleasant chore. Hence, the motivation to "train" him is always strong. On the other side, elimination is a function which is uniquely outside the control of the adult. A small child cannot eat unless food is provided by the adult; he can only accept or refuse the food. But within short time spans, apart from enemas and the like, the adult can neither make him defecate nor prevent him from doing it. Our suggestion is that this quality of being especially within the control of the child, along with the fact that the anus is capable of being eroticized, is the primary basis of its psychological significance. The child can express resistance or aggression either by refusing to defacate when expected to, or the other way around. But also, as Freud showed, defecation can acquire the significance of an expression of love, hence the feces become "gifts." The famous symbolic equation of "feces—child" seems very plausible in view of the reciprocity of role pattern between mother and child. Just as mother gives birth to child, so the child also "gives birth" to an object, he hereby in some sense is able to identify himself with his mother, symbolically to take her role.

We may now turn to certain problems on the object-categorization side of the picture. We have put it that at the mother-child identity stage the child has, in the action-system, already acquired a personality. He has not, however, yet acquired a "self," as a differentiated, autonomous "he who" actively does a variety of things. It is extremely important to make this distinction between the more autonomous and the more dependent parts as *objects* and with it to think of the evolving personality as now consisting in a *system* of more than one unit on the level of internalized social objects and need-dispositions, whereas at the earlier stage it was a system of which the units were organic needs only. This is to say that we have here the beginning of *organization* on a higher level of generalization with respect to the meanings of objects and hence behavior toward them. This, even more clearly than before, is a cultural-symbolic level. The mother-child system has elaborated and differentiated its common culture, part of which is derived from outside, but part of it and its specific meanings for the child built up in the course of the process of interaction itself.

What the child has now internalized is not merely an object, but a system of objects, which includes a set of *relations* between the component separate objects. In this sense we may say that in a much more definite way he has now internalized a set of *values* because it is a condition of the stability, both of the mother-child interaction system, and of the system composed of the two internalized social-object units of his personality, that the *relations* between the two object-components should be kept within certain limits of variation, which is to say, should conform with certain norms. The earliest inter-unit value-problem then is that of the proper balance between dependency and autonomy, or between care or nurturance and love. For this particular level of social system this is strictly a *moral* problem. For the developing personality it is the question of the relative strengths of the two major internalized object-motive units of the system. It is possible, then, for such a personality to deviate from the "norm" in either of two main directions. If the dependency need-disposition is relatively too strong the child becomes over-dependent. If the autonomous love component is too strong he is too independent, not able to accept the requisite amount of "care" from other persons. This means that he is compulsively "demanding" and hungry for "love," that is, for appreciation of his own diffuse autonomous performances, in a diadic situation.

This gives us, perhaps, a basis on which to venture an interpretation of what Freud meant by primary "narcissism." We have to think of a system of four units, two in each of the two interacting personalities. There are two main possible ways in which the integration of such a system can be disturbed. The first is the one just mentioned, that of an imbalance between the two qualitatively differentiated role or need-disposition types within the personality, cross-cutting the interpersonal differentiation. The other is a disturbance of the interpersonal relationship. This latter is the narcissistic case, as formulated from the point of view of the child. It is disorganization of the system by weakening the solidarity of ego and alter, from ego's point of view, minimizing the importance of alter, and hence tending to "go it alone." The tendency, then, will be, instead of depending on alter's sanctions, to use the complementary need-disposition unit of one's own personality as the sanctioning agent, which of course within limits is possible. Then the *internalized* nurturant "mother" is used to "take care of" the dependent element of the self. Similarly the "loving" autonomous component of the personality, instead of loving mother and looking to her reciprocal love, will tend to love only one's own personality and look to internal sanctions of self-acceptance. The more specific features of narcissism will vary according to whether the nurturant or the loving aspect has primacy in the personality. Thus we may suggest that the "hypochondriac" type of personality involves an important component of nurturant narcissism, while the overly "self-appreciative" type has a predominance of the autonomous love-motivation.

These considerations in turn call attention to a further problem about the structure of internalized object-systems. We have laid down as a fundamental proposition that what is internalized is a *reciprocal* ego-alter role-interaction pattern. Therefore, in internalizing "alter" as an object, ego also internalizes alter's orientation toward himself as an object (subject of course to possible distortions). The internalization of the nurturant "caring" mother includes the internalization of the object of care. It is only on such an assumption that turning of "libido" on to the self becomes understandable. Then we must say that in so far as the orally dependent child has internalized the mother as nurturant, he has also internalized "secondarily" her concept of himself as object of nurturance. He can thus take her role toward himself, or toward an alter. Similarly later, internalization of the mother as loving, also includes internalization of her picture of himself as reciprocally loving. Thus the idea of the internalized object as in some sense a "mirror-image" includes the idea of a "hall of mirrors" effect, namely the reflection inside the reflection, etc. The internalized personality establishment therefore, though originally built up through the experiencing of functions performed *for* ego by an alter, can from then on always serve as an agency of the performance of the same functions either in return for alter, or, in the role of alter, for ego himself. This seems to be the basic insight which Freud formulated with the concept of narcissism.

Finally, the idea of a personality which on the level of internalized social object relations has acquired a minimum of differentiated organization, seems very much to underlie a greatly enhanced capacity for symbolic manipulations and symbolic learning. It has already been suggested that the association of the first learning of speech with this period of development is not a matter of chance or merely of biological maturation. We suggest that capacity to converse with others is associated with awareness of self as autonomous agency, and that having a sufficiently complex personality is a condition of that internal conversation we call thought. Indeed one might go so far as to suggest that consciousness has its origin in the order of complexity of organization of the personality system we have described. The relation of consciousness to verbalization, and the difficulty of recovering pre-verbal memories even in the deepest psychoanalysis, are at least suggestive in this connection.[44]

The personality structure at the conclusion of each of the first two stages of development is graphically represented in Figure 7. It is more convenient, for purposes of exposition, to discuss the later stage first. The two need-disposition-object units are differentiated on the dual basis of power and of instrumental-expressive functions, with the instrumental primacy fused with the superordinate power role. Each unit then, involves a recip-

FIGURE 7

First Two Phases of
Personality Structure

A.
Oral Dependency
Personality

(1 unit)

Object—
    Parent-child identity

Need-disposition
    Oral dependency

Performance type
    "Asking" for care

Sanction type
    Passive reception of care

[Figure 7 continued on next page]

44. Cf. T. Parsons, "Consciousness and Symbolic Processes," *Problems of Consciousness,* H. A. Abramson, ed. (New York: Josiah Macy Foundation, 1954).

FIGURE 7 (contd.)

*First Two Phases of
Personality Structure*

B.
Love—Dependency
Personality

(2 units)

Superior Power

Instrumental

Objects:
   Cathected: Self
   Internalized: Parent

Need-disposition:
   Dependency

Performance Type
   Alter-oriented—Asking for and
      giving care
   Narcissistic—Self-indulgence

Sanction Type
   Alter-oriented—Accepting care
   Narcissistic—Self-gratification

Inferior Power

Expressive

Objects:
   Cathected: Parent
   Internalized: Self

Need-disposition:
   Autonomy

Performance Type
   Alter-oriented—Loving alter
   Narcissistic—Self-love

Sanction Type
   Alter-oriented—Receiving
      alter's love
   Narcissistic—Self-love

rocal role-relationship, which is presented as a cathected (situational) object and a corresponding internalized object. In the superior power-instrumental case the internalized object is the parent or mother, the cathected object is the dependent part of the personality which is cared for by the "parent." In the inferior power-expressive case the cathected object is the parent, the internalized one the autonomous self. The corresponding need-dispositions (motivational units) it is convenient to call dependency and autonomy. It is brought out that in each case there is an "alter-oriented" and a "narcissistic" possibility. It seems extremely likely that the development of a certain level of narcissism should be regarded as normal in order to balance the system, that pathological narcissism should thus be regarded as a disturbance of this balance, i.e. as *too much* attention to self as an object of orientation to the exclusion of alter.

In the case of the single-unit personality the situation is of course much simpler. The parent is cathected as the agent of care, but there is no independently autonomous self cathected. The child therefore is only a subsidiary object within the parent object; they constitute an identity. The single governing need-disposition is oral dependency, with the only active performance type is "asking" for care, while the appropriate sanction is passive receipt of care.

The Oedipal Phase

This brings us to the oedipal phase of child development which is the classical focus of psychoanalytic theory in this field. We may, therefore, regard our capacity to give a satisfactory account of the known facts of this phase and to produce additional insight, as a particularly crucial test case of the soundness of the approach we have adopted.

On the social system level, we regard this as the process of transition of the child from integrated membership in a two-member (autonomous) interaction system where power and instrumental-expressive differentiation are fused, to integration in a four-member, or basic role, system, where these two axes of differentiation have become segregated out from each other. In personality terms we regard it as the process by which in the internalized object aspect ego differentiates from a two-unit personality structure to a four-unit structure, by a process of bifurcation, on the instrumental-expressive dimension, of each of the earlier two into two more, making four altogether.

Seen in another perspective, the crucial event of this phase is the first stage of the assumption by the child of his sex role. The pre-oedipal child is, we assume, in the sense of fundamental personality constitution, sexless—as is in literal terms the "mother," since we assume that *for the child* the differentiation of the two parents as objects by sex has not yet on the requisite level been internalized.[45] Here we assume that the biological differentiations of the sexes provide ascriptive foci for allocation of the individual to one or the other socially institutionalized sex category. But they serve as symbols, in the same basic way that we have interpreted the oral and anal foci to serve. Freud referred to this as the "phallic" phase of psychosexual development, and this seems to be correct. The penis is the positive symbol of masculinity, and its absence, of femininity. The basic difference between it and mouth or anus in this respect is that for the first time, a basis is introduced for establishing a classificatory *difference* between children and not merely between parent and child. In the earlier phases there was only *one* ascribed role the child could assume—more or less satisfactorily. Now he must "choose" between *two*—though the pressure to choose the ascriptively right one is overwhelmingly great. In this first stage, however, sex role must not be interpreted primarily in terms of membership in the total society, but only in the family. We assume that beyond the family there is at this stage only an undifferentiated "non-we." Being a "boy" or a "girl" in the wider universalistic sense involves a further order of integration, this time in the peer group.

We may refer back to Figure 3 which shows the basic social structure of the four-role family as a system. Put in object terms, we have noted that the pre-oedipal mother-child system represented a two-member system, with a "you," a "me" and a "we" and the residual category of "non-we." Now "father" and "mother" are differentiated out from the earlier "you," and "self" (and/or sibling of own sex) and "sibling of opposite sex"

---

45. This is an important illustration of the point made above that it is dangerous to impute to the child common-sense *adult* categorizations of objects.

are differentiated out from the earlier "me." There is the further implication that an elaboration of the structure of "we's" takes place. There is still the old "we" of "mother and I." If the child is a boy, however, there is "father *and* mother," "we males," i.e., father, myself and brothers and "those females," mother and sister (s). Then there is the we of myself and siblings regardless of sex. Finally there is the overall "we" of the family as a whole over against the non-we of non-members of the family. We-ness then has become not a one-level structure, of the one autonomously interactive system, but a *hierarchy* of two levels, with a superordinate we-system, and a series of collectivity sub-systems, taking the possible permutations and combinations of each of the four basic roles, namely six. Because sex and generation are both mutually exclusive categories, ego can belong only to four of these six; two of them, the older generation, the parents, and the other sex, can be only "they" to him.[46]

On the psychological side, however, a personality system which can interact in any one of the roles in such a complex system, must be composed of at least four primary internalized object—need-disposition units, and must have certain relatively stable modes of organization of these units to each other. It is quite clear, for instance, that not all four of the six possible relational pairs in which ego participates directly can be treated equally and indiscriminately; they have to be ordered relative to each other as a condition of both social system and personality systems maintaining a relatively stable state. It is in connection with the importance of certain restrictions on their symmetry that we will attempt to interpret the significance of the repression of early eroticism, and its sociological counterpart, the incest taboo.

First, however, let us attempt to give a sketch of the developmental process at this stage comparable to those given for the two earlier phases of development. The best starting point is to recall that in the mother-child system it was the mother who played the predominantly instrumental role, whereas, in the wider familial system, of which the mother-child is, it will be

---

46. In terms of reference group theory here for the first time the distinction between membership and non-membership groups becomes positively categorized for ego. Cf. Merton and Kitt in *Continuities in Social Research*, Merton and Lazarsfeld, Eds., (Glencoe, Illinois: The Free Press, 1950).

remembered, a sub-system, it is the father. There is, therefore, a fundamental sense in which the father at the oedipal stage is the functional equivalent of the mother at the pre-oedipal stage. This is to say that the father is, symbolically at least, the primary source of the new "demands" for conformity and autonomous performance. The mother, on the other hand, this time as distinct "person," remains the primary source of "security" or "acceptance" in the love-relationship.

Permissiveness and support, then, tend to be focussed on the mother role in the form of continuing nurturant care, and expression of love. The more disciplinary aspect, however, focuses on the father role, above all the denial of reciprocity and the manipulation of positive rewards for adequate performance. This raises certain questions, particularly in connection with the American urban family, about concrete agency in relation to symbolic significance of the two parental figures, which we can take up later. The logic of the whole analysis, however, points to this broad differentiation of function in terms of its significance for the child.[47]

The new "demands" of course this time are differentiated by sex. They consist in the appropriate forms of behavior for a "big boy" and a "big girl" respectively, the symbolic significance of which will be taken up below. Both parents clearly act as socializing agents, as a team or coalition, hence their support is, from the point of view of the higher and more mature behavior standard, maintained "in spite of" continuing "childishness." The illegitimate strivings for which reciprocity is denied are above all dependency and aggression, but also premature adulthood, "precocity." There is reason to believe that the erotic sphere is particularly crucial in this whole connection. Clearly the trend is to shift the main supportive or security base from the mother as a person to the family as a collectivity, and to the parental pair as the responsible power-coalition.

47. In this connection the significance of the basic uniformity of structure of the nuclear family, discussed in Chapter VI by Zelditch, becomes evident. It is this basic uniformity of family structure which insures that the mother-figure is always the *more permissive* and supportive, the father the *more denying* and demanding. The basic problem concerns the roles of the two parents in the family as a system. If the boy is to "identify" with his father in the sense of sex-role categorization there must be a discrimination in role terms between the two parents. This is essentially a different question from that of agency in administering specific disciplines.

The higher level of differentiation allows a further very important phenomenon to appear at this stage. Since the "mother" can now be differentiated from an undifferentiated "parental figure," it is possible for both mother and child to act in representative roles vis-à-vis those outside the mother-child collectivity. This seems to be particularly important in the transitional phases. Before he has internalized the father as an object the child cannot be fully sensitive to his attitudes as sanctions. He can, however, be motivated to do things which please *both* mother and father and be rewarded by mother's love and nurturance. By some such process he comes to cathect the father—because mother both loves father and backs him up—and from this generalized parental object then a qualitatively different object can be differentiated out. In general we say that once this level of differentiation is reached, a transition to a next higher level always involves playing a representative role on behalf of the lower-order solidarity in its relations to the higher-order system. Here the significance of the dual role of the socializing agent becomes clear. Authentic participation in the lower-order system is a condition of adequately rewarding the child for his performance of the representative role in the earlier stages. At the same time participation in the higher-order system is essential to reinforcing the new demands necessary for learning the new role, including solidarity with other representatives of that new system. In this respect we may say, very broadly, that the mother role tends to be anchored *between* family and mother-child systems, the father role more between family and extra-familial systems.

The main structure of the new personality emerging at the end of the phase is graphically presented in Figure 8. It should be read with reference to the second part of Figure 7. The principle of its construction is simple bifurcation (vertically) of all the categories presented in the earlier figure on an instrumental-expressive axis. Calling attention first to object-categorizations, it will be noted that what was treated as the "mother" both as cathected and as internalized, in the two-unit personality is now divided into the two parental objects, "mother" and "father." We must understand this to mean that what to adults is the concrete object father was previously not discriminated, as a distinct, boundary-maintaining object system, but was part of the

FIGURE 8

The Post-Oedipal Personality Structure

	Superego	Id
	Instrumental	Expressive

Superior	Objects:
	  Cathected: Self (masculine)
	  Internalized: Father
	
	Need-disposition
	  Conformity
	
	External Orientation
	  Performance: Control of Alter
	  Sanction: Esteem
	
	Internal Orientation
	  P—Self-control
	  S—Self-esteem
		Objects:
		  Cathected: Self (feminine)
		  Internalized: Mother
		
		Need-disposition
		  Nurturance
		
		External Orientation
		  P—Giving pleasure
		  S—Response
		
		Internal Orientation
		  P—Self-indulgence
		  S—Self-gratification

Inferior	Objects
	  Cathected: Father
	  Internalized: Self (M)
	
	Need-disposition
	  Adequacy
	
	External Orientation
	  P—Instrumental performance
	  S—Approval
	
	Internal Orientation
	  P—"Reality testing"
	  S—Self-approval
		Objects:
		  Cathected: Mother
		  Internalized: Self (F)
		
		Need-disposition
		  Security
		
		External Orientation
		  P—Giving love
		  S—Acceptance
		
		Internal Orientation
		  P—Harmonization
		  S—Self-love

(Power: Superior / Inferior)

Adaptive functions } Ego { Integrative functions

undifferentiated "mother" or perhaps more correctly "parent" object. That at this stage, however, there should emerge two such differentiated objects is, in the light of our whole scheme of analysis, hardly problematical. Of course they appear in two places, as internalized objects in the upper row, as cathected objects in the lower.

It is perhaps somewhat more problematical that the autonomous "self" of the two-unit stage should also be treated as bifurcated, this time into what it seems reasonable to call a "masculine" and a "feminine" self, again both as internalized object and as cathected object. This treatment is nothing more than an application of the logic of the scheme. It does, however, have one immediate and interesting implication. This is, namely, that the differentiation of personality by sex does not involve a difference by presence or absence of certain critical motivational factors, but a difference in the *organization* of what are qualitatively the same factors or types of units. If this view is correct then we have deduced a basis of the "bisexuality" of the child which is independent of Freud's assumed "constitutional" bisexuality. The latter also almost certainly exists, but Freud's actual use of the concept certainly involved a good deal of ad hoc assumption. It seems to us entirely in line with the general view of personality development we are presenting that there should also be a psychologically independent factor of bisexuality.

Turning to the need-disposition aspect of the new organization, we have treated the "dependency" need of the earlier stage, corresponding to the parental object, as divided into the "nurturance" need and the "conformity" need, as aspects of the internalized mother and father objects respectively. Correspondingly the "autonomy" need-disposition of the earlier phase is treated as dividing into those of "security" as the expressively differentiated or "feminine" self, and "adequacy" as the instrumentally differentiated or "masculine" self-object.[48]

---

48. There is always a difficult problem of terminology in connection with this type of theoretical development. We have chosen terms all of which are current in social science and psychological literature, but have given them somewhat special meanings. Careful consideration, however, indicates that the meanings here are not very far away from current usage, always making allowance for the fact that current usage is far from consistent.

In order to avoid misunderstanding, however, it is best to try to state as specifically as possible what is here understood by these four terms. First, the term nurturance has already been used. Here we mean by it that component of the original dependency need-disposition which concerns the positively gratificatory aspect of the original giving of "care." It is the need for assuring segmental gratifications, relatively independently of their conformity with normative standards. As in all the types of need, it may be inwardly or outwardly directed, to self-gratification or the gratification of an alter. This is not the critical criterion, but rather the primacy of the segmental need, the motivational unit as object of attention. Again this may be relatively independent of the exact content of the need, but we may presume erotic needs are prominent. The term conformity on the other hand refers to the need-disposition to enforce or implement conformity with the highest level of normative standards which have yet been internalized—again either in ego's own behavior or that of alter. In schematic theoretical terms we may say that this differentiation separates the two aspects of the content of the latency cell of our general paradigm, the "tension management" aspect and the "pattern-maintenance" aspect. It should be noted that only when such a differentiation has taken place does moral or "superego" conflict over the legitimacy of indulgence, become possible.

The terms security and adequacy are given a parallel meaning. Security is that aspect of the earlier undifferentiated autonomy need-disposition which concerns the *relational* aspect of the significance of the cathected mother-object. It is the need to receive love or acceptance and to "show solidarity" in relation to an alter, or other members of a collectivity by virtue of their shared membership—as well as to "accept" other parts of the personality. Adequacy, on the other hand, refers to the autonomous *performance* aspect, the need and disposition to *do* specific things which are expected and acceptable. These clearly have to do with the differentiation between integrative and adaptive functions respectively.

This way of looking at the structure of the post-oedipal personality seems to have a most important relation to Freud's famous classification of the structural components of personality, namely id, ego and superego. The id, we may say, centers in what we have called the nurturance need-disposition. It is that motivational sub-system which has the most direct genetic relation to pre-socialized organic needs and to the earlier stages of personality development, in a sense the one from which newly organized subsystems have branched off. The erotic component is particularly important in it because of its significance for generalization of gratification and cathexis in the whole pre-oedipal period, but for example relatively uncontrolled hunger-drives would, according to this view also be treated as id-drives. The erotic component is however only part of the id and is itself internally differentiated even at this phase, into oral, anal and phallic components. In this view, the id is particularly closely related to the genetic history of the personality. It contains all the residua of earlier phases which have survived the branching off process of more recent differentiations. It contains more "archaic" elements than any other motivational subsystem. It is, however, of the *first* importance to our view that we do *not* define the id as a "constitutional factor," a bundle of "instincts" in that sense.[49] It is a part of the differentiated and organized personality system which as such has become organized by processes of learning.

The superego clearly comes very close to what we have called the conformity need-disposition, and the association with the internalized father-object clearly agrees with Freud. Finally Freud's ego, we suggest, comprises *both* components of the previous autonomy need-disposition. The "reality-testing" aspect of the ego clearly belongs to what we are calling the "adequacy" need-disposition. It is perhaps a little ambiguous in strict Freudian theory where the need for love or security in our sense belongs. But our schema makes it possible to distinguish it on the one hand from the nurturance needs and on the other from those for adequacy. Its relation to autonomy clearly, in spite of the differences, makes it logical to relate it to the adequacy motive. Perhaps this distinction between the adaptive and the integrative aspects of the ego may prove helpful. It may be remembered that each of these need-dispositions operates *both* internally and externally. Internally this security need-disposition then seems to relate to the integrating function in the

---

49. I believe this interpretation to be in accord with Freud's most mature view.

personality itself as a system—"insecurity" in this sense is a threat to this internal integration the source of "ego-anxiety." Freud clearly treated personality integration as ego-function. Externally, on the other hand it is the "affiliative" need-disposition, the focus of attachments and loyalties.

To return to our own more specific paradigm, our next step is to note two further breakdowns, that into the performance or "disposition" aspect and the "sanction" or "need" aspect of each need-disposition, and second that into the internal and the external reference. Here we encounter what is theoretically a most important emergent development, namely it turns out that the four "appropriate" sanction types for these four need-dispositions are the four basic sanction types which have played the primary role in our previous theoretical work.[50] These types have been worked out from the analysis of social interaction and hence their most direct relevance is to the type of *r*eaction expected (needed) from alter. Let us first run through them in these terms. *Response* we have treated previously as the attitude of readiness to provide segmental gratifications, to serve as a consummatory goal-object, or to serve as the direct agent of the availability of such objects. This clearly is the sanction-type most appropriate to the nurturance need as we have defined it. Secondly, *acceptance*—which at an earlier stage we called "love" —is (in social system terms) acceptance in terms of solidarity of membership in a collectivity, the diffuse symbolic expression of the attitude of recognition of belongingness. In the external reference this, we presume is what the sense of being secure means, to be unequivocally accepted as "belonging" by the significant alters.

Third, *approval* we have defined as the attitude appropriate to the positive sanctioning of functionally specific instrumental performances, in terms of their effectiveness or efficiency. It is the attitudinal generalization of recognition of attainment of standards of efficient performance. Finally, fourth, *esteem* we have defined as the attitude of positive overall evaluation of a

---

50. This was a wholly unanticipated development. For the most recent discussion of these problems cf. *Working Papers*, Chap. V. The origins of this classification go back to T. Parsons and E. A. Shils, "Values, Motives and Systems of Action" in *Toward a General Theory of Action* (Cambridge, Mass.: Harvard University Press. 1951), and extensive use was made of it in *The Social System*.

person, a collectivity or other object, in terms of universalistic standards by which it is measured in comparison with other objects, independently of its belongingness in a particular relational system. This is the appropriate positive sanction for conformity with the generalized standards which are institutionalized in the system of interaction.

Clearly the coincidence of such a generally important classification of sanctions with the differentiations from each other of the four basic familial role-objects as internalized in the personality, is a consequence of the generic significance of the structure of the nuclear family. It seems probable to us that this insight would not have been arrived at had the structure of the family continued to be treated primarily in terms of the biological specificities of generation and sex, without seeing that these are also *symbols* of much more generalized meanings.

Once given the classification of sanction types, the appropriate corresponding performance types can be directly read off from our fundamental interaction table. They are, clearly, for response, "giving gratification," i.e. being nurturant, to alter, for acceptance, reciprocal acceptance or love, or "showing solidarity," for approval, adequate instrumental performance relative to the specific given goal or function and, for esteem, adequate control or discipline to secure conformity with the given standards, not in one specific functional context, but overall.

This classification brings to light a most important and interesting asymmetry, which follows the instrumental-expressive distinction. It will be noted that on the expressive side of the table, performance and sanction are directly symmetrical with each other, mutual response, mutual acceptance. On the instrumental side, on the other hand this is not the case. This is because in the instrumental case the functional reference is *outside* the system, to its relations to its situation. The sanctioning agent, however, is *inside* the system. Hence what the sanctioner can give cannot be a direct exchange of the "same" thing for what the performer has given, because the latter has had to manipulate the relations of the system to external objects, independently of the sanctioner's activity. It seems evident that this is particularly important to the analysis of the functioning of representative roles. It is also important to work out its analogue for the personality as a system. In this respect we infer that superego functions and *adaptive* ego functions will have in common this asymmetry relative to id functions and integrative ego functions.[51]

Let us now take up briefly the problem of the relations between the external, socially interactive, and the internal intra-personality references of these object and motivational concepts. This is again the problem of "narcissism" on our present, more differentiated level of personality structure. Intrinsically, that is, each unit of the personality structure has an orientation to a situational cathected object—or class of such objects—and to an internalized object or class, one or more other units of the same personality system. This duality seems to be the direct result of the internalization of reciprocal role patterns and hence what we called above the "hall of mirrors" structure of personality organization. Thus the nurturance need is, as derivative from the internalized mother object, oriented to the "self" whom the mother historically has nurtured, and also to such external objects as may be "identified" with this self-object. In the one relation it is the "id-drive" which seeks self-gratification, that is not merely passive *asking* for gratification, but the internalized mother directly facilitating the gratification. Following through our genetic analysis shows that *both* these aspects were involved in the original internalized mother. In the other relation, on the other hand, it is the need to give gratifying responses to an alter, to a cathected external object. The balance of these two fields of operation of the need-disposition is clearly as important to concrete behavior as is its relation to other need-dispositions. The narcissistic case, we suggest, is the one where the self-gratificatory orientation has undue predominance over the alter-gratificatory.

Essentially the same order of analysis can be applied to the other three need-disposition units. Self-love, in this technical sense, is the cathexis of the internalized "mother" by the internalized "feminine" self as the need to love and be loved. This is in competition with the cathexis of external love-objects, which must in this specific context be regarded as "mother-

---

51. Essentially the same asymmetry has been shown by Olds in his analysis of the relations between love and approval as motives. Cf. James Olds, *op. cit.*, Chapter IV.

substitutes"; in a technical sense the cathexis of the actual mother as object has been generalized to the new object by the mechanism of substitution. Similarly self-approval involves cathexis of the internalized masculine self object by the internalized father-motive, whereas approval of others is possible by generalization of this through substitution from the masculine self to other objects "identified" with it, i.e. "brothers." Finally self-esteem is the cathexis of the internalized father-object by the internalized masculine self. Esteem of others, on the other hand, is generalization of this to others who function as "father-substitutes." In each case, we may say, the actual familial role-figure serves as a kind of a focus for the generalization process to operate, i.e., as a symbol.[52] Through internalization, the attitude appropriate to it comes to be applied to a component of the personality system, and through further generalization, it is extended from the original familial object to other objects which in the relevant respects are categorized with the familial object. Perhaps in this connection we may speak of "internalization" as a special case of the process of generalization, of which "substitution" is the other principal type.

These considerations give us a possible way of defining the controversial concepts of guilt and shame so that they are consonant with a generalized analytical scheme. From this point of view guilt would be internal "disesteem" and shame, internal "depreciation." Guilt, that is, would be the feeling centering in the internalized masculine self motive, that the appropriate attitude of the internalized father, the superego, was not deserved, i.e., its control functions in enforcing conformity with normative standards were not being adequately performed, or threatened not to be. Shame on the other hand would be the feeling, centering in the "feminine self-object" that the appropriate attitude toward the internalized mother-object, that of response or, in value terms "appreciation," was misplaced because this part of the personality was not performing its function of ensuring adequate nurturance, both of ego's own personality and of the alters involved. To be ashamed is to be "displeased" with oneself.

---

52. Cf. Parsons, "The Father Symbol" in Finkelstein *et al.*, Eds., *Symbols and Values: An Initial Study* (New York: Harper & Bros., 1954).

It seems probable that what we ordinarily mean by shame includes still a further component, namely a special sensitivity to the attitudes of alter. This can, we feel, be understood in terms of the more general structure of the personality system as seen in the light of its developmental history. The nurturant need-disposition complex is peculiarly associated with dependency on both the levels on which we have discussed this concept. In this sense "narcissism" focuses more on self-nurturance than any other of the four oedipal-stage personality-units. But, because of its history this is the least acceptable basis for "justifying" an orientation. Hence if it is the nurturant component which is felt to be "lying down on the job" there is a special motivation to refer to alter as the source of sanctions rather than to an internal source.[53]

Clearly it is central to the whole tenor of our analysis that the significant situational social objects acquire complexes of *meaning* to the chld. This is coming very close to saying that they become the centers or foci of symbol-clusters, the points around which such clusters are organized. The basic sense in which this is true of the familial objects of the nuclear family is, we suggest, that of expressive meaning. The familial objects may, then, be said to be the generically fundamental bases of the organization of the system of expressive symbolism for a personality. They are the prototypical expressive symbols.

The interpretation of such a statement may be followed up in two directions. First, specific and discrete nonsocial objects, physical objects, and above all the specific acts and bodily attributes of the significant persons, tend to acquire their expressive meanings primarily by their modes of association with the familial figures. This set of problems involves above all the processes by which a "complex object" on the one hand, the category of possessions on the other, come to be built up.

53. David Riesman in *The Lonely Crowd* (New Haven, Conn.: Yale University Press, 1950), has emphasized the tendency to "other-direction" in considerable numbers of the American population including many of those which are strategically placed, for instance in metropolitan communities. It may be suggested that the pattern of other-directedness is largely a manifestation of this set of mechanisms of personality—the strength of dependency needs and compensation for the temptation to narcissism by transfer of cathexis to others, perhaps in our society particularly a "generalized other." It would be expected that because of the strength of achievement values in our society this would be an important area of strain. It does not follow that this pattern is likely to become dominant.

The other direction of analysis concerns the implications of the placing of these familial objects in the genetic sequence of personality development. In this connection, we suggest that the basic framework of later, and hence more "sophisticated" expressive symbolism, develops by the "derivation" of different types of such symbolism from the expressive meanings of the familial figures. Therefore we would have the "father-symbol" cluster, the "mother-symbol" cluster, the "brother" and the "sister" clusters. For example it seems reasonable to suggest that in this genetic sense, religious symbolism—having to do with a "supernatural" toward which an "attitude of respect" is manifested—is derived from the two "parental" clusters. It is at least suggestive that in the Judeo-Christian tradition, a strong preference is shown for father symbols, sometimes of course directly using the kinship term, whereas it is at least tempting to suggest that in the "pantheistic" Oriental religions, the symbolism of the supernatural is primarily derived from the maternal complex.[54] There is no space to follow out this theme here, but attention is called to the possibilities which this unexpected correspondence of the familial object system with the four fundamental types of expressive attitude has opened up.

Returning to problems closer to the field of socialization, we may next raise again some of the questions involved in the concept of "identification." This has of course been a notably ambiguous and controversial concept in the literature of the field. Perhaps we can suggest some of the sources of the difficulties and a constructive way out of them. Freud, it will be remembered, introduced the concept in connection with what, above, we have called the "mother-child identity." The principal difficulty seems to arise from the attempt to use the same concept in relation to the processes which go on in the oedipal period, above all with reference to sex-role assumption. Thus a boy is often said to "identify" with his father at this period and a girl with her mother.

In our opinion the trouble comes from sticking to the attempt to deal only with the relation to *one* role-personality in a situation where multiple role-relations are already involved. In the case of "primary" identification there was only one object, the

---

54. This problem is particularly well handled in an unpublished memorandum by Robert N. Bellah, "A Typology of Religious Orientations."

nurturing or "caring" mother. Identification with this object could be treated as an adequate focus of the total internalization process. From the child's point of view, in the significant sense, he and the mother become one.

When it comes to the oedipal period, on the other hand, for the boy his father is only one of four basic types of object. The process of discriminating him as an object and developing a stable orientation toward him as distinguished from the mother, is *one part* of a more general process of reorganization of his personality system as a system in terms of an altered relation to an external social system. The essential point is that *both* of these are systems. One cannot treat the father as an isolated object and analyze the relation to him, without treating him as part of the nuclear family as a social system. Similarly he is not "internalized" or "identified with" out of the blue without reference to the pre-existing structure of the personality system.

What happens, then, is the reorganization of the total personality as a system. This involves the addition, *by fission,* of two new object-units, the father as discriminated from mother and the discrimination of ego from sibling of opposite sex. There is also a differentiation of the collectivity structure from the simple mother-child "we" to a familial "we" with six potential elementary sub-collectivities. The focus of a son's identification with his father is his self-categorization as belonging to the "we-males" subcollectivity—which is the same thing as saying that he and father share the category of "maleness." It means that this we is set over against a "they" of the females to which he *cannot* belong. But there is another they to which he also cannot belong, namely that of the "parents"—in *this* nuclear family—and his father does belong to this one. In this sense the boy cannot identify with, i.e., play the role of, his father, but only with his brother if any, and with respect to generation, not sex, his sister. It is, however, profoundly true that in this process *both* boy and girl internalize the father as an object. *This* aspect is strictly parallel with internalization of the mother in the primary identification, but the others clearly are not parallel, for the simple reason that in a one-unit system there are no analogies to many features of a four-unit system.

It should not be forgotten that, if our interpretation is correct, at the same time that the child is discriminating father as an independent object, he is also discriminating siblings, notably the sibling of opposite sex. This figure is also internalized, and ego is also categorized with the sibling over against the parents.

There is still another crucially important aspect of this whole problem. The self-categorization of ego as a member of a collectivity, we have seen, is, in the full sense of the internalization of that collectivity as an object, *the same thing* as the internalization of the common values of the collectivity as a social system, or this process is the focal part of this categorization process. In internalizing the father and sibling objects as discriminated from mother and self, and thereby internalizing the family as a collective object, therefore, he is internalizing *a new set of values*. The father is, for both sexes, the focus of this aspect of the process because, of the pair which possesses superiority of power, he is the *new* element vis-à-vis the earlier mother-child subsystem, he therefore, preeminently "represents" to the child the values of the wider system precisely in their *differences* from the values of the narrower system. This is connected with the fact that he, compared with the mother, plays the more instrumental role in the familial system, and vis-à-vis the outside, is more "responsible" for the family. This responsibility is focal to his "authority" to symbolize these familial values to his child.

We suggest that the term identification has tended to be used to designate a variety of these different aspects of the total complex, but that the complex as a whole has not been adequately analyzed. We can suggest a usage of the term which is free of ambiguity, namely that identification should designate the process of internalization of any common collective "we-categorization" and with it the common values of the requisite collectivity. In this meaning of the term, in the oedipal phase of development a child undergoes not one but *three* new identifications. Two of them are common to members of both sexes, namely internalization of the familial we-category, and of the sibling category, namely "we children." The third, by sex, differs for children of each sex, in this third sense the boy identifies with his father, the girl with her mother. It should also be noted that in none of these three senses does identification mean the internalization of a *concrete* role-type. The only basic familial role type which a child *can* share with another is that of son or daughter with the sibling of the same sex. To be sure he can prospectively become *a* father, but only in another nuclear family; he cannot assume *his* father's role in *this* nuclear family. It is precisely this impossibility which, in one sense, defines the oedipal crisis for the boy. To realize the goal of becoming a father, an elaborate further developmental process must be gone through.

Sex Role, Eroticism and the Incest Taboo

With this framework in mind, let us come back to the problem of sex-role assumption and the oedipus complex in Freud's sense. Let us start with the relevant aspects of the structure of the nuclear family as a social system. The mother-child, pre-oedipal system is of course a subsystem of this. The question is how this subsystem can, by a process of transformation, be absorbed into the larger system, through change in the structure of the roles, without disorganizing the family as a system. Maturation of the child and the cultural demands as to what kind of behavior is appropriate for a "big" boy or girl, make simple maintenance of the pre-oedipal status quo untenable. We will first assume that inertia will operate in the motivational systems of both mother and child, but more prominently the latter, because a lesser proportion of the mother's personality is invested in this particular subsystem. Regardless of the sex of the child, the "line of least resistance" would be to move the child into a role analogous to that of the husband (father). This would make it possible to preserve primary solidarity with the mother, especially advantageous of course for the child.

This of course is blocked by two main circumstances. The more obvious of course is that the role of husband is, in the normal case, already occupied, and this tendency would bring the child into direct competition with the father. In general, in view of the power situation, the outcome of such competition can hardly be in doubt, unless the mother is in such conflict with her husband that *she* gives the child priority over him. Something approaching this obviously does sometimes happen.[55] The second main reason is what, from the instrumental-expres-

---

55. In a seminar discussion Anna Freud was asked why the marriage solidarity of two parents was important to the development of the oedipal child. One principal reason, she said, was that it prevented the child from playing the role of

sive point of view, is the "tandem" relation of the three roles. The father-role is the more instrumental in the superordinate family system, the mother-role the more expressive, but in the mother-child system the mother-role is the more instrumental, the child-role the more expressive. Then one could say that assumption of the father role was particularly difficult for the child. Nevertheless the facts about children's, particularly of course, boys' deep sense of rivalry with their fathers, and jealousy of the father's position with the mother, seems to fit this situation and suggest that in fact there is a strong trend in this direction which has to be dealt with by strong counteracting forces. That the trend should be stronger for the boy is understandable in view of his developing masculine identification.

A second possibility, of course is that the child should attempt to take the role of the mother in relation to the father, again regardless of the sex of the child. That this is very much a possibility is indicated by the fact that the mother as object has been thoroughly internalized, and therefore the mother-role in relation to a child is in fact a need-disposition of the child's personality. In particular certain nurturant aspects of this role can relatively easily be generalized to other objects, as can the showing of love-solidarity. Again, because of developing feminine identification, it is particularly easy for a girl to embark on this path, which is the development of an "electra" complex in relation to her father.

A further consideration derives from the reciprocity of the mother-child relation in erotic as in other respects. The mother in fact *has* an erotic attachment to her child the renunciation of which she tends to resist. She may, hence tend to "aid and abet" the child in his "bid" for a "husband role." The erotic attachment of a father to his child is likely to be considerably weaker, but the components of it are clearly present as precipitates of his own developmental history and to some degree in his actual role. Hence he also may tend—unless there are adequate countermotives—to encourage the child's erotic interest in him.

On the basis of these considerations, we suggest that from the family point of view the primary function of the repression

---

spouse with either parent. She illustrated with the case of a five-year-old child of divorced parents who clearly was trying to be both a "husband" to her mother and a "wife" to her father—she saw both of them regularly.

of eroticism is to prevent the assumption of either parental role by the child or its encouragement by the parent. In the mechanisms involved on the social system level two points stand out. The first is the very general fact about groups, which Bales has brought out, namely that the stability of a small group is highly dependent, both on the differentiation of instrumental and expressive leadership roles and on a coalition of the instrumental and expressive leaders.[56] From this point of view denial of the child's impulses to assume either of the parental roles vis-à-vis the other (equally of the parents' complementary impulses) is a protection of the integration of the family as a system against a disruptive tendency. Secondly, the erotic relation between the marriage partners, is a primary symbolic focus of their solidarity. It both symbolizes the differentiation of their roles in the family system, and their integration with each other. The child's earlier erotic attachment to the mother can be defined as non-competitive with her attachment to the father, but beyond a certain point, particularly where the child's role becomes sufficiently active, this non-competitiveness tends to break down.[57] It is a well-known principle of differentiation of social structures, that competitive pressures can be eased by qualitative differentiation of roles (this was probably first stated by Durkheim). It can then be argued that repression of the child's eroticism has the function for the family of protecting the integration of the family as a system by enforcing a clear differentiation of roles. As the child grows in relative power and independence,[58] his role is forced in the direction of greater qualitative differentiation from that of either parent, particularly in relation to the other.

---

56. First reported by Bales in *Working Papers,* Chap. IV, and will be further developed in Chap. V.

57. This problem seems to be classically illustrated in Freud's famous case of "Little Hans." Hans' neurosis broke out after a summer spent at a resort with his mother. During the week Hans slept in the same bed with his mother, but on the week-ends the father arrived and displaced Hans as the mother's bedfellow. Could anything be better calculated to define the situation as one of rivalry?

58. In general this argument assumes a family system—in the most general sense, including the role of the incest taboo—as given. The problem then concerns the reasons for the universality of the conditions on which both family and incest taboo depend The relation of the taboo to the stability of the family was strongly emphasized by Malinowski (Introduction to H. Ian Hogbin, *Law and Order in*

What then, of the situation with respect to the child's personality? We have suggested above that a primary function of eroticism is as a vehicle of expressive generalization. At the oral stage it serves to bind together into a single complex the meanings of various segmental gratifications of which the mother is the agent. We may go on to suggest that, at the love-dependency stage this generalizing significance is extended in that erotic pleasure forms a link between the dependency and the autonomy sub-systems, thus serves to integrate the personality. Erotic stimulation, that is, particularly at this stage that type associated with diffuse pleasure on affectionate bodily contact, is a pleasure-gratification source. But *giving* such pleasure is also a manifestation of love as distinguished from nurturance, and serves as a symbolic acceptance-reward.

There is, however, in this generalizing function of eroticism, an inherent link to the more expressive aspect of the child's personality. In this wider respect it is associated with dependency. But the imperative developmental need at the oedipal stage is to build up the instrumental side, cognitive powers and knowledge, instrumental skills, independent responsibility and the like. The erotic need, precisely because of its paramount expressive significance, can be the most serious barrier to progress in this direction, it can serve as the primary focus of the inertia of the older personality system.

Thus we have, anchored in their roles in and responsibility for the family as a system, in both the normal parents powerful motivation not to allow the child to build up and extend his relations to them on an erotic basis. This motivation above all depends on the stability of the coalition between them and on the importance in their personalities of their extra-familial roles. "Seduction" of a child into erotic reciprocity by either parent is presumably very generally associated with disturbance in the marital relationship. On the child's side we have serious resistance to giving up his erotic investments, but at the same time, with proper parental functioning, powerful rewards for development of the instrumental side of his personality.

Polynesia, Christophers, 1934). A more general consideration of problems of the incest taboo will be found in Parsons, "The Incest Taboo in Relation to Social Structure and the Socialization of the Child," *British Journal of Sociology,* June, 1954.

Finally, it is of the greatest importance that this erotic need-disposition is repressed, but *not* extinguished. It presumably has some of the characteristics of "addiction."[59] It re-emerges as a critical aspect of the adult personality, but only when certain further conditions have been fulfilled. These conditions, we feel, involve successful carrying through of two further major steps in personality development beyond the oedipal stage. After we have sketched our interpretation of what happens in these steps we will return to this subject.

Now we can approach the question of the differences between the sexes with respect to erotic development. These result, on the above interpretation, from a combination of two factors, first having to fit as a "latency period" child into the family as a system, and second the operation, at this phase, of sex-role identification. We spoke above of sex-role identification as one of three identifications which have to be learned by the child at this period. Perhaps the most important difference of the sexes at this point lies in the fact that, as shown in Figure 9, for the boy neither of the two sub-identifications, leaving out the family as a family, coincides, personnel-wise, with the pre-oedipal identification with the mother, whereas for the girl, one of them does. We noted that there are, in the family system, two sub-collectivities to which a given member *cannot* belong. From the boy's point of view, i.e. both by sex and by generation, the mother belongs to both. From the girl's point of view she is excluded only by generation. Then we can say that the boy has to undergo at this stage a *double* "emancipation." In common with his sister he has to recognize that, in a sense not previously so important, he must not pretend to adulthood, he is unequivocally a child. But as differentiated from her, he must substitute a new identification with an unfamiliar and in a very important sense threatening object, the father, at the expense of his previous solidarity with his mother. He must renounce his previous dependency in a more radical sense. The girl, on the other hand, though she must internalize the father as object, does so only in his role as instrumental leader of the family

---

59. Cf. R. L. Solomon and L. C. Wynne on the unextinguishability of fear reactions in dogs once sufficiently firmly established in "Traumatic Avoidance Learning: the Principles of Anxiety, Conservation and Partial Irreversibility," *Psychological Review*, November, 1954.

as a system, not in the dual role which includes sex-role-model as well. Similarly, she remains categorized with her mother by sex, which coincides with the previous a-sexual (but not non-erotic) mother-child solidarity. Put a little differently, the boy must proceed farther and more radically on the path away from expressive primacy toward instrumental primacy. He is, therefore, subjected to greater strain.

FIGURE 9

*Basis of Sex-Role Identification
in the Nuclear Family*

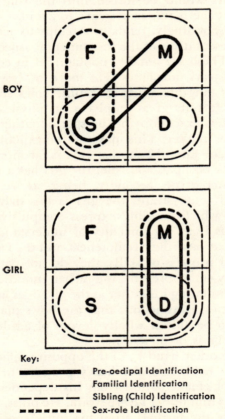

Key:

―――――――― Pre-oedipal Identification

――――・――― Familial Identification

―― ―― ―― Sibling (Child) Identification

■―■―■―■―■ Sex-role Identification

The impact of sex-role assumption is, in our society certainly, sharply emphasized in the differentiation of play interests in the early latency period. The girl, we must say, tends to act out symbolically precisely the *instrumental* aspect of the preoedipal mother role. Playing with dolls and playing "house" in the sense of household chores seem to provide the principal content. It is strikingly notable that in the main pattern no adult masculine object is present, she herself is the "mother" and her doll is the child, but there is no father in the picture. Does this not suggest that she is symbolically acting out the mother role in the *pre-oedipal* situation where the separate identity of the father as object was not prominent? One might say that if there were a father-doll the girl would be forced into the role of "wife" which is just what she is under pressure to avoid.

The boy, correspondingly, tends to attempt to act out what are symbolic representatives of the instrumental aspects of adult masculine roles. These are notably nonfamilial in content. He plays with trains, cars, airplanes. He more or less explicitly assumes relatively tangible adult masculine roles such as fireman or soldier. He puts great emphasis on physical prowess. But his play is a less exact copy of the specific father role than his sister's is of the mother. This may well be explained, partly at least, by two facts. First the mother role is far more uniform than the masculine occupational role; the girl has a rather specific role-model stereotype. Secondly, being, as we have suggested, under less acute strain, the girl is less driven to the kinds of symbols which tangibly express compulsively tinged sex-qualities. Thus both the difficulty of understanding many middle-class occupations—their remoteness, and the fact that not involving physical prowess or skills, they do not patently symbolize masculinity—may prevent the urban middle-class boy from so directly emulating his father as the girl does her mother. But it is nevertheless conspicuous that the boy's play-world at this stage seems to be almost wholly devoid of adult feminine figures, as the girl's is of masculine.

The girl on the other hand faces the opposite difficulty. The boy, we have just held, is under heavy pressure to achieve a degree and rate of emancipation from his dependency on his mother which puts him under severe strain. He must, as we have pointed out, move the farthest from his initial position. The girl, on the other hand, retains her sex-role identification with the mother, and of course also her categorization as child in common with her siblings regardless of sex. The problem here seems to be the obverse of that with the boy; it is how to push her hard and far enough to renounce dependency. It is further, socially more acceptable for a girl to maintain dependency than for a boy. Hence we would suppose that imperfections of adjustment would in boys tend to be manifested more in reaction-formation to dependency needs, in girls more in overt dependency. Furthermore one would expect girls and women to be more readily open to the directly regressive types of deviation from the normal pattern of development. We will return to the implications of this asymmetry again in Chapter IV.

These considerations seem to underlie the fact that, probably even cross-culturally, but certainly in our society, the "oedipus" complex is a much more pronounced storm-center than is the "electra" complex. In terms of the relations of the parents to child care the family is a fundamentally asymmetrical system, and this fact is reflected in these circumstances. This seems to explain why boys develop such a pronounced "tenderness" taboo and a variety of similar phenomena. It does not, however, imply that in the longer run strain is not relatively equally distributed between the sexes.

If this general analysis is correct, then the most fundamental difference between the sexes in personality type is that, relative to the total culture as a whole, the masculine personality tends more to the predominance of instrumental interests, needs and functions, presumably in whatever social system both sexes are involved, while the feminine personality tends more to the primacy of expressive interests, needs and functions. We would expect, by and large, that other things being equal, men would assume more technical, executive and "judicial" roles, women more supportive, integrative and "tension-managing" roles. However, this is at best an extremely broad formula and other things very often are not equal.

The above discussion throws some light, we think, on certain aspects of the incest-taboo and its functions for society. Starting again at the level of social structure, the universality, with very few qualifications, of the taboo highlights the fact that the nuclear family is *never* a complete society but only a special kind of sub-system of a society. The husband-father role, preëminently but of course by no means alone, must articulate into a more complex role-system which can be built up only out of members of many nuclear families and must involve a more complex system of differentiated functions than the nuclear family permits between persons. The familial roles thus, from the point of view of the society, are not "the" instrumental and expressive roles respectively, but *special types* of such roles which are differentiated in this way *relative* to each other. Put a little differently, in order to perform their socializing functions successfully, the parents must have personalities more complex than that of an immediately post-oedipal child. The fact of the extension of the network of social relationships beyond the family and that of the child's emancipation from his family of orientation are correlative facts.

The incest taboo then means, not only that erotic attachment within the nuclear family is repressed, but its revival is permitted *only* outside the nuclear family. The child is never permitted to assume the role of *his* parent but only of *a* parent. Psychologically we assume that this is associated with the fact that eroticism is an "addiction." Its connection with the surviving structures of infantile dependency is so close that free expression with any of the figures of the original drama as objects would tend to revive these remnants to the detriment of the more mature parts of the personality. The suggestion then is that eroticism is not all that is repressed. A much bigger complex of addictions, i.e., the "archaic" id, is repressed which it is never safe to allow free unregulated expression.[60] The erotic component can be safely freed from restrictions only when there is a double protection from revival of these other elements of the id. The first source of protection lies in the strength of the later and thus more mature elements of the personality structure, not only those laid down in the original oedipal period, i.e., the archaic superego, but those developed later through socialization in *extrafamilial* social systems, to the analysis of which we will have to turn presently. It is only as a full-fledged man or woman in this sense that one is allowed to love erotically in the "genital" sense. Secondly, however, the addictive significance of the older ties is such that a change of object is imposed, the original potential objects are taboo, only

60. Possibly just this free expression is the major specific content of interest in psychosis.

those to some degree universalistically *categorized with them* are permitted. This change of object is clearly a further protection against the return of the repressed.

Sociologically, however, through social evolution this psychological necessity has been constructively put to use in that this aspect of the "sex drive," attraction to a non-incestuous object, has been made one principal basis for establishment of *new* nuclear families.[61]

The two aspects are, apparently, very closely linked with each other.

In this whole connection a word should also be said about the other great erotic prohibition, namely the prohibition of homosexuality, which is nearly as much a sociological universal as the incest taboo. Freud made us aware of the presumably universal possibility of homosexual attraction. Most fundamentally, we suggest, the prohibition of homosexuality has the function of reinforcing the differentiation of sex roles, the earliest and hence in one sense most fundamental *qualitative* differentiation of role and personality. Put a little differently, seen structurally the taboo on homosexuality is the obverse of the intrafamilial incest taboo, in that it protects the monopoly by the parties to the marriage relationship over erotic gratifications within the family. From the societal point of view it serves to prevent competing personal solidarities from arising which could undermine the motivation to marriage and the establishment of families. In the case of individual psychology it reinforces sex-role identification very strongly. The relation of any erotically bound pair must be to some important degree analogous with the marriage relationship, given the immense importance of the latter in the social structure and in the socialization process. Then at least implicitly the question must always arise, which partner plays which role? This means, if it is a homosexual relationship, that *one* of the partners must be radically denying his sex role, while the other does so less drastically by admitting erotic attraction to the same rather than the opposite sex. Put very generally, homosexuality is a mode of structuring of human relationships which is radically in

---

61. A further and more general discussion of the incest taboo is given in Parsons, "The Incest Taboo in Relation to Social Structure and the Socialization of the Child," *op. cit.*

conflict with the place of the nuclear family in the social structure and in the socialization of the child. Its nearly universal
prohibition is a direct consequence of the "geometry" of family
structure.

All of these considerations make it quite clear how entirely
inadequate is the view which the common sense of psychology
has far from outgrown, that "sex" is most usefully treated as a
constitutionally given "drive" which is either "allowed expression" or "perverted" or "repressed." That there is such a constitutionally given component in normal heterosexual erotic
motivation seems beyond doubt, but that this aspect of the
matter can satisfactorily account for the kind of facts we have
been discussing, seems equally out of the question. Freud was
clearly very much on the right track, and in fact gave us the
foundations of the present view. But what Freud lacked was
a systematic analysis of the structure of social relationships as
systems in which the process of socialization takes place. It is
this which we are attempting to supply.[62]

Some General Questions

In view of the apparently critical significance of the oedipal
period and its outcome, this seems to be a good place to pause
from our outline of the socialization process and raise certain
rather general questions. First, though it has been implicit
throughout, it should be quite definitely stated that what we
have been attempting to present is a kind of general "norm"
of the socialization process. We have concentrated on the contemporary American family and have in no way attempted to
take account of either of two basic types of variation. One of
these is variation in the social structure of nuclear families, and
hence the implications of such variations for typical differences
of outcome of the socialization process. Such analysis would
have to take its departure from the kind of structural analysis of
variation which Zelditch presents in Chapter VI, and then in
the light of the above "norm" and of our psychological knowledge, attempt to work out the implications for personality of
the different kinds of variations found. Such structural variations in the family are of course found not only as between very

62. Cf. Figure 10 for a schematic outline of process in the oedipal phase.

different societies, but also within the same society, though presumably covering a considerably narrower range.

The other type of variation concerns the consequences, relative to any given cultural or subcultural norm, of deviant behavior on the part of the socializing agents, such as the "overpro-

FIGURE 10

Developmental Process in the Oedipal Phase

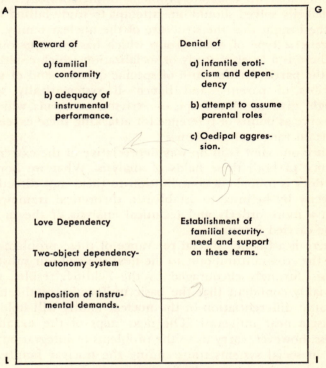

A

Reward of

a) familial
   conformity

b) adequacy of
   instrumental
   performance.

G

Denial of

a) infantile eroti-
   cism and depen-
   dency

b) attempt to assume
   parental roles

c) Oedipal aggres-
   sion.

Love Dependency

Two-object dependency-
autonomy system

Imposition of instru-
mental demands.

Establishment of
familial security-
need and support
on these terms.

L

I

Process Counterclockwise from L.

tective" mother, the "authoritarian" father and various others. This, preeminently, is the field of the etiology of psychopathological conditions, though it spills over into the other one.[63]

Both of these are, obviously, fields of enormous extent and complication and of course of importance. The main reason for not attempting to enter either of them in this chapter is

63. A brief discussion of a limited aspect of this field will be given in Chapter IV.

simply a matter of putting first things first and of the limitations of what can be done in a single attempt. It is our profound conviction that only when norms of the character we are attempting to work out here have been solidly established, can the lack of incisiveness of so much current treatment in both these fields be overcome. Essentially the requirement to enter and solve the other problems first would be analogous to the suggestion that only after the concrete problems of meteorology had been satisfactorily solved should one attempt to study falling bodies. It is the insight that the structure of the nuclear family is that of a *generic* type of small group which has given us our clue that there is a level of study of socialization which could transcend the particularities both of specific cultures and of specific behaviors of parents, and hence, if systematically worked through, give us some hope of arriving at norms which can *then* serve as points of reference for attacking these exceedingly important ranges of problems.

Hence our view is in no way depreciative of the extreme importance of both these fields of analysis. What we hope this essay does is to make a contribution to them, not directly, but indirectly by helping to establish a theoretical framework in which a more orderly and technical analysis of the problems can be carried forward.

There is a further special relevance of these problems, especially the cross-cultural one, to the next stage of our substantive analysis. Strongly encouraged by the Zelditch results, we are reasonably confident that the basic uniformity of the lines of structural differentiation of the nuclear family will hold up as at least a near universal. The next steps of the socialization process, however, carry us to the problems of integration of the child in social systems transcending the nuclear family. Here the problem of what is "culture-bound" becomes even more acute. This is a problem we will have to keep prominently in mind. Our procedure is to focus on the contemporary American urban situation—after all this *is* a going society and presents the nuclear family in a highly differentiated form. But the question of how far and in what sense we are stating a norm valid beyond this case will always be in the background, and will be brought up at a later time for explicit discussion.[64]

---

64. See Chapter VII.

These considerations have mainly to do with limitations on what has been done so far, and opportunities for further investigation. What can we say at this point about positive contribution to clarification of the general theoretical problem underlying this essay, namely that of the systematic relationships of social system and personality? The common sense of the sciences of behavior, it seems to us, has tended to use the biological frame of reference in a particular way, to think of society—or its subsystems—as an "environment" within which the personality itself developed without raising the question: on what *level* is the environment crucially relevant? At a considerably earlier stage of our own work there seemed to be good reason to question the adequacy of this formula. The basic reason for this was the realization that, as systems of action, personalities and social systems are not only interdependent, but *interpenetrate,* precisely on the level of social interaction in cultural terms. The role-expectation, that is, which is a unit of a system of social interaction, *is* itself also a motivational unit—an internalized object of the personality of the actor. When a person is fully socialized in the system of interaction it is not so nearly correct to say that a role is something an actor "has" or "plays" as that it is something that he *is*. It follows from this that the crucial components of that aspect of the structure of personality which interpenetrates with systems of social interaction are *the same* as those composing social systems. Within the frame of reference of action as we have been using it, these are "culturally" patterned and organized objects, invested with motivation, organized in terms of symbolic meanings, patterns of value-orientation and the like.[65]

Our whole approach to the problems of this essay has been dictated by this more general view. What we have been trying to do is to pin down in more specific and circumstantial detail than before, just what we mean by these more general propositions and show how they can fruitfully be put to use. The very simplicity of the structure of the developing personality in its early stages and of the nuclear family as a social system has given us an especially favorable opportunity to do this,

---

65. For a fuller discussion of this problem, see Parsons, "Psychology and Sociology," Chapter IV, *For A Science of Social Man,* John Gillin, ed. (New York: Macmillan Co., 1954).

since certain broad lines stand out with far greater clarity than they do in more complex cases.

We feel that our review of the problems so far in the first place strongly vindicates the fruitfulness of this approach. But over and above genetic understanding of the process of socialization, and a striking codification of psychological and sociological knowledge, it gives us an insight into certain basic theoretical relationships. Even on so simple a level these are not, however, easy to state. We may approach them by calling attention to the fundamental significance and connection of the facts first that personalities as systems consist in a *plurality* of need-disposition systems and subsystems which have originated in the internalization of significant social objects, whereas secondly societies also consist in a plurality of partial, qualitatively differentiated and hierarchically organized subsystems. Neither phenomenon would be possible without the other. But one aspect of the difference between them is that in the nature of the case they cannot exactly "match." The society must contain *more* significant subsystems that any one personality can implement in his role-expectation need-dispositions. The personality, on the other hand, must be built up through participation in a plurality of interactive social subsystems, in which socializing agents with several *differently* organized participations influence him. To take the simplest example, neither boy nor girl can, if our analysis is correct, be adequately socialized without a parent—or some substitute—of the *opposite* sex whose role pattern he can *never* assume. This "contrapuntal" interlacing of the structures of social system and personality seems to be of the essence of their relationship to each other. From the point of view of personality the social interaction system is a "buffer" placed between the individual and the physical environment. He can never experience the latter "directly" as child or adult but only in terms of the meanings of his culture and the perspective inherent in *his* place in the society.

The ramifications of the problem are wide. There is a sense in which the personality of the oedipal child is a "mirror-image" of the nuclear family as a social system. It literally "consists" of the four role-objects he has internalized. But this basic phenomenon is possible only because the parents as personalities are *more* than parents, have participations in a society transcending the family. Moreover the child's status in early latency is clearly unstable and inherently temporary. If he does not soon begin to "mirror" wider social structures than his family he becomes a pathological case; there is no standing still. Hence beyond the "mirror-image" idea we must clearly add the idea of *organization in depth,* the cumulative impact of a succession of social system-integrations, each simpler one an essential prerequisite of integration in the one of next higher order of complexity. It is clear that here the imperatives of integration of the personality as a system necessitate that there should be something more than the mirroring of any particular, or any random succession of social system-internalizations. There must be ordered sequence where *both* motivational and object-categorization continuity can be maintained, and in some instances "matched."

The aspect of this organization in depth which is most clearly visible at this point is the "branching tree" relation of the different principal motivational components of the personality of the oedipal child. In general theoretical terms we regard this as an application of a position stated earlier[66] that for purposes of the theory of action" motivation" should be assumed to be an "originally" undifferentiated energy flow. Structure of the motivational system, that is to say, is to be regarded as primarily a consequence of the development of a process of differentiation *in the system of action itself,* not a derivative from the structure of an independently given "prior" system-level. *Types* of motivational investment, then, we treat as developing out of the process of differentiation of the personality. The necessity of meeting the conditions necessary to "tap" the original motivational resources of the organism in such a way as to motivate culturally organized action, is in one sense the fundamental reason why personality structure has to go back to the single-unit stage and differentiate from there.[67]

Seen in these terms, the emergence, at the oedipal stage, of our four basic attitude-sanction types is of all the greater theoretical significance. What we have done is to show how these types, of such general theoretical significance, can be derived by a continuous process of differentiation, from our postulated

66. *Working Papers,* Chap. V, sec. vi.

67. It is, if we are right, intimately connected with the reasons why families are essential to human cultural-level societies.

undifferentiated motivational flow. This is the branching of the motivational stream which constitutes *one* major aspect of what we have called the organization of the personality in depth. This branching, as we see it, is a function of the *cathexis* of objects, i.e. of the investment with motivational significance of systematically differentiated *kinds* of social objects; the complementary role-objects in the social systems in which the child is socialized.

The complexity of the relationship, which is certainly great, should not be permitted, however, to obscure the fundamental character of the relationship itself. Clearly recognition of the fact of the internalization of values, that great independent discovery of Freud, of Mead and of Durkheim, inevitably leads to a picture of personality and its development, and its articulation with social systems, which is far closer to that sketched out in this essay than it is to the others which have tended to dominate the psychological literature, above all those which either attempted to derive the main structure from constitutional drive or "instinct" components, or from more or less random, situationally unstructured, processes of conditioning.

Finally, these relationships, and the very close analogies between personalities and social systems, put us in a position to say something about the nature of the *organization* as distinguished from the "unit-composition" of a personality system at the oedipal stage of structural differentiation. As in the case of a social system, we may say that the units must be *ordered,* both in terms of hierarchy or stratification, and of qualitative differentiation of the ultimate units. But this also involves a network of subsystems. The qualitative differentiation of the units has been the main theme of our previous analysis. The case of sex-role, to the point thus far worked out, will illustrate the problem of variability of organization, both with regard to the relations of subsystems, and with regard to stratification. Let us look at it in terms of the relations between Figures 9 and 8. For the boy, his inclusion in sub-collectivities of the family clearly focuses on the *combination* of "child" and "male." This new combination takes precedence over his previous solidarity with his mother. Essentially this means that, relative to the basic personality type of his culture, the instrumental need-dispositions take precedence over the expressive, i.e., superego and adaptive ego over integrative ego and id. It may further be suggested that his role as child in the family relative to his parents gives precedence to the adequacy need-disposition over the conformity one. One would, therefore, expect for the boy the following rank-order: adequacy, conformity, security, nurturance. This seems to be particularly appropriate to the American boy, though perhaps security sometimes competes with conformity in this case. How far it can be cross-culturally generalized raises questions, which can best be taken up later when we deal with the further stages of differentiation.

In the case of the girl it is the combination of her categorization as a child and expressiveness which is the focal one. If the case is parallel to that of the boy here it should be the security need-disposition which has the paramount place. The parallel logic would lead us to assume that nurturance should come next. There is an obvious problem here in that the girl as well as the boy must repress her older dependency needs. We suggest that in this case the repression is accomplished, more than in the boy's case, by turning the nurturance motive outward to *external* objects, that is, in this respect by taking the *role of* the mother. This we would regard as the primary significance of the symbolism of girls' doll-play; they take the instrumental-nurturant component of the mother role, but *not* the wife-role. The rank-order of the two instrumental components then is perhaps problematical, but one would suggest that categorization of the girl also as child would make for dominance of adequacy over conformity. This general interpretation is in harmony with the suggestion, in Figure 9, that the role the postoedipal boy is *farthest* from that of the mother; she is the one family member with whom he shares *no* subcollectivity identifications within the family, but only the overall familial identification. Correspondingly, the girl at this stage is farthest from the father role; she shares no subcollectivities with him. It seems legitimate to infer that this structural position vis-a-vis the role of the parent of opposite sex means that that parent as internalized object takes last place in the rank-order of need-dispositions. This "missing element" however is in a sense "restored" through the complementarity of marriage-partners.

This may be generalized in terms of a further point. The

"interlacing" of the patterns of social systems and of personalities of which we have spoken, is possible only on the basis that, among others, their structures share one particularly important common feature, namely what sociologically we know as the phenomenon of multiple roles. The same person, that is, participates, not in a single social system—except in the limiting case of his "society"—but in as many social systems as he has roles. Furthermore each role is divisible into "subroles" which are roles in the subsystems of the larger system with reference to which the "main role" was defined. Thus the postoedipal boy's role in the family system comprises a sub-role in the masculine subsystem, and one in the cross-sex sibling subsystem, and as we shall see presently, he also has extra-familial roles in school and peer group.

Turning to the personality then, we find a "mirror-image" structure in this as in other respects. The mother-child "identification" though it is transformed, does not disappear with the transition to the full oedipal personality structure. The "masculine self" is a participant in the total new familial object, in the masculine sex-role identification object, in the sibling object, and in the genetically prior mother-child object. From one point of view this is, as we will point out later, another way of saying that need-dispositions are genetically related through a "genealogical tree." Belonging on a given "branch" of the tree is to "participate" in all the genetically prior object systems of that branch. The same need-disposition is thus a "unit" not only in the personality system as a whole, but in a plurality of subsystems of that system on different levels.

This in turn, we believe, is to say that any need-disposition itself is composed of a plurality of sub-units; it is not a "unitary" entity but is itself a system. This, elsewhere, we have said to be characteristic of all units in systems of action.[68] Put somewhat differently, in the language of that earlier publication, what we mean by the multiple "participations" or "submotives" of a motivational unit is the "amplitude" of its "orbit." *Because* it is a unit in a system, its "pattern" of relationships to the other units must change, it cannot always "move" in the same direction. It must be a different *kind* of motive according to

68. *Working Papers,* Chap. V.

the phase of its orbit. Its overall characterization, i.e. as internalized masculine self, is only, in the relevant system reference, in this case of the four-unit "internalized family" system, the characterization of its *furthest* direction of movement relative to the others. But at one phase in its orbit it is "closer" to the internalized father than at another, at one phase closer to the feminine self, etc. Put in general terms of our four-dimensional spatial frame of reference, the significant properties of a system unit (besides its power or intensity) designate its position on the coordinates of a space. This position is not a constant through time except in a "resultant"sense. A closer view always reveals a pattern of repetitive change in location within certain limits. It is "role" in the superordinate system which prescribes these limits.

Finally, the internalization of the family collectively as object and its values should not be lost sight of. This is crucial with respect to a main feature of the next stage of development, namely the assumption of representative roles outside the family on behalf of it. Here it is the child's family membership which is decisive, and thus his acting in a role in terms of its values for "such as he." This becomes the major overall framework for the organization of his personality at this stage.

The Latency Child in Family, School and Peer Group

This last point may serve as our point of departure for starting the next phase of our analysis. Internalization of the familial "we" clearly implies the significance of at least a residual category of the "non-we." It is from this non-we that the further differentiated categorizations have to be carved out.

We have several times emphasized that in the nature of the case the nuclear family cannot constitute a complete society; the incest taboo is one prominent confirmation of this view. Put in terms of the theory of social structure, this implies that the nuclear family constitutes one particular type of collectivity subsystem of a society. Compared to most other groups, in pattern variable terms, it is above all characterized by particularism, and quality-emphasis or ascription of roles, notably from the child's point of view his role is completely ascribed, and is defined, as we have considered it so far, only in relational terms, with reference to the other three basic familial role types, and by no other criteria. Essentially the problem of further steps of differentiation is that of how these features of familial roles, and of the family as a collectivity, come to be placed in a wider context so that they are discriminated from other role-types and collectivities, and these discriminations internalized.

We have suggested above that the next major discrimination is that between the particularistic and the universalistic aspects of objects, and their differential categorization in terms of relative primacies. Our principle is that such discriminations develop by bifurcation of the previously significant object-categories, and corresponding differentiation of orientation to the newly discriminated types of object. In discussing the oedipal internalization of the familial role-objects, we have used the ordinary kinship terminology. This can have misleading implications because these terms are in ordinary usage clearly formulated from the adult point of view and imply discriminations which we are sure the child has not yet made. To an adult, a boy's father is of course only one instance of the universalistically defined category of "man." But to the oedipal boy the discrimination of "father" and "man" has not yet been made, similarly of "mother" and "woman," "self-brother" and "boy," "sister" and "girl." The question, then, is what social structures present these discriminations to him in such a way that as subsystems they can be treated as socializing agencies, performing all the functions we have outlined, as pertaining to such agencies.

It is manifestly clear that the family cannot perform these functions by itself, because it does not have the necessary level of structural differentiation. We have suggested above that family, school and peer group should, in our society, for this purpose be treated as a *single* social system, comprising the whole range of the pre-adolescent's significant social participations.

With respect to the two primarily significant subsystems in which the child has not previously become integrated, it may be suggested that the school is *primarily* focussed around the generation differentiation, whereas the peer group is organized around sex categorization. This is to say that in school the child is thrown with others of his age in the same class—and of course greater refinements of age-grading are emphasized by the fact that a school has a whole series of grades. But the generation line is clearly emphasized by the differentiation of teachers' and pupils' roles, with both authority and superior competence vested in the teacher. In the peer group on the other hand, the dominant structural characteristic at this age level is, by contrast with most American schools, the sharp restriction of membership to one sex—it is significant that this is clearly not imposed by adult authority. It seems, however, to be an important characteristic of the latency peer group that its membership covers a certain age range; there is an opportunity for the older members to socialize the younger before they themselves pass on to a higher age grade.[69]

Let us remember that the internalization of sex as a category in the oedipal period proceeded only part way. It concerned only that aspect which enters into the role structure of the family itself, that which a boy has in common with his father and brothers. Though this intrafamilial aspect cuts across the generation line it does not transcend the familial "we." The association with boys from other families, and the sharp discrimination of them, and their activities from girls, regardless of family membership, is the dominant feature of this peer-group activity. It is what "we boys" (or girls) *as distinguished* from "we Joneses" do. In this case it is striking that in American society such peer groups form into something closely approaching corporate groups which are in a position to inculcate a very strong sense of solidarity.

Of course a variety of other things are going on in the peer group at the same time. Various kinds of skills are being practiced and sanctions apportioned to the various levels of achievement—prominent among these are the skills of physical prowess for boys. The group itself develops a differentiation of roles, particularly with respect to leadership. But even here one may suspect that "prowess" in various symbolically significant types of activity is more important than is the particularistic aspect of group leadership as such. This would be an important field for research.

69. As compared with European cases the American system seems to constitute a more advanced level of differentiation in this respect. The age and sex components are not fused (through sex-segregation of education) but differentiated out from each other to a greater degree.

In American society particularly the masculine peer group apparently forms the primary focus of the phenomena of "compulsive masculinity" at this age. The contempt of boys at this age for the "softness" and gentleness of girls and one suspects, reinforcement of each other's reaction formations against repressed dependency needs, constitutes one principal source of the bond of solidarity between them. Where the symbolic significance of the mother and the woman teacher combine as threatening dangers, in this sense, it is easy for this masculine peer group to become a center of revolt against adult expectations, particularly those of the school. In situations where delinquency is prominent, through truancy, and through positively defiant activities, it becomes the growing point of the delinquent subculture. But short of this its instrumentalism is strongly emphasized, and instrumental leadership reflects only *part* of the father role.

The school institutionalizes another aspect of the universalistic values of the society. The specific content of school work, is of course one part of it, but only part. In addition there are standards of dress, deportment, etc., which are inculcated as suitable for children of this age in this community. It may well be suggested that the coeducational composition of the typical American school is significant in that it serves as a counterbalance to the peer group in emphasizing the things *common* to the age grade across the sex line. The sex differentiation is to be sure sharply symbolized in the first instance by clothing, in the schoolroom, and in certain other respects such as separate toilets for the sexes. But in the school room, the content of subject matter and the general standards of deportment are made deliberately identical, e.g., in the proper way of addressing the teacher and the like. The importance of this aspect of things is stressed by the very strong emphasis in the teacher's function on her ability to handle the disciplinary problems of her class effectively, e.g., to keep order.

Both with respect to school work and to deportment, however, it is important to note that the basic standards are *ascribed* at this point. The emphasis is on what the children of that age grade in that community should know and do. In the earlier and, in this sense, more basic grades there is no option of taking different subjects. The children are, to be sure, marked, but caution should be taken not to interpret this too much in "achievement" terms. The one with high marks is simply a "better" boy or girl than the one with the lower, better in living up more fully to the common, universalistically defined age-appropriate standard.

The crucial difference from the intrafamilial standards is with respect to universalism, not to achievement as values. Here the child is put in explicit comparison with children who represent a sample of the families in the community. From one point of view it is a test of the family, the meaning of which is made very clear by parental sensitivity to the child's record and behavior in school. The child is playing a representative role in the school vis-à-vis his family. He is, to an important degree, responsible to his family for "being a credit" to them, and positively, he is motivated by a desire to please them, and to get their love, approval and esteem.

In fact this example brings out with special clarity the connection of this type of representative role with the mechanisms of learning. So far as the family as a system was concerned, the child could not play this type of role before the instrumental components of his personality had become sufficiently developed. For, it will be remembered, it was specifically these which concerned, in the role structure of the family itself, functions vis-à-vis the external situation. He must have internalized both the familial we and its values, and instrumental motives. Then he is motivated to implement these values as a *representative* of the family, and with familial support to learn new values in his interaction with persons outside the family. Gradually, then, his sensitivity to sanctions from the new socializing agents, teachers and his older peers, increases, and his role in these other groups becomes less representative vis-à-vis his family. Indeed his parents alter their roles since their reference gradually comes to be not to familial membership so much as to universalistic appraisal of the child's behavior. They sanction more and more as members of the community rather than as parents of this particular child.

The outcome of this phase of the process for the personality of the child is, we assume, another bifurcation and corresponding reorganization of his internalized object and need-disposition system. Each of the four previous units subdivides, producing the "mirror-image" of the eight-fold differentiation of role types shown in Figure 4. It should be remembered that the father, at the earlier stage, was the prototype of *both* technical expert and executive. Now we presume that, the teacher and the older, superior peer, become above all figures of technical expertness in that they above all command the adaptive skills the child has to learn and can serve as role models in this respect. There comes to be an internalized attitude, "admiration" or "respect" for the person who "can do things" regardless of *who* he is. It is certainly highly significant that, precisely at this stage, both actual "culture heroes" and phantasy figures of universalistic prowess become prominent objects of preoccupation. The athletic hero is a particularly important one for boys, but also the "superman" type of phantasy figure is very prominent.

The essential point is, that with variations of relative primacy, in the first instance by sex, but of course in other respects, the child himself *becomes* all of these eight types of object, in that to one degree or another he becomes capable of assuming all eight types of roles in his interaction with others. For example, "loyalty" is a new category because it can be discriminated from what here is called being "accommodating." The prototype of it, presumably, is the difference between the obligations of support of fellow-members he assumes in his capacity as a family member, and the obligation to be "nice" to other people relatively independent of any collectivity memberships he shares with them. But clearly this distinction is soon generalized to the peer-group, and perhaps somewhat more palely, to the school. The boy, particularly, in our society tends to develop an intense loyalty to his "gang." If the personality is well balanced, however, this should not too far outweigh his universalistic attitudes, his willingness to be accommodating to non-members.

It will be remembered that we called attention above to the presumption that the earlier phase of language learning was dependent on successful establishment of the love-dependency relationship with the mother. A second phase of intellectual development seems to be clearly associated with the completion of the oedipal phase and growth of the object-systems which are universalistically categorized. Such authorities as Piaget[70] and Wallon[71] strongly emphasize that the development of logical thinking occurs, with individual variations of course, essentially during this period, not getting notably under way before the ages of five to six and continuing until about twelve. There seems to be an important connection between this timing and the fact that in social object terms it is in this phase that universalistically categorized social objects, specifically as differentiated from those which are particularistically categorized, are first clearly internalized. It is presumably not altogether fortuitous that in Western countries formal education begins about the age of six. It may also very well be that the higher levels of abstraction involved in the use of written as distinguished from spoken language, perhaps particularly the elimination of the expressive cues given with tone and cadence of voice, pronunciation, facial expression and gesture, can only be attained when the kind of elaboration of personality structure we refer to has occurred. In particular a spoken communication is relatively inseparable from *who* says it in what specific context. A written communication focuses attention much more specifically on the meaning-content itself. This is surely more universalistic.

In an important sense, logical thinking always involves both conjunction and disjunction of objects as many modern logicians put it.[72] And perhaps the latter is most characteristically logical. Thus, for example, in adding together four different things to a sum of four, the child is reasoning by conjunction: I plus 1 plus 1 plus 1 makes 4. But at the same time he is reasoning by disjunction in the sense that each one of the things is *identical to each other* in the abstract sense that it is one more *thing* to be counted.

Disjunction denotes this "or" relation between objects which makes A or B substitutable, i.e. identical, not in the concrete, but *for some abstract purpose* like counting. Disjunction implies a cognizance of the criteria of similarity between the two con-

---

70. Jean Piaget, *Language and Thought of the Child* (London: Routledge and Kegan Paul, Ltd., 1926), and other works.

71. H. Wallon, *Les origines de la pensée chez l'enfant* (Paris: Boivin & Cie., 1934).

72. Ralph M. Eaton, *General Logic* (New York: Charles Scribner's Sons, 1931), pp. 366-367.

crete objects which are disjoined. (As the teacher often says to a schoolchild, you cannot add oranges and apples and come out with a meaningful sum unless you make explicit some other criterion of classification.) But, because disjunction implies this cognizance of criteria of similarity, it implies that there be an abstract concept instantiated equally by all the disjoined objects.

Now, the conjunction-disjunction dichotomy (both terms of which are required for abstract thought, plus a discrimination between them) is so closely related to our particularism-universalism pattern variable as to be, probably, another way of talking about the same distinction. For particularism is the consideration of objects as related to one another by common membership in one group; e.g. objects A & B & C make up family *I*. A & B & C are particularistically related as members of the family. All of them added together (and systematically related to one another) make up the family. We could not say A or B or C is the family *I*; we must rather say A & B & C is the family *I*. Thus, particularism denotes a conjunctive relationship of terms.

Universalism, on the other hand, is the consideration of objects as related to one another by abstract similarity; e.g. object D *or* E *or* F (not *and*) is a man. Objects D, E, F are universalistically related by the concept man. Any one of them taken separately, i.e. one at a time, makes up a whole man. We *could* say D or E or F is a man; but we must not say D & E & F is a man (because it is not, it is three men.) Thus, universalism denotes a disjunctive relationship of terms.

We can regard the following set of facts, therefore, as an extremely important set of inter-validations: (1), we find the internalization of the universalism-particularism discrimination to be the primary feature of this stage of child development; (2), Piaget and Wallon find a new level of logical thought to become possible at precisely this stage; (3), logicians find the conjunction-disjunction pair to be at the root of all logical thought[73]; and (4) we find the conjunction-disjunction distinction to be identical to the universalism-particularism distinction.

We may now approach another problem which probably has particular significance in connection with the peer group

---

73. *Ibid.*

structure. The two fundamental axes of differentiation of the nuclear family as a small group are, in their impact on self-categorization of the child, in one major respect different from each other. Categorization by sex, which of course is relative, is under human conditions, indelible. A person can never "outgrow" his or her sex; presumably this is one reason why we are so prone to believe the major features of sex role must be "inborn" and not have any important learned component. Relative power, however, is not fixed once and for all, but may change, and above all the normal child is destined to become an adult and fulfill the role of parent in a nuclear family. It is true that he cannot do so in his own family of orientation, but his growing "too big" to continue in a subordinate position is one reason for his extrusion or emancipation from the family of orientation. The question is, what is the process by which the capacity to assume a role as equal or superior is built up? This question is often discussed under the heading of attitudes toward "authority" but this formulation seems to us too narrow.

The school is like the family in that it is fundamentally adult-controlled. The teacher is hence, in the nature of the case, a "parent figure." But in the peer group for the first time a child encounters a whole *system* of significant social objects in which superiority-inferiority relationships are not institutionally ascribed by norms transcending the group. Even between siblings birth order imposes such a differentiation, and the closeness to the parental superiority to all children in the same family makes for a basic difference from the peer group. Even so, the nearest familial analogy to the peer group is the group of siblings, particularly those of one sex. It is not fortuitous that Freud and many others have used the group of "brothers" as the prototype of such a grouping.

One fundamental feature of the peer group in this respect is that, relative both to family and to school, the power-differential is enormously narrowed. Furthermore, we may suggest that the absence of previous particularistic ties between the members tends to put a premium on universalistic categorization of status. Also our assumption should be remembered that ascription and achievement have not yet been significantly differentiated. Hence we may suggest that both what a member *is* in terms of his qualities and what he can *do* can serve as criteria of differentiation. The peer group, with relatively manageable limits, therefore provides a range of status-power differentiation among its members to which the child can orient himself in a much more minutely selective way than was true in the family. (Of course there are similar features in the composition of the school class—leaving the teacher aside —and these have a similar significance and generally overlap in personnel.)

Now it will be remembered that, as we attempt to show above, the child has already internalized the differentiation between parental objects and his own personality or self as an object. In so doing he has internalized the *reciprocal* role pattern of the relationship. It would seem to follow that when interacting with an alter who is unequivocally in a superior position relative to him, he will tend to assume the attitude appropriate to that of child to parent, i.e. one of deference, obedience, etc. Where, as is seldom the case except perhaps with younger siblings and pets, the relationship is to an alter clearly inferior to him in power and status, he tends to assume a parental type of role, to control, give nurturance, accept obedience and deferrence, etc. But in either case, his actual behavior is a *resultant* of the internalized parental and child-self components of his motivational system.

When he is faced with a situation where he and the object are peers or nearly so the presumption is that the pressure of the learning process will be to retain the qualitative distinctions between those motivational components, but to balance out their relations to the power factor. Essentially this will have to mean that the control function and the nurturance function are made mutual. Instead of, as in the parent-child situation, the lion's share of the nurturance and enforcement of conformity being on the parent's side, that of the showing of adequacy and security (trust) on that of the child, as between peers, the amounts of control and of nurturance on each side must be about equal, and similarly with "adequate" performance and mutual acceptance.

In this situation a very important relation to universalism appears. Universalistic categorization makes it possible to translate the mutuality of control and nurturance into *common* subjection to a *general rule*. Control and nurturance—as the "parental" functions—need no longer be carried out by virtue of a particularistically defined status, but may be related to universalistically defined qualities and capacities, and to the generality and impartiality of the rule. Then such differentiations of power as do remain and develop can be legitimized in universalistic terms and accepted on this basis. The greater knowledge or physical strength of an older boy are cases in point. The individual by this path can come to be emancipated from the rigid alternative of either being deferent to superiority in the child role, or reversing it and becoming dominating by assuming a parental role in relation to others. He can fit into a graded system of superiorities and inferiorities in different universalistically defined respects. He need not act wholly as one or the other in all respects.

Perhaps it is legitimate to interpret Piaget's[74] distinction between cooperation and moral realism in this context. In the case of moral realism an obligation of obedience is attached to the source of authority as such. In that of cooperation, the rules of the game are subject to revision in the light of the interaction of the players, defined as peers. The age-range of these phenomena as Piaget reports them fits with this interpretation. Freud was somewhat less clear on this problem but the transfer of cathexis from the "father" to the community of "brothers"[75] seems to be open to essentially the same interpretation.

The Adult Community Structure: Family of Procreation and Occupation

The next and, on a comparable analytical level, last stage of the binary differentiation process we are following is the one which leads through the adolescent crisis to full maturity or "genitality" and which involves the discrimination of quality and performance-categorized objects, or in social structure terms of ascription and achievement. The first question to ask, following previous procedure, is, what are the strategically significant social structures which constitute the reference system for this phase of the socialization process? We suggest that they

---

74. *The Moral Judgment of the Child* (New York: Harcourt, Brace & Co., 1932).

75. James Stachey (trans.), Sigmund Freud's *Group Psychology and the Analysis of the Ego* (London and Vienna: The International Psychoanalytical Press, 1922).

are the major structures of the "adult" society, which in our own society may, in a highly simplified way, be treated under the three headings of family of procreation, "community" and occupational system.

By saying family of procreation instead of just "family" it is meant to emphasize that whereas the oedipal child was being socialized into the role of "latency child" *in* his family of orientation the adolescent is being socialized "out of" his family of orientation into a different concrete family, a family of procreation, in which he is to play the dual role, not of child, but of spouse and parent. For this to be accomplished his own parents, though still among the socializing agents, must play quite different roles from their previous ones; they are in a sense in representative roles vis-à-vis the "community," and their roles must be shared with other agents, other parents, teachers, and "influential" people in the community. At this phase, furthermore, in our society certainly the accent is on the role of spouse, of adjustment to persons of opposite sex in such ways as lead up to marriage.

The case of the occupational system in our society is particularly clear of course for the masculine role. The adolescent boy must begin to think about what he is going to "do"—a very significant linguistic usage in our society. He can no longer rest content with his ascribed statuses, but must "take responsibility" for his future. In an older phase of our society the girl had no such problem; in the present phase, however, the pattern seems to have shifted to the point where she plans at least for education beyond early adolescence and very often if not generally for a "job" beyond that. Here one can say that for the boy the occupational role has primacy over the marital role, for the girl, vice versa, but both are tending to become typical for both sexes. For the occupational role the socializing agents are, in anticipation, parents, older peers, teachers, and people a boy "knows about" or knows who can "steer" him. Of course once in an actual job, especially not very late in adolescence for many lower class boys, it is the "boss" and the older peers actually acting in the job situation.

The "community" is included in the above enumeration, not only as the superordinate system comprising both families and occupational roles and organizations, but because it comprises a set of residual roles not directly included in these two categories. There is, above all, the whole network of "friendship" relationships, the role of "citizen," and the role in church and in a variety of possible associations or organizations. Participation in most of these is broadly age-graded and they serve as socializing agencies with the older members or participants as the personal socializing agents. Those may of course interpenetrate in various ways with the "proto-family of procreation" (courtship institutions) and "proto-occupation" (usually mainly education) as well as actual occupation. Hence at this level the problem of a clear delineation of the social structure in which socialization takes place is much more difficult than at the earlier levels.

We have already noted the sense in which the category of achievement was relatively irrelevant to the object-internalizations of the earlier phases. In the family this is nearly obvious. Who a child's parents and siblings are, therefore what objects he is to internalize and hence who *he* is, is completely determined independently of anything either he or they do. Performance is relevant only to *how* things are to be done, which means essentially how well the ascriptive standards are fulfilled. We have tried to argue in the last section then that, contrary to certain appearances, this is essentially still true of the latency period school and peer group object systems. The fact that, in our community system, a child should go to school, should be in a given grade determined by his age, etc. is almost wholly ascribed. Also that he should have friends from among his peers is pretty much ascribed. There is more choice open as to whom he should select as friends, but broadly it is still true that they are the friends he is "naturally thrown with" above all schoolmates and the neighbor's children. Relative to a given neighborhood—and a primary school is usually a neighborhood institution—the organization of peer-groups is mainly "horizontal" rather than clearly stratified at this time. In adolescence it becomes quite different.

Returning to the main argument, we will now take each of these three subsystems in turn and analyze its relevance to the discrimination of performance and quality as object-categories. It should of course be remembered that the previously significant socialization-systems remain as bases of operation in which ego plays a representative role in relation to the systems in which he is becoming newly involved. Regressive motives tend to be anchored in the cathexes of these systems, and the permissive-supportive sanctions to emanate from the significant figures in these systems in the earlier stages, but progressively less so.

First, then, let us take the family of procreation. We have noted that in the latency period, either, as in the peer group situation, the sexes tend to segregate drastically, or, as in school, to associate on a plan on which differentiation by sex is largely irrelevant. Adolescence, in this sense, is practically defined by the awakening of a different order of interest in persons of opposite sex, an interest which includes sensitivity to specifically sex-categorized qualities, beauty and "charm" for example in girls, and an undercurrent, which may emerge into overtness at any time, of erotic attraction. On the one hand, then, sex and its attendant sub-qualities, becomes a newly significant quality-category. No matter, for instance, what good manners he may have or how interesting he is to talk with, a fellow adolescent male cannot serve the function of being "my girl." This of course is taking up and utilizing the components of the ascriptive category of sex which have been developed in the two previous stages. But at the same time, the establishment of specifically *significant* cross-sex relationships comes to be a matter of a specific type of achievement, what in another connection we have called a "human relations" achievement.[76] This may be defined as "getting" the partner to consent to and engage in a special type of relationship which of course has many levels and variants, but in its individualized form may be called "going with" the alter of opposite sex. The important point is that sex, and possibly various sub-qualities, are essential ascribed prerequisites of eligibility for such a relationship. But exactly who is to go with whom and on what terms is not ascribed but is left open to the initiative of the individual, though of course regulated in pattern.

It is important that in adolescence early ventures in this direction are usually attended with great anxiety, and that for permissiveness in expressing that anxiety, and in various other

76. *Working Papers,* Chap. V, sec. viii.

respects, the individual tends to fall back primarily on his own-sex peer group. This indicates that the representative role pattern is repeated here, that an individual tends to approach the opposite sex in his role as a representative of the peer group (in some societies it may be a kinship group). One of the most striking portrayals of this situation is that given in Waller's classic paper on the "Rating and Dating Complex."[77] The situation portrayed there is somewhat extreme, but nevertheless brings out the main elements present in this situation. "Dating" the right person, is clearly regarded as an achievement by both peer groups involved, and it is most important to validate that achievement by public appearance, which legitimizes the giving of the requisite approval as a sanction.

"Dating" of course is one item in a series which, with many vicissitudes, can go on with the same or different partners to the stage of "going steady," to engagement, and finally to marriage. But all these stages have in common the accent on achievement, on what has been accomplished, with whatever help and support may be received from peer group and possibly family. It is regarded as the individual's "own doing," on his own initiative and responsibility, and is made possible by his own skills in making himself attractive to the partner, aided or handicapped of course as the case may be by the relevant ascriptive qualities. Finally, in our society marriage is clearly defined as an achieved status, and our definition of its obligations and responsibilities revolves about that fact; of his own free will one agrees to marry this person and to assume the obligations flowing from that act. Of course there is an ascriptive base in that it is "normal" to marry and to marry within certain status-ranges. But on that base it is an achieved status.

Marriage is, of course, particularly important for the girl since as an adult her status in the family of procreation is the primary focus of her general social status. The fact that getting married and the selection and persuasion of the partner are so definitely defined as achievements in our society has much to do with the special character of the feminine role in it. There is a special power situation involved in the fact that the partner who has the greater stake in the outcome, is the one who is

---

77. Reprinted in Wilson and Kolb, *Sociological Analysis*, pp. 611-618.

institutionally expected to take the more passive role in the process of courtship. The balance is partly redressed by the specialization of the feminine role in the expressive direction, hence the presumptive effectiveness of "charm" as an instrumentality. But none the less this is a major focus of strain related to such phenomena as the "glamor" pattern.

What is the contribution of this process to the development of the internalized object system and hence the personality? It is essentially, we may say, the discrimination between the universalistic, but ascriptive sex-category instance, boy-girl maturing to become man-woman, and the specifically sex-role relevant instance of the category of achievement, "man-performing as male in relation to woman as female" and vice versa. The roles of marriage partners are, we may say, the prototypes of these sex-achievement roles, and genital eroticism is a central symbol of it. These are, however, the central types of a cluster of such achieved roles, and hence sub-objects. That the normal end-product of the process is actual marriage is of course of fundamental importance to the form the process takes, and the basic structure of the two types of object in relation to each other.

That the marital role, and associated with it that of genital eroticism, is basically focussed on achievement, even cross-culturally, is dramatically symbolized by the psychological importance of "virility" or "potency" in men and sexual responsiveness and fertility in women. A man's anxiety about his virility involves the question of what he is *able to do*. Similarly there is a predilection, probably in most societies, to "blame" the woman for childlessness. Then naturally the assumption of parental roles introduces a further achievement emphasis. The concept of responsibility in this connection is clearly central.

The case of occupational roles for the male as the goal of this stage of socialization in our society is so clear as to need relatively little comment. In boys' education there is a continual shift from emphasis on the more ascriptive elements of "what a boy should know" to "preparing" for the future, predominantly what he is planning to "do." Evidence from the study of mobility cited above shows that even the decision whether or not to enter the college preparatory course during Junior High School (in the New England Public School System) is heavily

oriented to expectations of occupational future, and to judgments of capacity for occupational achievement. The reasoning
runs, "can he do well enough to get into a good college, and in
turn do well enough there to qualify for the kind of job he
wants?" If he cannot he had best be more modest in his am-
bitions.

Here we may say that the object-category "man" which is
defined mainly ascriptively within the horizon of the significant
community status range, and from the boy's point of view above
all by age-status, comes to be differentiated into he who is a
"man" in the ascriptive sense, no matter what he does, and
he who "does" or expects to do certain kinds of things, to be
a lawyer, a business man, or a mechanic. It is quite clear that
the expectation of an adult, responsible occupational role in
which the man "does something worth-while" and "earns a
living" is very strongly ascribed in our society. But *what* he does
is not ascribed; it is "up to him."[78]

Finally, there is the residual category of adult community
relationships. Because of the diversity of things included, it is
difficult to be very definite about this. But no adult in our
society participates only in family and job. He and his wife
have some circle of friends with whom they have reciprocal
social relations in the narrower sense. They very likely belong
to a church, and may in their respective roles, be "active" in
its affairs. They take some interest in political affairs on various
levels, in recreation, sports, the arts, music, etc. Even outside
the occupational roles which have largely this community reference, like ministers, public officials, entertainers, performing
artists, etc. there is a very wide range of achieved statuses and
of people who acquire a community status because they "do"
something felt to be important. This is, in the American middle
class, particularly important for the feminine role as an antidote
to the stigma of being "just a housewife." The same general
kinds of themes therefore run through this sector of the object-
world as the other two.

This last major category-discrimination, that between quality

---

78. Cf. Bakke, *The Unemployed Man* (New York: E. P. Dutton & Co., 1934), for
an excellent analysis of this aspect of the occupational role at the labor level in our
society.

and performance, stands out particularly sharply in American society because from the ascriptive base which is necessarily given with socialization in the family, the emphasis on achievement of statuses is much stronger than in most societies. On this account it may be illuminating to use our society for illustrating certain forces that make for a balance of these categories. There is of course a sense in which, although from a status of origin point of view many statuses in our society are achieved, once within a collectivity, this membership serves as an ascriptive basis for further treatment. This is obviously true of the family of procreation, symbolized for instance by the married woman being known as "Mrs. John Smith." It is also true of an occupational status once well established: "Oh, yes, he is that lawyer!" But in the adolescent and post-adolescent youth culture it is notable that a whole stratified system of ascriptively significant groups, membership in which is achieved, comes to be established. Thus while the latency peer group tends, as we noted, to a "horizontal" relation to others, the members of adolescent peer groups tend to be extremely sensitive about how, as groups, they "rate," and whether theirs is "the right crowd." This may range all the way from very informal groupings to the highly formalized fraternity and sorority systems of many colleges. This seems to be, in a highly achievement oriented society, an "adaptive" structure which preserves some of the functions of more ascriptive categorizations. The same is true of course of the stratification of pupils and students within secondary schools and colleges as units.

It is an extremely important hypothesis of our analysis that this new object-discrimination, like the ones which precede it, is not localized in the personality system, but operates "across the board" through all the object-systems. This is one main reason why it has been so important to trace it through several of ego's role-participation contexts. The essential point is that the same "principle" operates in his sex and marital life, in his occupational life—or preparation for it—in his community affairs life, in other words in all the principal contexts in which his main need-disposition subsystems are engaged. Only on such an hypothesis, we maintain, is it explicable that, with all the differentiation of both personalities and social systems, there should be sufficient consistency in their matching to make adequately integrated functioning of either system possible. We will take up this problem in the next chapter in connection with further considerations about the organization of personality as a system.

CHAPTER **III**

The Organization of Personality as a System of Action

BY TALCOTT PARSONS

In the chapter just finished the discussion was organized about the process of child development using the chronological sequence of phases as the main frame of reference. The treatment of this familiar sequence in our special theoretical terms, particularly the continual emphasis on the social structure of the socializing agencies, and the internalization of their role-units as objects, has raised a whole series of more general theoretical problems. These concern the organization of the personality as a system and the nature of its "fit" with the systems of social interaction in which it is enmeshed. These problems involve a sufficient change in the level of discourse, and in extensity of ramifications, to justify a separate chapter for their consideration.[1]

---

1. In one sense this chapter and that following may be considered as attempts to revise Chapter II, "Personality as a System of Action" of the monograph "Values, Motives, etc. . . . by Parsons and Shils in Part II of *Toward a General Theory of Action, op. cit.*

The Significance of the Oedipal Transition

We may start by reviewing the principles on which, in the last chapter, our analysis of the succession of stages has been built up, and introduce certain additional considerations of theoretical interest. It is only for the last two stages of discrimination, the 8-fold and the 16-fold stage, that we have explicitly used the pattern variables as the major framework of our analysis of the differentiation process. But we would like to make the suggestion now that the whole process can be formulated in pattern variable terms. We suggest, that is, that the first fission, from the one to the two-unit stage can be said to constitute establishment of the discrimination between adaptation and integration with special reference to the attitudinal aspect, namely specificity and diffuseness, while the second in a similar way establishes that between affectivity and affective neutrality.

It will be remembered that in discussing the mother-child love-dependency system as a system, we spoke of the two variables which have later become differentiated out, power and the instrumental-expressive focus, as "fused" and of the mother as playing *the more instrumental role*. This latter is the crucial point. Though relative to the specificity of the discrete organic needs which it has organized, the mother's "care" is diffuse, relative to the mother-child system as a two-member system, the *adaptive function* is clearly mainly in the hands of the mother. She must be concerned with the specificity of situational exigencies which the system must meet. It is precisely the main point that this differentiation of role makes it possible, indeed because of the power difference, imperative, for the child to *specialize* his own role in a diffuse direction, by developing a capacity to love as a contribution to the *integration* of the system. Of course since this is only a two-unit system this specialization cannot go very far. There are furthermore of course components of diffuse "executive" responsibilty in the mother role, and of more or less directly specific "tension-management" in that of the child. But the broad pattern seems to be clear; it would not be possible to make a good case for the reverse thesis.

But if the child's own role is specialized in one direction as characterized in pattern-variable terms, then the fact of thus discriminating his role from mother's underlies, as we have seen, his discrimination between them as types of object, and the internalization of both and the discrimination between them in his personality system. In this connection it is instructive to recall the function we have attributed to childhood eroticism, namely that of generalization of affect, or of expressive symbolization. The importance to the child of erotic pleasure, and thus the fact that the mother can reward him with this sanction, is a fundamental aspect of the mechanism of establishing a diffuse attachment to the mother—which is the same as his playing a diffuse role in the mother-child system. It is his *love for her* which primarily comes to be rewarded with erotic pleasure, not his making this or that specific contribution to her or his own welfare. Unless the discrete specificity of the different organic gratifications could be broken through with some pattern of generalization of *pleasure* as a reward, it is difficult to see how the child could be motivated to love as distinguished from a process of "exchange" of specific reciprocities for specific gratifications. The priority of diffuse love then shows the importance of integrative orientations as a "matrix" within which more specific ones can differentiate.

The second fission, we suggest, involves the internalization of the discrimination between the latency and goal-attainment dimensions, again with special reference to the attitudinal aspect of affectively and affective neutrality. The critical change is that the instrumental-expressive distinction comes to be differentiated out from the power axis. Here for the first time, in a comparable way, in a context which is dissociated from the power axis, the necessity for the disciplines of inhibition is borne in, the differentiation between the contexts in which "acting out" is permissible and the ones where sacrifices must be made for the sake of larger gains and future rewards. It is in adopting an autonomously instrumental role that this new patterning is imposed. Clearly this cannot have the same significance as the internalized mother figure of the earlier stage because of the "oral" mother's association both with control by superior power, and with the child's own expressive interests. Indeed this is the critical achievement of the oedipal period. It is not difficult to see, not only how important this is to the development of the higher instrumental skills and the like, but precisely to logical thought, since longer chains of reasoning must involve the capacity to resist the more immediate associations which always crowd in when a stimulus has been presented. It is suggestive that the properties of "prelogical" mentality and of Freud's "primary process" both seem to fit this pattern.[2] Essentially the point seems to be that these concepts describe the flood of affectively toned associations which are activated by a stimulus, unless there is a capacity to "keep them back" while a disciplined process of reasoning is being carried through.

The next two stages we have already interpreted in terms of the establishment of pattern-variable discriminations, this time with reference to the "object-categorization" side. If the above interpretation is correct, the very important question now arises of what is the significance of this pattern of order, namely the fact that the attitudinal aspects of the discriminations come first, the object-categorization aspects later. Furthermore, since we have interpreted these four pattern-variable distinctions to be reducible on a higher level of abstraction of two pairs, the four dimensions,[3] the question arises whether in this context our separation of the attitudinal and the object-categorization aspects is legitimate at all?

Clearly, according to our interpretation, the oedipal stage, i.e. its successful completion, constitutes a transition of fundamental significance. What is this significance? Our suggestion is that the need-disposition structure up to the fourfold stage constitutes in a special sense the main framework of the personality as a system, which corresponds to what, as sociologists, we call the main institutional structure of a social system. The essence of an action system is cultural *generalization* from the specificity of the multifarious concrete objects of the environment, and the corresponding specificity of reactivity of the lower organisms in relation to such objects. The primary functional requirement of such a process is the development of motivational structures which are capable of handling this

2. Cf. the relevant works of Lévy-Bruhl, Piaget and Wallon as well as those of Freud and other psychoanalytic writers.

3. Cf. *Working Papers*, Chaps. III and V.

multiplicity without reverting to organic specificity in modes and levels of reaction.

We presume that no such motivational unit can be built up without an internalized object or object system constituting an aspect of it. But the "strategy" of the socialization process seems to be to keep the object-aspect as the *simplest* possible level, and to use these extremely simple object relations to build up powerful motivational systems, including a very deep internalization of the *discriminations* between the elementary need-disposition types, and of course of the elementary but generalized relations between them. This is done by placing the child in an "artificially" stabilized and simplified social object world, both with respect to the infra-social aspects, i.e. those relevant to physical care, and to the all-important social aspects. Therefore the child's "problem" is not complicated by having to develop motives in relation to a complex and varying system of objects until he has firmly established those which relate him to a simpler and stabler one. From this point of view we can say that the primary function of the very first step is to get the specific organic needs adequately under control, so that on the action level there is established a genuine boundary-maintaining system. Only then, and at first only in a diffuse undifferentiated sense, is it safe to let the child develop autonomous motives of his own. The point is that this is in the normal case, done in such a way as *not* to reactivate the autonomy of the infra-social motivational components. There is a *single* autonomous love motive, while dependency on the continuing care of the mother exerts a controlling force on these organic submotives. Then, when this single autonomous motive has become sufficiently firmly established, it is allowed to differentiate into a sphere where more than two types of objects must be adjusted to and where the child assumes autonomous responsibility on a much higher level for "handling his own tensions." We suggest that the central significance of affective neutrality at this point lies in the fact that in this sphere, for the first time, a range of activities is opened up in which the child handles his own regressive needs without the direct help of the mother. The earlier mechanism, that is, operates through dependency. When faced with "temptation" to break through the essential disciplines the child is restrained by the fact that his dependency is so strong that he "does not dare" risk losing or jeopardizing the care or the love of his mother. But gradually he is "weaned" from this dependency and takes over responsibility for self-enforcement of discipline. This, of course, is the function in the first instance of the superego.

The basic reason why the fourfold, nuclear family internalization stage is so crucial is, we believe, that here for the first time the personality has attained a level of development which makes it a relatively complete system. Put in technical terms, it now has a thoroughly established need-disposition subsystem specialized in relation to each of the four basic system-problems. It can perform "adaptive" functions, through its "adequacy" motivational subsystem with relatively little interference from "irrelevant" or conflicting needs. In a similar sense through the security system, it can perform integrative functions, through the "nurturance" system, goal-gratification functions, and through the "conformity" system pattern-maintenance and tension-management or in a special sense control functions. From this point of view it is not a matter of chance that only when this process has come to a certain closure is it felt safe for the child to venture in a highly autonomous way outside the family—though of course he is still "protected" to a substantial degree by his family. But now, in a sense in which it was not at all true before, he is capable of coping with a more complex world, and learning its further complexities without the attendant strains driving him into regression.

Our answer to the broad question, then, is that attitudinal structure has priority, because motivational stability, on the requisite levels, is a precondition of coping with and internalizing a more complex object world. To reverse the order would not be possible for a *personality* system, because there would be no way of dealing with the differentiated object categories in any motivationally stable way.

This, of course, is in no way to suggest that the differentiations of the situational world formulated in the other pair of pattern variables, is irrelevant at this stage. The idea that all the pattern variables are involved in four universally relevant dimensions is not disproved by the above analysis. But object-discriminations are "controlled" in a very specific way. They are not permitted to dictate the structure of the *significant* social object world for the child; this world, as we said, is "artificially" simplified. All of these object-discriminations, that is to say, up through the oedipal period, *apply to aspects of all four of the objects.* The artificial simplification we referred to consists precisely in the fact that the child is not permitted to treat one of the four or two objects as universalistic only, another as particularistic only, in its significance for him (similarly with quality and performance). Only when he can fit such discriminations into a *motivationally* differentiated personality system can they safely be internalized as applying to *different classes* of objects. Otherwise these discriminations would "cross up" the basic structure of his personality as a system. The personality could not achieve functional integration as a system without such discriminations being fitted into an attitudinal organization. Essentially this consequence flows from our insight that personality is a system of differentiated motivational flows or currents *organized* about the structure of an internalized object system, or system of systems.

If this interpretation is correct it seems to have an important implication for certain possibilities of pathology. We suggest that where the attitudinal level of organization of the personality is defective, either because it has not developed or because the object-categorization discriminations have been pushed too early, the pathological syndrome will revolve about the interference of object-category discriminations with motivational functioning. Thus to suggest a simple case, instead of spreading superego control relatively evenly through the whole personality system, a person may activate it highly in relation to particularistically categorized objects, but keep it in abeyance when the object is universalistically categorized. The man who is most fanatically conscientious in fulfilling his obligations to his family or his friends, but sees nothing wrong with cheating outsiders at any opportunity, might fit into such a type.

The primary focus of integration, thus, is on the motivational aspect of the personality as a system. The stability of this integration must be protected if a fundamental functional prerequisite of complex social systems is to be fufilled, namely that the typical individual member should be capable of performing multiple roles. The multiplicity of roles means that the same person must be oriented to several different classes and types of social object. These in turn must each get their "share of attention," there must, that is to say, be order in the ways in which they are treated, the obligations accepted and the like. This order is established mainly in terms of the cathectic or expressive meanings of the objects, their rank orders or organization of overall importance in the individual's life, and the organization of the different components of motivational investment going into each. It is, we may suggest, a primary function of a sufficiently differentiated and integrated motivational system to make this orderly relation between object-involvements or roles possible. The fact that this set of functional needs takes precedence in the organization of personality, while the organization of objects takes precedence in the structure of the social system, is the basic origin of the "symmetrical asymmetry" of the pattern variable system to which we have often called attention.[4]

Let us now take note of another formal property of this pattern of succession of the four pattern-variable discriminations. Put in dimension terms, there is a repetition, with attitudinal and object-categorization primacy respectively, of first the adaptive-integrative pair, then the goal-gratification-latency pair. What is the broader significance of this? We think our account of the learning process as corresponding to our "counter-clockwise" phase process gives the explanation. The "goal" or "function" of the learning process is to establish both new goal-specifications and new internalized normative or regulative patterns. These two aspects of a system—or system-unit which on the next level "down" is of course also a system—are those which directly characterize its intrinsic "nature," relatively independently of the exigencies in which it is placed. Adaptive and integrative patterns, on the other hand, are a direct function of these exigencies, on the one hand those external to the system as a whole, on the other those internal ones which concern the relations of the unit in question to the other units of the system. In performance processes, the system goal and normative patterns take precedence; adaptive and integrative considerations define *conditions* to which the successful attainment of the goal and maintenance of the pattern are subject. In the case

4. Cf. especially "Values, Motives and Systems of Action," Chap. I, in *Toward a General Theory of Action, op. cit.*

of learning processes, on the other hand, goal and pattern are not yet established. These are *derived* from the adaptive and integrative aspects of the situations in which the system and unit are placed. The basic "strategy of socialization" to which we referred above was to hold this object system "constant" and thereby force and help the system to *adapt* to the given conditions, and in turn the various units of the system to attain a certain level of integration with each other in relation to those conditions. Then the internalization of the *new* goal specifications and normative patterns follows, provided of course the necessary conditions have been fulfilled. Hence we conclude that in a larger sense the adaptive-integrative discriminations are more "elementary" in the socialization process than are the other two.

This conclusion can be restated in terms of Freud's scheme. It will be noted that what we here call the adaptive-integrative problem foci constitute, according to the interpretation put forward above, the basis of organization of the Ego, whereas the Superego concerns the pattern-maintenance function of the personality system. It is certainly one of the fundamentals of Freud's account of personality development that a process of ego development, following the primary identification with the mother, must take place before the superego can develop.

Early in the previous chapter we attempted, for preliminary purposes, to fit the process of socialization through the adolescent crisis into our four-stage paradigm of the learning cycle (cf. Chap. II above, Fig. 2). What we have actually come out with is a *five*-stage scheme, and this discrepancy needs a word of comment. From the point of view of the pattern variables this constitutes an asymmetry. What we set forth as the first stage, from the birth to establishment of oral dependency, does not directly involve, according to our interpretation, any of the four "fundamental" pattern variables. The next two stages establish the two basic attitudinal discriminations, whereas the two object-categorization discriminations are compressed into what, on the basis of that paradigm, is one final stage, that from Freud's latency through adolescence to maturity.

This, in our opinion, is another consequence or aspect of the symmetrical asymmetry. It is undoubtedly significant that the attitudinal discriminations in the paradigm stand squarely "in the middle" of the socialization phase process. They are preceded by one fundamental phase, and succeeded by one fundamental phase. Another way of putting this interpretation of the last phase is to say that the discrimination of the two object-categorization phases we have traced is not marked by a clear difference of stages in overt *psychosexual* development. This we must interpret to mean that it does not involve a comparably critical reorganization of the child's internal *motivational* system, but centers on his orientation to objects.[5] It is, however, in our opinion highly significant that the represssion of eroticism is not lifted until *both* of the subphases are approaching completion. This means, as we will argue, that there must be a clearly established basis of discrimination between legitimate and illegitimate new objects of erotic attraction.

It was just said that none of the "fundamental" pattern variable discriminations was involved in the first phase of socialization as this has been interpreted here. This is meant of course to refer to the four which we have brought into the dimensional scheme. But readers familiar with the pattern variable scheme will have noted that the dichotomy of "self- vs. collectivity" orientation has been conspicuously missing from our analysis so far. We wish to advance the suggesion that this does in fact formulate a fundamental feature of the outcome of the first major phase.

In relatively recent work[6] it has become increasingly clear that this variable had to do with the relation *between* systems, rather than with the internal constitution of a system itself. Its importance derives essentially from the system-subsystem relationship which we know to be so important in the whole field of action. What it does is to formulate the difference between two modes of integration of a subsystem in a superordinate system. The collectivity-oriented case is that in which a role or function in the superordinate system is directly *constitutive* of the goals of the subsystem. Thus, to use a familiar example, the physician's goal is to facilitate the recovery of

---

5. We believe that there is in fact a latent psychosexual problem on this phase. The prominence of the one-sex peer group at this stage suggests that the pattern is homosexual but that to allow it overt expression would interfere with developing sex-categorization.

6. Cf. *Working Papers,* esp. Chap. V.

his patient, which is also as such the primary goal of the physician-patient system as a social system. In the self-oriented case, on the other hand, the functional requirements, and hence norms, of the superordinate system are not constitutive but *regulative;* they define the limits of acceptable variation of behavior which are compatible with "membership in good standing" in the superordinate system. Again, a common example is that of the market relationship. The rules against fraudulent practice, enjoining the maintenance of contracts, etc. do not prescribe *what* an actor shall want, but only certain rules of *how* he shall or shall not go about getting it. Such rules clearly have the function of preventing both the disorganization of the system, and interference with the other units in the system.

The undifferentiated, single-unit motivational system of the oral dependency stage is a system, but its units are not need-dispositions in the action-system sense, but are organic needs. The relevance of the self-collectivity pattern variable at this stage we conceive as formulating a fundamental relationship between these two system-levels. On the one hand oral dependency is a directly constitutive need-disposition unit. We may suggest that it is the basis of the motivational significance of the supportive attitude of the mother on this level which makes it possible for her to impose frustrations on the child in the form of new "demands" and still not risk "turning him against her," i.e. losing control of him. In this sense the motive unit is constitutive of the mother-child system as a collectivity. On the other hand, the organic needs have not been absorbed and their distinctiveness has not been destroyed; they are units in a system. But the fact that it has become a boundary-maintaining action system means that they are subjected to *regulation* in terms of the norms of the system. Thus the hunger-need is more than simply an "aspect" of oral dependency; it is an independent entity. But there is a difference between its operation here and in the unsocialized neonate; it has become integrated in a system of control so that it seeks (and obtains) gratification only under certain conditions.

Since, from this point of view the single-unit system is a complex entity, not just a "monolith," there may be important differences of balance in the organization of its components.

What we are formulating in applying the self-collectivity pattern-variable to this stage is the proposition, that for the later developmental process and its outcome the most important alternatives of organization at the oral dependency stage concern the balance between constitutive and regulative integration of the organic-need units in the need-disposition system. If the balance is on the constitutive side, i.e. the collectivity side, the later tendency will be for a "tighter" control over organic need elements underlying the action-organization of behavior, whereas if it is on the regulative side, it will be more in the direction of the "laissez-faire" type of control. In the first case gratification of an organic need will more often have to be positively *justified* by its direct contribution to system function, whereas in the second case it will be tolerated so long as it does not "interfere" with other interests. Thus the "puritan" attitude that food is justified as the "fuel" that makes it possible to work, may be contrasted with the acceptance of gustatory enjoyment as good in itself so long as it does not become gluttony. Of course such a discrimination presumably comes to be generalized from control of organic need-components to the patterning of relations between system and unit on all levels.[7]

These considerations lead on to another suggestion which will only be very briefly mentioned here but will be somewhat further elaborated on in the latter part of the present chapter. and in the next. A very important part of the general conceptual scheme with which we have been working is what we have called the "deviance paradigm," the classification of directions in which action may lead to a disturbance in the stable state of a system.[8]

7. We believe that the above analysis of the relevance of the self-collectivity pattern variable to this earliest stage of personality development is relevant and sound so far as it goes, but that it does not exhaust the subject. The use of the pattern variables for the analysis of the subsequent stages concerns the problem of the points of reference for the differentiation relative to an already established internalized value system. In the case of the first stage, differentiation is not in question, but rather the establishment of a *value system* without reference to to differentiation. The self-collectivity variable we feel adequately formulates one aspect of the status of such a system, namely that of the relation of the values in terms of priority, relative to the "interests" or "needs" of the component units. But there is no reason to believe that this aspect is exhaustive of the problems at this level. To go farther with the problem would, however, lead into fundamental considerations of the status of this aspect of the pattern variable scheme, which cannot be undertaken here.

8. Originally fully stated in T. Parsons, *The Social System* (Glencoe, Ill.: Free

This conceptual scheme involved three dichotomies of the direction of deviance which, when put together, yield an eight-fold table of possibilities; one combination of four, it will be remembered, converges with Merton's well-known paradigm of social structure and anomie. The suggestion here is that these three dichotomies formulate, not as do the pattern variables, the *types* of stable state at each of the first three stages of personality development, but the types of *deviation from* a stable state at these stages. Conformity-alienation we suggest is directly relevant to the success of imposing the very first action-level integration as control of organic need-motivation. There is *no* action system without a normative aspect; hence we argue that successful establishment of this normative control will minimize resistance to it. This is the conformative case. On the other hand resistance, if it becomes established or is not successfully overcome, will introduce an alienative element in the orientation system.[9] Presumably alienation can develop at any time, but this is the "deepest" level on which it can appear and if not overcome would have the most ramified consequences for the personality. The connection with the problem of anxiety seems to be very clear. This, it seems, is the only one of the three components which can make sense at the oral dependency level.

The second dichotomy of the deviance paradigm was, it will be remembered, that of "activity-passivity." The connection with the problem of the balance between dependency and autonomy at the two-unit stage seems clear. Essentially, we suggest, the family culture will establish norms as to the proper balance in this respect. Deviance in the passive direction then will, *relative to the norm,* be associated with overdevelopment of the dependency need-disposition, while activity-deviance will be related to relative overdevelopment of the autonomy motive, i.e. inability to tolerate and give adequate expression to, the dependency need. Finally the dimension of deviance which we have referred to as distinguishing emphasis on the "normative pattern vs. those on social objects" seems to focus at the third stage. Deviance in the direction of emphasis on normative

Press, 1951), Chap. VII. Hereinafter called *The Social System*. It was further developed in *Working Papers,* Chaps. III and V.

9. The most primitive expression of this we assume is "oral aggression."

patterns at the expense of social objects then would relate to overemphasis, *relative to the norms,* on the affectively neutral need-dispositions, while social-object oriented deviance would be overemphasis on the affective ones.

If this correspondence between the components of the deviance paradigm and the developmental stages holds up, it will represent a great advance toward effective use of it in personality theory, above all in linking the scheme of developmental stages with the analysis of the etiology of pathological states. It seems inherently reasonable that the foci of the deviance problem should be found in the stages having to do with the organization of the basic *motivational* components of personality structure rather than with the object-categorization components. A deviant tendency then in social interaction terms, is a lack of motivational integration of an actor with the role-expectations of the social system. It is a matter of motivational predisposition. The intra-personal case is essentially the same in structure.

The "Genealogy" of Need-Dispositions

We may now take up a series of problems concerning the fully developed personality and its articulation with the social system through common value patterns and interaction in roles. Let us begin by considering some of the implications of the pattern of genesis of the need-dispositions which we have followed throughout the present analysis. The main principle is that of differentiation by the process of binary fission. From this point of view we can consider each need-disposition unit at any stage to be located on a "genealogical tree," with a system of branches all going back to the "trunk" of oral dependency (with organic needs as the "roots"). While the motives which were the growing points at various earlier stages are no longer in the same sense "active," they are still there in the form of the genetically prior object frameworks within which "families" of currently active need-dispositions are to be located. They may therefore be said to define the boundaries of these genetically significant subsystems.

What can we say about the bearing of what has been determined at each of the successive fission points which carries over into the later personality structure? Three propositions stand out as probably correct. The first has formed a main framework of our whole discussion, namely that a division once made is irrevocable in the sense that a *direction* of specialization or qualitative differentiation becomes established which then is irreversible. This is to say that, once separated, the "lines of descent" of need-dispositions do not cross again. If this is true it has extremely important implications, in that the distinction between qualitatively differentiated components of the adult motivational system should be traceable to definite sources in genetically prior stages of the system, and the genetic stages and hence approximate time period at which any given differentiation was determined, located.

But besides qualitative differentiation there is another major aspect of the organization of a complex personality as a system, namely the hierarchical aspect. We can define this as concerning the *relative strength* of the different motivational units, and subsystems of units. Our second proposition is that these relations of relative strength derive from the *balances* established between the components at each of the important stages of the process of differentiation. Thus at the two-unit stage we may speak of the relative strength of the dependency and the autonomy components as variable. While the fact that such a differentiation takes place is universal, this is not true of the balance between the resulting components. We have illustrated this most directly for the next stage in the case of sex role differentiation, arguing that the difference, initially, lies primarily in the relative balance of the instrumental and expressive components, and that this relative balance is determined primarily at the oedipal period. From this point of view the masculine and feminine personalities do not differ in the *kinds* of need-disposition units which make them up, but in the relative strengths of different subsystems of their personalities. We will assume also that this determination of relative strength is, once made, broadly irrevocable.

When these two considerations are combined, we have a way of "locating" a motivational complex of the mature personality system in the personality structure as a whole, and characterizing both its derivation and its major characteristics in terms of our genealogical scheme. For convenience of reference, the scheme as a whole is set forth in Figure 1.

But still a further set of considerations must be brought to to mind. The most important contexts of concrete action for many purposes are role-interaction relationships. In analyzing the learning process we have stressed throughout that the situation which was significant for socialization was not composed of one object, but a *system* of objects. This is vividly illustrated by the case of the nuclear family at the oedipal stage. The child there internalized a new system of relationships to four familial figure-types, including himself. The effect of this was not only further to differentiate his need-disposition system, but to *order* the differentiated units, as illustrated by the sex-role case.

Turning this around for the performance case as distinguished from that of learning then we may say that what is "engaged" in a role-interaction process is not just one need-disposition unit of the personality, but some kind of a *subsystem* of them, very possibly not the whole personality in any direct way, but probably an important though selected *set* of parts of it. This is true whether the object be a single alter or a plurality who constitute a differentiated system. There will have to be an organized grouping of motivational units implicated, which will have to include a minimum number of properly differentiated units covering the requisite range, and will have to be organized in terms of a priority scale of relative importance *in this role*. Thus in addition to qualitative differentiation, and relative strength, or "stratification" we have *a third basic principle of the organization of the personality* as a system, the set of "cross-ties" which bind diverse motivational components together in role-expectation subsystems.

We would like to attempt to illustrate with two types of role which are important in modern society, the adult familial roles in the family of procreation, and the adult masculine occupational role. We should start by locating the role type in the general society and characterizing it. If in previous analyses we have been correct about the urban American Family,[10] its functions in the society have become specialized as predominantly expressive, even non-integrative (from the point of view

---

10. *Working Papers,* Chap. V. See also Chapter I of present study.

FIGURE 1

Genealogy of Need-Dispositions

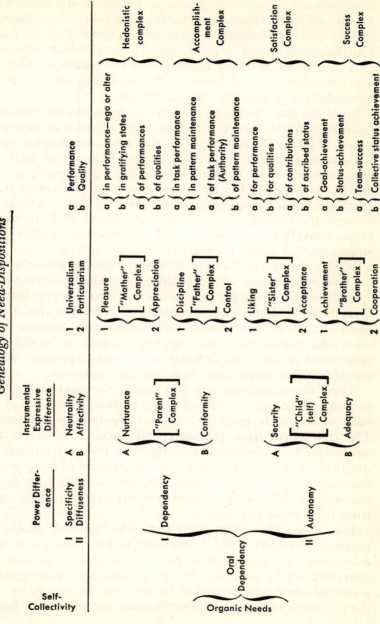

of the society); they belong, that is, largely in the latency cell. For its adult members, that is, the function of the family is mainly tension-management within the context of an institutionalized normative pattern system, for children, of course, it is mainly socialization which places far greater emphasis on the normative control element. Its functions for the society operate *through* personalities, not directly.

Since the adult members comprise only the marital pair, apart from socialization functions, then, their relation to each other becomes primarily expressive in the tension-management and pattern maintenance sense. We have briefly analyzed, in the last chapter, the process of courtship leading up to marriage, with special reference to the role of achievement motives in it. On marriage, however, quite definitely (a good deal less definitely before), the marriage pair becomes a solidary collectivity, and presumptively in the institutionalized sense, more than this, a subsystem of a larger collectivity, the new family.

Within the new familial collectivity the marital sub-collectivity has the system goal of optimizing "tension-management" or "gratification" of the partners. Since it is a collectivity, however, there must be both a differentiation of roles and the involvement of at least two *primary* need-disposition components on each side. Furthermore, as a system, we suggest its *differentiation* must involve one or both of the two elementary axes of differentiation, power and instrumental-expressive.

These considerations give us clues to the motivational composition of the marital roles. They constitute *derivatives of both sides* of the early mother-child love-dependency relationship. The differences from the genetically prior case derive from two major considerations; first that the power relationship is drastically altered and second that now, instead of monopolizing the total personalities of either, the components most directly involved in the marital relation are only part of the derivatives from these respective sources.

Let us take this latter point first. The "genital" erotic relationship is clearly a focal symbolic factor. The erotic need-disposition, we suggested in the last chapter, is at this stage characterized by performance or achievement orientation, by universalism, by affectivity of course, and by specificity. It is the prototype of "pleasure" gratification and important because perhaps the most generalized form of it. It is, according to our "genealogy," a derivative of maternal "care" via "nurturance" via a universalistic pleasure-motive. But at the same time the marital relationship involves "commitment" to alter as a person, "acceptance" or in this affective sense "love" of alter as co-member of a solidary collectivity. The "pleasure" motive therefore is interdependent, in the personalities of *both* parties, with the love motive. This latter is a derivative of the autonomy motive at the mother-child stage, via "security," and *particularistic* acceptance, and finally its ascriptive sub-type. Marriage in our society is an achieved status, but once entered into, it constitutes an ascriptive base for subsequent action.

Considered as a social system, the marriage relationship is clearly a differentiated system. The fact that sex (as category) is constitutive of it suggests that, of the two "primary" axes, the instrumental-expressive one here takes precedence over that of power. From this point of view, though the general functions of this collectivity in the superordinate systems are expressive, the *more* instrumental role in the subsystem is taken by the husband, the *more* expressive one by the wife. This is to say that externally, the husband has the primary adaptive responsibilities, relative to the outside situation, and that internally he is in the first instance "giver-of-care," or pleasure, and secondarily the giver of love, whereas the wife is primarily the giver of love and secondarily the giver of care or pleasure. The husband role, that is, is prototypically closer to the "mother" role, that of the wife, to the "child" role. But both are both "mother" and "child" to each other.[11]

11. When seen in this context the symbolism of the act of sexual intercourse is striking. The man, we suggest, has the primarily instrumental role. He is the main initiator and, with his penis as instrument, the main active "giver of pleasure" to both partners; he is thus acting in the "mother" role. The woman, on the other hand is not only typically more passive and receptive, but by admitting the penis and "embracing" it in her vagina, she may be said to be symbolizing her acceptance of the relationship and of her partner in it; in this sense she is acting in the role of the loving child. At the same time, however, the obverse aspect of the roles is also symbolized. The man embraces the woman with his arms and the woman, by caresses, movements, etc., actively contributes to the giving of pleasure.

Further, Freud's well-known "equation" of penis and child from the woman's point of view fits in. Complementing the man's "mother" role as giver of pleasure is *her* "mother" role in embracing and thus loving, him in his "child" capacity. The penis thus not only symbolizes "masculinity" in its instrumental aspect but at the same time the "child in the adult man."

Compared with the mother-child situation, however, the power relation has been very greatly, if not completely equalized. We suggest that this has happened by a process similar to that analyzed in the last chapter in relation to the attitudes toward rules in connection with the emergence of universalistic orientations. This involves a high degree of internalized superego control in relation to an institutionalized set of universalistic values. It is probably not a matter of chance that this equalization of power has gone very far in the American marriage relationship and that this has occurred in a society with an exceptionally strong general accent on universalistic values (there are of course other factors).

This control function in relation to power illustrates the involvement in the motivational structure of the marriage relationship of motivational components other than the two to which we have given primacy. It is also notable that in this case there is universally a strong accent on collectivity-orientation. Both giving pleasure to alter and loving him or her are positive obligations. Clearly there must, since this is a system, also be components derived from the "adequacy" and the "conformity" complexes, since there are in the nature of the case adaptive problems of the system.

The next set of considerations which is also very important, concerns the fact that institutionally the marriage relationship is a subsystem of the nuclear family. The parties' roles as parents therefore must be integrated with their marital roles. Here, as we have seen in instrumental-expressive and possibly in power terms, there is an important complication. The husband-father has the predominantly instrumental role in connection with the *family* as a collectivity, not only the marriage, he not only "supports" a wife, but a family. The wife, however, in spite of her *more* expressive role in the family as a whole, which we may say above all centers on her acceptance or love complex of motives, in her role of mother of specific children,

---

It is finally suggestive that it is nearly universally true that the sexual pair feel it very important to be alone with each other. This may be interpreted to symbolize the prototypical experience of early childhood, regardless of the sex of the child, of "possessing" the mother when alone with her. Only in this situation can the mother-child solidarity take undisturbed precedence over the other roles of the concrete mother.

must for the mother-child subsystems, take the predominantly instrumental role. From this point of view the pre-oedipal child is the terminal member of a *series* of role relationships which combine system-subsystem memberships and instrumental-expressive differentiation.

Because of his principally instrumental responsibilities in his familial as distinguished from his marital role, the husband-father needs a relatively more highly developed instrumental complex of motivational components than does his wife. But in turn it is evident that he must also have this specialization in order to serve his function as a socializing agent at the critical oedipal phase, as the primary symbolic source of the superego. The wife-mother, on the other hand, needs the predominance of expressive motivational elements in her total mother and familial role, in the case of the former because young children do not have highly developed instrumental motive systems and are not capable of responding to them. But because the mother must take relatively instrumental roles in relation to her children, and of course in important ways in relation to the family as a whole, those expressive motives must be balanced by those on the instrumental side. To take only one example, we have seen how essential it is that both parents should present a united front in imposing disciplines on their children. If the mother herself did not have adequate superego control, she would obviously be subject to easy "seduction" by her children. Particularly in our type of society where the father is absent so much of the time, the deleterious possibilities of such a situation are evident.[12]

One further balance is interesting. In the marital relationship, we have argued, the more instrumental role of the husband makes him more the "giver" of "pleasure," from the facilities necessary for his wife and for the marital collectivity to have "nice things," all the way to erotic pleasure. But in the mother role the wife, in turn, is the primary giver of pleasure to her children. This suggests an important relationship of balance in the feminine personality. It follows from our analysis above that the expressive primacy in the feminine personality

---

12. On some aspects of this problem, see T. Parsons and R. Fox "Illness, Therapy, and the Modern American Family," *Journal of Social Issues,* May, 1953.

and her greater difficulty in achieving emancipation from de-pendency would, other things equal, make for a greater direct vulnerability to the regressive motivational elements comprised in the "nurturance" complex, which, according to our analysis, is the primary location of the Id. If her pleasure needs were allowed to be too greatly turned inward, to become too narcis-sistic, this presumably would tend to activate regressive needs. The mother role, however, motivates a woman to turn nurtur-ance needs outward to the child. This strongly suggests the importance of the mother role to the personality-equilibrium of the woman.

Finally, a word of further interpretation may be said about adult or "genital" eroticism. It should, by this time, be clear how fundmentally the adult situation differs from that at the oedipal stage. Eroticism here for the man is ideally a direct factor in only one out of a ramified system of roles instead of being, as it was in the early relation to his mother, constitutive of the one fundamental social relationship in which he was then involved. Moreover, even this is carefully hedged in by the importance of other motives, his love for wife and family, and the whole instrumental need-complex. We may say that it is the fact that eroticism is now only part of a far more extensive solidly established motivational system which makes it safe to lift the repressions imposed at the oedipal period.

For the woman the situation is somewhat different. She is allowed a *plurality* of erotic relationships. But in the first place we note that she did not have to undergo so severe an oedipal strain as her brother did, and secondly, in their place in the role-systems, the different modes of erotic expression open to her are *qualitatively* differentiated. Moreover, she has to have strong enough superego and other non-nurturant mo-tives to be able, on her part, to renounce the erotic compo-nents of her attachments to her children as they come to the oedipal period. It may be that one important aspect of the father role lies in the fact that, since he in general has a much weaker erotic attachment to his children than does the mother, he is less likely than she to be seduced into allowing them to continue in a state of pre-oedipal dependency. If it were not for his role in the family it would be more difficult for the necessary disciplines to be imposed.

As a second example we may take the adult masculine occupational role. Here clearly the primacy lies on the instrumental
side since the occupational system is heavily specialized on that
side in the society as a whole. The connection with the relative
instrumental specialization of the masculine personality and
correspondingly of course the predominance of men in the
occupational world, is patent. In American society, furthermore,
we presume that by and large there is a stronger accent on
functions calling for derivatives of the adequacy complex than
of that of conformity.

However, occupational activities are carried out in a context where there are in turn also differentiated roles within the
relevant subsystems. The range of structural sub-types is so
wide that it is not possible here to give such a definite picture
as we gave for the marriage relationship and its involvement in
the family of procreation.

In line with the general principle that derivatives of both
the dependency and the autonomy motives tend to be involved
in reciprocal role relationships, we can suggest that the "adequacy" complex tends to have a certain priority, but that the
sanctions of approval require for their effectiveness a source
of moral authority. This must be a derivative of the "father-
conformity" complex. As between equals this is, we suggest
usually given in the general way we suggested above in connection with the internalization of universalism in the peer
group, as exemplified by Piaget's "cooperation." Two or more
cooperating persons, relative to an instrumental goal, are on
the one hand striving for "success," i.e. the attainment of their
group task. Success, however, must be measured by reference
to internalized standards. So far as there is equality and reciprocity, these have been "depersonalized" and mutually applied,
through the sanction of approval, to each. Esteem then, does not
go specifically to the individual actors, but to the group achievement itself and to the collectivity as a whole, e.g. "a swell outfit."
But each, through his superego, implements the esteem sanction.

There may, then, in our system, be further differentiations
from this base line. Leadership as autonomous performance
may involve simply greater contributions to instrumental goal
attainment, either in a universalistic "technical" role, or in a
more particularistic "executive" role. It may, on the other

hand, emphasize the conformity need on both sides more, that is when its incumbent is in a superior position, be the role of an "authority figure," again either in universalistic or in particularistic terms.

Finally, there is the "human relations" aspect of the occupational role. Internally to the organization as a system this is the integrative and tension-management role, externally, the role of "negotiator" and "public-relations" man—notably of course the salesman. Here the capacity to deal with alter's "feelings" is of the first importance, and the interplay of needs to like and be liked, giving pleasure, appreciation and acceptance are all important. In the occupational world, on the whole, however, these tend to be subordinated to the instrumental role components and hence motive-systems.

Perhaps we can generalize by saying that a role tends to utilize, not one specialized motivational subsystem, but *an organized complex* of motivational units. Of the more basic ones it seems that in every role—at least every one of major importance in the personality—derivatives of *all* primitive internalized objects become involved. Thus in both of our examples we have maintained that derivatives of both dependency and autonomy sources are involved, and secondarily in these cases of both instrumental and expressive components. Again, as so often, the principle seems to be that the motives involved in different roles are not "different in kind" but represent different modes of *organization* of the same components, at least on the "deeper levels," above all these organizations have differing *stratification* structures of the same elements.

If this is broadly true it has an implication for the nature of the problems of "social control," i.e. of motivating the individual to conformity with institutionalized expectations in roles. This is the consideration that very great importance attaches to the maintenance of the balances between the motivational components which go into a single role-motivation complex. Deviance, we suggest, comes at least as often from disorganization of the complex, as it does from direct and positively conflicting motive. This analysis obviously barely opens up a complex and very important field. There is no space to pursue it farther here.

Personality and Social Value-Systems

We may now turn to a more general set of problems concerning the organization of the personality as a system, namely the nature of the balances between the different components we have analyzed, including the relations of the individual's several role-expectation systems to each other. For a starting point we can go back to the problems of why the oedipal crisis is of such paramount importance, and to the nature of the difference between the personality in the periods before and after it. The major framework of the immediate postoedipal personality as a system, which in one sense continues in effect, is constituted by the four need-disposition clusters characterized by the special relevance of the attitudinal pattern variable combinations. But these do not constitute the framework for the values of *any* social system the structural differentiation of which goes beyond the level of the nuclear family as such. We have consistently argued that the nuclear family not only is not, but *cannot be* a complete *society* on the cultural level.

We have further argued that the other pair, the object-categorization pattern variables, characterize the main framework of the structure of societies as social systems. It is in these terms that the common value-systems of societies must be formulated. It follows that when we speak of the common values of the society as internalized in personalities we speak primarily of those elements of the value-system of the individual which become differentiated out in the postoedipal period.

Basing ourselves on the evidence from the study of small groups and from the comparative study of kinship, as illustrated in Chapter VI, we argue that the nuclear family is a universal structural component of all societies, and that its range of structural variability is limited first of course by maintaining the power differential between parents and children in favor of the former, and second by maintaining the husband-father role as *more* instrumental than the wife-mother, and vice-versa, the wife-mother as *more* expressive. This latter is the more controversial of Zelditch's theses, but we feel he has presented adequate evidence to justify its use for our specific purposes.

Then what can be the relation between the structural variability of nuclear families and that of the wider society in their impact on personalities? We suggest that the institutionalization of the societal value-system will lead to a "tipping" of the balance between the familial roles. Hence the paramount American value system, which we hold to be broadly characterized by a universalistic-performance pattern, will tend to narrow the power differential between the generations in the nuclear family, and to "instrumentalize" the role of the wife-mother, "pulling it over" toward the more instrumental pole, but leaving it of course still more expressive than her husband's role. This balance, then, will tend to be reflected in the balances between the four internalized object systems of the child. He will tend to be more "success-oriented" in adequacy terms, and less superego-dominated than a child socialized in a different kind of family. The girl will be more "independent" and less "nurturant," than those socialized in another type of family system.

To sum up, the family is part of the larger society and must be integrated in it. The basic point of reference for analyzing the structure of the society is this institutionalized societal value system.[13] In social system terms this means that, within limits, the family type will vary as a function of the kind of wider social structure, and hence value-system, in which it is integrated. This is reflected in the balance of the four fundamental need-disposition components of the oedipal personality, which in turn forms the basis on which the societal value-system can be internalized and the differentiations of role-participation within it worked out.

Is there any basis on which the nuclear family can vary structurally within the same society? Of course there are several, but one is struck by the paramount importance of the relation between the power structure of the family and the stratification system of the society. We suggest that in order for attitudes toward superiority, inferiority and equality to be fitted into different points in the range of social stratification, the structure of the family must be differentiated on this axis by class. Very, very roughly, the socialization process must operate so that

---

13. We have attempted to show this elsewhere, cf. *Social System*, Chap. V, and *Working Papers*, Chap. V.

those socialized in upper class—in a very broad sense—families will tend to assume more "parental" roles toward most others, whereas those socialized in families at lower levels tend to assume more "child" roles. The spread of these attitudes may of course vary greatly; American attitudes tend to be relatively egalitarian of course, which means that in an important sense the middle class is the "norm."

These considerations give us some points of reference for an approach to the problem of "national character." We suggest that there is, in a society, only in a very abstract sense a trend to a "modal personality" type which is independent of sex, class, and some other variables. However, if these two categories are treated as variable in the way indicated, it is considerably more realistic to speak for instance of a modal upper-class masculine and feminine personality type, and a modal lower-class type for each sex. Again very broadly we suggest, that with the "slant" given them by the societal value system, the upper class personalities will tend to a greater superego-nurturance focus, the lower to a greater adequacy-security focus.

Of course such a very general statement tends to assume a "perfectly integrated" social system, which we know to be a limiting case. A little more concretely we may distinguish between those social status-positions which engage for most purposes the "whole" personality, and those which engage clearly differentiated roles. Sex and class are preeminently the type cases of the former sort, whereas occupation and marriage are type cases of the latter. But such categories as ethnic group and local—or regional—community may approach the former. Hence it may make sense to speak of a negro personality type—differentiated within itself of course by sex and class—of an "American-Jewish" personality type, or of a "New England," or a "Texan" type. The focus on sex and class therefore is not meant to draw an absolute empirical limit to the differentiation of modal points of reference for the analysis of personality uniformities, but to suggest that these are of a different order of significance than are the finer differentiations of status within a society.[14]

---

14. The foci we have in mind as points of crystallization of differentiated modal personality types are mainly those we discriminated earlier (*Social System,* Chap. V) as the "diffuse solidarities" in the social structure. Of the four mentioned there,

Value-Systems and Specialized Roles

We can suggest, then, that the common value system of the society, duly differentiated by sex and class, etc., is in a vague undifferentiated form, internalized by the time of the oedipal resolution. But not all who share that value system, in norm terms, even, are destined to perform the same roles as adults. What of further differentiations? The structural point of reference for its analysis concerns the "intermediate" or "segmental" role-participations of the adult world, of which occupation may serve as a prototype, but also includes churches—in the denominational pluralism type of organization—associational memberships, "social life" in the narrower sense, and a good many others. We can state certain general principles of the relation between these and our concern with personality.

The society must be considered to be made up of a complex series of subsystem-subsubsystem relationships. Following our general line of analysis, to be treated as a subsystem, a complex of interactive relationships must be treated as having an institutionalized (more or less, of course) value system *common* to its members. This value pattern of the subsystem system must be treated as a *differentiation from* the common value system of the society as a whole. Its direction of differentiation is defined by the primary function of the subsystem for the larger system of which it is a part. Thus we may say that a business firm is a subsystem which belongs primarily to the "economy" as that subsystem of the total society which has the function of facilitating its adaptive processes, through "production" increasing the supply of disposable possessions, i.e. "wealth." The primary function of the firm (from the point of view of the society) is to "produce" one or a class of goods or services. The common value system of its participating members then, management, technicians, workers, etc. *in their roles* as employed by the firm, is a "spelling out" in a more specific context of the general universalistic-achievement value system of the society. (It is the case of "economic rationality." Or, to take another example, a university belongs in the first instance to the cultural

kinship, community, ethnicity and class, only kinship seems problematical. Essentially it places nuclear family in the place of sex. This is perhaps justified in social structure terms whereas sex is the relevant category for the typing of personalities.

subsystem of the total society; its primary function is represented in the "latency" cell; it is the maintenance (hence transmission) of certain basic values of the society in the fields of "learning," and their creative further development. Secondarily it produces new facilities which can be put to technological or other "practical" use, in the form of new knowledge and of the skills of people trained by its agency. This is a differentiation from the main overall value system in the direction of implementing those which are pattern elements relatively independent of specific and temporary situations yet which are necessary to stabilize and develop *this type* of society. Again all those who have roles in the university, faculty, administrative officers, students, and even buildings and grounds personnel, to some degree share this subsystem value system, *in these roles.*

A society as an ongoing system must, so far as it becomes sufficiently differentiated, develop subsystems in this sense which meet all of its functional requirements as a system. Analogous to the case of personalities as we have discussed it above, societies differ from each other in the degrees and directions of their structural differentiation and they differ in the ways in which the structural components are organized to constitute the system, but *at a given level of differentiation they do not differ in what structural components are present or absent.* Thus even if the socialization function could be cut loose from the biologically constituted family, if we are right, it could *not* be performed without placing the child in a small group the structure of which was *generically* the same as that of the family, *no matter what* the values of the society. This in turn means that it must be possible for the people who play one or more of the functionally essential roles in the society, also to share the value system of the society as a whole, with those performing what are, qualitatively, quite different roles.

This is accomplished in the society in part by the organization of its differentiated subsystems as a *hierarchy* of more and less inclusive subsystems which can be progressively more highly differentiated in function in the total society. Each subsystem then has a value system which is a "derivative," for the requisite functional area, from the societal value system, in a way which is analogous to the sense in which each of the later need-dispositions of the personality system is a derivative from its genetically prior "ancestors."

It follows from this analysis that in the social system sense a role does *not* embody or institutionalize a value system which is differentiated from those of the other roles in the *same* social subsystem at the same level, and which as roles are differentiated from it in terms of functions for the system. As part of the process of learning the role, the common value system must be internalized; this is true. But this *only* defines the commitment undertaken by assuming *membership* in the system or collectivity. The role, in addition to this, defines expectations of the respects in which ego's behavior will be *different* from that of alters who play roles complementary to his in *the same* system of interaction. This difference is *not* defined by the common value system, but by the *relation* between it, the exigencies to which attainment of such system-goals is subjected, and the values which regulate the functions of dealing with these exigencies, not specifically in *this* social system but in the society as a whole.

To internalize a role-expectation, then, the individual must internalize the social system as a superordinate object, *and* his own role as an organization of motivational components involving levels of his own internalized object system *other than* those involved in the relevant social system as object. The *further* crucial fact, then, is that the differentiations of role within the system will involve internalization of *other* common values than those common to the members of the system in question. Thus a technical man working in a business firm, may be a member of the collectivity of the engineering profession. In *this capacity* he is concerned with the implementation of the values of his professional group rather than with the business success of his firm. This particular subcollectivity value system is *not* shared with all the other members of the firm, such as the "boss" or the ordinary "workers." This criss-crossing of system memberships and value-commitments is the *fundamental* mechanism which stabilizes the role-differentiation within any one collectivity.

Let us attempt to illustrate more or less systematically. We have argued above that in American society the nuclear family is specialized far over in the "expressive," tension-management and socialization directions. The family then has a value-system, which is a differentiated derivative of the common value system of the society as a whole, but which defines *its* system-goals and norms in a relatively specialized way relative, for instance, to a business firm, a political organization or a church. The fact that these must be integrated in a larger value-system does not in any way detract from the importance of their differentiation from other components in that larger system. The marriage relationship then is, as we have seen, a subsystem of the family with its own further specialization of common values, this time with reference to tension management as a system-goal as distinguished from socialization.

Then each of these, system and subsystem, have, though they are few, a plurality of differentiated roles. The marriage relation is the simpler, because it is a two-member system. As we have seen the husband role is specialized *more* in the instrumental direction than the wife's, the wife role, more in the expressive direction. They share the marital system values of maximizing mutual and collective gratifications and satisfactions but their roles relative to these common values are differentiated. Broadly, the husband specializes in meeting the adaptive exigencies, the wife, the integrative. But these specialized aspects are not, in our own or any other society, met in uninstitutionalized ways. The husband is *expected* to be a "good provider," to be able to secure for the couple a "good position" in the community. The wife on the other hand is *expected* to develop the skills in human relations which are central to making the home harmonious and pleasant for both. She is expected to be "attractive," "charming," etc. This is also an institutionalized pattern composed of values she shares with other women as her husband's is shared with other men. Then both sexes cooperate in differentiated roles which are institutionalized in terms of values common to other collectivities to which they respectively belong, *but do not share.* The derivation of these from the adolescent peer-group involvements is clear.

Each, however, in addition to the marital role, plays a parental role in the family. The turning of the feminine instrumental functions in the direction of child care and care of the household which is common to husband and children, reinforces the general expressive trend of the feminine role. On the other hand, the instrumental responsibility for adaptive functions, not only on behalf of the marriage relation but of the family including the children as well, reinforces the instrumental specialization of the man's role. Of course a distinctive feature of our social structure is the extent to which both these adaptive responsibilities focus on the occupational role of the husband-father. It is the internalization of the value-system of the occupational world and whatever subsystems of it he is involved in, which is the focus on the masculine side of the *difference* of the husband-father role from that of the wife-mother.[15]

These considerations enable us to give an interpretation of the differences of the sex roles in their relation to values. It is, in our view, not tenable to assert, as is sometimes done, that in a broad and generalized way the sexes have fundamentally different value-orientations. This would be incompatible with the paramount necessity, if their roles are to be integrated with each other, for them to *share common values*. For example, in their roles as parents they socialize their children in common values, the mother does not inculcate one, a feminine value system in her daughters, the father another, a masculine system in his sons—unless of course the family is badly integrated (but even then the conflicting values need not be "sex-typed.")

As "citizens" in the broad, not the narrowly political sense, i.e. as members of the overall society, men and women share the common value system of that society. But they typically have *differential* participations in the subsystem structures of the society, and each of these participations carries with it a differentiated subsystem of the generalized value system. On this more differentiated level, wherever men and women cooperate in solidary collectives they *must*, however sharply differentiated their roles, share the values of the relevant collectivity,

---

15. Even where married women are gainfully employed, which is becoming increasingly common in our society, the *relative* difference still tends to hold. The fact that in status and income the husband's job tends to be higher than the wife's —almost universally true in the middle classes—means that it has greater adaptive importance for the family as a collectivity. Where this ceases to be true the repercussions on the family may be profound, as there is some tendency to find particularly on lower class levels. In particular cases there may of course be counteracting forces.

so far as it is integrated. But because their participations are different, these various sub-value systems have different orders of importance in the typical personality structures of men and of women. It is another case of our old principle that the difference between two types of cases is not, as it is so easy on common sense grounds to assume, a matter of presence or absence of certain components, but of different *combinations* or weights of the *same* components. Perhaps, then, we may put it that the sexes tend to have different "interests" and "sentiments" but in most respects *the same values*. The significant difference does not lie in what is held to be "good" or not good, independent of ego's personal situation, which is what is usually meant by a difference of value-orientation, if the term is not further qualified. The difference lies, rather, in the different levels of *personal commitment* to the implementation of different sub-categories of the overall shared value system. This is a function of *role* which, in this as in various other cases, is differentiated within the same system. It would, therefore, be in our sense misleading if we were to speak mainly of sex-value differentiation. We recognize that, since value-internalization is an essential aspect of role-assumption, the concrete internalized role value-pattern component of the personalities of the sexes is different *in organization*. But it is *only* that particular aspect of value-orientation which is a function of the roles, which is involved. It is not because the sexes have different values that they tend to assume different roles but, being socialized to assume different roles, they must organize their *common* value-heritage differently in order to implement it effectively in their respective roles.

We have taken the relation between values and sex role as an example because the essential problems are highly visible in this case. The same principles, however, apply in other cases though, because the spread is narrower, they may not be so easy to trace. Let us merely again recall the case of the relation between business and "professional" roles in the same organization, say a business firm. There is no doubt that both the business executive who is primarily responsible for the financial welfare of the firm, and the engineer, share common values. They both want to produce a "good product" according both to technological standards and to those of "customer satisfaction," and to "get it accepted" in the sense of a good sales record. Understandably, however, because of the allocation of responsibilities, the engineer is more interested in "efficient production" while the executive is more interested in selling, market relationships, and the financial balance sheet. One is integrated in the "technical production" value-system, the other in that of "business."[16] Clearly an analysis of the functional needs of a highly developed economy will make clear that *both* are essential functions, if the superordinate system-goal of increased and "properly distributed" facilities i.e. production in the economic sense is to be attained. Clearly the "interests" and hence the "sentiments" of the technician and the business man are different, and where there is strain this may well eventuate in important ideological differences and conflict (analogous to the "battle of the sexes"). But this is a problem, not in a simple sense of "different value-orientations" but of integration of sub-values within a superordinate value-system. It is the "reflection," in the value sphere, of the problems and difficulties of the integration of a complex social system.

Need-Dispositions and Role-Expectations

From the discussion of these last two sections a very important principle of the organization of systems of action, whether they be social systems or personalities, or their subsystems, seems to have become increasingly clear. It is by no means new, but we can now state it with greater clarity and generality than before.

This principle is, we think, a matter of new light on the integration of systems of action. Because action is process in time, oriented to situationally specific objects, it is tempting to look at it primarily in terms of a plurality of temporally ordered series, each leading up to a discrete goal-state.[17] But this is only one of two equally important aspects of the matter. The other is the way in which these discrete "means-end chains" come to be organized into systems by a series of "cross-

16. Cf. the old antithesis between "business" and "industry" which was so prominent in Thorstein Veblen's thinking. See his *Theory of Business Enterprise* (New York: C. Scribner's Sons, 1904).

17. This is, we may hold, the predominant tendency of "utilitarian" theory, most conspicuously spelled out in the economic field

ties" between them. Essentially these cross-ties consist in the internalization or institutionalization—according to the type of system involved—of *common* value-patterns which, as we have repeatedly insisted, is the same thing as a social object considered as an object rather than as a system of interacting units.[18] The essence of a system of action, then, is that it consists of motivational or need-disposition units each with its differentiated goals, interests and sentiments, but bound together with other units by serving the interests of the same value patterns, each of which mobilizes a plurality of different motivational types, or units. Seen in personality terms these value-systems are strategically the most important properties of internalized social objects.

A system of action can be stably organized only when these two "principles of organization" criss-cross each other. Only when motives have clear orientation to relevant goal states *through time* can the system function. There must, that is to say, be adequate investment of motivational energy in attainment of the complex network of system and subsystem goals. But, at the same time, "left to themselves" these motivational units tend to "fly off in all directions at once." They must be held together as a team, in the "service" of the system as a system. This is what we mean by integration of a system, and it now becomes clear that the primary function of *common* values is to achieve this integration. Without common values there is no *order*.

But equally important with the well-established principle of the necessity of common values as a basis of order, is the newer one that a *single pattern* of such values is not adequate, there must be a ramified *system* of such patterns, the structure of which matches the differentiations of structure of the relevant systems of action, both personality and social systems.

The fundamental significance of the concept of role is that it formulates the *points of intersection* of these ramified and criss-crossing sub-value systems. A role is only possible as a unit of an integrated system of social interaction in so far as, first, the incumbent internalizes the value system which is con-

---

18. This is, we believe, the same as the distinction Olds makes between "temporal systems" and "object systems." Cf. James Olds, *The Growth and Structure of Motives* (Glencoe, Ill.: The Free Press, 1955).

stitutive of the relevant collectivity or other subsystem and held in common by its members, but second and *in addition* he has internalized *at least one,* and possibly more, common value systems which are constitutive of other subsystems, which are *not* shared by those who play *different* roles in the same subsystem of which his role is a unit. In general this value-system will be shared with persons playing cognate roles in other subsystems.

The same principles of organization apply, with appropriate change in perspective, to the personality as a system. The principle on which the need-disposition units are differentiated from each other is that of temporally ordered, goal-directed, motivational systems. The very principle of their irrevocable differentiation from each other of which we have made much, however, makes clear that in the process of their establishment, the problem of their integration relative to the needs of the personality system as a system has not been solved. This only becomes possible when the necessary "cross-ties" between them have been established. This, essentially, is what roles on the mature level of personality development establish. We have emphasized throughout that action in a role is motivated by a *plurality* of need-disposition components. A role does not provide an opportunity for the "acting out" of *one* need-disposition, but a way in which a *subsystem* of need-disposition operates in an organized way. The internalization of the social value systems, differentiated by subsystem memberships, is the basic mechanism by which this organization is established.[19] In the personality system, then, motivational entities are not related to each other *only* through their "genetic" ancestry, in that they "tap" the same streams of motivational energy. They are also related in that they are organized in the same role-expectation units, but these two modes of relation criss-cross, so that the total structure is mutually reinforced. A motivational source cannot be strengthened or weakened in such a way as to affect only one role-participation but will affect all of those

19. It may be apropos to suggest the metaphor of a structure of steel-work. If the structure is to be stable and capable of withstanding heavy stress, it is not enough that there should be beams or girders covering the dimensions of the building—i.e., that it should be built high, broad and deep enough. It is necessary in addition, that these units should be, sometimes elaborately, cross-braced.

into which the same stream feeds, whereas on the other hand, participation in a role does not depend on only one motivational source, but can tap many, all of which feed into it. Through substitutability there is far greater flexibility than would be the case if the personality were only—as psychoanalytically oriented writers sometimes tend to suggest—a "linear" branching system of motivational strands which then operate independently of one another.

On this basis we come around again to the importance of the oedipal transition. Up to the successful resolution of this phase, differentiation of the object—hence role—system has been subordinated to establishment of the fundamental motivational differentiations. After this, the primarily significant process is the combination and recombination of these motivational resources with reference to a progressively more differentiated object system. This is attended by further motivational differentiation, but the recombination aspect begins to have predominance.

In a slightly different aspect, one may say that with greater maturity the superordinate collective object progressively shifts. The nuclear family as "we-object" is critical because it articulates directly with the more differentiated adult role-structure; the parents as *full adults* are crucial participants in the latter. The two earlier object-systems are too protected and remote to serve very usefully in orienting to the exigencies of adult situations.[20] Only when the motivational system has come to be organized relative to a more complex object system can such exigencies be met.

It also becomes clear here why organic need-motives or primary drives not only do not, but *cannot* serve as the primary basis for the organization of personality as a system. We can put it that, if this were the primary structure, there would be no adequate way of "matching" motivational components with object-categorizations and value systems in roles. The functional

20. In the case of the mother role, the fact of her having been fully socialized, and hence become a full participant in marriage, family and community systems is, as we have suggested, a fundamental prerequisite of her being an effective socializing agent. She must be an authentic participant in the preoedipal interaction systems, but she equally must not be "seduced" into upsetting the balance with her other roles. This can easily happen through the tendency to reactivate her own regressive motive systems.

exigencies of systems of social interaction *must* have primacy over the functional requirements of the organism as a physiological system, if this is to happen. These latter must be adequately "met," but they must not be controlling. This is why the *first* fundamental necessity of socialization is to establish *control* through social interaction over the significant organic need system.

Figure 2 illustrates graphically how these various elements are conceived to fit together. The point of departure for its construction is the dual classification of value-pattern types, first with respect to object categorizations, second with respect to attitudes.[21] The object-categorization (or performance type) value table is placed at the top of the figure (p. 172), the attitudinal (or sanction type) table at the bottom (p. 173). This separation in turn, it will be noted, is simply a breakdown of the general system paradigm to which we have referred so often (fig. 2 of the same series).

The four tables in the middle, then, are classified according to the four basic motivational types differentiated at the oedipal stage. These, as we have seen, correspond with the attitudinal types through their relation to sanctions. Each cell of the four sub-tables thus characterizes a need-disposition type, with the performance and sanction or disposition and need aspects distinguished. It is equivalent to looking at Figure 1 from the differentiated end with the four clusters arranged in a square instead of "strung out." The sub-tables are arranged in this way because our primary focus of interest in this chapter is on personality. If it were on the social system, the sub-tables would constitute types of social object, i.e. status-categories in the social structure.

The internalization of the overall societal value system discussed above would in one aspect be represented by the rank-order or stratification of the four basic need-disposition clusters. Thus in the American system we presume that the adequacy cluster is stronger than the others. The organization of these clusters in turn would be reflected in the differentiations of the "national character" by sex and class. Thus in the American feminine personality the two expressive clusters, nurturance and

---

21. *Working Papers*, Chap. V, Fig. 5, p. 203.

security, would be relatively stronger than in the masculine, but still the total personality type would be more instrumental than in a quite different, much more expressively oriented culture.

The cells in the sub-tables then constitute the motivational components which go into the more specialized role-expectation subsystems of the personality. As we noted above, the principle of their organization is the selection of at least one from each of the clusters, and their organization in terms of rank order and in certain other respects. Thus the "technical" type of occupational role would tend to mobilize mainly from the upper left-hand corner, with first rank given to A-1, Goal-striving, and approval for goal-success. The other cells of the A table would also be involved in subsidiary ways. But we presume that such a complex cannot operate without motivational components from the other sectors of the personality system, i.e. segmental pleasure in achievement, and response from others.[22] Some components of the security and the conformity clusters must also be involved.

All of these sub-units then must be organized relative to each other. Maintaining order in this sense rather than in that of relative strength in the system as a whole is the function of what above we have called the "cross-ties" provided by internalized *social* value-patterns. One might suggest the metaphor that the table of highly differentiated need-dispositions constitutes a kind of "keyboard." A given role-orientation is a "tune" played on that keyboard. Many different tunes will strike the same notes but in different combinations, and some will be altogether omitted from some tunes. Some will be louder than others. The "pattern" of the tune is not deducible from the structure of the keyboard, but it is not possible to play a tune for which the requisite notes are not provided on the keyboard. The composer's standards of a "good tune" are the analogue of the social value-patterns, while the keys and their arrangement are the analogue of the genealogical tree of the need-disposition system. It is small wonder that persons whose attention is fixed overwhelmingly on one basis of organization find it difficult to see its relation to the other.

---

22. In interpreting this it is most important to remember that *every* goal-oriented motive in its consummatory phase yields pleasure or direct gratification.

FIGURE 2

Values and Need-Dispositions in the Personality System

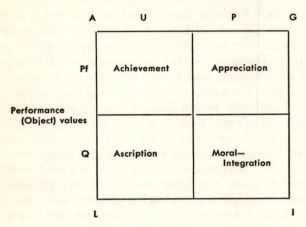

	A U	P G
Pf	Achievement	Appreciation
Q	Ascription	Moral— Integration

Performance
(Object) values

L   I

Adequacy ND
(Achievement—Approval)

A

1	2
P. Goal- striving S. Goal success	P. Team contribution S. Team success
4 P. Status striving S. Status recognition	**3** P. Team loyalty S. Recognition of loyalty

SUCCESS GOALS

Nurturance ND
(Gratification—Response)

G

1	2
P. Giving seg- mental pleasure S. Receiving segmental response	P. Pleasure to solidarity member S. Response from solidarity member
4 P. Pleasure in quality or state S. Response to quality or state	**3** P. Same but in partic- ularistic setting S.

HEDONISTIC GOALS

FIGURE 2 *(contd.)*

Values and Need-Dispositions in the Personality System

Conformity ND		Security ND	
1	2	1	2
P. Creative Accomplishment or pattern-maint. S. Esteem for acc. or p.m.	P. Active Exercise of Authority S. Respect for authority	P. Intrinsically satisfying (influential) performance S. Being liked for "nice" acts	P. Supportive activity S. Conditional acceptance
4	3	4	3
P. Embodiment of status qualities S. Status-deference	P. Particularistic prestige expression S. "Filial" piety	P. Int. satisfying qualities & their expression S. Liking for "nice" qualities	P. Ex. of supportive acceptance of status S. Unconditional acceptance
(Accomplishment—Esteem)		(Satisfaction—Acceptance)	

L
ACCOMPLISHMENT
GOALS

I
SATISFACTION
GOALS

	A	G
S	Approval	Response
D	Esteem	Acceptance
	L	I

Sanction (Attitudinal) values

Inputs, Outputs and the Generalization of Goals

The distinction of two cross-cutting aspects of the organization of the personality system, gives us a basis for interpreting somewhat further two central problems which have concerned us in our previous work. The first of these is the analysis of the inputs and outputs of a system of action.[23] The second is the problem of the nature of what we have called "situationally generalized goals."[24]

Input and output we defined as the comparative "state of the balance sheet" of a system of action as between an initial and a terminal state relative to a process over a time period. It concerns *differences* of the two states with respect to valued properties of the system. Thus if we take the personality of the child as the system of reference, we can attempt to draw up an inupt-output balance as between the beginning and the end of, for example, the oedipal phase.

What are the "assets" available to a personality system at a given time? These fall, we suggest, into the two basic categories of "motivation," which we conceive as a kind of energy, and of "information" in a very broad sense, which, looked at a little differently, consists in significant *relations* to object as facilities, which includes both their cognizability and their manipulability. Each of these in turn may then be subdivided according to whether its significance to the system-process is immediately current in the realistic or "situational" relation to objects, or is "internal" to the system, i.e. significant to internal equilibrium and control processes, because the relevant objects are "internalized."

Situational objects, in immediate relation to the action process, i.e. as perceived and manipulated, are reward-objects in the gratificatory or consummatory phase; in the instrumental-adaptive phase they are "facilities." As internalized, on the other hand, objects can serve as sources of tension-reduction through their relations to other internalized objects, i.e. motive systems, whereas they can also serve to stabilize the system by providing the patterns the system is committed to maintain.

---

23. *Working Papers*, Chap. V, Sec. vi.
24. *The Social System*, Chap. VI.

To sum up, then, motivation ("tension") and information or object-relations, situational and internalized, can be combined and utilized in four fundamental ways: (1) through establishing a goal-state relationship with a situational object as a situational reward; (2) through manipulating the situational object-world to bring one or more goal-states nearer, i.e. increasing "facilities"; (3) through internal system-processes using one motivational-object-unit to reduce the tension of one or more others, i.e. providing "narcissistic" rewards; and (4) to maintain or "improve" the patterns of the system in the sense of the intactness of order among the internalized objects. If the "fundamental" inputs are motivation and information, then these are the four fundamental types of combination of these inputs with objects, situational and internalized.

These four categories of input then correspond to four already familiar categories of output. So far as the output of a personality system consists in consummatory reward through relation to a situational object in a goal-state we call it *gratification*. So far as it consists in narcissistic, internal reward derived from internal reward-relations between motivational subsystems we call it *satisfaction*. So far as it consists in maintenance or improvement in situational object-relations in their instrumental significance as facilities, we call it *achievement*,[25] and finally, so far as it consists in maintenance or improvement of the *internalized* object system as value-patterns we call it *accomplishment*. These relationships are graphically represented in Figure 3.

The relations between these input-output categories and the picture of the structure of personality presented in Figure 2 are clear. The types of input-output concern the balances within each of the four basic motivational subsystems of the personality. The G subsystem (Figure 2) is the primary source of gratification but in order to produce it requires an adequate input of reward-objects from *outside* the personality system. The I subsystem is the primary source of satisfaction, but requires an adequate input of narcissistic rewards, i.e. the "cooperation" of the different need-disposition units of the per-

---

25. It will be noted that this is a special use of the term achievement, which should not be confused with others.

FIGURE 3

Input-Output Factors for the
Personality System

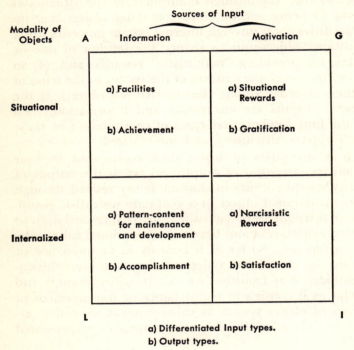

a) Differentiated Input types.
b) Output types.

sonality.[26] The A subsystem is the primary source of achievement but requires an adequate input of facilities from outside, and finally the L subsystem, as the source of accomplishment, requires an input of patterns of internalized objects, either from the system's own past (memory) or from the situation in the form of models for identification.

The functioning of a personality as a system is dependent both on the quantitative rates of flow of inputs in each of these categories, and on the maintenance of the balances between

26. The problem of the relation between the balance of narcissistic rewards and ego's relations to external objects will be taken up in Chapter IV, pp. 248 ff.

them with respect to each of the fundamental system-problems and subsystem problems. The cross-ties of which we have spoken, as internalized objects, are the forms of the primary stabilizing mechanisms with respect to these balances.

This brings us to the second question, that of the meaning for personalities of the concept of "situationally generalized goal."[27] Concrete goals of the personality system are *not* the goals of the need-disposition units we have discussed so often, but are role-expectation goals, or derivatives of them. They therefore each mobilize a *plurality* of such need-disposition units and organize them in a system. *This system as a system* has gratificatory interests and needs, needs for satisfaction, for achievement and for accomplishment.

From the point of view of personality, each of the need-disposition units is both a subsystem of the larger personality system and of the role-expectation system as a cross-cutting subsystem of the personality system. As a unit-subsystem it of course has its own goals and gratification needs and all the other types of needs. A situationally generalized goal, then, is the goal of a role-orientation subsystem of the personality. This will be specified by the pattern of *organization* of the motivational units which make it up. There will tend in each case to be a paramount *type* of need-disposition unit which has the "leadership role" in the system, which "sets the tone." This will determine the class of goals to which the subsystem goal belongs.

If this view is correct, there are many levels of situational generalization of goals. The point of reference for determining them is the place of the role in question *in the social system,* not the place of the qualitative types of motive in the personality. But they are the goals of personalities, and formulated in such terms. On the most general level, there are four generic types of situationally generalized goal, differentiated according to the four basic types of social system function. These, obviously, are A—"success" or achievement goals, G—"hedonistic" or gratification goals, I—personality integrative or "satisfaction" goals, and finally L—pattern-maintenance or as the case may be "creative," i.e. accomplishment goals. These, however, can be

27. Cf. *The Social System,* Chapter VI, pp. 236 ff.

subdivided according to the same general principles we have repeatedly employed (cf. Figure 2).

To illustrate, we suggest first that gratification and satisfaction are relatively more important to the feminine personality whereas success and accomplishment are more important to the masculine. On a more differentiated level, our old friend the "profit motive" is a situationally generalized goal which is a sub-type of the success goal. Within this (cf. Fig. 2) it is a sub-type of A-1, essentially in that it takes a situationally given type of sanction, namely money earnings, as the significant symbolic reward object. The focus of gratification, then, is the degree of attainment of a consummatory relation to a particular class of reward-objects.

We can thus see that the concept of situationally generalized goal is one of the essential links between the two basic modes of organization of the personality as a system. It is such links which make possible the ordered articulation of the personality with the social object system on the mature levels when the object system is no longer "artificially simplified" to conform with the organizational patterns of the genealogical tree of need-dispositions. If the personality could not cathect situationally generalized goal-objects it would be at the mercy of the shifting currents of stimulus-influence from the environment.

It should also be quite clear once more that *neither* the need-disposition organization of personality *nor* the role- or situationally generalized goal aspect is derivable from the organic need system as a structure. To account adequately for social motivation, we must depart from the organic reference point, not by only one fundamental step, but by *two*. Here again we see the importance of the shift from the "attitudinal" emphasis of the oedipal personality, to the "object-oriented" emphasis of the more mature personality.

Modes of Disorganization of Personality Systems

The main theme of our discussion for a considerable period now has been the *organization* of the personality as a system. Perhaps we can pull the main threads together and relate them to another very fundamental problem area, that of "deviance" as seen in relation to the social system, and "disorganization" or malintegration as seen in relation to the personality as a system.[28]

It seems to us that there are four major conditions of the integration of a highly differentiated personality as a system. One of these, the basic stability and internal consistency of the internalized pattern system, may be considered as a point of reference which is not basically problematical for *our* particular purposes. The other three can, in our terms, by slightly restating our previous classification, be formulated as follows: The first is the "level of differentiation" of the need-disposition system in its relation to the structure of the situation, as we have analyzed it for the personality in terms of the genealogy of the need-dispositions. This is, thus, essentially an aspect of the way in which the personality responds to the situational object system, matching its significant structure with an appropriate organization of responses. There is, at any given stage of development and within any given situational object system, an "optimum" of such differentiation, which of course in the personality structure aspect is differentiation of the *internalized* object system.

The second concerns the problem of the "relative strength," as we have put it, of the different need-disposition components. This is their "power" relationship or perhaps better, their relative positions in a system of *internal stratification* of the personality as a system. Again, given the developmental history and other conditions, there will tend to be an optimum organization in this respect. Finally, third, there is the problem of the stability of the "cross-ties" to which we have referred, the value-pattern components which organize genetically dissimilar motivational elements in role-orientation systems. Again there is, with respect to the system as a whole and to any given subsystem, an optimum structure of such cross-ties or values.

We suggest that these four aspects of organization can be formulated as problems of how the four "system problems" from the perspective of the personality as the system of reference are to be solved. Furthermore, we suggest that the optimum in each case is the relevant application of one of the four

---

28. This theme will be discussed again in Chapter IV, pp. 243 ff.

"principles" of action process we stated in *Working Papers,*[29] and that the deviance pardigm states, for the *social* system case, the directions of departure from each of the four, except for the one which is taken as a point of reference, in a "too much" and a "too little" direction respectively.

We will attempt now to justify these statements, and to extend them by showing the relation between the social system and the personality references of these categories. The system problem which is taken as the point of reference is latent pattern-maintenance. The relevant principle is *inertia.* A change in the inertial base is by definition a change in the "structure of the system." In social system terms there is deviance only *relative* to such a structure and similarly in personality terms disorganization is so relative.[30]

Given this inertia of the structure of the system, the problem of the appropriate level of differentiation of the system then is, in the present context, the relevant aspect of the adaptive system-problem. The system must have a structure which is sufficiently differentiated to "cope" with the complexities of the significant situational object-system. It has been a major theme of our analysis of the process of socialization that where the internalized object-system is insufficiently differentiated, a process of further differentiation takes place—if the proper conditions for it are given. Where there are adaptive strains, however, it is possible to deviate from the relevant optimum either by extending the differentiation of orientation to situational objects or by suppressing the operation of differentiations already established. In the paradigm for analysis of deviance in the social system, this is the range of deviance which we designated as that by overemphasis on norms, or on social objects respectively. *Relative* that is, to motivational orientation to the situation, the actor may attempt to fulfill the value-expectations as he interprets them, even though he has not properly differentiated and cathected the relevant objects (which are very often collectivities). On the other hand he may attempt to concentrate his motivation on an oversimplified

29. Cf. Chapter III, pp. 102-3.

30. It should be clear that our reference here is to the inertia of the units of the system in their respective orbits, not of the system as a whole relative to other systems.

"definition of the situation." This is, we may say, the problem of the "moral complexity" of adaption of situations.[31]

In personality terms the cognate directions of malintegration may be called "precocity" and "regression" respectively. In the first case the individual attempts to meet the strain by a more "sophisticated" orientation of the situation than he is "emotionally" prepared for. The case of internalizing the universalism-particularism discrimination in relation to social objects *before* successful resolution of the oedipal problem, cited in the last chapter, is an example. The effect is a "skewing" of the symmetry of the genealogical tree of need-dispositions. The opposite case, regression, is more familiar. It consists essentially in resorting to *less* differentiated treatment of objects than the situation calls for. This seems to be on one level what happens in the development of the transference in a therapeutic relationship. The patient to a considerable degree loses the capacity to discriminate his therapist as a professional role-person from the "figures" of his early socialization experiences. In this case, however, regression is used constructively to help reorganize the personality. More generally, then, "precocity" consists in giving the situation too much weight in personality process without the internalized personality organization being able to cope with it; on the other hand regression blurs and distorts the situational object system in the interest of maintaining internal equilibrium.

Of our four principles of system-process it is that of action and reaction which is directly relevant here. These types of disorganization are disturbances of the balance between situational stimulus and motivational response; in the one case the stimulus is allowed too great weight relative to the mechanisms of response, in the other the motivational need to "act out" prevails over the appropriateness of the response to the situation.

The next organizational problem, that of relative strength of the units or internal stratification, concerns the system-goal attainment or gratification problem. The essential question is which of the motivational units which make up the personality

---

31. This is in one perspective, to say that the main *adaptive* problem for an action system is set by the structure of the norms (expectations) of the system immediately superordinate to it.

is to have what degree of influence or weight in determining the goals which the system as a system will strive for. There must be order in this respect as well as in the interplay with situational objects. This is the problem formulated in our social system deviance paradigm as involving the two types of departure from an optimum balance which we have called "activity" and "passivity." Deviance in the active direction consists in the actor in a role-interaction system attempting to secure too much influence on the process relative to the definition of his role, while passivity means the opposite, having too little influence, tending to withdraw from initiative and responsibility when it is called for.

There are cognate modes of departure from the optimum balance in the personality system. Unfortunately there do not seem to be terms current in the psychological literature which designate over- or under-assertiveness of motivational units *within* the personality, regardless of what qualitative type they belong to. Perhaps for the counterpart of activity we can use the term "compulsive need" while for the counterpart of passivity, "overinhibition" comes fairly close. It is clear, then, that these concepts designate disturbance of the internal balance of the personality by one, or a subsystem of need-disposition units—in terms of the genealogical tree—tending to claim either too much or too little power or attention in determining the processes in the personality *relative* to a standard of integrated organization.

Of our four principles of system process this problem range concerns what we called the "principle of effort." In the compulsive need a case a greater amount of motivational energy than is "normal" is invested in this particular need-disposition (or subsystem) and this affects the balance of activity in the system as a whole in proportion to the increment of energy. The case of overinhibition is the obverse where some of the normal quota of motivation is withdrawn from a motivational unit.

Finally, the fourth problem of organization of the system, that of the stability of the "cross-ties," concerns what in the narrower and more technical sense is the problem of system-integration. In social system terms it is the problem of maintaining "solidarity." Departure from it can be either in the direction of over-conformity with the values which define the cross-ties, i.e.

overcathexis of commitment to the obligations of membership, or of underconformity or "alienation." In social system terms, we have seen, this is always an attitude both to a collectivity as an object and to patterns of value. With respect to the personality as a system, this concerns the problem of the *relation* between the pattern-structure of the internalized object-systems and the internal cathexes of the motivational units. The disturbance of the optimum balance in the direction of over-integration at the expense of the independent cathectic interests of the units, we may call "compulsive control" or "rigidity," (of the system, not inertia of the unit). The opposite direction is "compulsive acting out" which seems essentially the same as "psychopathy." Another way of putting it is that compulsive control involves not an overpowerful, but an inflexible superego.

The principle of system process involved here is of course that of system-integration. We have stated this as follows: "a *pattern* element within a system of action will tend to be confirmed in its place within the system or to be eliminated as a function of its contribution to the integrative balance of the system."[32] The two types of malintegration we have distinguished tend to interfere with this selective process. Compulsive control tends to the *retention* within the system of pattern elements which in a better integrated system would be dysfunctional. This is because the disintegrative pressures are so great that they cannot be dispensed with—e.g. "compulsive rituals." Compulsive acting out on the other hand tends to the *extrusion* of control-patterns which are functionally needed, but cannot be tolerated because of the alienative motivation toward them.

The relation of these problems to the other of the developmental process as we analyzed it in the last chapter may be pointed out. As we have discussed them just now they follow the scale of "regression" downward. Thus the problem of exposure to a complex situation for orientation in which the personality is inadequately differentiated becomes most acute on emergence from the family of orientation into a situation which is no longer "artificially simplified," as we put it. Again

---

32. *Working Papers,* p. 103.

this concerns proper discrimination between occasions for overt affectivity and for affective neutrality in relation to situational objects. Furthermore regression is most likely to occur from this point because there is "farther to go." The problem of activity-passivity, or internal stratification, then is especially related to the next earlier stage, the balance between dependency and autonomy. This is, according to our analysis, the first point as which the problem of relative strengths of motivational units could have arisen, and presumably lack of integration in this respect can be propagated onward from there. Finally, the conformity-alienation problem, or that of integration, we found arose at the very earliest stage, and tendencies established at that stage continue to affect the processes of the personality.

Of course this developmental order does not mean that only at each of the respective developmental stages can the corresponding type of disorganization arise. We can say only that the danger is presumably particularly acute at that time, and that a "susceptibility" in one of the areas may be "inherited" which may underlie incapacity to withstand particular types of strain later.

These relationships are graphically represented in Figure 4.

Two important basic relationships of this analysis to our previous discussion need to be pointed out. We have taken as our model for working out this classification of the possible modes of disorganization of the personality system, the paradigm previously used for the analysis of deviance in the social system. This has not only been possible and fruitful because, both being systems of action, they have fundamentally the same order of functional problems. There is a more intimate connection. This lies in the fact that it is the person acting in a role which is the basic unit of systems of social interaction. Then what elsewhere and in the following chapter we call the "mechanisms of adjustment" of the personality are in fact *the obverse* of the mechanisms of social control in the social system. The types of deviance in social interaction are the consequences of the types of solution of personality problems and strains which operate through changing relations of the personality system to the external situation. The problem of maintaining the internal stable state of the personality as a system then is cognate with that of adjustment to the situation. What we have just reviewed are the points of reference for an analysis of the mechanisms which operate in both these spheres. It is notable that the problem of adjustment concerns role-expectations as

FIGURE 4

Modes of Disorganization of Personality
and Correspondence with Social Deviance Types

A   G

a) Action and Reaction	a) Effort
b) Level of Differentiation	b) Relative strength, or internal stratification
c) +Emphasis on Norms —Emphases on Social Objects (old object)	c) +Activity —Passivity
d) +Precocity —Regression	d) +Compulsive Need —Overinhibition
a) Inertia Points of reference: b) Institutionalized Norms c) Structure of Personality as a system.	a) System-integration b) Stability of "cross-ties" or internalized social values c) +compulsive conformity —alienation d) +compulsive control (rigidity) —compulsive "acting out" (psychopathy)

L   I

a) System-process principle.
b) Personality organization "problem."
c) Social Deviance type + = "too much"; — = "too little").
d) Personality Disorganization types.

subsystems of the personality and their relation to situationally generalized goals. The problem of internal stabilization on the other hand treats the need-disposition systems and subsystems as the primary units. Thus we come back from another angle to our distinction of the two cross-cutting aspects of the organization of the personality as a system.

The second set of general considerations concerns the relations of these problems to the analysis of inputs and outputs which we sketched above. Either for the total personality as a system or for any unit as a subsystem, the maintenance of a stable state depends on the balancing of inputs and outputs over time. The four principles of system-process tell us the basic nature of these connections. Inertia thus tells us that given a rate of motivational flow it must work itself out in some balance of gratification and satisfaction over time. Overactivity of the system or of any unit through compulsive need is possible only by "borrowing" energy and creating a deficit somewhere, unless there is a change in the inertial level itself; correspondingly underactivity or overinhibition is building up motivational force somewhere which tends to "break through." "Precocity" involves an excessive input of "information," i.e. of facilities, which the personality does not "know what to do with," whereas regression involves the mechanism of shutting out information to the point where stable adaptation is not possible. Compulsive control involves an excessive input or retention of value-pattern components so that functional needs other than "conformity" are not adequately met, whereas compulsive acting out involves under-internalization of pattern elements. We merely mention these problems here, but will take them up in considerably more detail in the following chapter dealing with the mechanisms of the personality.

CHAPTER **IV**

The Mechanisms of Personality
Functioning with Special Reference
to Socialization

BY TALCOTT PARSONS
AND JAMES OLDS

The two preceding chapters have dealt more with structural patterns, in the process of socialization itself and in the personality as a system, than with process. The aim of the present chapter is to take up more systematically than has yet been done, the analysis of the processes of learning themselves and the bearing of this analysis on the classification of the types of process which go on in the personality system at any stage of its development.

The primary key to this analysis we think should be looked for in the concept of mechanism, which has been discussed extensively in previous publications.[1] It has been defined as a

---

1. Cf. T. Parsons, *The Social System*, Chapter VI (Glencoe, Ill.: Free Press, 1951). Hereinafter referred to as *The Social System*. Also T. Parsons and E. A. Shils, Eds., *Towards a General Theory of Action*, Part II, Chapter II (Cambridge: Harvard University Press, 1952). Hereinafter referred to as *Towards a General Theory of Action*.

[*187*]

generalization about motivational process formulated with reference to the significance, for the system in which it occurs, of different alternative outcomes of that process. Hence, as we see it, an attempt to consider the mechanisms of personality functioning, both in the process of socialization and more generally, should logically follow, not precede, the "morphological" analysis of the relevant systems. This is why we have postponed their treatment until after the presentation of the last two chapters. Or, putting it in a slightly different way, only after we have successfully established certain types of "norm" does it make sense to inquire into the nature of the processes by which these norms are "fulfilled" or fail to be fulfilled.

Any treatment of mechanisms in the sense we have in mind, should of course take the fullest advantage of the established knowledge of the laws of motivational process which we possess, as for instance in the field of learning. But there are two primary reasons why a treatment of process on the levels with which we are most concerned cannot simply be made an "application" of available knowledge of psychological laws. The first is that we are dealing with a shifting set of references of systems, both on the level of personality and of systems of social interaction; we are concerned with personality as a developing system the structure of which does not remain constant relative to its own initial base and to the relevant social systems. We must, therefore, establish the necessary structural points of reference in order to make our treatment of laws relevant to our particular problems.

The second reason is that the available knowledge of laws is too fragmentary to meet our needs. Some of the gaps may, however, be filled by relatively well established empirical generalization if only we have the points of reference from which to make their relevance clear.

We should like to suggest that the psychology of learning, so far as it deals with mechanisms in the sense in which we have just defined the concept, may for our special purposes be divided into the following three areas of concern: 1) The mechanisms of "simple learning" as it is sometimes called, which concern the learning of specific cognitive items, or specific instrumental procedures or cathectic associations without reference to any total system of boundary-maintaining organized action on the cultural level; 2) The mechanisms involved in the original transition from the state of "pure organism" of the human neonate, to the first establishment of a stabilized interaction orientation, as we interpreted it in Chapter III, of the mother-child identity or oral dependency; and 3) The mechanisms which are involved in every process of differentiation of an already established internalized object-motive system by binary fission to form a new and more complex differentiated-integrated system.

Our main attention in this chapter will be focussed on the third of these problem areas of the analysis of the mechanisms of learning behavior, since this is closest to the level of the treatment of personality as a system which has concerned the two preceding chapters in this volume. We will naturally have to take a good deal of knowledge of the other two levels of the study of mechanisms for granted, and will, early in the chapter, give a brief summary of what to us are the most critical assumptions we need to make in these fields. In presenting these we will of course try to keep as closely in accord with established psychological findings in these matters as our knowledge and the difficulties of interpretation and adaption to our particular purposes allow.

The main organization of the chapter will be as follows: We will start by outlining the presuppositions both with regard to the social structure of the socializing system and with regard to psychological processes, which we feel are necessary for an analysis of the kind of process of socialization discussed in Chapter II. Then we will attempt to outline in rather meticulous detail the stages of process involved in a single cycle of differentiation and integration within the personality system, trying to relate systematically to each other processes in the relevant systems of social interaction and the relevant personalities. Having done this we will take up the problem of classification of the mechanisms which the analysis of a socialization cycle has revealed to be in operation. We will then attempt to relate the results of this classification to our previous analysis of input-output relations in systems of action, and to apply these results to a variety of problems such as the relations between mechanisms and structural parameters in learning and performance and in normality and pathology. We will finally use the paradigm to work out a very tentative classification of pathological syndromes.

Sociological and Psychological Presuppositions

The first of the important assumptions on which this analysis is based, which in turn is a generalization from the analysis of Chapter II, is the proposition that, in certain fundamental respects, the process of socialization must be considered to be *discontinuous*. It is not, if we are right, a continuous linear process of successive approximation to an end state of "maturity," but would be represented by some kind of a "spiral," in such a way that at times the development would, if interpreted by extrapolation alone, appear to be going way from maturity. It is the establishment of reference points for the main elements of discontinuity which we consider to be one of the main contributions of the previous analysis, above all in bringing together Freud's conceptions of the stages of psychosexual development, and a sociological analysis of the successive series of social relationship systems into which the child is socialized. This discontinuity of course occurs within a larger framework of process which might be called "growth" and marks "stages" in it.

Once the first internalized object-system[2] has become estab-

---

2. We use, from time to time, a number of terms referring to the internal structural elements of behavior and personality systems. To avoid confusion we will try to explain here what we mean by the principal ones. *Motive* or *motivation* we use more or less indiscriminately, to mean either the general concept of motivational energy without specific reference to structures, or any such structure which has come to be invested with motivational energy. (Cf. *Toward a General Theory*, Part II, Chap. II). *Need-disposition* we use to refer to a structural element where motivational energy is *organized with* cognitive object-categorization of some sort and to some degree. A need-disposition is thus never motivational energy as such alone. We tend, however, to use this term when the emphasis is on the motivational aspect and its relations to the "genealogy of need-dispositions" in the development of the motivational system of personality. *Internalized object* or *object-system* refers to the same kind of entity, but seen from the other perspective of the cognitive structuring which relates it in an organized way to the situational world. It will be remembered that in the last chapter it was held that many need-disposition components come to be organized in the same internalized object-system. Finally by *concept* in this usage we mean such an internalized structure with special reference to its function in ordering cognitive orientation to the situation. It relates especially to what later we will call the reality-testing mechanisms.

lished, we conceive the process of personality development in any one of these discontinuous phases to be organized around a process of differentiation and integration relative to the system of social objects in which it is integrated and with which it interacts. First, then, let us recall the generic features of the social structure of this interaction system which are relevant to any stage of the process of differentiation, since this provides the indispensable situational points of reference for the analysis of the mechanisms in the individual personality.

The first essential key lies in the fact that the relevant *social* structures constitute a "nesting series." If we take any two contiguous "levels" in this series, the "higher" one will be more complex than the lower; it will be a social system of double the number of role-units of the lower one. An obvious example is the four-role nuclear family as distinguished from the two-role mother-child "love attachment" system.

Secondly, the key socializing agent or agency, which may be a single personality-in-role or a collectivity, is at the beginning of one of these phase cycles of socialization a full participant in *both* the relevant interaction systems. This fact concerns the "duality" of the role of an agent of social control to which attention has been called on several occasions. The participation of the socializer in the system in which the socializee has not yet begun to participate is an essential basis of the "leverage" which can be exerted upon the latter.

A third primary feature of the relevant interaction system is that the roles of socializer and socializee should be differentiated from each other in a double respect. First, there is a hierarchical dimension of the differentiation; the socializer is the more powerful of the two, has a greater degree of control of the system of interaction which involves both as a system. Second, there is differentiation on the instrumental-expressive axis; the role of the socializing agent is the *more* instrumental of the two. We will make use of all of these structural features of the socialization situation as we go along.

For the moment let us rest content with pointing out the relation of these considerations to the structure of objects which have to be internalized. At the outset of a phase of the process we assume that the socializing agent, in his role in the *lower* of the two levels of system, has been internalized as an object, or more precisely, the actor-object relationship *pattern* has been internalized so that there is both the cathected and the internalized object aspect of the relation to alter. This lower-level system is, however, to be regarded as a subsystem of the higher-level system with which it is articulated. Then alter as object in his role in the lower-level system is a "special case" of the category of his more general role in the higher-level system; "mother," in relation to the child in the mother-child subsystem is thus a special case of the more general category "parent" in the nuclear family.

One aspect of the importance of the dual role of the socializing agent then lies in the fact that this provides the structure of the "vehicle of generalization" for the formation and internalization of new objects. Cathexis and, hence, internalization of the new object occurs by way of extending the cathexis of the old object from the lower-level role alone to the inclusion with it of the higher-level role. Then the new object becomes "meaningful" as another instance of the same category of object as the old one, redefined as an instance of the higher-level category.

What we are presenting here is simply a restatement of the discussion in Chapter II of the relationships between "I," "you," "we" and "they." The residual category of "they" is residual so far as ego, the socializee, is concerned. But it is not purely residual seen in terms of the structure of the situation of ego from the point of view of an observer. This is because alter, the socializing agent as a person not only functions as "you," as the complementary role in the lower-level interaction system, but also as a participant in the "they" system in his role in the superordinate structure. In other words, of all the indefinitely numerous possible subcategories included in "they," the social structure presents *one* specific one, that of the parental collectivity in the illustration we have cited, as the one which is to be treated as *significant* at the stage in question. The psychological importance of this lies in the question of what determines the specific paths along which psychological mechanisms of generalization will operate, both in the cognitive and the cathectic or expressive meaning of generalization.

The Psychology of Learning

As a next set of preliminaries before entering on our main analysis, we need to recall to the reader's mind a few essentials of the psychology of learning on the more elementary levels. We assume that in the early stages of socialization before the processes of differentiation in which we are primarily interested begin, two fundamental steps in the learning process must already have taken place. Both of these involve the well-known mechanisms of discrimination and generalization, but not differentiation and integration in the specific senses with which we will be concerned.

The first of these steps is that involved in the transition from the case in which environmental stimuli operate simply as "trigger releases" which activate constitutionally built-in mechanisms, to the development of responses specific to the "motive-situation pair."[3] This implies the learning of a discrimination among stimuli, not on the basis only of their "intrinsic" appropriateness to trigger the response, but of *experience* of relative success or failure in attaining the goal. This is essentially to say that the *structure* of the stimulus situation has, in an elementary way, begun to be significant in the organization of behavior. This is what is ordinarily understood by "conditioning." The presumption is that these processes of conditioning are continually going on within the higher orders of organization with which we are concerned.

Certain basic conditions which enter into the mechanisms of discrimination become visible even on this elementary level. The discrimination must follow from adequate differentiation of the "cases" in both cognitive and cathectic or motivational respects. For the cognitive aspect the essential condition is the presentation of sufficiently clear and stable cues to stabilize the discrimination.[4] In the motivational aspect, on the other hand,

3. The trigger-release case is thus to be regarded as a limiting case from the point of view of the theory of action.

4. The same pressures-to-discriminate are known to have abnormal consequences if no adequate cue for the discrimination is available. The classic experiments on difficult discriminations were done by Pavlov; a careful modern version of these is reported by N. R. F. Maier in *Frustration* (New York: McGraw Hill, 1949). Rats are put in a position where reward and punishment are reciprocally related to two different response systems, but no adequate cue for discrimination is available. The position of the rat is this: (a) he cannot remain on a jumping

there must be, with respect to the original basis of "interest," *relative* deprivation of sufficient intensity between the two cases. The simple point is that if both types of stimulus situation were equally gratifying to the motive in question there could be no *motive* to act differently in the two stimulus situations with any consistency. This seems to us to be a simple application of the principle of inertia which we have invoked so often. Implicit in these two conditions, but extremely important, is the condition that there must be an element of significant and consistent *incompatibility* between the two stimulus situations which are to be discriminated. Cognitively there must be a sufficient difference of properties so that they are not confused. Motivationally there must be conflict, in the sense at least that one of them produces a level of gratification which the other does not. If, that is, in a sufficient proportion of cases, of course, ego tries to secure the wished-for gratification by the wrong route he will fail.

For the order of differentiation which is most important to socialization to take place, we believe that this must be a sharper and more pronounced difference of cues than is ordinarily necessary in most cases of the elementary learning of instrumental techniques. This is because we assume that ego will have a powerful emotional investment in the old object system and its inertia will be so strong that very striking differences will be required to "shake him out of it."

We believe that when learned discriminations have become established in such a way that a stimulus which originally produced gratification has been learned no longer to do so and, vice versa, one which originally did not do so, has been learned to be a gratifying stimulus, it is correct to speak, in an elementary sense, of the internalization of a situational object-system. The crucial criterion, as we noted above, is that the

stand because an airblast drives him off; therefore, he must jump to one of two platforms, A or B; (b) if A is the reward-platform in a particular trial, A-approach will be rewarded, B-approach will be quite violently punished; (c) if B is the reward-platform, the opposite circumstance occurs. However, the animal is provided with no basis for making the discrimination: at this point an abnormal fixation ensues almost invariably. That is, the animal fixates either A-approach, or B-approach, and this fixation cannot be broken, even when the situation is later changed so that the fixated side is always negative, and the other side always positive.

actor-object *relationship* has become an independent system, the situation is no longer *only* a set of "trigger releasers" for for a preestablished set of mechanisms in the organism.[5]

A second major step must, we believe, precede the type of differentiation which we have in mind. This is the internalization of a *social* object which we have postulated first occurs with the establishment of the mother-child identity. The psychological principles involved do not seem to be different from those operating on the more elementary levels. The difference is rather, as we see it, a matter of the *organization* of the system in which they operate. Two fundamental features of this case are of particular importance. The first of these is what we have in Chapter II called the "artificial stabilization" of the child's situation of action over an area substantially wider than would be possible without organized human agency. The second is the sensitization of the child to the *attitudes* or intentions of the mother (or other socializing agent), and the corresponding development of a capacity for organizing generalized attitudes of his own. This seems to be an essential component of what we mean by "dependency." Later we will try to establish a critical relation between this and the differentiation of the role of the socializee in a power-inferior and expressive direction to which we have just called attention.

In general discussions of social interaction we have made much of what we have called the "double contingency" of the interactive situation. This is potentially a source of extreme instability. But it is one of its most important features that it may, under certain conditions, lead to a far wider *range* of stabilization than would be possible without it. In the present case the essential point is that the mother uses the extreme physical helplessness of the child and his expressive investment in the relationship as a lever of control to impose an *ordered* set of stimulus-situations on him. These are of course conditioned by, and adapted to, the physiological needs and rhythms of the child-organism, but only conditioned by them,

---

5. James Olds in *The Growth and Structure of Motives* (Glencoe, Ill.: The Free 1955), (Chap. I) has shown that even on the elementary S-R level, behavior can advantageously be analyzed as the operation of systems of action in the full technical sense. This, we feel, includes the internalization of situational objects. The same publication (Chap. II) treats the elementary mechanisms of integration, so we need not go into them here.

not wholly determined or "governed." This, we assume, is an order which meets the basic conditions of learning we have just outlined. There are above all two major features of it. The *agency* of the mother becomes significant probably in the first instance because of relatively consistent cues for discrimination between the situation in her presence and in her absence and secondly, because of the relative deprivation this entails. In sufficiently critical respects gratification comes to be associated with her presence. Hence, by and large her presence is gratifying and her absence relatively frustrating. By some such process, in which we may assume that holding, fondling, etc., as well as feeding, play an important part, there is a process of generalization by which this agency of gratification comes to be "interpreted" as what we have called[6] a single "complex object" on the true social interaction level.

It has then become an "object system" in the full sense in which Olds as elsewhere[7] used that term. There is a plurality of units of that system; these are Olds's "temporal systems," such as the hunger-gratification system, the safety-protection system, the erotic system, etc. Further, and highly important, the system itself should be interpreted as being involved in a process of phase movement. The internalized "mother" is not always in a consummatory phase, but is sometimes latent—most obviously in sleep—sometimes in an instrumental phase, and sometimes in an integrative phase dealing with the inter-relations of the constituent organic need units.

The "relative deprivation" of which we speak must, we feel, have two properties which go beyond the more elementary case of one alternative simply producing more gratification than the other. The first of these is that instrumental behaviors which in the earlier situation were successful, on the new basis must be unsuccessful, so that there is a contradiction or conflict between the consequences of behaving in a certain way in the two situations, which goes beyond a quantitative difference of gratifying results. That is, the *same behavior* which in one situation produces gratification, in the other must not just

6. T. Parsons, R. F. Bales and E. A. Shils, *Working Papers in the Theory of Action* (Glencoe, Ill.: Free Press, 1953) Chap. II. Hereinafter referred to as *Working Papers.*

7. *The Growth and Structure of Motives, op. cit.*

produce less gratification, but positively *impede* goal-attainment and/or bring on punishment. Thus the infant must cry to get attention and food in the mother's absence, but in her presence, after a certain point in socialization, the same kind of crying will annoy her and cause her to withdraw rewards. The second point is that, in connection with the importance of the *attitudes* of alter, ego should come to be oriented to the *polarity* of attitude structures. He must have learned that not only can failure to fulfill alter's expectations lead to withdrawal of rewards, but it may lead to *punishment*. This may, as we shall see, become a very important focus of anxiety as motivation to learn. The polarity of reward and punishment has much to do with constructive use of the duality of phantasies of gratification and aggression in the reorganization of motivation.

We may sum up the main conditions of the process of learning on each of these levels in terms close to our general conceptual scheme as follows: There must be frustration of previously established expectations of gratification. This frustration must be "comparable" with a continuing source of gratification; there must, that is, be *"relative* deprivation." Second, these two aspects of the situation must be cognitively discriminable by adequate cues, so that the source of deprivation becomes associated with *different* perceptions and cognitions from that of gratification. The "experience" of relative deprivation must link up with the "cognition" of the discriminated objects.

Then we assume that, in addition to this process of discrimination or differentiation, there must be processes of generalization in two respects. First, cognitively, there must be generalization from the old significant object into the "residual" area so that some part of it comes to be defined, no longer as a purely residual "they," but as somehow cognitively linked with the significant object of the earlier system-level. We have already suggested that this takes the form of definition of a more generalized or abstract category of which the old object is an "instance" in such a way that there may be other instances which are similar to the old one and yet differentiated from it.

Second, on the cathectic or expressive side, there must also be generalization so that there is no longer the exclusive investment in the specific old object, but a capacity to include new objects—at least one—as well. But in expressive meaning these new objects must be "classed" with the old object.

In this way we arrive at a paradigm of the elementary mechanisms of the learning process so far as it is significant to our problem. In logical structure this paradigm is generated from two fundamental distinctions which we have continuously used. The first is that between cognition and cathexis; in relation to objects between cognitive and cathectic or expressive aspects of their *meaning*. It will be remembered that we have argued that an object always has *both* kinds of meaning if it has any meaning at all.[8] The distinction is an analytical one; there can be differences of primacy of the two aspects, but never cases exclusively of the one or the other as a distinct entity. The second distinction is that most commonly put forward in psychology as between discrimination and generalization. This distinction has usually been interpreted in a cognitive context, but we suggest here that it is equally applicable in both cognitive and expressive contexts: it is general to the category of meaning. The two distinctions then generate a four-fold table as shown in Figure 1.

FIGURE 1

Paradigm of Learning

Relations of Objects	Aspects of Meaning	
	Cognitive	Expressive
Discrimination (Differentiation)	Cognitive Discrimination	Relative Deprivation (Selective reward and gratification)
Generalization (Integration)	Cognitive Generalization	Generalization of Cathexis

8. *Working Papers*, Chap. II.

This paradigm, we suggest, constitutes a generalized statement of the major aspects of learning which we have just reviewed. In the upper left-hand cell we formulate the condition of significantly discriminable cues as between two situations. In the upper right there is the condition of motivationally significant differences in comparable respects. In the lower left is the extension of cognitive categorization to include both the old object and a new one which is also an instance of a common generalized category and, finally, in the lower right, the generalization of cathexis to include the new object as well as the old under a single "rubric" of expressive meaning.

It cannot but strike the reader that in this paradigm we have produced another version of the general action-system paradigm which has emerged so often in our work. In particular we may regard it as a special case, adapted for the analysis of learning, of the revised paradigm of input and output relations which was presented in Chapter III, Fig. 3. It is that special case which, on the one hand takes the personality system as the point of reference, and on the other, emphasizes learning rather than performance. This we assume to be the major framework for the classification of the personality mechanisms with respect to socialization.

The Problem of System-References

A further preliminary step is necessary. We must now attempt to relate together the different system-references which we must take into account, and their relation to the order of phases of the process in which we are interested. At a minimum we must keep in mind four distinct but interdependent and interpenetrating systems. For clarity's sake we shall consistently use the illustration of the transition from the mother-child love relationship system through the oedipal crisis to the state of integration in the nuclear family system. Then we have two systems of social interaction: 1) the mother-child system; 2) the four-role nuclear family; and we have further at least two personality systems, 3) that of the mother with the dual role of member of *both* interaction systems both initially and at the end, and 4) the personality of the child who at the beginning is a full-fledged member only of interaction system 1.

Several times in our previous work we have called attention to the phase processes of action systems and in particular to the fact that, in some sense, the order of phases in the ordinary "task-solution" processes of systems of action and in processes of socialization and social control was reversed.[9] The problem of relating the multiple system-references involved in our problem to each other brings us up against the problem of what exactly is meant by this double character of phase structure and how it bears on our problem. Only a few remarks will need to be made on this subject.

The ordinary task-solution process, as we understand it, presumes a stable state of the system which among other things assumes that the goal is given. The primary "problems" are the adaptive-instrumental problems of coping with situational exigencies to bring about the consummatory goal-state; secondarily there are problems of coping with the integrative consequences of these activities. From this point of view the kind of learning process undergone by the personality, which we have in mind in this analysis of socialization, does not differ in the basic phase-pattern, but constitutes a case of disturbance of the stable state so that full attainment of the given goal is prevented. The personality in question then does not function "autonomously" to attain a goal, but in special ways is "manipulated" in the system of social relationships in which it is involved.

From the point of view of the superordinate of the two social-interaction systems, the socialization process may also be regarded as that of a task-oriented system, with the successful achievement of this particular phase of the total socialization of this child as its goal. This entails treating the mother-child subsystem as in certain respects part of the situation in which the superordinate family system functions. The mother is thereby put in the position of treating one of her own roles as situational relative to the other—of the two we are considering. This system then, we assume, also goes through a normal task-oriented phase pattern as part of the process we have in mind.

What we have elsewhere interpreted as the reversal of the "normal" phase pattern must, therefore, now be understood

_____

9. *Working Papers,* Chap. I, Sec. vi, and Chap. IV.

as the pattern involved in the *relation* between this superordinate socializing system and the personality of the socializee,
through the role of the socializing agent who participates in
both systems. The problem can be somewhat simplified by calling to mind the fact that *concretely* we are dealing with only
three, not four action systems. This is because in what for us
are the significant respects, the personality of the child and
his roles in the socializing systems are identical. He has not
yet reached the stage where there is interpenetration with the
socialization system only for certain role-expectation subsystems
of his personality.

This then serves to localize the difference in the role of the
socializing agent who is the common member of the two interaction systems at the beginning. This difference is a question of
a *pattern of sanctions* as administered by the socializing agents,
which is specifically different from that involved in cooperation
in the attainment of a system-goal where all parties are "responsible" cooperators. Broadly we may summarize the differences
as follows: First in a task-oriented group a "leader" i.e., a
member in a superordinate power and instrumental responsibility position, does not deliberately and "unnecessarily" frus-
trate the attainment of the "personal" goals of another group
member. Second, in the face of resultant "inadequacy" of performance, he does not act permissively and supportively in the
sense of suspending normal negative sanctions and "going out
of his way" to "accept" the delinquent regardless of his short-
comings. Third, he does not deny reciprocity to "overtures"
which are appropriate to the given goal-orientation of the system and, finally, he does not make positive rewards conditional
on performances which would not have a place in the system
in question. We may state the same points in terms of norms.
First by acting as an agent of frustration, and then suspending
the normal negative sanctions for inadequate performance, the
socializing agent violates the latency-phase norms of the system.
Then in being what by the relevant standards is oversupportive,
he violates the integrative norms; then he violates the goal-
gratificatory norms by refusing positive sanction to relevant
contributions and finally the adaptive norms by sanctioning—
rewarding—performances appropriate to *another* system. But
these are "violations" only in terms of the norms of the *sub-*

ordinate interaction system. They are legitimized by the higher "mandate" to break up that system in the interest of integrating the child into the superordinate system. From the point of view of the values of the latter system they are not deviant, but on the contrary conformative actions.

A Cycle of the Socialization Process

We shall now attempt to sketch in a broad way the main events of an idealized single cycle of differentiation and integration which occurs in the course of the socialization process. We shall distinguish five phases instead of the usual four, the first and fifth being initial and terminal stable states respectively. We shall also attempt to give the main facts about the state of each of the systems we have to take into account. We shall, however, attempt to simplify this somewhat by dealing first: (a) with the superordinate socializing system, e.g., the nuclear family; second (b) with the roles of the dual-participating socializing agent e.g., the mother; third (c) with the role-personality of the socializee, the child. We will label the phases in order, $T_1 \ldots T_5$.

T_1 We start with a stable state. (a) For purposes of illustration let us assume throughout this discussion of a socialization cycle, a "normal" family with two parents and, besides ego, the socializee in question, one older sibling of opposite sex who has already passed the oedipal phase. We are thus concerned with illustrating this general model by the oedipal transition but our primary interest is in the *general* model of the phase cycle. The stable state means that the family accepts the mother-child subsystem as a subsystem asymmetrically related to it; mother is most directly responsible for ego and it is understood that he is a "little child" primarily attached to and dependent on her. By the rest of the family he is treated more nearly as a valued "possession" than as a "member." They "take care of" him to a considerable extent and are "pleased" with him.

(b) The mother stands in the dual role of (i) family member, as wife and mother of the older sibling, and of (ii) mother of ego. In the former role at this stage she is primarily concerned with maintaining the proper limits of the mother-child system, tolerance for its special immunities and the limits these place on her relations to other family members; but equally not permitting it to claim too much. In the later role she gives the proper balance of instrumental care and love to ego, fulfilling his expectations in these respects. She of course acts as a disciplining agent, but within the limits of the defined stable state of this system; she does not "expect too much."

(c) Ego is well-integrated, both in interaction with his mother in his role, and internally as a two-unit personality system. The more recent unit, the "autonomous self" is satisfactorily gratified in cathexis of the mother, loving her and being loved in return, whereas the internalized mother cathects the "mirror-image" of himself in the concrete mother and there is here a reciprocity of nurturant care. The inequality of the two roles is most pronounced in this area. There is further, as an aspect of the integration of the personality, a reciprocal cathexis by the units of each other expressed as "narcissistic" self nurturance and self-love. Ego's "dependency" consists both in his need for care, centering in the internalized mother object, and his need to give and receive love.

T_2 This is the phase in which this "Garden of Eden" stable state is disturbed, and the immediate consequences of the disturbance dealt with. Empirically the disturbance may come from a variety of sources. Most broadly, we may say that it comes from a combination of two factors; first the bio-social maturation of the child himself whereby he becomes capable of higher levels of performance and in respects relatively independent of the main structure of his personality, learns new skills etc.; second, the expectations of his family of how a child who is "getting so big" should behave.

This question of the empirical source of the disturbance should, however, be distinguished from that of its *meaning* with reference to each of the action systems with which we are concerned. For it is the meaning which events acquire for a specific action system which defines the inputs into that system for which they will be responsible, and this is the problem in which we are interested.

(a) For the family as a system, the essential process is the transition from a state of latency, with respect to this particular task-oriented sequence of its socialization function, to the adaptive-instrumental phase. It consists in taking changes in the child, both in his physical features, like size, and in his behavior, as "signs" that he ought to be treated differently because he is "growing up." Empirically there may also be pressure from him, but we will ignore this since we have assumed a stable state of the mother-child system. In terms of meaning this takes above all the form of changing the role of the mother, from her role in the family propagating into a change in her role in the mother-child system. Because she is the primary link between the two systems, she plays a *representative role* on behalf of the family in relation to her child. Whatever different members of the family do empirically in relation to the child, by him she is "held responsible" and vice versa, the family holds her responsible for her treatment of the child.

(b) In terms of meaning, then, the disturbing influence is propagated into the mother-child interaction system, the main channel being through the personality of the mother from her "familial" or parental role to her "mother-of-this-child" role. The main alteration of this role, in turn, we presume consists in the withholding of part of the "care" which has been the main focus of her more instrumental role in the system. For reasons we will take up presently it does not seem probable that there is a comparable withholding of the "love" component of her role. The effect of this withholding, plus perhaps an increase in the incidence of negative sanctions for unacceptable behavior, is a disturbance in the system, which is felt most severely in the role-personality of the child, because he is the less powerful member of the system, in that sense more dependent. We should not forget, however, that there is some disturbance of the personality of the mother, since there is an inertia in her role and personality also. We presume, however, that this will be less severe in her case, partly because she is "stronger" in her leadership role in the system, but partly also because of her anchorage in the family system and in still other systems superordinate to that, all of which serve to "legitimize" her action. Related to this is that she foresees the terminal state, accepting its achievement as her own personal goal.

So far as the values of the superordinate systems have been

internalized in her personality her own internal control mechanisms will thus tend to counteract the disturbing factors. In coping with the consequences of the disturbance this helps to make it possible to be permissive and then supportive. Permissiveness, we assume, consists primarily in the withholding of negative sanctions which would otherwise be imposed in reaction to the "inadequacies" which appear in the child's behavior as a consequence of the disturbance.

(c) The change finally reaches the child—in a "wave" which presumably begins gradually and gathers force, finally to recede —and constitutes "frustration" to him. Its primary aspect is the absence of certain gratifications which he had come to expect in the role-expectation sense, and hence to feel he "had a right" to. As frustration it is also *relative* deprivation, because relative to a standard of internalized expectations and values, from the source from which he expects a given gratifying treatment he fails to get it.

At this point the question of the psychological reactions to frustration become relevant. We approach this through the conception of inertia. Frustration we hold to be a psychological aspect of the disturbance of an inertial system, a system in a relatively stable state. The general tendency of inertia is to maintain and/or restore the original stable state. In so far as action is directed towards objects external to the system, we may divide this tendency into a positive and negative aspect. The positive aspect is to cling to the desired relation to the object which, especially, focusses on the consummatory goal-state of this relation. Where its attainment is objectively impossible we have the phenomenon of phantasy-gratification, or in common parlance "wishful thinking." The negative aspect is removal of what is "felt" to be the source of the disturbance, which we take to be the root-phenomenon of what is ordinarily called aggression. These may be further differentiated, by different objects or classes of them, and different phases of the relationship to them, but these concepts will suffice for the present.

At the same time it must not be forgotten that there is an internal aspect of the impact of frustration or disturbance. On the positive side there are, as we have seen in Chapter II, limited possibilities of turning from external object-gratification to narcissistic gratification. On the negative side, similarly, there can be interpretation of the source of disturbance as internal and hence aggression is directed against part or all of the self. Very broadly the distinction between the internal and the external aspects of the impact of frustration is the basis of the fundamental distinction between the mechanisms of adjustment and the mechanisms of defense which we will have to take up later.

But apart from these relatively specific possibilities of reaction, there is apparently very early a generalization of the state of disturbance in a personality system which we usually refer to as anxiety. Anxiety may be thought of as the impact on the expectation system of ego of the effects of the experience of frustration. It is a generalized predisposition to "expect the worst" in any uncertain or contingent situation, and hence to "take measures" to forestall it. High level and generalization of anxiety may be thought of as a general component of tendencies to a "deviant" solution of any situation of "strain," whatever the type, and to activate mechanisms which short-cut the "risky" parts of a "normal" process of action.

We thus expect our child under frustration to show active phantasies, outward-directed aggression, narcissistic tendencies, self-aggressive tendencies and anxiety.

We further expect the consequences of this disturbance to be reflected in inadequate or deviant behavior in ego's role in the mother-child system. He will not "do his share" presumably in both the instrumental and expressive aspects of his role, but particularly, perhaps, the element of aggression will interfere with what is his main function, giving love. This is the point at which the main function of the permissive element of the mother's role becomes evident. The withholding of negative sanctions, within limits, prevents tension levels from rising so high that the capacity to learn would be blocked. There must, however, also be a limit to permissiveness, and we presume it is essentially that which is well known in psychotherapy. There is a high degree of permissiveness for "symbolic" expression of deviant motives, including phantasy gratification of dependency wishes, but this does not extend to permission to "act out," the impulses to which must be controlled.

We must remember that the most important aspect of the mother as an object to ego is the social aspect; this means that her *behavior* in relation to ego has priority over anything else. Alteration of her behavior, therefore, means that the most important part of the situation for him has changed. Put in our technical terms, this means that there has entered into his role-personality as a system, an input of cognitive information. Ego perceives that there is an aspect of his mother's behavior, hence of her as an object to him, which is *different* from what he has been accustomed to. She has presented him with a set of cues for making a cognitive discrimination. But such a discrimination is only possible if *some* aspects of her as an object remain essentially unchanged; he must, that is, be aware both of the "new mother" and of the "old mother."

On grounds of general learning theory, we know that this discrimination will not be learned unless differential behavior in relation to the two different objects is rewarded differentially. If, as in the case of Maier's rats, the mother either indifferently rewards in the same way reaction to both aspects of her—to ego—dual personality, or indifferently fails to reward both, cognitive-instrumental learning will not take place, but fixation will occur.

But in order to give her an opportunity to introduce stable and systematic differentiation of treatment in relation to the two objects, ego must be motivated to positive action in relation to the new object, i.e., the new aspect of mother, and the presumption is that since the initial experience of it is one of frustration, his initial reactions are negative, aggression toward her and withdrawal into narcissistic gratifications. There would also be generation of anxiety about the future of the relationship. In other words, the frustration would provoke a crisis of the integration of the mother-child system. This is partially alleviated by the permissive attitude of the mother we have already discussed, but we can presume that this is not sufficient to resolve the crisis. How this can be done is the subject of the next major phase of the process, to which we now turn.

T_3 (a) There is a problem of the synchronization of the phases of the different system-processes we are attempting to analyze together. The evidence from the study of small task-oriented groups tends to show that the adaptive-instrumental phases are of considerably longer duration than the primarily integrative phase. We suggest, therefore, that what is the pri-

marily integrative-supportive phase in the subordinate socializing system of mother-child coincides in time with the latter
part of a prolonged instrumental phase of the superordinate
system where the primary function of this latter system is to
facilitate the former, literally by providing facilities for the
performance of its function. This, we think, occurs in two
principal ways. First, the fact that the changed element of the
mother's behavior toward ego is in accordance with the values
of the family system, means that, in this role she is "identified"
with the family, particularly the parental couple as the superordinate "leadership" element in it. Above all the function of
the father is to "back her up" by making his behavior consistent
with hers, so that they present a "single object" to ego. This
means, in the cognitive context, that there is a coordinated and
consistent input of cues presented to the child for his discrimination. Secondly, however, this system is involved in the policy
of permissiveness. On the one hand, permissiveness extends to
a very natural mechanism of ego; namely, displacement of his
aggression on the other member of the parental couple, the
father, thereby easing his own tension. At the same time, it is
presumably the father's role to help ease the corresponding
tensions of the mother by an "understanding" attitude toward
her. We presume that this basic orientation of the "family"—
which includes the mother in her familial role—begins in the
T_2 phase but continues through T_3 for the mother-child system.
Thus the facilities provided by the superordinate family system are, first, information as to the character of the "new object"
and, secondly, strengthening of the mother's capacity to be permissive and supportive in the face of strains which otherwise
would tend to diminish her capacities in both respects.

(b) The most important change in the mother-role vis-à-vis
ego is the shift from the more negative attitude of permissiveness
to positive support. Essentially this involves taking cognizance
of the threat to the integration of the system to which we referred, and counteracting it by a positive extra input of support.
By this we mean "acceptance" of her child in spite of the inadequacies in his role-behavior which have developed during
the previous phase. Since we hold that in this period there are
two primary components of her total role in the mother-child
system, we may put it that she tends to make up for the deficit

of instrumental "care" by an increase of "love." This, we suggest, puts a "floor" under any tendency for the threat to integration to develop into a vicious circle. Put another way, its primary function is to relieve ego's anxiety.

(c) Ego has been brought to the point where he has, as a personality system, been "shaken out" of the old equilibrium, but is, in the relevant respects, left in a disturbed state. He has been denied what had been essential gratifications, and been given information which, however much he has "perceived" it, he is not yet able fully to "digest." He has been forced into the residual area of the "they," but has no positive basis for defining specific significant objects in that area, and no motivation to do so. Since we presume the essential cues for discrimination have been presented, the primary problem is motivational. He has, as a first contribution to this, been given some tension release by permissive treatment.

We assumed above that the primary locus of frustration was in the area of the instrumental functions of the mother for the system she and ego comprise. Now we assume that, by her supportive attitude, she partly "compensates" for this by giving stimulation to the other main component of his motivational system, that of "love." By rewarding his show of love with *more* affection than he had been accustomed to expect, she stimulates his own autonomous love need-disposition.

The critical importance of this lies in the fact that whereas the needs which have been frustrated are, in the relevant sense *specific* i.e., in terms of frustration in the system in question, the love need-disposition is *diffuse* relative to that system. We speak, therefore, of a disposition, a tendency and capacity, to cathect the object in question in *all* possible relevant aspects. This, we suggest, provides the basis for the generalization of positive cathexis beyond the "mother" in the sense of the role-participant *only* in the initial mother-child system. The concrete mother is, after all, one organism and one behavioral system as personality, so that the step is not impossibly difficult.[10]

But we must be clear in what sense and by what paths a new object can be cathected. We have left ego in a dilemma. Cogni-

10. This is based on the law of motive growth as discussed more fully by J. Olds, *The Growth and Structure of Motives, op. cit.,* Chaps. I and II.

tively he is confronted by a mother who, in part of her meaning to him, i.e., the impact on him of her behavior, is a *different* mother from the one he has been used to. Cathectically this has involved deprivation of previously enjoyed and expected gratifications, though only some, not all. So far the only new positive element is an increase of love-support from her. We suggest that in this situation he cannot directly and immediately cathect and hence internalize a "father" as an object and personality distinct from the mother. This is particularly true because of the probability that some of the aggression and anxiety generated in the situation have been displaced onto the concrete father to relieve the strain in the mother-child relation.

As we have already suggested, the obvious path of generalization of the cathexis is by way of the common element between the old and the new objects. Precisely this is the value-pattern of the role of the mother in the *superordinate* familial system; it is the mother in her "parental" as distinguished from her "mother" role, in the role which she *shares* with the father. We suggest that the "construction" of this object and its cathexis as "continuous" with the original nurturant mother is an essential step in being able to construct and cathect the father-object.

As Olds, in particular, has tended to put it, ego must, after his initial shock "return to" the old object, but this time with a *diffuse* cathexis which can comprise both the old and the new "aspects" of it.[11] The mechanisms by which this occurs have to do with what he has elsewhere called the "law of motive growth" whereby, after being deprived in certain respects of gratification through an object, one comes to want it more intensely and more "unconditionally" than before. We may explain this in terms of inertia. Short of radical disorganization of the system, disturbance of equilibrium builds up forces tending to restore the old equilibrium. Under certain conditions, which we have tried to specify, these can be used to guide the transition to a specific kind of new equilibrium rather than either restoring the old or resulting simply in cumulative disorganization.

These considerations give, we think, the basis of a more specific insight than we have previously attained into the

11. Olds, *op. cit.*

functions of eroticism in socialization. With differences at the different stages, eroticism functions, we feel, as a primary mechanism of the generalization of cathexis from an agent of specific instrumental care to an object of diffuse attachment. Through lending diffuse meaning to somatic pleasure, erotic gratification becomes a primary *symbol* of love or acceptance. In making the transition from the primarily instrumental role of T_1 to the more supportive-expressive role of T_3 the mother relies heavily on the erotic component of her child's attachment to her, that, e.g., being fondled gives him a diffuse pleasure which serves as reinforcement in the building up of his own attitudinally diffuse love-motive system. But in turn, this eroticism is specifically bound to its integrative function in the lower-order system. Hence, if it is allowed to continue in force it will interfere with the integration of the child in the higher-order system. This, we suggest, is why every transition to a higher order system is marked by a crisis in the erotic sphere, the "oral aggression" crisis, the "anal" crisis and the oedipal crisis. In each case a "ladder" which has been essential at one stage of the climb, must be "thrown away" because it becomes an encumbrance from then on.

T_4 (a) For the superordinate system the consummatory phase may be considered to fall here. It is the phase in which the actual goal is approached and its attainment marks the close of the phase and transition to another. The child, we assume, has completed the preliminary adjustments and is actively engaged in the construction and internalization of the new objects. From the family point of view this means that father and sibling[12] are now actually being treated by him as significant objects and must be expected to reciprocate appropriately. The essence of this reciprocation consists in the maintenance of the proper balance between denial of reciprocity for ego's "overtures" and positive reciprocation, i.e., rewarding of them. The primary reward-type, according to our paradigm, should be response-gratification for specific performances in relation to the new objects. For power reasons the father is, of course, the most important of these objects; he should, there-

---

12. For the sake of brevity we will not treat relation to the sibling here. The analysis presented in Chapter II applies. We assume that *both* prior internalized objects bifurcate.

fore, be pleased at his child's new levels of achievement and responsibility, but equally, he is selective in his bestowal of his reward. The mother, in her "parental" role must of course also be positive in other than the old supportive ways. Secondarily, the family must continue to "back up" the mother in her gradual transition from being a supportive "mother" to being a selectively rewarding "parent." From one point of view this is a second source of frustration where integration in the old system is no longer encouraged.

(b) What from the point of view of the superordinate socialization system is the consummatory phase, is for the old subsystem what may be called the phase of "liquidation." In proportion as the integration of ego in the superordinate system takes place, that in the older one must give way. The mother as the more powerful member of the old system has the primary responsibility for guiding this process. This takes the form of consistently holding the relevant cognitive cues before the child, and gradually, according to his capacity to "take it" without undue anxiety, withdrawing the lower-level support and substituting for it support or "acceptance" on the "parental" level and specific gratifications as rewards for adequate performance in the new context.

It should be remembered here that in the family as a system the mother plays the more expressive leadership role. Therefore, we presume that the child's diffuse attachment to her on the lower level is generalized to her other role. His altered attachment to her remains his main focus of acceptance in the—to him—new system, supplemented by attachment to a sibling. We further suggest that a main feature of the mother's changed role consists in the withdrawal of stimulation of her child's erotic need, paving the way for its later repression.

A further aspect of what happens in this system may be described in sociological terms by saying that both mother and child act in representative roles in relation to the superordinate family as a system. Already from the beginning she has had a dual role. As the child begins to acquire his new role in the new system, her interaction with him takes place progressively more in her familial role, with the role-elements of the old role gradually disappearing. We can see that this process would be accelerated by the presence of a younger sibling coming into a preoedipal love relationship with her.

(c) We have presumed that the effect of support in the previous phase has been to stimulate motivation to act positively on ego's part. This will include activation of the aggressive components and of the older dependency needs in the old system. But it will also include considerable "trial and error" behavior in relation to the previously residual area. This is guided in the first instance by the system of cues for discrimination, in sociological terms including role-models. But on the one hand the manifestations of the old system must not be reinforced by reciprocation. This applies in particular to the awakened love-need on the old level as well as to aggression. Secondly, in the trial and error area only the overtures which "fit" the new object-definitions must be rewarded. This process, we presume, goes on by mechanisms general to all kinds of learning. The appropriate paths are learned by finding reward at the end, whereas the inappropriate ones are either not rewarded or directly punished. This is the obverse of the relative deprivation with which the process started.

It is in this process that we conceive the actual "fission" of the old internalized object system to take place. There has been a cognitive perception of the mother's role in the family, as well as in the mother-child system. The father is also cognitively perceived as "belonging" to the family, and with mother together constituting ego's "parents." Cognitively then there is the superordinate "parental" object, and the new subobject "father." But this fission of the old mother does not leave her unchanged; as "mother-parent" she has changed her character, though she is still the "more expressive" and hence responsive-supportive of the two.

On the cathectic side we presume that the diffuse cathexis of the old mother has made it possible to comprise her "parental" role in the wider cathected object. Generalization of positive cathexis then continues further to include the father as "also parent." Then as part of the total reorganization of this system the "old mother" is restructured to become mother-parent-in family as distinguished from father-parent. There are new elements of this mother; namely, her parent role which was not part of the old system, but also old elements have to be eliminated from here which are incompatible with the new

system. On psychological grounds one would suggest that some
of these old elements are extinguished. But we have given
reason to believe that some of them are of the character of
"addictions" and cannot be extinguished.[13] In this category,
apparently, belong some components at least of childhood eroticism involved in the love attachment to the mother. In the
absence of extinction these elements are separated off and "repressed" to appear later with the emergence of genital eroticism,
but in very different form and company. The motive persists but
there is substitution of a new object. Also repressed are presumably various other elements, notably certain anxieties which
have never been "overcome."

In the above discussion we have concentrated attention on
the fission of the internalized self-object in its relation to the
cathexis of the mother. But it is our hypothesis that with respect
to this particular case the fission extends through the whole
personality system, including the internalized mother-object
in relation to the cathected self-seen-in-mother. The essential
difference is that the external object which is discriminated
from this aspect of the concrete mother-image is not the father
but the sibling. For our present purposes it is not necessary
to attempt to follow out the complications introduced by the
presence of this additional object. We will also not attempt
to carry the analysis into the field of sex-role identification. On
both points the reader may be referred back to Chapter II.

T_5 (a) For the superordinate family system this may be
thought of as the phase of integration following consummatory
goal fulfillment which includes, it should be clear, the reorganization of the family which is entailed in the "admission" of a
new member. This consists in consolidating the support—i.e.,
the acceptance given to the newly socialized member, a support
which we have given reason to believe centers on ego's relation
to his mother. It entails protecting him against rivalries for the
positive sanctions belonging to his new position from jealousy
of siblings or possibly of the father, because the more mature
love of the mother for her postoedipal child may be more
threatening to the father than was that on the less mature
levels. It also entails the readjustments of the other family
members to each other. With the completion of the phase the

13. Cf. Chap. II.

family goes into latency so far as this cycle of socialization of this child is concerned.

(b) For the old mother-child system T_5 is "latency" in another sense, the final dissolution of that system. It is one of pattern-maintenance in terms of the value-patterns of the new system, what started as the superordinate system, and it is tension-management as far as the old system is concerned in the sense of management of whatever residual motivational elements appropriate to the old but not to the new system, have been left over. For the child it includes keeping residua of his dependency needs, including the erotic component, success-fully repressed and continual reinforcement of the new pattern. For the mother there may also be a problem of not "forgetting" that the child is no longer 'little."

(c) Finally, for the new personality system of the child this is the phase of "consolidation" of the newly formed structure. It is the successful completion of a process of "adaption by integration"; what was only "situation" to the child has now become a system in which he has a role, the culture of which he has internalized. What we have elsewhere referred to as the "manipulation of rewards" consists essentially in the stabilization of the sanction system in which his new level of functioning fits. The most important new elements in it are the importance of sanctions of approval as *differentiated* from response, and of which the symbolically central source is the father, and esteem as differentiated from acceptance. These are the rewards most important to the new "adaptive ego" and "superego" sub-systems of the child's personality. But the most important thing is the *balance* between the different types of sanction which is the primary condition of stabilizing the balance of his differentiated need-dispositions. Psychologically the centrally significant process is reinforcement.

We have gone to considerable lengths of meticulous care in outlining all five phases for three system references in a determinate order, because only in this way could we be sure to place the problem of identifying the mechanisms involved in its full setting. We have explicitly included the processes in the relevant social interaction systems, as well as in the personality of ego, *because we feel that this structural setting is the key to the identification and discrimination of the different mechanisms.* Only by seeing ego in this social setting can we understand what the "problems" facing him as a personality are, and hence define the possible ways in which he can attempt to "solve" these problems.

We are fully aware of the fact that what we have presented is not a realistically documented account of a concrete process of socialization, but a schematic model. The justification for selecting the ingredients we have to put into the model must rest with the justification of the general analytical scheme with which we are working; they are the ones which wide experience in the use of the scheme suggest to us are strategically the most important ones. Furthermore we may remind the reader that our selection of the transition from the mother-child love-relationship to the postoedipal integration in the family system for empirical discussion was for purposes of illustration only. We intend our model to be sufficiently general to apply to any case of differentiation of a prior personality structure by binary fission, and to the solution of the resultant problems of reintegration of the system.

The Gross Classification of the Mechanisms

With this dynamic model before us, let us now attempt to approach the problem of classification of the mechanisms involved in the socialization process more analytically and technically. For this purpose we may return for our point of reference to the paradigm presented in Fig. 1 on page 198 of this chapter. This, it will be remembered, we held to be a special case of the more general paradigm for analyzing the inputs into and outputs from a system of action, first presented in *Working Papers,*[14] and in a further refined form in Chapter III, Fig. 3.

This paradigm constitutes a classification of the functional "problems" which a personality system must confront and solve in order successfully to traverse a single cycle of internal structural change, of differentiation and integration as we have put it. Looked at in terms of the relation of the system to the situation it also presents a classification of the principal conditions which must be fulfilled in the situation if this type of

---

14. *Op. cit.,* Chap. V, Figs. 7 and 8.

process in the system is to take place, with the results postulated.

Each of these "problems" is that of "coping" with or reacting to the conditions set in the situation on the one hand and the "internal" conditions given in the state of the system at the time on the other. We conceive each of these four problems to constitute a focus of a cluster of mechanisms. We can analyze the cluster and thereby discriminate the different mechanisms in it by constructing a sub-paradigm for each of the four sub-phases of the main phase process we have been considering. Let us, first, however, run through the main process in more technical terms and then proceed to discuss the further analytical breakdown within each subphase.

Figure 2 is a revision of the original paradigm of Figure 1 in terms of its relevance to our problem of mechanisms. We con-

FIGURE 2

Gross Classification of the Mechanisms

Learning	Object-focussed Mechanisms	Motive-focussed Mechanisms	Performance
A			G
Mechanisms of Differentiation	(1) Mechanisms of Primary Adaptation Conversion of old structure into motivation Cognitive discrimination and reactions to frustration	(2) Mechanisms of Relative Deprivation Reorganization of motivation by stimulus of diffuse attachment and inhibition of other motives	
Mechanisms of Integration	(4) Mechanisms of Reinforcement Consolidation of new structure Autonomy of norms relative to new situations	(3) Mechanisms of Internalization Conversion of motivation into new structure Generalization of cathexis to new objects	
L			I
Performance			Learning

ceive the process with which we are concerned in a broad way to be analogous to the processes of transformation between matter and energy, which have been so important in physics, only here the relevant terms are "structure" and "motivation." Starting as we have from an initial stable state, we assume that first the old "structure" of that stable state has to be broken down. This breakdown results in the "release" of energy, i.e., of motivation. But initially the enhanced motivation is "unorganized" and must be "channeled" into new patterns of organization which eventually come to be "crystallized" in what we think of as new structure. The "pattern mold" into which this new motivation is "poured" is, of course, the structure of the situationally presented object system as we have reviewed it. We have, it will be noted, already mixed our metaphors; we do not mean to argue by analogy but only to try to give some indication of the broad kind of process we have in mind.

After the imposed situational change which in its beginning marks the transition from the stable state of the old system (T_1) into the new "adaptive" phase (T_2), the primary "problem" of the system is that of adapting to an altered situation and developing a meaningful cognitive orientation to the definition of *what* it is that has changed. This is a matter, we have said, of discrimination between two different aspects of the old object system. At this stage we assume that the problem is primarily cognitive, but the change cannot have *only* cognitive consequences. It is not only change, but frustrating change, as we have argued above, so that this is the phase in which the more immediate consequences of frustration develop. The primary cognitive starting point is what we will presently call the "perception of error" in the sense that the presumption of gratifying experience within a certain situation proves to be in error, and first this has to be "taken in" as a "fact." We may call the mechanisms operating in this phase those of "primary adaptation"—primary because from a broader point of view the whole process is one of adaptation.

If we were dealing with an ordinary process of "learning by experience" on a fully autonomous basis there would be no significant changes in the situation from here on except as controlled by ego. But we assume that in this case the order of frustration is too great for ego to cope with without help.

The first order of help he receives is permissiveness toward the manifestations of his disturbance, but then (in T_3) a more positive help which we have called "support." This consists in giving enhanced positive gratification to *part* of the old motivational system, which is followed by a set of reactions to the selective character of this gratification within the personality system and in its relations to objects. We may refer to this cluster as the "mechanisms of relative deprivation."

The third phase (T_4) is that in which the new structure definitely emerges as part of the personality. It involves the reconversion of "free-floating" motivation into structure, this time, however, *new* structure. For the first time the new objects, in our example the "parental" object, the father, and the "new" mother, and the new self object and the sibling, are positively cathected. We may call this cluster, then, that of the "mechanisms of internalization." Finally, in the last phase (T_5) the newly internalized structure is consolidated and reinforced. We presume that it is stabilized by its main structural outlines taking on definitely *normative* character in the sense that there is a progressively increasing independence of the continual presence of the older situational stimuli, hence an increase in capacity for self-regulation of the personality system. It involves the growth of motivation to organized positive activity in terms of the new goals and values. We may adopt the psychological term and speak of this cluster as that of the mechanisms of "reinforcement."

The various logically possible ways of grouping these four clusters of mechanisms lead us, as indicated in Figure 2, to an interpretation of certain of the current categories for the classification of mechanisms. Thus if we take the horizontal division of the table we can formulate the distinction, with which we have continually been working, between the mechanisms of differentiation (1, 2) and those of integration (3, 4). Essentially this means, in the terms we have used, the distinction between differentiation as comprising the processes involved in the breaking down of old structure and the motivational reorganization preparatory to the development of new, while on the other hand, integration is the actual building up and then the consolidation of the new.

If, then, we take the vertical line of division of the table we have another distinction which is less familiar, but we feel equally important. The left-hand column (1, 4) comprises those mechanisms with reference to which the cognitively meaningful properties of the significant objects have primacy over motivational or cathectic meaning. In the case of the adaptive mechanisms it is the significant situational objects which are the focus, in that of the mechanisms of reinforcement, the newly internalized object system. We may then call these two clusters together the "object-focussed" mechanisms.

The right-hand column on the other hand, (2, 3) constitutes the mechanisms where motivational reorganization problems have primacy. In the first case (2) they concern how the motivational consequences of frustration are handled, in the second (3) how the newly presented and significant object-structure is endowed with motivational significance. These we may call the "motive-focussed" mechanisms.

A further set of important problems arises concerning the significance of the diagonals of the figure, that is the combinations of adaptive and internalizing mechanisms (1, 3) on the one hand, of relative deprivation and of reinforcement (2, 4) on the other. We suggest that this differentiation has to do with the old distinction between learning and performance. On previous occasions we have consistently held that, like so many others, this familiar distinction was not one of absolute either-or but of relative primacy.[15] Both performance-processes and learning-processes go on continuously in all systems of action, but their relative significance will vary in different processes and in different systems.

When we speak of the A-I diagonal, that is the cluster of mechanisms involved in the adaptive and the internalization groups (1, 3) as constituting learning mechanisms, we mean that the learning problem focusses at these points. In the first case, it is a matter of the severity of the adaptive problem faced by the system relative to its prior capacity to cope with this problem. In the second, it is a question of the magnitude of the internal reorganization of the object-motive systems which is necessitated by the consequences of this adaptive strain. When on the other hand we speak of the other, the L-G diagonal

---

15. *Working Papers*, Chap. V, Sec. vi and *Toward a General Theory*, Part II, Chap. II.

(2, 4) as comprising the performance mechanisms we mean that these will be the more prominent problem foci where the process is mainly one of performance, and these mechanisms will figure more largely than the others. Performance focusses on the one hand, on the stability of the internalized object system and the ways this is maintained (4) on the other hand, on the selective gratification of motives (2). This is perhaps another way of saying that all concrete processes involve all classes of mechanisms, but in different relations of relative significance.

Before going on it may be useful to summarize two other important features of the phase cycle on this broad level. First, it is clear that the phases of the role of the primary socializing agent correspond with these phases in the relative importance of different mechanisms in the personality of the socializee. In fact, they constitute the definition of the situation in which these mechanisms operate. First then, in the transition from T_1 to T_2 and throughout the latter the role of this agent, alter, will be characterized by the combination of the imposition of frustration, primarily by withdrawal of rewards, and permissiveness relative to the symptoms of disturbance on ego's part. In T_3 there will, on alter's part, be a gradual increase of selective support, while still maintaining the old frustrations. In T_4 then, there will be a selective treatment of ego's "overtures," one main aspect of which is the "denial of reciprocity" for those of ego's overtures which do not fit the value-pattern of the role into which he is being socialized, but do involve reciprocity for those which fit. Finally, T_5 alter's role comes to be focussed on "manipulation of rewards" in the sense of selective reinforcement of ego's *new* level of role-behavior, by treating him as the "big boy" he now is.

Second, we may relate this to the classification of sanctions with which we have been working for some time, and which has been shown in the preceding two chapters to be of central importance in personality development, as well as elsewhere. In T_2 we suggest that the first change is the withdrawal of certain of the positive sanctions appropriate to the old interaction system. In this place is put the "model" of the conditions for full membership in the new system which we may state as if alter said to ego, "if you behave in the ways that are now

FIGURE 3

Detailed Classification of the Mechanisms

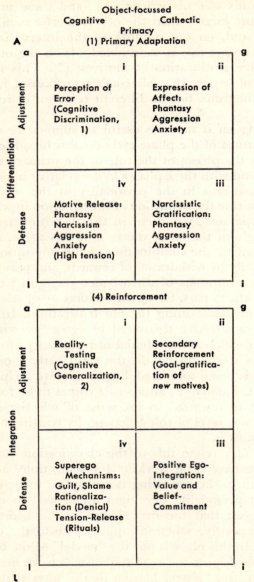

FIGURE 3 *(contd.)*

Detailed Classification of the Mechanisms

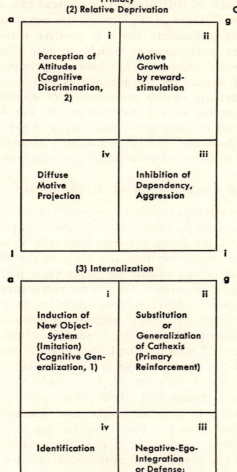

Motive-focussed

Cognitive   Cathectic

Primacy

(2) Relative Deprivation

a		G
	i	**ii** g
	Perception of Attitudes (Cognitive Discrimination, 2)	Motive Growth by reward-stimulation
	iv	**iii**
	Diffuse Motive Projection	Inhibition of Dependency, Aggression
I		i

(3) Internalization

a		g
	i	**ii**
	Induction of New Object-System (Imitation) (Cognitive Generalization, 1)	Substitution or Generalization of Cathexis (Primary Reinforcement)
	iv	**iii**
	Identification	Negative-Ego-Integration or Defense: Extinction Repression Isolation, etc.
I		i

being held up to you, you will earn the right to be *esteemed* as a fine big boy." This "offer" provides the legitimation for the frustrations which are imposed upon the child. Secondly, in T_3 the predominant type of sanction comes to be that of *acceptance* which in this illustrative context can appropriately be called "love." Then in T_4 though the negative sanction of denial remains prominent, there is positive *response*-sanction for satisfactory performances which, in our illustrative case we may presume because of her more expressive role in the family system, center on the mother as agent. Finally, in T_5 there is an increase in the prominence of *approval* sanctions which in meaning at any rate focus on the father.[16] The concrete content of these sanctions, that is to say, what the appropriate symbols are, will of course vary according to which specific phase of the total socialization process is in question.

The Detailed Classification of Mechanisms

Now we can attempt to break down each of these four clusters of mechanisms into its more differentiated components. As we suggested above, in doing this we shall take as our operating hypothesis the suggestion that the basis of the differentiation is a subcycle of phases within the larger cycle pattern which is a microcosm of that pattern. Or put into structural terms, each cluster will again be differentiated according to the four functional problems we have been continually discussing.

The breakdown we wish to present is schematically indicated in Figure 3. Let us start with the cluster of the mechanisms of primary adaptation operating in T_2 of our larger cycle. Since the system is faced with an adaptive problem, the first and major impact of change will fall at the adaptive "boundary" of the system and will present in the *first* instance a cognitive problem. Relative to previous expectations the focus of the relevant cognitive mechanism is the "perception of error," in the sense that the perceived situation differs from the expected one. Put into more positive terms, the primary focus of this subcluster of mechanisms is one aspect of the process of discrimination in the mainly cognitive sense.[17]

16. Only in the oedipal phase, of course. In earlier phases it will be on newly significant *aspects* of the concrete mother.

17. We may remark here that our concept of mechanism implies that there is

The rest of the mechanisms in this cluster concern the impact of this frustration on the rest of the system, and its other boundary-relations. We have said that it "shakes up" the already present structure of personality or internalized object system. Then in the "latency" cell of this subparadigm we would place what we have already discussed as the psychological reactions to frustration—namely, production of phantasies, aggression, narcissistic needs and anxiety. This we regard as a subcluster of the mechanisms of primary adaptation which have the common characteristics of together producing an increase of tension-level, and an incipient "differentiation" relative to the established base. This differentiation we have already defined as involving two primary cross-cutting "axes," first the external-internal axis, and second, that of positive and negative attitude.

The other two subclusters we think of as functionally concerned with the "management" of the tension which has been built up in this way. From the perspective of ordinary task-oriented performance, we have assigned the function of tension-management to the "latency" part of the system. But we presume that it is one of the defining characteristics of socialization that the controls which make this possible are broken through. This breaking through is what we mean by the "conversion" of structure into motivation. There must, therefore, be mechanisms which outside this "encapsulated" area of the old structure, somehow "cope with" the newly released motivation. In the external reference we think of these mechanisms as those of symbolic *manifestation* or expression vis-à-vis the situation, which means alter as the significant object, of these products of frustration; namely, of phantasies, aggression and anxiety. This is made possible by the permissiveness of alter and results in some reduction of tension and hence of anxiety as one main index of tension.

But the break-over of newly released motivation will not be confined to the external reference. The old personality was

---

no intrinsically inevitable "correct" unit of a system of mechanisms. When we speak of "a" mechanism we are bringing together the elements of a process which has certain characteristics as a process. But we can always treat it as a "cluster" if we wish to separate out these elements from each other.

a structured system in which the units were boundary-maintaining subsystems. This means that there is also a break-over of these boundaries vis-à-vis each other, and hence we presume an "internal permissiveness" and some tension and anxiety reduction through previously "forbidden" narcissistic gratification of phantasies and aggressions.

The four subclusters which belong in the general class of mechanisms of primary adaption are (i), the mechanisms of perception of error, or one part of cognitive discrimination; (ii), the mechanisms of symbolic manifestation or expression; (iii) the mechanisms of narcissistic gratification, of phantasy and aggression; and (iv), the mechanisms of "motive release" resulting in the production of phantasy, narcissism, aggression and anxiety.

Next, let us turn to the second major subcluster which we called the mechanisms of relative deprivation. Here the primary cognitive mechanisms concern the stabilization of the perception and conceptualization of the new situation, including the newly supportive attitudes of alter. Since the general emphasis has, by virtue of the motivational repercussions of the initial frustration, shifted to the motivational side, we may speak of these as the mechanisms of "perception of attitude" as distinguished from perception of error. They may be considered as the second subclass of the mechanisms of cognitive discrimination. The keynote is to establish the cognitive basis for relative deprivation by a clear cognitive orientation to the two discriminated aspects of the old object situation.

The second subclass concerns the mechanism of response to alter's supportive attitude. We may speak here of the mechanisms of "motive growth," using a term which Olds has found convenient in a general context of the psychology of learning.[18] These are the processes of preliminary restructuring of motivational orientation resulting from the fact that certain old outlets were blocked on all but a symbolic-expressive level and that the supportive attitude of alter gives positive gratification to another sector of the motivational system. The effect of this is to focus the expectations of gratification on alter as an object, and organize the high tension relative to this object.

18. Olds, *The Growth and Structure of Motives,* Chaps. I and II.

Third, the "motive growth" which is stimulated through these mechanisms makes it possible to end the phase of permissiveness, both external and internal. But because of the supportive attitude of alter, the time is not yet for a primary external emphasis in this direction. Internally, however, we think that the growing strength of positive motivation makes it possible to begin to *inhibit* other motivational elements which do not fit with the complex which is growing. This includes those elements of the old system which are not gratified, and aggression both internal and external, and anxiety particularly as directed toward alter. This cluster, which has an integrative significance, we may call that of the mechanisms of *inhibition*.

What then do we conceive as happening to the "structure of the system" as conceived in terms of the latency cell? Essentially, the consequences of the initial "shaking up" have been brought under control. The most important feature of the system is no longer the tendency for motivation to break over the boundaries of previous organization in all directions at once, but it has been organized and channeled so as to give it a certain directionality. This consists in the disposition to follow the lead of the object of diffuse attachment, alter, in the positive cathexis of new objects. Since we conceive that so far this is mainly a "readiness" and the process of actual generalization of cathexis has only begun, we may speak here of the mechanisms of diffuse "motive-projection." We use the term here in a sense close to that of Murray when he speaks of projection as occurring in the use of "projective techniques."[19] Projection in this sense is a readiness to endow a previously unstructured, i.e., uncathected, object with a certain cathectic meaning when it is presented in a certain context. This is, of course, a state of the personality organization which is a resultant of the operation of the other three subclusters of mechanisms in this larger class.

The four subclusters of mechanisms which we place in the general category of mechanisms of relative deprivation, we hold to be: (i) the mechanisms of perception of attitude, a subclass of the mechanisms cognitive discrimination; (ii) the mechanisms of motive growth; (iii) the mechanisms of inhibition; and finally (iv the mechanisms of motive projection. It

19. Cf. H. A. Murray, *Explorations in Personality* (New York: Oxford University Press, 1938), p. 529 ff.

should be clear that we consider both the mechanisms of primary adaption and those of relative deprivation, including all eight subclasses we have distinguished, to belong primarily in the general class of mechanisms of differentiation. We turn now to the other great subclass, the mechanisms of integration.

Starting with the mechanisms of internalization, then, the first, the subclass which has primarily cognitive-adaptive functions, comprises those concerned primarily with the cognition of the newly significant aspects of the object system, those which are in process of internalization. We may perhaps call these the mechanisms of "induction," since ego is in the relatively passive role, coming to understand what is "presented" to him. The difference from the mechanisms involved in cognitive discrimination is that, here, the premium is placed on the positive significance and relationships to each other of objects, not on the negative aspects of their relation involved in discrimination. We presume that the mechanisms usually referred to as imitation belong in this cluster. What is provided by these mechanisms is the "definition of the situation" or the set of paths for the generalization of cathexis from old to new objects. It is one aspect of cognitive *generalization*.

The next set of mechanisms at the G phase of this subcycle are those involved in the actual cathexis of new external objects. These clearly are the mechanisms of substitution, if we conceive these in a sense which places the emphasis on capacity to cathect new objects and on continuity of meaning between an old object and the new object. They might equally well be called mechanisms of generalization of cathexis. The classical case of substitution, where what, concretely, is the old object ceases to be cathected at all, we regard as a special case. The psychoanalytic concept of sublimation presumably belongs here. The mechanisms of substitution constitute the actual process of "pouring" motivational content into the new "pattern mold." It may also be considered to be the place in our more complex system which corresponds to "primary reinforcement" in the processes of elementary conditioning.

The third subcluster of mechanisms of internalization have to do with the consequences for the integration of the system of these new cognitions and cathexes. Since we assume that the new object system as a system comes to constitute the total structure of the personality on the relevant new level, this becomes a question of "dealing" with those motivational elements which do not fit the new structure. The "ideal" process of course is extinction (which shades into sublimation), and we presume that this is prominent. This subcluster, however, is the locus of many of the classical psychoanalytic "mechanisms of defense." Repression may be considered the center of the cluster. Repression is necessitated by the failure of extinction and sublimation. Most of the others in turn may be considered to be consequences of the failure of repression to be completely effective. It would include the possibilities of displacement, isolation, etc. We shall return to this question presently in a slightly different connection. In general terms, we may refer to these as the mechanisms of "negative ego-integration."

The last of the subclusters belonging to the larger one of internalization concern the new "state of the system" as described in the latency cell. This is the end-product of this phase of the socialization cycle and seems to us to be the appropriate place to use the term *identification*. This essentially means that internalization of the new object system has been successfully completed. The structure of ego's personality system now consists in the *system* of identifications which have become established, in the sense in which the term was used in Chapter II. This means that from now on ego's major "predispositions" or "orientations" are to act in terms of the newly internalized object-system and the motives which are organized in it. Its internal structure is that of the *system* appropriate to the stage of socialization in question. We have discussed this at great length, so that it need not detain us further now. We may remark only that this system is still a "tender plant" which requires stabilization through reinforcement before it can resist serious pressures or frustrations.

The mechanisms which belong in the cluster which we have called that of internalization fall into four subclusters as follows: (i) the mechanisms of induction of new object-systems; (ii) the mechanisms of generalization of cathexis or substitution; (iii) the mechanisms of negative ego-integration, or defense coping with motivational elements in conflict with the new internalized object-system; and finally (iv) the mechanisms of identification.

The last of the major clusters of mechanisms is that which

we referred to above as the mechanisms of reinforcement. We presume here that in all its structural essentials the new personality system is already complete. What remains is to stabilize and "harden" it, so that it can function independently of some of the situational supports which it has previously enjoyed. At the cognitive-adaptive boundary we may speak of the sub-cluster of the mechanisms of *reality testing*. This involves *use* in an active way of the cognitive aspects of the new internalized object system, as a system of "concepts," and the "verification" of these concepts through actual dealing with the external situation. The essential question is how far the "image" of situational objects and of self, arrived at by what we called "induction" in the previous phase, proves to be "true." By such processes, we presume, "ideas" about the situation come to be hardened into "convictions."

The second set of mechanisms constitute the focus of the process of reinforcement at their "core." It is what in learning theory is usually called "secondary" reinforcement. This is the set of experiences with respect to consummatory gratification of the *new* goal-orientations. We suggest on established psychological grounds that steady experience of gratification in conformity with expectations is particularly important at this point. The rewards must, however, be *conditional* on adequate performance, in order for the newly internalized norms not to be upset; unwarranted reward independent of such performance would be just as unsettling to the new system, by stimulating the revival of regressive motives, as would over-severity in the form of withholding rewards which according to the new standards had been earned. The central type of reward at this point, we have argued is that of *approval* on the part of the significant objects. At the oedipal phase the father should be the symbolic focus of this reward-complex, regardless of the sex of the child.

The third subcluster of mechanisms concern the positive integration of the newly-formed personality or internalized object-system. In the corresponding subcluster of the last group we emphasized the importance of the negative aspect of this integration, the coping with the elements which did not fit the new structure. We assume that as this problem approaches solution there is a gradual turning to a more positive emphasis, to strengthening the internal ties between the different elements of the new structure. We may speak of the mechanisms involved here as those of belief- and value-"commitment." By this we mean that, in so far as this positive internal integration gains force, the different units will come to constitute an integrated system so that the units will be capable of being "mobilized" in support of each other in an orderly way. As this process proceeds, the new personality becomes progressively emancipated from dependence on situational support. The strength which comes from appropriate motivational reinforcement in the g subcluster of this group is "shared around" within the personality system to reinforce the cross-ties within the personality, to which we referred in Chapter III. This is the internal counterpart of external reinforcement. Perhaps the most appropriate term would be mechanisms of *positive ego-integration*.

Finally, for the last time we raise the question of the "structure of the system." We presume that this is now fully developed and growing progressively stronger. The function of the last subcluster of mechanisms is to "hold" the gains thus made, by bringing together the pattern-maintenance and the tension-management functions of a stabilized system. This constitutes, we believe, essentially what psychoanalysts are accustomed to call the *superego* mechanisms. We can think of a negative and a positive aspect. On the one hand, there must be self-imposed sanctions against violation of the internalized normative system. We feel, following up the view taken in Chapter II, that guilt and shame belong here; guilt so far as the primary reference is to the internal relation between motive-unit and internalized value, shame so far as the reference is "external" to the actual or probable orientation of valued and cathected social objects. On the other hand, there must also be a positive aspect which in turn may have more a cognitive or more a motivational emphasis. Where the cognitive aspect is paramount we may speak of rationalization, which we assume has the primary function of striving for consistency in the belief system as part of the internalized culture; it means that cognitive processes are understood in their relation to this problem of consistency rather than to cognition of external objects. When, on the other hand, the motivational aspect is paramount, we may speak of mechanisms of tension-release in which what in the narrow sense is "symbolic" behavior and "rituals," will be prominent.

Thus in the more general cluster of mechanisms of reinforcement, we have again distinguished four subclusters as follows: (i) the mechanisms of reality-testing; (ii) the mechanisms of secondary reinforcement; (iii the mechanisms of positive ego-integration; and (iv) the superego mechanisms.

We have now completed the review of our suggested detailed classification of mechanisms. We have, as the reader will note, adhered strictly to the general action-system paradigm used throughout this volume, using particularly the version of it we felt most appropriate to our present purpose which we introduced as Figure 1, Page 198. We feel that the results are closer to relatively established usage in the psychology of personality than we had any reason in advance to expect. One major result of our work is, we think, to show that the different mechanisms which have been discussed in the literature lie on several different levels in their relation to the processes of personality as a system. Thus some of them, like inhibition, substitution and identification, we have been able to fit in as each matching directly one of our own categories on the more detailed level. Other cases like differentiation, integration, learning and performance, we feel, as is the general tenor of the literature, are more macroscopic *classes* of mechanisms, comprising in each case several of our more detailed classes. In the cases of cognitive discrimination and generalization, we feel that the common usage fits *two* of our classes, namely 1-i and 2-i, perception of error and perception of attitudes, and 3-i and 4-i, induction of new objects and reality testing respectively.

It has become evident in the course of our analysis that a large number of commonly identified mechanisms are best treated as more special "cases" under the rubrics we have defined even in our more detailed classification. Thus we placed production of phantasy, aggression, narcissism and anxiety all in class 1-iv "motive-release" or reactions of the internalized structure to disturbance. Similarly in 3-iii, in which placed many of the classical mechanisms of defense, we included extinction, repression and by implication several others, and under 4-iv, superego mechanisms, both guilt and shame, and rationalization and tension-release as well. We feel that, in one or another of these ways, we can come very close to finding a reasonably satisfactory place for all except a few of the currently discussed mechanisms. The exceptions we have in mind are cases, such as displacement, projection in the sense of ego attributing what is really his motive or belief to alter, and reaction-formation. These we think are not cases, either of our own categories or of members of classes either in the logical sense superordinate to or subordinate to any of them. They are, rather, "complex" mechanisms involving combinations of several different classes on the level on which we have treated them. We shall discuss these briefly a little later in this chapter.

We are quite frank that we have not yet been able to take the time for a thorough checking with the accepted "classical" definitions of all these mechanisms and beyond that the ways in which the concepts have been used in the most authoritative sources. This would be an obvious next step in the process of codification to which we hope this chapter is a contribution.

Before leaving the question of classification as such, we may point out another general distinction which only emerges at the more detailed level of breakdown which we have just reviewed. This is the distinction between the mechanisms involved in relating the system to its external situation on the one hand, (i, ii, in each of the main clusters and those involved in its internal processes (iii, iv in each cluster). We suggest that this distinction is essentially that which has been current in the literature as that between the mechanisms of adjustment and the mechanisms of defense, in one meaning of the latter term. This was the meaning which we understood by these terms in *Toward a General Theory of Action*.[20] Our present analysis, however, has shown that a large proportion of what, in the literature of psychoanalysis and circles influenced by it have been called the mechanisms of defense, fall in one of the four subcategories of this latter class (3-iii) or are of the "complex" character to which we have just referred. On the whole we prefer a terminology which would reserve the unqualified term "defense" for the larger class, and then refer to mechanisms of superego defense, positive and negative ego-

---

20. T. Parsons and E. A. Shils, *op. cit.*, Part II, Chap. II.

defense, etc. But what we are here mainly concerned with is pointing out the problem which current usage poses.

Problems of Input and Output Relations

From time to time throughout our discussion we have referred to the bearing of the analysis of system-process in terms of inputs and outputs on our problem. We are now in a position to sum up this aspect of the problem for a cycle of the socialization process. On an earlier occasion[21] the input-output point of view was defined as that of assessing the "balance sheet" of a system by comparing its state at the beginning and at the end of a time-segment of process. We then try to assess what, in that time segment has "gone into" the system and what has "come out," and to compare the two.

Inputs are, according to the paradigm as refined in Chapter III, Figure 3, of two main classes and in turn come through two main channels, yielding four categories. The two classes we distinguished were there called "information" and "motivation." The channels are the situation external to the system (external objects) and the internal state of the system at the inception of the time-period (internalized objects). The classes of positive output in turn have a similar and corresponding structure. They consist in improved relations to external objects through command of facilities (achievement) and changes (improvements) in the internalized object system (accomplishment) on the one hand; in "consumption" of external object-values as rewards (gratification) and "consumption" of internalized object-values or rewards (satisfaction).

In terms of this schema, let us summarize each of the four main phases of our socialization cycle in turn. We think of the process, starting with the system in a stable state, as characterized by a certain *rate* of input in each of the four categories. This implies relative stability, both in the situation and in the internal state of the system, and a corresponding stability of outputs.

The first change consists in alteration in the balance of situational inputs. There is both an added input of new information (alter is behaving differently and this is perceived)

21. *Working Papers*, Chap. V, Sec. vi.

and a decrease in the motivationally significant input, in that rewards previously expected are not forthcoming. This combination of new information and diminished reward, in interaction with the original internal structure, leads to the disorganization of the latter, with production of deficits in both "satisfaction" and "accomplishment" which are in turn reflected in lowered achievement. As these effects appear the disorganizing pressure is somewhat slackened by alter's permissiveness.

The second phase opens with alter's supportive action, the effect of which is an increased input of motivational stimulation. It is assumed that the rate of input of information remains approximately constant. The increased gratification produced by the input of support in its effect on motivation, mitigates the internal deficit of satisfaction and, therefore, the motivational effects of the internal disorganization. This permits a restructuring which mobilizes some of the motivation released from the older object system into a process of motive-projection oriented to the diffuse cathexis of the supporting object. This in turn produces an important new output of satisfaction with the effects of diminution of anxiety and development of "self-confidence."

In the third phase the motivational input from the situation is again turned into a deficit, lest it over-stimulate motive-projection. The mechanism of this is denial of reciprocity. Input of information again takes the lead, this time positive information about the new object-system. The motivational output stimulated in the last phase is thereby guided to the cathexis of the objects and hence their internalization. This is the first stage of new internal structuring, hence of increase in the output of accomplishment as compared with earlier phases. Finally, in the last phase there is a resumption of the external motivational input, this time in the form of rewards for satisfactory achievement in the new role, so that the higher accomplishment level is manifested in enhanced achievement and gratification of the newly formed achievement motives.

The relations of input and output and their fluctuations are schematically shown in Figure 4. We assume T_1 as the base line. The signs, zero, plus and minus in each box refer to relative changes, in T_2 relative to this T_1 base, in each subsequent phase relative to the one immediately preceding. They

FIGURE 4

Input-Output Relations in a Socialization Cycle

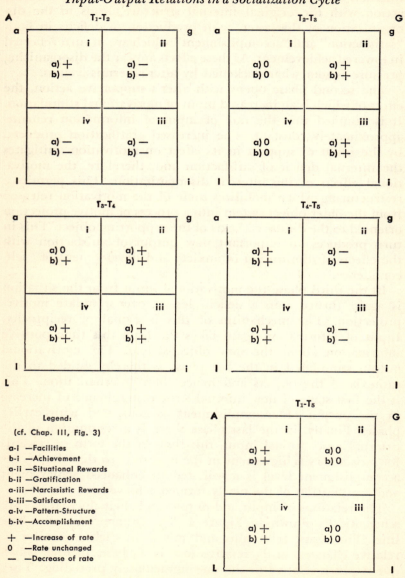

Legend:
(cf. Chap. III, Fig. 3)

a-i —Facilities
b-i —Achievement
a-ii —Situational Rewards
b-ii —Gratification
a-iii—Narcissistic Rewards
b-iii—Satisfaction
a-iv—Pattern-Structure
b-iv—Accomplishment

+ —Increase of rate
0 —Rate unchanged
— —Decrease of rate

constitute, that is, *changes of rate* of input and output in the different categories, not absolute quantities. At the end is given a table of net changes over the whole process. It consists, that is, in a comparison of the T_1 stable state with the stable state attained at the conclusion of T_5.

It will be noted that we have assumed that in a normal socialization process the *net* total changes are confined to the "information" side of the input and output balance. It is for this reason that we have used the convention of entering O instead of plus or minus in certain cells, i.e. 2-i, iv and 4-i of the detailed table, and ii and iii of the general table. Essentially what we are saying for the detailed breakdown is that in T_{23} and T_{45} as compared with the phases preceding them there is a slackening of informational input, but not necessarily to a point below the base-line rate for the previous state of the system. In the case of motivation, on the other hand, we assume that there is a wider "swing" between phases in the relative quantities of input.

This in turn relates to the way in which we have schematically portrayed the overall balance. The essential point of this is that the *net* change is found in the "stored" informational content of the system. This is, we think, another way of saying that the change is a *cultural* change. This is in accord with a view we have several times stated,[22] leaning on Durkheim's view, that "progress" does not consist in or lead to an enhanced level of "happiness" (gratification plus satisfaction), but to a change in the *structure* of the system. It is for this reason that we have left the net balance of motivational inputs and outputs at zero.

It should be kept clear that this is not meant to be a balance sheet of the total concrete process of socialization, but only of the "action" aspect of one cycle of it. We have often said that the source of motivational energy lies in the organism.[23] The socialization of the child coincides with the biological maturation of the organism. Since the organism is growing bigger and stronger, it is reasonable to assume that it produces an increasing output of energy into the personality system. When we say, therefore, that there is no net balance of motivational

22. *Working Papers,* Chap. V, p. 218, note.
23. *Ibid.,* Chap. V, Sec. vi.

input over a socialization cycle we mean, as made available by action mechanisms and relative to a given curve of concrete motivational growth from organic sources. But the informational net input is one which in the nature of the case *cannot* come from the organism, but only from the "accumulation" of the culture, or by additions to it from the situation.

This question relates to another which may have concerned the reader. We have several times stated that it seems probable that motivational energy cannot be transferred from one personality system to another, but that motivation available to a personality system comes exclusively from the particular organism of the person in question. What, then, do we mean when we speak of situational rewards as a source or channel of the input of motivation? Our hypothesis is that situational rewards constitute mechanisms which regulate the boundary-processes between the organism and the personality. A positive reward then, we suggest, acts to stimulate the organic energy-flow into the personality, or to remove inhibiting factors, whereas a deprivation has the opposite effect. Internal rewards on the other hand, we think of as regulating the *allocation* of energy within the personality system as between different object-motive units.

The Mechanisms and Personality Structure

We are now in a much better position to discuss two questions which have been in our minds since the beginning of this chapter. The first question is, what are the *changes* in the mechanisms which occur as a function of the progressive differentiation and integration of the personality system through the stages of socialization? The second, what are the limitations on generalization of our analysis of the mechanisms imposed by the fact that we have analyzed them in relation to a cycle of socialization, not to ordinary "performance"?

Throughout this and the two preceding chapters we have consistently held that the first construction and internalization of a complex social object, in the human socialization case the establishment of the "mother-child identity," constituted a fundamental turning point, and the beginning of the socialization process "proper." Only from then on can we conceive the process as one of binary fission of already internalized object-systems.

We feel quite confident that the order of differentiation of the *mechanisms* from each other which is given in our more detailed classification is in force from then on. We could perfectly well have chosen the first process of fission, from mother-child identity to differentiation of dependency and autonomy need-dispositions, as our basic illustration, or alternatively one of those subsequent to the oedipal phase. We do not thereby mean to suggest that there is no significant change in the system of mechanisms which is a function of stage in the developmental process. We suggest only that such change leaves untouched the order of differentiated structure of the system of mechanisms which we have outlined. We think that the changes have to do mainly with two aspects of the operation of the personality system.

The first concerns the level of differentiation of the internal personality system as a system of objects. This means that the empirical parameters, which must be ascertained before the more abstract generalizations which constitute what we have called mechanisms can be used for concrete explanation or prediction, will change from stage to stage of the process. This change involves not only the sheer number of differentiated structural units which must be taken into account, but at least two other features of the structure they constitute. One of these is the genetically derived hierarchy of superordinate-subordinate object-relationships. When a process of fission takes place the prior internalized object does not "cease to exist," but, as we have seen, it is *transformed* to constitute the superordinate framework within which the newly differentiated pair of objects, or classes of them, fit. Thus the original internalized mother differentiates into a new mother and a "self." This "mother" in turn differentiates into the two internalized "parent" objects, while the self differentiates into a masculine and a feminine self, as we put it in Chapter II. It is only on the hypothesis of the persistence, through these processes of transformation, of the genetically prior internalized object systems on each level, that we can account for the continuing integration of the more differentiated system. Essentially then, what we have is the differentiation of a system into a more and more complex network of

subsystems. The *structure* of this network constitutes one variable element in the parameters of application of the mechanism
concepts.

But we have seen that this is not the only structural hierarchy
which constitutes internal structure for the personality. There
is also the internalized *social value* component, which is the
"cultural" component as such. In order to get the process of
internalization started, the two have to coincide in the earliest
stages. The first internalized mother-object is in one aspect
the value pattern of what in one sense is a very "low-level"
subsystem of the society. The two-unit system of the next stage
is a little less low level subsystem—it is the first genuine collectivity—and the nuclear family still less so; indeed it is ordinarily
recognized sociologically as a "unit" of the society. But the order
of hierarchy in this case is the reverse of that in the case of
the genetic series of priorities. The child starts by participating
in a very highly differentiated subsystem of the society and
progresses from there to participation in, hence internalization
of, as objects, more and more superordinate systems until, when
fully mature, he can be said to be a member of the "society"
as a whole, and to have internalized *its* values. We have seen
that once the differentiation of role begins, with the beginning
of sex-categorization in the oedipal period, these two orders
of object-internalization no longer coincide but cross-cut each
other. They constitute as it were "warp" and "woof" of the
structure of the personality. What in this sense are the internalized social role-values constitute just as much variant parameters
for application of the concepts of mechanisms as do the genetically ordered objects.

The mechanisms then, as we understand them, are formulated
so that the empirical results of their operation are *relative* to
the concrete internalized and situational objects within and
between which they operate, or to concrete motives and meanings of objects relative to those motives. But we have been able,
taking over most of the actual concepts we have used from
current psychological theory, to formulate them as a *system*
independently of these particular parameters. It is this which
makes it possible to speak of what, on one particular level we
believe to be a general theory of psychological process which
does not have to be restructured to take account of every con-

crete variation in the structure of different personalities, or of the same personality over time.

The second field in which development of the personality may be held to influence the mechanisms, concerns what above we called the "complex" mechanisms which involve two or more of the subcategories which we outlined in our detailed classification. We presume that resort to these is a function of the complexity of the personality as a system, and that some of the more complex of them could not operate on the earliest levels. We cannot, however, attempt to enter into this complex set of questions here, but must rest content with taking note of the problem.

We said that we were confident that our classification, even on the detailed level, was applicable to the whole range of socialization processes, once the internalization of a single culturally formed complex social object had been achieved. We are less confident that the same classification is equally relevant for the process leading up to the first internalization, or in sub-human cases where the cultural level of social interaction is not involved. We cannot attempt to explore these questions here, but wish only to note that Olds's work on the relevance of the action schema to the field of behavior psychology[24] is suggestive that in this as in various other respects, the theoretical gap is not so great as has often been supposed. If even the S-R-S sequence can be analyzed as process in a system of action, the presumption is that the analysis we have presented of the mechanisms is not wholly irrelevant even to this level. Indeed we have borrowed freely from experimental psychology for a number of our formulations. But the thorough exploration of this problem area would lead farther afield than we can go in this chapter.

The second of the major questions we raised above was whether what we have put forward is only a classification and analysis of the mechanisms of a cycle of the socialization process, or something more general. We have already foreshadowed our answer to this question, which is that we think our scheme, so far as it is valid at all, is valid for all types both of learning and of performance processes in a cultural-level personality

---

24. Cf. Olds, *The Growth and Structure of Motives, op. cit.,* esp. Chap. I.

system. The difference between what is concretely called a learning process and one of performance is, we suggest, a difference in the parameters of the problem, not in the mechanisms involved. It is true that differences in the parameters will lead to differences in the relative importance of different mechanisms for the particular cases, but not to a totally new set of mechanisms which operate in one kind of situation but not in the other. This view is in accord with the whole tenor of our theoretical analysis in the field of the theory of action.

We may illustrate. We interpret a cycle of socialization as beginning with a relatively large input of new information and a relatively large deficit of motivational input through withholding of rewards. A "routine" performance process would start with mounting tension in the latency cell and hence behavior "seeking" a gratifying relation to a goal-object would ensue. So long as the process remained routine there would be no large input of new information and no deficit of reward beyond "orbital" expectations. Hence there would be relatively little activation of the mechanisms of perception of error and of reaction to frustration or motive-release. If, however, the situation had changed, thus a particularly difficult "task" had been set from outside, then the operation would resemble that in the early phase of a socialization cycle much more closely.

We suggest then that within the limits we have formulated, our analysis of mechanisms is completely general and not in any way specifically bound to the socialization situation.[25] We regard the latter, however, as a particularly favorable focus for this general analysis because of two features of it. In the first place in the early phases of socialization the major set of parameters, the structure of the object system, both internalized and situational, is relatively simple, so we are in much less danger of confusing questions of difference of mechanism with those of parametric variation than if we attempted to take performance processes in the adult personality as our field of empirical analysis. Secondly, in socialization we have a major process of *reorganization* of the personality system going on. It

---

25. We think that some of our specific formulations and terminology have been influenced by the fact that we have analyzed a socialization process. At a later stage of refinement any such bias might be removed in favor of more general formulations.

is much more likely that here the whole range of different kinds of mechanisms will be prominently and actively involved than is the case where something like "routine" performance processes are going on. From this point of view the only comparably favorable situation for study is that of the disturbed personality; but here the first of the two advantages just referred to would not exist.

Disorganization and the Pathology of Personality

There is one further large theoretical field which we have not yet touched. So far and quite deliberately, we have dealt with an idealized picture of the socialization cycle. But what of the analysis of deviations from this idealized picture or model of a cycle and their bearing on the analysis of the mechanisms? Our central thesis in this area is that such deviations *do not concern the mechanisms at all,* but are matters of input and output and their balancing, that is to say again, that the problems are parametric. Put somewhat differently, the *same* mechanisms will produce "normal" or "pathological" consequences, according to whether, given the previous state of the personality and its conditions, including the relevant capacities of the organism, the inputs are within certain limits or not. There is in this sense no such thing as a distinction between the "mechanisms of normal development" on the one hand and the "pathogenic mechanisms" on the other. The distinction is one of conditions, that is of parameters. Essentially for this reason we have not built the distinction between "positive" and "negative" meaning, as it is used for example in the analysis of sanctions in the interaction process, into our classification of mechanisms. This distinction belongs to the input-output category. Positive sanctions are the source of increased inputs into the personality of the "target" actor; negative sanctions correspondingly of decreased inputs, relative to the previous rate and in the relevant category of course.

A mechanism, then, establishes a *relation* between an input and an output—or a combination of several mechanisms does. Let us start this part of the analysis with a brief discussion of some of what we have called the "complex" mechanisms. A simple one to take first is that of *displacement*. By this is meant the cathexis, positive or negative, of an "inappropriate" external object and the corresponding behavior in relation to that object. How do we analyze this?

We presume that the cathexis of the "real" object is part of an internalized motivational system which includes the internalization of the actor-object relationship, hence then an internalized object—of any level of "abstraction"—is bound to a situational object. Somehow, however, cathexis of this external object and the appropriate behavior are in conflict with other motivational subsystems which are strategically more important to the personality. Then the first set of mechanisms involved belong in category 3-iii of Figure 3, mechanisms of negative ego-integration. We presume that extinction has failed and there has been an attempt at repression, but this is only partially successful. The motive is too strong to be denied all expression. Hence, secondly, there is substitution, that is generalization of cathexis to another object which, in motivationally meaningful ways, is sufficiently similar to the original object, or otherwise associated with it, but the cathexis of which does not come so sharply into conflict with other motivational systems. But because the original motive is neither extinguished nor completely repressed, the substitution, like the repression, remains incomplete, so the manifest cathexis of the substitute object is "not what it seems." The repression of the connection can go "below the threshold of consciousness" without being complete.

Displacement is a rather simple case of a "complex" mechanism and hence a good one to begin with. Now let us take a somewhat more complicated one, namely *reaction-formation*. Here we start with the same set of conditions, a motive-system which is in conflict with other more important systems in such a way that the cathexis of the external object is imperfectly repressed. But in this case instead of displacement of cathexis to another external object, we suggest that what happens is the substitution of cathexis of another motive as an *internal object*—whether this should be called displacement or not is an open terminological question. In any case it is a "narcissistic" solution. This internal object, being more acceptable in the total system than the external object "originally" cathected by the partially repressed motive, is in some sense and to some degree "opposite" to or in conflict with the latter. By receiving narcissistic gratification (1-iii) then, it is stimulated or strengthened and this results, within the relevant part of the personality, in motive growth (2-ii), and eventually motive projection (2-iv). The essence of reaction formation is internal rather than external "displacement" followed by the stimulus, growth and projection of the stimulated motive system, hence the strengthening of *its* cathexis of external objects.

Finally, let us take up the case of *projection* in the "classical" sense of ego's attribution of part of his own motivational system to alter. We suggest that this also starts with essentially the same situation as the other two, the imperfect repression of an unacceptable (to ego) motive system. Possibly because for some reasons the other possibilities of displacement and reaction formation are closed, or because of the importance of cognitive aspects of his personality integration, the next step is, we think, a special case of rationalization (4-iv). Here it takes the drastic form of *denial* that this motive system is part of ego's personality. This then throws the "problem" into the adjustment category in the external object field. Here there may be involved elements of two sets of mechanisms, on the negative side insufficient reality-testing (4-i), and on the positive a special form of what we have above called "perception of attitudes" (2-i). The difference from both displacement and reaction-formation of course lies in shifting the "solution" from a primarily cathectic change, to one which is primarily cognitive, but retaining the character of the motive unchanged.[26]

These complex mechanisms, if those we have discussed constitute a fair sample, constitute ways in which the operation,

---

26. As an example we may take a case reported in R. W. White's *Abnormal Personality* (New York: Ronald, W., 1948), pp. 81-90. The patient repressed his own sexual timidity, and his deviant sexual wishes. This allowed him to conceive of himself as an exceptionally fine person; one whom the world should praise. But, instead of praising him, people around tended to treat him as something of a 'Milquetoast' character. He explained their treatment by constructing a delusional system (which eventually hardened into a complete rationalization of life) wherein there was a conspiracy on the part of these others to control him, and confine him, for devious purposes. This explained the deprecatory attitudes of those involved in the conspiracy; and it even allowed him to express deviant sexual wishes without taking responsibility for them, for they were attributed to electrical manipulations of him by his persecutors.

Here we see the repression of certain sexual motives, then the rationalization of the self-image, then the construction of a delusional system with special reference to alter's attitudes.

partial or complete, of one or more elementary mechanisms, which itself is occasioned by a surfeit or deficit of input somewhere in the system, propagates the consequences of this input-situation to other parts of the system. We can, then, construct such more complex mechanisms if we have sufficient knowledge of the interconnections of the input-output relations between the different subsystems of the personality. These mechanisms thus involve somewhat higher level generalizations than the elementary mechanisms; they, therefore, require more precise specification of conditions before they can be reliably used for explanation.

We can now attempt to generalize the bearing of these considerations about input and output in relation to the mechanisms for the problem of the equilibrium of the personality and hence the balance between "normal" and "pathological" trends. In doing so, we wish to attempt to make use of the distinction between the mechanisms of defense in the broad sense discussed above and of adjustment, and the relation of the latter to the patterns of deviance in the social system, as discussed in the last section of Chapter III above.

The essential starting point is the proposition that equilibrium or a stable state depends on an optimum balance of inputs and outputs in each category. The consequences of any given combination of inputs for the corresponding outputs should of course be traceable through the mechanisms. For a stable state there will, with respect to each category of input be an optimum, hence there will be deviation in either a "too much" or a "too little" direction.

The first point of reference for analyzing this equilibrium is the state of the internalized object system as we have thought of it as defining the content of the latency cell of our paradigm. This we assume to be relatively stable and this fact is the reason why, for the ordinary analysis of performance processes, we assume it to be given. But this is only a relative stability and we have seen how, in the analysis of socialization, we think it possible to account for fundamental changes in this state. Such stability as there is is maintained by continual equilibrating processes. But, we assume that, so long as it is stable, these processes are focussed on the next level down from the analysis of the personality as a system; they are processes of the stabilization of internalized *units* as systems. We have previously described[27] the main character of this stabilization function in the formula that it combines "pattern-maintenance" and "tension-management." We further assume that the main channels of input and output of this system are not directly related to the situation external to the personality but rather to other "parts" of the personality as a system. There is one exception, the boundary vis-à-vis the organism where the regulation of rates of motivational input occurs. This subsystem of the personality involves what we call, beyond a certain level of differentiation, the "superego," and hence the mechanisms which we called superego mechanisms (4-iv) principally operate in this field.[28]

There are, then, three other principal loci of boundary-processes of the system. The first is that "specializing" in the input of facilities from outside, and the corresponding output of what we have called "achievement." Here the essential condition of stability is the "matching" of the inflow of information about the external object system, and the orientation to the latter of the internalized object-motive system. We have spoken of this[29] as a matter of the "level of differentiation" of the personality system, relative to the structure of the system of significant objects in the situation. The case of too much input is illustrated by the early phase of the socialization cycle; ego is asked to react to discriminations to which his internal motivational system is not adapted. He can "perceive error" but cannot make the appropriate use of the "unfamiliar" objects. The case of too little on the other hand would be the one where external objects did not expect of him differentiated orientation up to the level of his established motivational system. This would be illustrated by the reversion of a mother, when the oedipal cycle was nearing completion, to treatment of her child as if it had never started.

The second boundary-process vis-à-vis the external situation concerns goal-gratification of the personality as a system and the corresponding level of input of situational rewards. Here

---

27. *Working Papers,* Chap. V.

28. If we are correct in this view of the superego as a principal subsystem of the personality, it should have a particularly important relation to psychosomatic processes.

29. See Chap. III.

the "too much" is a question of overstimulation by reward which is excessive relative to the equilibrium level—a case would be oversupport in the socialization cycle which ignored the importance of denial of reciprocity, i.e., of continuing to deprive the motives destined for extinction or repression. The "too little" case is that where there are not enough rewards to produce a balanced input relative to the other conditions. The effect is to produce a motivational "glut" which cannot find expression.

The inputs of facilities and rewards constitute the most obvious ways in which sanctions from the external situation influence the personality, but a third is of great importance; this concerns the integrative balance within the personality itself and thus the allocation of internal rewards among its units. But a balance in this respect, connected as we have held it to be with the internalized social value-systems, is open to situational influence not only through the above channels, but also independently of them through the processes of expressive communication. This is possible because of the interpenetration of personality and social system which we have often discussed. In terms of personality structure, the essential phenomenon is the internalization of the *pattern of relationship* between ego and a cathected object. Hence an object which "fits" with this relationship pattern can, by the appropriate symbolic action, influence the internalized counterpart. The mechanisms concern generalization of cathexis and the balance between external and narcissistic object-cathexes. We suggest essentially that a negative sanction in this category stimulates a narcissistic reaction, thus rewarding another internalized object, whereas a positive sanction tends to draw cathexis to the external rewarding object. In our analysis above this is illustrated by the withdrawal of supportive rewards in favor of denial of reciprocity; the effect we think is to make the motivational energy in part available for the cathexis of the newly internalized objects.[30]

Essentially, this is what we mean by the integrative balance of the personality system. Expressive communication with alter constitutes a governing mechanism which can influence this balance by influencing the transfer of cathexis between external

30. It will be noted that we held this mechanism to be involved in reaction-formation.

and narcissistic objects. The optimum balance is one in which a certain relation between them obtains. The case of "too much" input means that certain internal objects are overly-cathected to the detriment of good "adjustment" to external objects; conversely, "too little" means that certain internal objects are "impoverished" and the corresponding external objects overcathected. The bonds of "solidarity" are given preference over the integration of ego's own personality.

This review now gives us the basis for a more general statement of the relations between the mechanisms of adjustment of the personality, and the patterns of conformity and deviance of the social systems in which ego participates. Broadly, mechanisms of adjustment are mechanisms of "coming to terms" with the sanctions which a given mode of behavior will tend to produce in the action of alters. They constitute ways in which the elementary mechanisms come to be used and organized as part of the role-expectation units of the personality-system as we analyzed these in Chapter III. At the level of organization most of them belong, therefore, in the category of what above we called the "complex mechanisms" in so far as they completely account for a role-orientation.

These complex mechanisms are *not,* as such, "patterns of deviance" or of conformity from the point of view of the social system. This is because the structure of the personalities which have to come to terms with a given sanction system is not uniform for all personalities who are incumbents of "the same" roles. This basic fact underlies the well known observation that it is quite possible to conform with social role-expectations for highly "pathological" motives, and vice versa to deviate for "normal" motives.

The "ideal type" of stable equilibrium in social systems requires stable personalities where the values of the social system are fully internalized in all of them. Relative to this model, a deviant act on the part of one, ego, affects the input-balance of the others on whom this action impinges. Their reaction may then either tend to restore the balance in his (ego's) own personality or drive it further from an equilibrium which is compatible with the stability of the social interaction system. The mechanisms of adjustment then may operate to maintain relatively high levels of "conformity" with social role-expectations *at the expense* of internal tension within the personality system which requires strong "defenses" to prevent breakdown. Or, on the other hand, they may act to relieve internal tensions at the cost of role-conformity and hence somehow work out a way in which the necessary price in the form of negative sanctions—or withdrawal of positive—can be paid. It should not be forgotten furthermore that deviances may be complementary, so that two or more deviants may mitigate the personality cost of their deviance by meshing with each other. This phenomenon, as we know, is important in the development of many forms of socially structured deviance such as the delinquent gang.[31]

In so far as a personality structure can justifiably be called "pathological," this is because the operation of the mechanisms of defense in the broad sense is such as a) to operate to maintain a low level of internal integration and/or b) to impede the operation of the boundary-adjusting mechanisms; hence, an additional burden is thrown on the personality from the point of view of its relation to the external sanction system. The consequence is either that "normal" inputs cannot be tolerated and the mechanisms of defense operate to close the personality to their reception or, conversely, that there is an excessive need for input beyond the normal level. Thus we suggest that in one sense rigidity is a characteristic of all pathological personality conditions. The "trouble" centers in the latency cell of our paradigm. There is too much energy consumed in pattern-maintenance and tension management, and a corresponding inadequacy in the adjustive processes.

The Principal Pathological Syndromes

The input-output balances at each of these main boundaries of the personality as a system may then be regarded as resultants of the operation of many of the elementary mechanisms we have reviewed. Now we would like to suggest that the nature of these balances is a primary focus of the familiar pathological syndromes. As in all such problems, a classification of concrete types must be based on a rank order of relative importance of the various mechanisms, and on organized combinations of

---

31. Cf. *The Social System*, Chap. VII.

them, not on their absolute presence or absence. In general, a pathological syndrome may be considered to be the adjustive aspect of a mode of organization of the personality system which has developed a sufficient investment in internal mechanisms of defense so that the interest in their maintenance outweighs the cost in negative sanctions and deprivations incurred in the adjustive context.

The boundary where the facilities-achievement balance is the primary one is, we suggest, the focal point of what is ordinarily called the paranoid-schizoid group of pathological syndromes. The main clue to this is the prominence of cognitive mechanisms in the pathology of this area. Broadly, we suggest that the paranoid group have to do with the handling of an excess input of information (excessive relative to the capacities of the personality), which is extruded again, as it were, by the mechanisms of projection. This means that the internalized object system is not capable of coping with aspects of the situation which yet cannot be ignored.

The schizoid group, on the other hand, we feel, is characterized by the opposite, what is relatively, too little, input in this area. The personality has somehow built up defenses which inhibit the perception of error relative to the situation, and simply turns to predominantly narcissistic solutions of its problems, shutting out a large part of the external world to which normal people are sensitive. The extreme of course is the catatonic variety. These considerations would help to explain the extreme difficulty in the therapy of schizophrenics, since it is the input of new information, activating mechanisms of the perception of error, which starts a reorganization process going. Putting it somewhat differently, it is extremely difficult to impose the right order of meaningful frustration on a schizophrenic. We suggest further that "paranoid schizophrenia" may involve a cyclical alternation between the two modes of disturbance of balance in this area, leading to paranoid handling of the occasional break-through of otherwise excluded information.[32]

---

32. We would like to make clear that placing the focus of interpretation of the schizophrenic syndrome in the mechanisms of cognitive adjustment, and placing the critical period so late as the oedipal transition, is not incompatible with

The second boundary-process concerns the balance between reward-input and the cathexis of external objects, which is related to what, in the social context, we have called the activity-passivity dimension of deviance. We suggest that this is the focus of the "manic-depressive" group of pathological syndromes. The manic case is that of overcathexis of external objects and hence an excessive level of activity in the personality which cannot be sustained. The depressive case is that of the withdrawal of cathexis and a very low level of activity. These, more than the others, seem to be linked in a pattern of cyclical alternation, so that manic-depressive psychosis is a familiar clinical entity. They can, however, appear independently, particularly in the case of depression, and they are certainly different states of the personality system.

Finally, third, the input balance of internal reward as involving expressive communication mechanisms may be said to be the focus of the two familiar syndromes usually called "psychopathic personality" and "compulsion neurosis" or compulsive personality respectively. We associate this area with integration of the personality as a system and the patterns of social deviance we have called alienation and compulsive conformity. We think that the case of psychopathic personality involves the inability to tolerate the restrictions imposed by certain internalized patterns in the normal personality, which precisely are those which have internalized the value-patterns of the social system. The mechanisms of defense, like repression and those clustering about it, do not operate effectively and, therefore, the only way to handle tension is to "act out." The

---

the common psychiatric view that very primitive phantasies are central in the actual content of schizophrenic pathology. Indeed, we think this fits with our interpretation. We have held that the critical initiating factor was the blocking of cognitive input, the assimilation of which would be necessary for adequate growth of the personality. This, then, throws ego back on the "regressive" alternative in the solution of his adjustment problem (as distinguished from the "precocious" one —cf. Chap. III). Narcissistic gratification of his more primitive motive systems, precisely the ones which in normal development are destined for extinction and repression, is, therefore, his principal recourse. More generally, it is very important in relation to any pathological syndrome to distinguish between the boundary-process which is the focus of the adjustment-difficulty, and the "structure of the system," the content of the latency cell. We think that in the literature, classificatory criteria are sometimes drawn from one source, sometimes from the other, without making the distinction clear.

"compulsive" personality, on the other hand, is subject to too "tight" an integration; his personality is rigid and not capable or normal levels of flexible adjustment because of the threat to this integration. The psychopath is too susceptible to expressive communication focussing cathectic interests on the integrative significance of external objects, the compulsive not sufficiently susceptible.

It is perhaps significant that Freud's early insights were particularly concerned with the compulsive type. Here we would assume that the mechanisms of negative ego-integration, namely, repression and its associates, would be most prominent. This then would be a particularly favorable vantage point for studying the problem of the "unconscious."

In the present state of knowledge of this field in general, and of the development of our conceptual scheme and of its working out in the personality field, any such classification as the above must remain highly tentative. All we can say is that this seems to put a more meaningful order into the relations between the principal clinical syndromes of psychopathology than any other basis of classification with which we are familiar. Validation will require an immense amount of work in this, as in many other fields.

We will attempt to make only one further suggestion here, for development on some other occasion. The problems of etiology of these conditions are certainly complex, but we feel that the suggested classification just reviewed, combined with the considerations brought forward in the last chapter about the relation of problems of strain and input-output to the time-sequence of the developmental process, are at least worthy of serious attention because of their possible implications in this direction.

We suggested in Chapter III that the conformity-alienation problem was the most critical one in the very first phase of socialization. If this is correct, then psychopathic and compulsive types would presumably have the sources of their difficulties concentrated in the early relationship to the mother. The activity-passivity problem then was associated particularly with the second major phase-cycle, the development of the mother-child love relationship. We would expect the etiology of manic-depressive disorders to depend particularly on events at this stage. Finally, the informational input problem we held was most acute at the oedipal phase. We would therefore expect the paranoid-schizoid types to have undergone particular severe strain in this period. The established clinical association between paranoia and homosexuality fits with this interpretation.

Figure 5 give a schematic representation of this classification of pathological syndromes. The plus sign in each of the three cells (excepting L) means that the critical problem around which the primary adjustive mechanisms are organized is the

FIGURE 5

The Principal Pathological Syndromes

	A		G
Decisive Crisis: Oedipal Phase	+ Paranoia — Schizophrenia	+ Mania — Depression	Decisive Crisis: Anal Phase
	Internal Object-Motive Structure Impeding "Normal" Adjustment (System of Defenses)	+ Compulsion Neurosis — Psychopathic Personality	Decisive Crisis: Oral Phase
	L		I

Critical "Problem"   + = Excessive Input   — = Insufficient Input   in relevant category

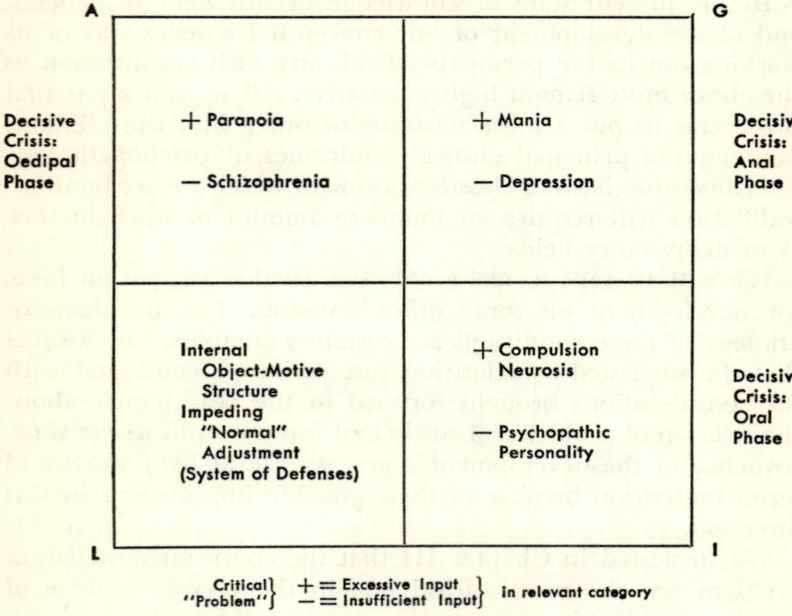

handling of what, relative to the internal object-motive structure indicated in the latency cell, is the capacity of the personality system. Thus, in the paranoid case information will be pressed on the personality which can only be handled through the pathological mechanism of projection. In the schizoid case, on the other hand, and this is general where the sign is minus, the system of defenses necessitates exclusion of information which would be necessary for normal adjustment. We have also indicated in the margins what we think is the period of socialization in which the decisive crisis probably occurred for each case.

We may, finally, attempt to spell out just a little what we feel to be the kind of analysis which can be made of this process of determination of pathological tendencies at each of the critical stages. First, we maintained (in Chap. III) that the problem of the first major phase was the establishment of the order of integration which is given with a genuinely internalized object-system. This was a matter of getting the organic need system under control. But it is control in the sense of integration of a system, *not* of suppression of the units of which it is composed, and therefore there is an optimum level of this integration.

We have suggested that the compulsive personality is one characterized by too rigorous a control, the psychopath by too loose a control. If our hypotheses, both about the crucial time and about the crucial class of input are correct, the primary foci are on the relation to the mother in the first year or two of life, and on the input of integrative control through expressive communication. The compulsive tendency, then, would be derived from what was, *relative* to the needs and capacities of the organism (it must be remembered that these will vary independently of culture and family structure) too severe frustration. While initial frustration may be too severe, we suggest that the critical thing is over-denial of reciprocity at the phase of internalization itself. Perhaps relatively strong support must be assumed in order to account for strong internalization. The effect would be, according to the principles we have used above, overcathexis of the internalized object. This points to the relatively strict and severe, but basically loving mother. Psychopathy, on the other hand, should be associated, perhaps with relatively little initial deprivation, but still more with too strong a reciprocity; i.e. too little contrast between the supportive and the denial phases, so that cathexis is drained away from the internalized object to the situational mother or rather the segmental gratifications she controls. This points to a rather "laissez-faire" and indulgent mother, who tends to gratify ego's wishes as they arise without presenting a strong object for identification.[33]

The second main stage is that of the fission of the original internalized mother-child identity to form the two-unit personality system of what we have called "dependency" and "autonomy" need-dispositions. This is the phase during which the "anal" crisis occurs. We suggest that the critical input in this case is that of support. The manic case is likely to be the one who has been "oversupported" at this stage, relative of course to the other components of an optimum balance. He would be likely also to have remained underfrustrated. This is the overdependent child with a weak autonomy motive; he is compulsively in need of gratifications but little motivated even to the reciprocation which is possible to a child of that age, in terms of his own love-motive. This points to what is often called the "overprotective" mother. In the case of tendency to depression, on the other hand, we suggest undersupport at this stage as the critical input defect; often, probably, combined with overfrustration. This leads to too rapid development of the autonomy need, but it is insecure because it does not meet adequate reciprocation from the mother. This type of child wants to love but is afraid of rejection and tends to repress or otherwise erect defenses in this area. He thus tends to become compulsively independent. The case points to the underprotective mother, the one who pushes her child too hard and too early to "stand on his own feet."

Finally, the paranoid-schizoid pair, we suggest, are particularly related to the oedipal crisis. Here for the first time the relation to the father is of *direct* central importance. The critical problem is that of the informational input and its relation to the reactions to frustration. The paranoid type is, we think, likely to have been, relatively to his capacities so far, excessively frustrated by the withdrawal of too large a proportion of earlier rewards and the holding up of a father-object too drastically different from the mother he has been attached to. Then her support is not sufficient to build a bridge to the adequate posi-

---

33. It is our suggestion that the genesis of the psychopathic personality comes the closest which is possible to the behaviorist's picture of the process of personality development; namely, the progressive conditioning of discrete primary drives without reference to their integration into a system.

tive cathexis of the new father object. It points to a parental relationship in which there is too wide a gap between the roles of the two parents and not an adequate relation of solidarity between them. The case of the "authoritarian" father, perhaps particularly as combined with the submissive mother as in the "classical" German family pattern, comes to mind.[34]

The schizoid case, on the other hand, involves too little new information and resultant frustration, so that there is not sufficient shaking up of the old system and hence a tendency to fixate on it. This is related, we suggest, to an insufficient differtiation of the roles of the parents, so that there are not adequate cues for the critical discrimination. It could be associated with an excessively dominant mother combined with a "Milquetoast" father, or it may involve a father who is remote and inaccessible —such as some American middle class fathers tend to be—leaving the mother alone in charge of the field. We are aware that this sketch of possible hypotheses about pathogenesis is at best a mere beginning. We have entirely failed to take up the sequence of probable influences which would flow from socialization in a given *type* of family structure, or to attempt to trace the ramifications of what we have treated as the critical source of strain through the personality. We have gone even this far only to make our suggestions a little less baldly speculative than they would be without any illustration, and to suggest possible directions of work in further codification and in new research, which cannot be followed out within the limits of this chapter.

Essentially the same general kind of analysis would, we feel, be fruitful in attempting to work out a classification of normal personality types. Here, however, the primary focus would be on differences in the value-system aspects of the social objects which have been internalized. We cannot attempt to carry out this analysis here, but the reference points worked out in these last three chapters should help in making progress in this important problem area.

---

34. Cf. E. H. Erikson, "Hitler's Imagery and German Youth" in Kluckhohn & Murray, *Personality in Nature, Society & Culture,* 1948 edition, pp. 485-510.

CHAPTER V

Role Differentiation
in Small Decision-Making Groups

BY ROBERT F. BALES
AND PHILIP E. SLATER

Introduction

One important aspect of the social organization of groups which endure over any considerable time is the fact that usually roles within the organization are differentiated from each other. The members of the organization possess a common culture, part of which consists of the expectations they have developed as to how each person will behave. When roles are differentiated, overt acts of certain qualities are expected of certain persons at certain times, while overt acts of other qualities are expected of other persons at other times. Furthermore, there is some permanence in the expectations which apply over extended time periods.

In a more general sense, however, one can think of "differentiation" as a process of development by which such a constellation of roles comes to be recognizable. Presumably, high degrees of differentiation generally trace back to more simple beginings. There may even be a kind of "evolutionary tree"—

a branching process of development in which certain divisions or differentiations are not only primary in time for a given group, but also functionally more fundamental, and so likely to be similar from one type of group to another.

In the present chapter we report certain data on differentiation between members in small decision-making groups.[1] The degree to which differentiated roles in the fully developed structural sense appear in these small decision-making groups is perhaps a moot point. Certainly some of the characteristics are present in some of the groups. On the other hand, data on certain aspects, particularly direct measures of expectations are not available for this study. Expectations in the present analysis are inferred from consistencies in overt behavior, consensus in ratings, and congruence between behavior and received ratings. Furthermore, the time periods involved are short, so that the degree of permanence is relatively slight.

But in any case, degrees of complexity, clarity, and permanence are surely relative matters. The aim of the present analysis is to catch role-differentiation "in the making" from some minimal level, in the hope that the character of the minimal phenomena may give clues as to very general forms and reasons for development of role differentiation. We hope that a study of the most general aspects of differentiation in small groups through microscopic time spans can provide a useful conceptual model for understanding role differentiation on a more complex structural level.

The Experimental Setting and the Sample

A number of other reports have preceded this one.[2] The sample used for the present study overlaps in part with that used in previous studies, but not completely. The cases used for

1. The research was facilitated by the Laboratory of Social Relations at Harvard University, and completed with funds from The RAND Corporation, Santa Monica, California.

2. Robert F. Bales, *Interaction Process Analysis, A Method for the Study of Small Groups* (Cambridge, Mass.: Addison-Wesley Press, 1950).

Robert F. Bales, "A Set of Categories for the Analysis of Small Group Interaction," *American Sociological Review,* Vol. 15, No. 2 (April, 1950), pp. 257-263.

Robert F. Bales and Fred L. Strodtbeck, "Phases in Group Problem Solving," *Journal of Abnormal and Social Psychology,* Vol. 46, No. 4 (October, 1951), pp. 485-495.

the present study are part of a larger series that will include groups of sizes two to seven inclusive, four groups of each size, each group meeting four times. The present sample consists of four 3-man groups, two 4-man groups, four 5-man groups, and four 6-man groups, or fourteen separate groups. Each group was observed through four sessions, making a total of fifty-six sessions.

All of the groups in this sample were composed of paid male undergraduates at Harvard, recruited through the student employment office. Every effort was made to insure that none of the subjects knew one another, but there were a few pairs where this condition was not met. The subjects were not introduced to each other by name, and no leader was appointed by the experimenter. The aim was to start the members on as equal a footing as possible, and leave them to solve all of their problems of social organization by themselves. We wanted to observe the development of role differentiation from some minimum starting point.

The task given to each group was the same. They were told we were interested in group discussion and decision-making, and that the physical facilities had been designed to make our observations as easy as possible. Microphones were pointed out, the subjects were told a sound recording would be made, and that they would be observed from an observation room divided from the discussion room by a one-way mirror, in order to avoid distracting them with observers. Each subject was given a five page written summary of facts about an administrative problem of the sort familiar in college case discussion courses. They were asked not to show these summaries to each other. The summaries

Robert F. Bales, Fred L. Strodtbeck, Theodore M. Mills, and Mary Roseborough, "Channels of Communication in Small Groups," *American Sociological Review,* Vol. 16, No. 4 (August, 1951), pp. 461-468.

Robert F. Bales, "Some Statistical Problems of Small Group Research," *Journal of the American Statistical Association,* Vol. 46, No. 255 (September, 1951), pp. 311-322.

Robert F. Bales, "The Equilibrium Problem in Small Groups," Chapter IV, in T. Parsons, Robert F. Bales, and E. A. Shils, *Working Papers in the Theory of Action* (Glencoe, Ill.: Free Press, 1953). Hereinafter this study is referred to as *Working Papers.*

C. M. Heinicke and Robert F. Bales, "Developmental Trends in the Structure of Small Groups," *Sociometry,* Vol. 16, No. 1 (February, 1953), pp. 7-38.

were collected after they had been read by the subjects individually.

The subjects were asked to consider themselves as members of the administrative staff of the central authority in the case. They had been asked by their superior to consider the facts and return a report to him which would give their opinion as to why the persons involved in the case were behaving as they did, and their recommendation as to what he should do about it. They were to take forty minutes for the discussion, and in the final one or two minutes to dictate their decisions for the sound record. They were asked for a "group decision" without further specification as to what this meant or how they were to arrive at it.

The host experimenter left the room at this point, taking the written case with him. The discussion was recorded and the interaction observed by Bales' set of categories.[3] At the end of the session the host experimenter returned and the subjects filled out a questionnaire which included the following questions:

(a) Who contributed the best ideas for solving the problem? Please rank the members in order. *Include yourself.*

(b) Who did the most to guide the discussion and keep it moving effectively? Please rank the members in order. *Include yourself.*

(c) How well did you personally like each of the other members? Rate each member on a scale from 0 to 7, where zero means "I feel perfectly neutral toward him," and seven means "I like him very much."[4]

Each group met four times at intervals of one week, in order to get a sample of developmental trends. Four similar cases were used, given in a rotated order from group to group in a latin square design in order to compensate for differences in the case material. The questions above were answered at the end of each of the four sessions. At the end of the fourth session an additional question was asked:

(d) Considering all the sessions, which member of the group would you say stood out most definitely as a leader in the

---

3. Described in detail in Robert F. Bales, *Interaction Process Analysis, op. cit.*

4. A different form of question was used for the earlier part of the sample, but both forms were reduced to rank order of liking for the present study.

discussion? How would you rank the others. *Include your-self.*

Overt and Latent Aspects of Differentiation

It is worth pointing out that the methods of measurement chosen rest on certain preconceptions about the nature of differentiation. The measures are of two general kinds, first, measures of overt behavior, the social interaction and, second, measures of certain attitudes of members toward each other which the subjects report in writing to the experimenter. In choosing to make both types of measurement we assume in the very beginning that a fundamental aspect of differentiation is a differentiation between overt behavior and underlying attitude.

It is impossible, of course, to avoid all beginning assumptions. There may be some readers, however, who would prefer to avoid making the particular assumptions we make. For this reason it seems desirable to start on a very concrete level and show how the assumptions seem to arise as one tries to think consistently about the problem. This section is an attempt to present, in a developmental manner, some of the basic assumptions underlying the measures used.

Let us start with the simple observation that for any single organism which can be said to "behave" or "act" (including subhuman animals) a *range* of characteristic types of overt behavior will be observed, not simply one type. As one continues to observe, the organism will be seen in time to change its behavior from one of its characteristic types to another. For example, an animal may hunt, eat, sleep, wake, yawn, and so start the cycle again. Time is required for the organism to go through its complete repertoire. It is impossible for the organism to behave in all its characteristic ways at once. The potentiality for the complete range, given the appropriate environment, is somehow retained and carried by the organism through time, but at any given time most of the potentialities are latent and only one or a few are in active execution.

It requires the physical "facilities" of the organism (activation of neural pathways, muscles, organs, etc.) to put one of its potentialities into overt action. As compared to the requirements of the complete range of potentialities, the physical resources of the organism within a given short span of time are always limited. All behavior has an "economic" aspect in this sense. Within a given small span of time behavior involves the selection of a given alternative from a larger range of potentialities and an allocation of limited resources to the selected alternative. The constriction of resources in this fundamental sense may be said to force a differentiation in the quality of activity in time. It thus becomes possible for the observer of even a single organism to distinguish a series of types of activity, and to note that the type changes with time. This is a general and fundamental aspect of differentiation.

The constriction of time resources for activity holds also for the organization of activity which appears when a number of persons interact with each other. This is especially obvious in small discussion groups where persons take turns in talking so that when one talks the others keep silent (or nearly so). If the communication is to be successful each member must spend some time listening as well as talking. While a given person is listening his tendencies to talk must be held latent, at least to a large degree. The range of potentialities for action is distributed among different individuals. Hence, if a social group is to achieve an organization of activities so that even the major tendencies have a chance to issue into overt action the activity must not only be distributed in time but also must be distributed among members. This is a second very general and fundamental aspect of differentiation.

In social systems the members do not only "act" individually vis-à-vis the physical environment. They "interact" vis-à-vis each other and communicate. They attempt (at least part of the time) to make their activity "add up to," or "refer to" something they want to achieve or keep in common. We recognize here a third major type of constriction—the condition that the series of acts should have some kind of "connectedness" or "consistency," that they should either "fit in" to an existing state of affairs considered desirable to maintain, or else "get somewhere" in modifying the existing state of affairs in some desired direction.

But the acts will not add up to anything the members *know they have in common* unless each attempt to communicate or each proposal for an addition to the common stock is "reacted to" by one or more of the others. The consistency can not be maintained over any long period unless actions are acknowledged by reactions, and unless actions and reactions somehow "hang together" in relation to some concept held in common. This is a fourth type of constriction in behavior systems; namely, that one-way communication is typically not enough, and that some time must be diverted to acknowledgment, that is, communication about how the overt behavior of one member fits with the attitude of the other.

"Action by one person" followed by "Reaction of the other" appears to be about the simplest possible set of categories which recognizes any differentiation in the total process of a system of social activities at all. But it will be noticed that this set of two categories is already fairly complex. At least three aspects of differentiation are implicity recognized: (a) a differentiation in *time* of occurence; (b) a differentiation in *who performs* the activity; and (c) a differentiation in *quality* or type of activity.

But if these are aspects of social differentiation on the overt level of behavior, it must make sense to ask: of *what entity or unity* are they differentiations? The observer who claims he can make these distinctions must have some concept or frame of reference in terms of which the differentiated parts or aspects are supposed to be related to each other. He assumes that overt acts which appear do have something in common, namely, common membership in some larger class of events, of which they are each a part. We can call this larger class of events, classed in the mind of the observer, the *concept of a social interaction system.* At minimum the acts are two, the persons performing them are two, and the number of time units involved are two. In general the observer feels impelled to regard the events as interrelated because he intuitively feels or "perceives" (rightly or wrongly) that the two persons involved each see the acts as interrelated in roughly the same way that he, the observer, does.

The observer assumes that the two persons have a "common concept"—at least one common concept, but typically, of course, a great many. This common concept is latent, that is to say, the concept is not the same as the present overt activity as such, but an internal process in the mind of each which each assumes to be sufficiently similar to the process going on in the mind of the other to be called "common." The overt acts "refer to," "express," "symbolize" as well as "constitute" parts of an interrelated system because of the fact that they have relevance for, that is, an effect upon, the common concept. We have many words which refer to various aspects of that which is common—common meaning, common values, common goals, common fate, common definition of the situation, common norms, common culture, etc. Differentiation implies some common latent base, out of which, or with reference to which the more differentiated state develops. Thus the complete social interaction system includes both a latent aspect and an overt, or manifest, aspect. The concepts "Action by one person" followed by "Reaction of another" imply a fourth aspect of differentiation in addition to the three mentioned above; namely, (d) a differentiation between that which is *overt* during some small time span, and that which is latent.

In the next section we shall describe some characteristics of overt interaction, how it is differentiated in quality, and how its quality changes in time, as observed in the present sample. In the following sections we shall examine the relation of overt interaction to the ratings subjects give each other. The ratings are reports by the subjects of their attitudes. The attitudes themselves are, by comparison with overt behavior, latent.

Differentiation in Overt Interaction

The method used to observe and classify interaction starts with the assumption outlined above, that probably the simplest possible set of categories we can imagine involves: (a) a discrimination in *quality* or type of activity (at least the distinction of "overt action" and "no overt action"); (b) a discrimination in *who performs* the activity; and (c) a discrimination in *time* of occurrence.

If these discriminations are taken as the starting point, perhaps the next step in refinement consists in the development of a finer qualitative classification. We wish to make further distinctions which will reduce the degree of abstraction and include more information.[5] Figure 1 shows a set of categories for the classification of acts of communication which have been developed with

---

5. The further distinctions involved are best described in *Working Papers* pp. 194-202, where it is shown that they are essentially the distinctions made by Parsons' "pattern variables."

criteria of this sort in mind. It is still a highly schematic classification system, but is believed to be logically exhaustive at its own level of abstraction. There are four major sections of qualitative

FIGURE 1

A: Positive Reactions	1. Shows solidarity, raises others' status, jokes, gives help, reward
	2. Shows tension release, shows satisfaction, laughs
	3. Agrees, shows passive acceptance, understands, concurs, complies
B: Problem Solving Attempts	4. Gives suggestion, direction, implying autonomy for other
	5. Gives opinion, evaluation, analysis, expresses feeling, wish
	6. Gives orientation, information, repeats, clarifies, confirms
C: Questions	7. Asks for orientation, information, repetition, confirmation
	8. Asks for opinion, evaluation, analysis, expression of feeling
	9. Asks for suggestion, direction, possible ways of action
D: Negative Reactions	10. Disagrees, shows passive rejection, formality, withhold help
	11. Shows tension increase, asks for help, withdraws "Out of Field"
	12. Shows antagonism, deflates others' status, defends or asserts self

types: Questions (Categories 7,8,9), Problem Solving Attempts[6] (Categories 4,5,6), Positive Reactions (Categories 1,2,3), and Negative Reactions (Categories 10,11,12). Each section in turn is sub-divided into three types. Each of these types in turn sub-sumes a great multiplicity of sub-types.[7]

The distinction of who performs the act is made by identification numbers assigned arbitrarily to the subjects. An apparatus has been constructed which provides a paper tape moving horizontally, over which the vertical list of categories is placed. An action is recorded by writing down on the moving paper tape an identification number designating the person speaking, followed by a number designating the person spoken to. The score is placed on the tape in a vertical position which indicates the category of the act. The time order is provided automatically by the horizontal order of scores. The behavior unit scored is a single simple sentence of verbal communication or its non-verbal equivalent as understood by the observer. The scoring is continuous. Every act which occurs is thus classified as to its quality, who performed it, toward whom, and when.

Let us first examine the way in which the quality of an act is related to its place in a time order. When the observations are kept in time sequence and identified by author, as described above, one can easily identify each place in the time series where the authorship of the activity changes. Acts which occur immediately after a preceding act by a *different* author we call "Reactions." When the author of the present act was also the author of the preceding act, we call the act a "Proaction." Interaction consists of one or a series of Proactions by one person followed by the Reaction of a different person. If the same person continues to talk after his first Reaction, his next act becomes Proactive. Thus the classification of action by time position changes from Reactive to Proactive as the same person continues. It changes from Proactive to Reactive as the authorship changes hands.

---

6. In previous publications called "Attempted Answers." The change is made here to make the exposition easier to follow. "Problem Solving Attempts" will be considered to consist of both "Initial Attempts" and "Attempted Answers to Questions."

7. An extensive breakdown of further subtypes will be found in *Interaction Process Analysis*, Appendix, Definitions of Categories, pp. 177-195.

Figure 2 shows how the *quality* of activity tends to differ according to this basic positional division. The data are obtained from all the men in eight five man groups through four sessions each.[8] Groups and individuals differ in detail, but the general tendencies seem to be clear. Proactions (as defined by time position)

FIGURE 2

*How the First Act Differs From Later Acts
of the Same Contribution*

(Proactive and Reactive Percentage Rates in Each Category of Interaction. Based on 8,881 Proactions and 15,300 Reactions from 8 five-man groups, 4 sessions each.)

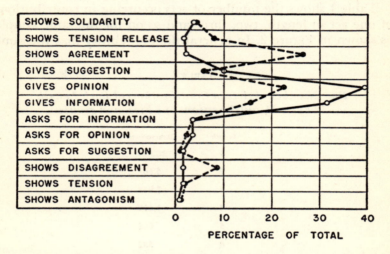

[The first act when a person begins a message is often a positive or negative reaction to what the other has said, as indicated by the dotted line. If he then continues speaking he tends to shift to problem solving attempts, as shown by the solid line.]

are heavily concentrated in the Section of Problem Solving Attempts. In other words, as a person continues to talk he tends to specialize in the task area of activity, giving opinions, citing facts, making inferences, presumably building out a more or less logical argument or connected series of acts, of which a suggestion is a logical termination.

8. Data are not available for the total sample, because of the labor required by this kind of analysis. The eight five-man groups include the four used in the present sample, along with four run previously under only slightly different conditions.

Reactions (as defined by time position) differ markedly in qualitative specialization from Proactions. Reactions are specialized particularly in showing agreement, disagreement, and tension release, and possibly to a minor degree in showing solidarity, antagonism, and tension. Acts in the reactive position are (relatively) low in Problem Solving Attempts. Of the Questions, only asking for orientation is as frequent in the reactive position as in the proactive position.

In view of the marked changes in quality as the authorship of activity changes hands it is interesting to inquire: How long on the average does a given member "hold the floor"?

Table 1 shows the number of acts occurring in contributions of one act in length, two, three and so on for the same sample as shown in Figure 2. In general the probability that the same

TABLE 1

*Raw Number of Acts in Contributions of Each Length
32 Forty Minute* Sessions of 8 Five-man groups*

Length	Observations
1	10,739
2	5,667
3	2,945
4	1,693
5	868
6	562
7	377
8	280
over 8	647
Total	23,778

*Each session equated for time.

person will continue for another act drops with each succeeding act in his sequence and, in the situation we report here, quite rapidly.

If there were only chance connections between one act and the next it would be as likely at each act that a given man would stop speaking as that he would go on. A chance model can be constructed on this assumption. From the numbers in Table 1 the observed probability after each act that the man already speaking will continue can be constructed and compared with the chance model just mentioned. This comparison is shown in Table 2.

TABLE 2

Number of Instances in which Runs Longer than a Given Length Occur, Compared to a Chance Model

Runs Longer Than:	Raw Numbers		Percentage (Probability)	
	Observed	Model	Observed	Model
0	23778	23778	100.00	100.00
1	13039	11889	54.84	50.00
2	7372	5945	31.01	25.00
3	4427	2972	18.62	12.50
4	2734	1486	11.50	6.25
5	1866	743	7.85	3.12
6	1304	372	5.49	1.56
7	927	186	3.90	.78
8	647	93	2.72	.39

It is evident that in general the runs or lengths of contributions are longer than would be expected by chance. Differences between the two curves, tested on a non-cumulative basis with a Chi-Square goodness-of-fit test are significant at far beyond the .001 level. By reference back to Figure 2 it can be seen that when a man does continue (a Proaction) after his first act (a Reaction) the probability is very high that the quality of his activity will fall in the area of Problem Solving Attempts. One would suppose that in verbal communication the demands of logic are such that in order to make a connected inference or argument, more than a single act in succession will often be required. The demand for connectedness thus gives rise to contributions, not only longer than chance runs, but at the same time so long that any tendency to balance each act of problem solving quality immediately with one of reactive quality must be to some degree postponed or inhibited.

And yet in the long run there does seem to be some tendency to balance each act of problem solving quality with one of reactive quality. When all of the acts of each of the twelve types are added together for a large number of groups, without regard to who performed them, or in what order, an interesting pattern of rates appears. The raw numbers and percentage rates are shown in Table 3.

TABLE 3

Observed Total Raw Numbers of Acts and Percentage Rates in each category of Interaction, Twenty-four Groups, Sizes 2 to 7, in 96 Meetings

Qualitative Category	Raw Numbers	Percentage Rates
1	2458	3.4
2	4295	6.0
3	11886	16.5
4	5705	8.0
5	21595	30.1
6	12855	17.9
7	2535	3.5
8	1720	2.4
9	755	1.1
10	5592	7.8
11	1916	2.7
12	526	.7
Total	71838	100.1

It will be seen that the total number of problem solving attempts (categories 4,5,6 . . . giving suggestion, opinion, and orientation) add to 56 percent, or slightly over one half the grand total, leaving 44 percent for questions and acts of a reactive quality. Yet we know from the data on lengths of runs reported above that there are many instances in which the runs are so long that the balancing, if any, can not take place immediately. It must take place, if at all, at some other specialized sub-period in the interaction, during which reaction follows reaction rapidly, with only minor intervention of proactions. Empirically we observe that sequences like this typically do occur, particularly toward the end of sessions, in periods of protracted joking and laughing.

The fluctuation of quality of action by sub-periods within meetings, and the final balance of rates at the end of meetings, suggest that the members feel that Problem Solving Attempts on the part of one member require an adequate Reaction by some other in order to reach a satisfactory "closure" or sense of completion. The reaction may be postponed, or suppressed, to allow the proposer to build an argument, or for other reasons, but sooner or later it tends to appear. A final period of joking and laughing at the end of a session does much to build up the total rate of low participators, and to increase the final rate of positive reactions, which may have fallen low in the heat of the discussion. There appears to be something underlying the observed overt behavior which has a continuity and persistence through time. It seems to act something like an "accounting system" which takes account of deficits and surpluses that appear within given small time spans, and acts in such a way as to tend toward restoration of certain balances in quality and distribution of action among members over longer time spans. In other words, the act, or series of acts, that occurs in a small time span is like a differentiated part of some longer or more inclusive whole.

We may hypothetically identify this "something underlying the overt process" as the latent state of the total system, i.e., the attitudes, values, goals, expectations, inhibited affects, etc., which exist as internal processes in the minds of the members. We assume that the observed balances of rates appear as an end result of members going through many short series of acts which somehow "make sense" to them as parts of a larger whole. In general it appears that "requirements of connectedness" tend to force a specialization in quality and authorship of activity by sub-periods in time. Coherent task oriented problem solving attempts require longer connected blocks of time than do reactions. Some reactions, on the other hand, such as laughing, typically occur simultaneously by all members with no mutual interference, and thus are economical of time. In general, however, the ability to inhibit, and thus "store" tendencies to act and react is fundamental to the time patterning of overt action.

The quality of overt participation of a particular member is thus presumably constrained, in part, by the way in which the things he would like to say or do "fits in" to a larger latent structure of ideas, feelings, and expectations as that structure develops over a long time span of interaction. What the particular member does overtly depends in part also on *when* in the time order he is able to enter the overt process, and upon *how long* he is able to "hold the floor." In so far as particular members of the group are restricted in the time at their command (for example by a felt lack of prestige relative to other members), they will tend to be forced toward activity of a reactive quality. Conversely, in so far as members do tend to specialize overtly in one way or another, others generalize from their behavior and develop expectations about future behavior. Thus further constraints are built into the latent state to affect overt behavior.

At this point in the analysis one can begin to see how the microscopic and general phenomenon of differentiation of acts by time and quality (which occurs for each single individual) may be related to the development of more permanent role differentiation by person. As the analysis proceeds it will be shown that the profile of overt activity of persons rated high on performance of task functions tends to approximate the "proactive" profile, whereas the person who is best liked, but not highest on task ratings emphasizes activities characteristic of the "reactive" profile.

Consensus in Subject's Ratings

Role differentiation in the fully developed sense rests on the existence of a culture common to the members of the system. The expectation members have as to the specialized roles each will perform are only a part of the common culture, but they constitute an important part of it. Possession of a common culture, in turn, implies some degree of *consensus*. There are degrees of consensus. All, or only some of the members of the system may have similar expectations. All may have similar expectations, but not yet "know" that they are similar. And so on, with many degrees of complication.

The existence of consensus, of whatever degree, of course does not imply that all members are necessarily expected to behave alike on the overt level. Indeed, when role differentiation develops the consensual expectation is precisely that the overt behavior of members will differ. The expectations are "common," "shared," "consensual," but the content of the expected overt performances are "different," "contrasting," perhaps "complementary." This is one of the fundamental paradoxes that has occupied social theorists from the very beginning of serious thought about the nature of social systems, particularly in relation to the division of labor.

The distinction is nicely illustrated in certain operations used in the present study for obtaining an "Index of Status Consensus" as described below. The content of the judgments subjects make of each other after a session asserts that a rank order of *differences* exists between members according to an evaluative criterion such as "who had the best ideas?" However, the subjects may make highly similar judgments and thus be in *consensus* as to the nature of the criterion and the relation of members to it. One would suppose that a certain degree of consensus in this sense is a precondition of the persistence or stability of a set of differentiated roles on the behavioral level. Conversely, it seems probable that a certain degree of congruence between the overt behavior of each member and the way others expect him to behave is a precondition of the stability of consensus.

In a previous study of developmental trends over four sessions,[9] it was found that groups differ markedly in the degree to which the members are in consensus as to the rankings they assign each other in response to questions asked at the end of each session. Perhaps this is due to the degree to which the subjects happen to hold common values, and hence have a common basis for evaluating each other. Possibly it is also a function of the amount of conflict arising in the course of the discussion. Whatever the underlying factors, the developmental trends in groups seem to differ according to the degree of consensus in rankings as determined at the end of the first meeting.[10] Groups high in status consensus at the end of the first meeting show a decline in status consensus at the end of the second meeting,[11] a trend which is reversed in the later meetings.

9. C. M. Heinicke and R. F. Bales, *op. cit.*, pp. 7-38.

10. *Ibid.*

11. This decline, while not statistically significant for the Heinicke and Bales sample, was significant at the .01 level for the groups now under consideration.

However, the status *order* remains substantially the same throughout the four meetings even though the degree of consensus about it undergoes a decline and recovery. In groups where the consensus in rankings is low at the end of the first meeting, high consensus is never achieved, and these groups tend to suffer constant turnover in the top ranks.[12]

What does this imply about the development of role differentiation? Does it imply that groups with low consensus are never able to discover or develop a common latent base in terms of which differentiation by person is acceptable and integrative in its end effect? This is one of the hypotheses suggested by the following analysis. In any case, the two types of groups show tendencies so different that we feel obliged to analyze them separately.[13]

The measure used to represent the agreement of a given set of rankings of members of each other is based on Kendall's "Coefficient of Concordance"[14] which he calls "W." It is obtained from a matrix of rankings, each individual (placed in vertical order on a series of rows) ranking each individual (placed in horizontal order on a series of columns). The formula follows:

$$W = \frac{12\,S}{m^2\,(n^3 - n)}$$

S equals the sum of the squares of the deviation of the column totals from the grand mean, and *n* equals the number of individuals ranked by *m* observers. In our rankings $n = m$, since everyone in the group ranks everyone including himself. When agreement is perfect, W is equal to one; when there is no agreement, W is equal to zero.

For our measure, W is obtained for rankings on questions (a) above ("Who had the best ideas") and separately for question (b), ("Who did the most to guide the discussion"), for each group. These two W's are then averaged, and the measure

---

12. *Ibid.*

13. This distinction was not made in the preliminary analysis reported in the *Working Papers,* and is undertaken here as an extension of that analysis.

14. M. G. Kendall, *Rank Correlation Methods* (London, 1948), pp. 160 ff. See also F. Kraüpl Taylor, "Quantitative Evaluation of Psycho-Social Phenomena in Small Groups," *Journal of Mental Science,* Vol. 97, No. 408 (October, 1951), pp. 690-717.

is called the "Index of Status Consensus." When the average index for a group for all four sessions is .500 or above, the group is classed High on status consensus. When the Index is below .500 the group is classed as Low.

Our sample breaks down as follows (each group runs four sessions):

High Status Consensus ($W > .500$)		Low Status Consensus ($W < .500$)
3 man	2 Groups	2 Groups
4 man	2 Groups	None
5 man	2 Groups	2 Groups
6 man	1 Group	3 Groups

The High groups are on the average a little smaller in size. On the basis of other data, we regard this as accidental, and do not suppose that this effect constitutes a serious bias in our present findings, but this question can be settled with certainty only when the design is completed.

Differentiation in Subject Ratings

Measures of how much a man talks and receives are obtained from the interaction records. Measures of how the members judge each other's ideas, guidance ability, and how much they like each other are obtained by questions after each meeting. A simple measure of the degree to which these measures may tap different aspects of differentiation can be obtained by asking the question: How many times do we find a rank one man on a given one of these characteristics who is not rank one on any other of the four remaining characteristics? A "specialist" might be considered to be a man who achieves isolated prominence in only one of these areas. Similarly, if there is any characteristic in which this kind of specialization occurs more often than in the others, this characteristic might be considered to identify an "axis" of differentiation. Table 4 presents relevant data.

The principal type of differentiation revealed in Table 4 is a *separation of the rankings on likes from the rankings on other measured characteristics.* Apparently there are more cases in which the best Liked man holds top ranking in only that one characteristic than cases of any other sort of isolated prominence.

TABLE 4

Number of sessions* out of a possible 56 in which a given person holds top position in one and only one rank order out of five possible rank orders

	High Groups 28 sessions	Low Groups 28 sessions	All Groups 56 sessions
Talking T	3.0	3.0	6.0
Receiving R	2.5	4.0	6.5
Ideas I	1.0	6.0	7.0
Guidance G	2.6	5.5	8.1
Liking L	9.0	13.8	22.8
Total	18.1	32.3	50.4

*The decimals arise from ties in rankings

For all groups, the difference between this characteristic and the others is significant at the .001 level, using a Chi-Square test. In the High groups alone, the difference is significant at the .01 level, in the low groups at the .001 level.

The probability that the person holding top position on one of the "task characteristics" (Idea and Guidance rankings) will be the same person who holds top position on the Like rank order appears to be higher in the first meetings than in any meeting following. One can calculate the percentage of cases in which the same man holds top position in both rank orders by sessions and find out whether there is a decrease. Data are shown in Table 5. The trend toward separation of top position on Idea rank order and being best Liked is significant at the .05 level, but the trend toward separation of Guidance and Likes is not.

TABLE 5

Percentage of cases in which the same man holds top position on Liked ranking and either Idea or Guidance Rankings at the same time, by sessions

Coincidence Between:	Sessions			
	1	2	3	4
Ideas and Likes	52.1	8.6	16.4	8.6
Guidance and Likes	34.3	25.0	12.1	23.6

Profiles of Idea Specialists
and Best Liked Men

This tendency for the best Liked man not to be the man chosen as having the best Ideas—a tendency which seems to increase over time—raises the question as to whether men of these two types, high on one characteristic but not on the other, will show congruent differences in overt behavior. The following procedure was followed for obtaining cases: (1) All sessions were eliminated in which ties for top rank occurred in either the Idea or the Like ranking. (2) All sessions were eliminated in which the best Liked man was also top man on the Guidance or Idea ranking. (3) The remaining 23 sessions constituted the sample. About two-thirds of the sessions in the sample are drawn from Low status consensus groups, and about two-thirds are drawn (in equal numbers) from five and six man groups. In most of the sessions the top man on the Idea ranking also holds top position on the Guidance ranking.

Table 6 shows the composite profiles in percentages of own

TABLE 6

*Composite Profiles of 23 top men on Idea ranking and
23 top men on Like ranking for the same sessions**

| Interaction | Initiated | | Received | |
Category	Idea Men	Liked Men	Idea Men	Liked Men
1. Shows Solidarity	4.19	4.79	2.90	3.68
2. Shows Tension Release	5.97	7.71	8.40	10.38
3. Shows Agreement	14.60	14.97	22.92	17.88
4. Gives Suggestion	8.66	5.68	6.14	6.36
5. Gives Opinion	31.30	27.20	26.28	28.86
6. Gives Orientation	17.90	17.91	15.24	13.73
7. Asks Orientation	3.66	3.43	2.78	3.01
8. Asks Opinion	2.39	2.73	2.00	1.98
9. Asks Suggestion	.98	1.58	.72	.33
10. Shows Disagreement	7.31	8.43	9.5	10.21
11. Shows Tension Increase	1.97	3.67	1.30	1.37
12. Shows Antagonism	1.07	1.90	1.74	2.21

*Differences between the two men were tested on the following sets of categories. Levels of significance are shown in parentheses:

Initiated: 1+2 (.05 level)
4+5 (.01 level)
10+11+12 (.05 level)

Received: 1+2 (.05 level)
4+5 (Not significant)
10+11+12 (Not significant)

initiated and received interaction for the twenty-three top men on the Idea ranking and for the twenty-three top men on the Like ranking obtained from the same sessions. Note that the man in the top Idea position is higher in giving suggestions and opinions whereas the man in the top Liked position is higher in giving and receiving solidarity and tension release. The Idea man seems to receive more agreement. The Liked man, perhaps somewhat paradoxically, shows more negative reactions although he does not receive significantly more. The Liked man also may be slightly higher than the Idea man in asking for opinion and suggestion. These differences may perhaps be best summarized by saying that the Idea man shows a concentration of activity in the task area, whereas the Liked man shows a concentration in the socio-emotional types of activity, both positive and negative.[15]

The problem of testing the significance of these differences is a vexed one, largely because of the problem of interdependence among the categories. The use of raw scores, which would minimize this effect, would be misleading, since the Idea man tends to both initiate and receive more interaction in absolute terms than the Best-Liked man. We have therefore resorted to performing correlated t-tests on individual percentage profiles. We assume that, since the tests were performed on only three groups of categories, comprising about half of the total, the dependence effect will not be too great. Although these tests do not directly test the differences in Table 6, which are based upon composite profiles of raw scores rather than means of individual percentage profiles, we assume that the differences are of the same order and the tests therefore relevant. The results of the tests are shown in Table 6.

15. A recent study by Richard Mann, based on two much larger samples of groups of the same kind as reported here shows that this general type of differentiation is not confined to those with the highest positions. A comparison of the position of a man on the two criteria of task ability and being liked yielded two types. Subjects who are evaluated by their peers as having a *higher* position on task ability than on being liked are found to have "giving suggestions" as significantly more characteristic of their behavior than the other type, whereas those subjects whose position on being liked is higher are found to have "showing tension release" as significantly more characteristic of their behavior. Unpublished honors thesis, Harvard College: *The Relation of Informal Status to Role Behavior in Small Discussion Groups.*

A different test of significance may be made by constructing an index for each man, based on his own raw profile, including all categories of action given and received, arranged to fit the actual differences between the different profiles. The numerator will include all categories in which the Idea man scored higher in the composite profiles than the Liked man, while the denominator will include all categories in which the Liked man scored higher than the Idea man. The higher the index for a given man, the closer he approaches the hypothetical Idea type. Using this method, the mean index for the twenty-three Idea men is .766, and for the twenty-three Liked men it is .597. The difference between these means is significant at the .01 level.

A simpler and less ad hoc index may be constructed for each man by placing in the numerator the raw number of positive reactions (Categories 1, 2, 3) he initiates, and in the denominator the raw number of task oriented attempts (Categories 4, 5, 6) he initiates. This index is the reverse of the other—the higher the index for a given man, the closer he approaches the hypothetical Liked type. Using this method the mean index for the Idea men is .458, and for the Liked men it is .582. The differences between these means is significant at the .01 level. That there are real differences in the quality of overt behavior between the men in these two status positions seems fairly clear from these findings.

In the present section we have found that of the several rankings examined the two which diverge from each other most markedly are the ranking on "who has the best ideas?" and the ranking on "how well do you like each of the other members?" On this basis two status types can be recognized. It has been shown that men occupying one of these status positions but not the other show significant and complementary differences between the types of overt behavior they tend to initiate and receive.

We are now in a position to note a fact which suggests that this type of differentiation is of more general significance. It was shown earlier in Figure 2 that the quality of behavior shifts markedly from the last act of the contribution of a given member (his Proaction) to the first act of the member who responds to his contribution (the Reaction of another). This is perhaps the most striking phenomenon of differentiation on the microscopic behavioral level.

The remarkable fact is that the behavior differences between the two status-types occur along the same axis of differentiation as that which distinguishes the Proactive Profile from the Reactive Profile. In other words the differentiation of activity that appears in the behavior of the *same* person, as he passes from the reactive to the proactive phase of his own participation in a microscopic time span is essentially the prototype of a more macroscopic differentiation in the activity of *two different* types of persons, as measured by the ratings of members of *each other* in post meeting reactions. This congruence between microscopic and macroscopic levels of differentiation suggests that the cause for this type of division may be common to behavior systems at several degrees of molarity, and is in this sense fundamental.

Interaction Between Specialists

The complementarity of the two patterns of behavior characteristic of the Idea man and the best Liked man strongly suggests that a good deal of interaction may take place directly between the members of this pair. They may, in some groups, constitute a dominant or central pair, supporting each other, and dividing between them the performance of the major activities necessary for the task accomplishment and social-emotional recovery of the group.

The study of pair relations within the group can become exceedingly complicated, and analysis of this kind is only beginning. However, in the present context it would be particularly interesting to know: (a) whether the Idea man and the best Liked man interact more with each other than with other members; (b) whether they agree more with each other than with other members; and (c) whether they are the top two interactors. These questions apply, of course, only to sessions where these two statuses are held by different members. Any differences between High and Low status consensus groups will be of particular interest.

Table 7 shows the results of such a study. All of the characteristics examined are in the expected direction, and all except

TABLE 7

Characteristics of Interaction between Top Ranking Men on Ideas (I) and Top Ranking Men on being Liked (L)

Characteristic of Interaction Observed	Percentage of cases in which characteristic occurred		Significance Level for High and Low Groups Combined
	High Groups	Low Groups	
I *interacted* with L more than he did with any other member	57.1	52.9	**
I *interacted* with L more than any other member interacted with L	64.3*	50.0	**
I *agreed* with L more than he did with any other member	57.1	44.1	*
I *agreed* with L more than any other member agreed with L	75.0**	44.1	**
L *interacted* with I more than he did with any other member	92.9***	47.1	***
L *interacted* with I more than any other member interacted with I	71.4**	32.4	*
L *agreed* with I more than he did with any other member	85.7***	44.1	***
L *agreed* with I more than any other member agreed with I	46.4	29.4	—
Percentage expected by chance	32.1	28.8	

Level of significance:

No asterisk: non significant
       * : .05
      ** : .01
     *** : .001

one are significant when the data for High and Low groups are combined. When the Low groups are examined alone, however, not one of the characteristics reaches the .05 level of significance. The High groups are markedly different. In these groups it is very characteristic that the best Liked man talks more and agrees more with the top ranking Idea man than he does with any other member. No other member is likely to talk as much to the Idea man as the best Liked does, but sometimes some other member may agree more with the Idea man than he does. Apparently, simply saying "yes" to the Idea man is not enough to make one best Liked. The Idea man on the other hand, talks more and agrees more with the best Liked man than any other member does typically, but does not confine his attention to the best Liked man, and sometimes talks and agrees with other members about as frequently as with the best Liked man.

The general picture is clear. In the groups with High Status consensus particularly, a heavy traffic of interaction passes between these two specialists, and it is of a generally supportive nature. In the Low status consensus groups there is some tendency in this direction, but the pattern in every respect is less clearcut and frequent. Inter-specialist support in overt interaction is a phenomenon associated most frequently with High status consensus.

One is led to expect, by the nature of the findings, that both specialists must generally be high interactors, perhaps the first and second high interactors in the group. The average Talking rank for Idea men in this sample is 1.6 (1.1 in the High groups), and for best Liked men 2.9 (2.6 in the High groups). The expectation thus holds better for the High groups than for the Low. However, there is also an indication that the best Liked man is third or lower in a fair number of cases, and thus may be interacting with the Idea man more frequently than his own interaction rank would warrant.

Activity, Task Status, and Liking

The fact that the qualitative difference between the Idea man and the Like man is the same pattern of difference that distinguishes the Proactive Profile from the Reactive Profile leads to an inference that quantity of participation is an important variable in producing the qualitative difference. It was shown earlier that Proactive runs tend to be markedly specialized in the task area, in giving orientation, opinion, and suggestion. It may be inferred that if a man, for any reason, prefers to specialize qualitatively in the task area and attempts overtly to do so, he will tend to make runs longer than chance. If he is permitted or encouraged to specialize in the task area, he will tend to make more such runs and so tend to build up his total amount of participation.

Should we expect, then, that a high ranking on total amount of participation would always be associated with a high ranking on Ideas, since a high ranking on Ideas is also associated with specialization in the task area? This conclusion would follow, perhaps, if overt attempts to specialize in the task area were always met with acceptance, and answered with agreement. But we know that this is not always the case. When a serious disagreement occurs, an argument often follows which tends to build up the sheer amount of participation initiated and received between two or three of the participants to a considerable degree, and yet one of them may have had no support from other members, and may come out far down on the rank order in the final judgment as to the quality of Ideas. Or the group may remain divided, and the consensus as to who had the best Ideas may be very low.

This line of reasoning suggests that in groups with Low status consensus we might expect a low degree of congruence between the amount of talking a given member does, and the final esteem in which his opinions and suggestions are held. In groups with a High status consensus, on the other hand, there may be a higher congruence, since, if a man receives agreement and is allowed to specialize in the task area, this tends to require more and longer periods of Proaction. To put the hypothesis most simply and crudely, it requires talks to communicate ideas, but sheer amount of talk does not guarantee acceptance. The relationship between amount of participation (both "Talking" and "Receiving") and the post-meeting ratings on Ideas, Guidance, and Liking are shown in Table 8.

Each of the mean correlations[16] for both High and Low status consensus groups is significant at the .01 level (using a correlated t-test) with the exception of the correlation of Liking with

16. The use of rank order correlations here involves serious statistical problems, due to the small sizes of our groups. Clearly, a *rho* drawn from a three-man group mean very little, and *rhos* from even the larger sizes are not too reliable. In dealing with this problem two different techniques were used: (a) Median values were computed; (b) Means based on the raw *rhos* of all but the three-man groups were computed. While these methods yield identical results, neither is entirely satisfactory, and we suggest that the reader accept these findings with reserve.

TABLE 8

Intercorrelations between Talking, Receiving, and ratings on Ideas, Guidance, and Liking. Mean rank order correlations of 40 sessions (size 3 excluded)

High Status Consensus Groups

		T	R	I	G	L
Talking	T	.90	.83	.73	.46	
Receiving	R		.76	.73	.55	
Ideas	I			.82	.46	
Guidance	G				.53	
Liking	L					

Low Status Consensus Groups

		T	R	I	G	L
Talking	T	.69	.36	.46	.10	
Receiving	R		.41	.49	.10	
Ideas	I			.77	.16	
Guidance	G				.18	
Liking	L					

the other four variables in the Low groups. In the groups with Low status consensus there is no significant correlation between how well a man is Liked and how much he Talks or Receives, or with ratings he receives from the other members on Ideas and Guidance. In the groups with High status consensus there is a tendency for Talking, Receiving, being judged high on Ideas and Guidance, and being well Liked, all to go together to some extent. But being well Liked is the least stable characteristic of this combination. Even in the High groups Liking tends to split off as a separate factor from the factor which combines the other four characteristics. The correlations in the Liking column are significantly lower than most of the correlations in the other columns.[17] In the Low groups the tendency for Liking to split off as a separate factor is accentuated to the extent that it no longer shows any significant correlations. Again the correlations in the Liking cluster are significantly lower than most of the other correlations.[18]

But in addition to this, another difference appears as the Low groups are compared to the High groups. In the High groups Talking, Receiving, Ideas, and Guidance are all highly intercorrelated, as if they tended to constitute a single factor. But in the Low groups, while Talking and Receiving are still highly correlated with each other, they are *not* highly correlated with ratings on Ideas and Guidance. In fact the correlations of both Talking and Receiving with Ideas are significantly lower than the correlation of Ideas with Guidance. But the correlation of Ideas and Guidance is still relatively high.[19]

---

17. To list the significant differences for the High groups: The correlation of Liking with Talking (LT) is lower than the following correlations at the noted level of significance: TR .01, IG .05, TI .01, RI .05, RG .05. The correlation of Liking with Receiving (LR) is lower than TR at the .05 level. The correlation of Liking with Ideas (LI) is lower than the following correlations at the noted levels of significance: TR .01, IG .01, TI .01, TG .05, RI .01, RG .05. The correlation of Liking with Guidance (LG) is lower than the following correlations at the noted level of significance: TR .01, TI .05. Thus of the twenty-four possible comparisons fourteen show a significant difference. In making these comparisons, the Link and Wallace procedures for setting allowances were used. See, R. F. Link, and D. L. Wallace, "Some Short Cuts to Allowances." Princeton University (unpublished).

18. To list the significant differences for the Low groups: The correlation of Liking with Talking (LT) is lower than the following correlations at the noted level of significance: TR .01, IG .01, RG .05. The correlation of Liking with Receiving (LR) is lower than the following correlations at the noted level of significance: TR .01, IG .01, RG .05. The correlation of Liking with Ideas (LI) is lower than the following correlations at the noted level of significance: TR .01, IG .01, RG .05. The correlation of Liking with Guidance (LG) is lower than the following correlations at the noted level of significance: TR .01, IG .01. In addition, the Low Groups show two more significant differences: TI is lower than IG at the .05 level, and RI is lower than IG at .05 level.

19. Parenthetically it may be noted that all of the correlations in the Low groups appear to be lower than those in the High groups. In itself not much is to be made of this, since the low groups are distinguished by the fact of low agreement between raters, which statistically is equivalent to low reliability of measures, which results in generally lower correlations. A series of t-tests shows that all of the differences between High and Low groups (including the Talking-Receiving correlations which are based upon interaction scores rather than ratings) are significant at the .05 level or better, with the single exception of the difference between the two Idea-Guidance correlations. Ratings on Ideas and Guidance thus display a fairly strong tendency to hang together even in the Low groups. This fact, along with

Thus in the Low status consensus groups there seems to be some tendency toward three separable factors. (1) Talking and Receiving hang together, but are not highly correlated with (2) Ideas and Guidance. (2) Ideas and Guidance tend to hang together, but are not significantly correlated with (3) Liking. (3) Liking in turn is not significantly correlated with (1) Talking and Receiving. This is the picture we were led to expect by the line of reasoning above. When status consensus is Low, sheer amount of Talking and Receiving is a poor index of the esteem in which a man's Ideas will be held, or how much he will be Liked.

The question may be raised as to whether one is justified in speaking of a specialization by particular persons on the basis of the rank order correlations presented in Table 8. Some additional light can be thrown on the problem by asking not whether the whole rank order of men on one characteristic is correlated with their rank order on another, but rather, what is the percentage of cases in which the *same particular person* in a given group holds top position in the rank order of men on each of two characteristics.

Data obtained in this manner are presented in Table 9. These data are obtained from the total sample (including three-man groups) of 14 separate groups, each through four sessions, or a total of 56 sessions. Those percentages which are significant (using a Chi-square test) are indicated by an asterisk.

The picture obtained by this method is similar to that of Table 8, but with certain interesting differences. The relation of Liking to the other variables still tends to be the lowest in both the High and Low status consensus groups, while the Task measures tend to be more highly interrelated.

But there tends to be less overall difference in Table 9 as compared with Table 8, between High and Low groups in the degree of interrelatedness. Guidance now shows a somewhat stronger tendency than the other characteristics to be associated with Liking in the High groups, while Liking now shows a stronger tendency to be associated with Talking and Receiving

other differences we have found between High and Low groups, many of which are unrelated to the correlations, leads us to believe that few of the differences between High and Low groups in role relationships are due to unreliability of Low group measures.

TABLE 9

*Percentage of Total Number of Sessions (56 sessions) in which
the Same Person holds Top Position in two rank
orders at the same time**

High Status Consensus Groups

		T	R	I	G	L
Talking	T		55.3*	69.6*	36.1	22.5
Receiving	R			46.4*	43.2*	33.2
Ideas	I				52.1*	27.5
Guidance	G					38.6
Liking	L					

Low Status Consensus Groups

		T	R	I	G	L
Talking	T		57.1*	39.3	42.9*	33.2
Receiving	R			26.8	39.3	40.4*
Ideas	I				55.3*	15.4
Guidance	G					8.9
Liking	L					

*Chance expectation for each cell is 24.6% for High Groups, and 22.5% for Low Groups. Those percentages significantly higher than this chance expectation, using a Chi-square criterion, are followed by an asterisk in the Tables.

in the Low groups. As in Table 8, Ideas is much less strongly associated with Talking and Receiving in the Low groups than in the High groups.

With the percentage coincidence method, as well as with the correlation method, Talking in the Low groups is associated with Receiving, and Ideas with Guidance to the same degree as in the High groups. This is another indication perhaps that differences between High groups and Low groups are not due to unreliability of Low group measures.

In the High groups, then, the man who receives the highest ratings on the performance of task functions (Ideas and Guidance) tends to be the same person who Talks and Receives most. In the Low groups this congruence tends to break down. More often there is a separate individual who Talks and Receives most but fails to achieve top rating on task ability. Apparently in the groups with Low status consensus we have a somewhat passive task specialist along with a more aggressive individual who fails to achieve highest task status. The task specialist in the Low groups is almost never best Liked—if anything the probability is below chance—while the more active participator achieves this position about one time out of three.

The Attribution of Leadership

How do the subjects in these groups conceive "Leadership"? It will be recalled that at the end of the last session the members were asked: "Considering all the sessions, which member of the group would you say stood out most definitely as a leader in the discussion? How would you rank the others? Include yourself." To investigate the relationship between "Leadership" and the five other measures we found the top man for all four sessions taken together, on each measure, and then found the percentage coincidence of top position on Leadership with top position on each of the five rank orders.

By this method it turns out that top position on Leadership coincides in 50.0 percent of the cases with top position on Talking, in 60.7 percent with Receiving, 59.3 percent with Ideas, 78.6 percent with Guidance, and only 14.3 percent with Liking.[20] The highest association is with Guidance.

Leadership might best be described as a generalized role. It is perhaps the most unspecialized and diffuse designation of high status that can be found in a small group situation. When members of a group designate a particular individual as "leader" in answer to a question such as the one above, that individual

---

20. These figures were subjected to a Chi-square test in the following manner: The raw coincidence figure for the Like role was tested against the total for Talking, Receiving, and Ideas combined. It was significantly lower at the .02 level. The figure for the Guidance role was also tested against difference at the .05 level. The High groups and Low groups were tested together, since no difference appeared between them.

is perhaps felt to possess those qualities which best serve to solve both the task and social-emotional problems of the group. Since different groups emphasize task and social emotional problems in varying proportions, the attribution of leadership will depend not only upon the choice of one person over another but also upon the differential stress placed upon these group problems by the group. The group problems might thus be conceived as factors, with weights assigned to them by the group according to some elementary kind of value consensus.[21] One group, e.g., might attribute leadership on the basis of, say, .7 task ability, .3 likeability; another might reverse the weights. Consensus on leadership attribution according to this notion would depend upon (a) the amount of group agreement upon the weights to be assigned (value consensus), and (b) the amount of group agreement upon ratings given each members on each factor (rating consensus). Leadership would thus be thought of as tending to "bridge the gap" among the more specialized roles, and perhaps also to "shift in time" being attributed now to one sort of specialist, now to another, according to the most pressing problems or the major values of the group.

The fact that Liking coincides so seldom with Leadership suggests that in our present sample Likeability is given a rather low weight, possibly because of the heavy task demands placed upon the group by the experimental situation. Among the task characteristics those that seem to coincide most often with Leadership show some signs of being the least specialized. Table 9 suggests that in the High groups at least, Guidance shows some tendency to bridge the gap in its degree of association with other measures, being associated most of the time with

---

21. We are indebted to Arthur Couch, Research Assistant in the Laboratory of Social Relations, for this conceptualization. There may well be other factors in addition to the two mentioned—the findings for the Low groups suggest amount of participation as a third.

A factor analysis by Couch and Carter of some nineteen different sorts of ratings of individuals made by observers of groups somewhat similar to those in this sample indicated three orthogonal factors: (1) a "group goal facilitation" factor which is probably similar to our variable of task ability; (2) an "individual prominence" factor which is probably similar to gross participation rate, and (3) a "group sociability" factor which seems very similar to our Likeability measure. See Launor F. Carter, "Leadership and Small Group Behavior," in M. Sherif, and M. O. Wilson, *Group Relations at the Cross Roads*, (New York: Harper & Bros., 1953), Chapter XI.

Ideas, but also fairly often with Liking. In the Low groups it is rather Receiving which seems to bridge the gap in this manner. Unfortunately there are too few cases to show any clear trend as yet, but we propose the tentative hypothesis that attribution of Leadership will tend to be associated with prominent performance of highly generalized rather than with highly specialized functions.

Personality Factors and Relations Between Specialists

The Low groups, according to the findings above, tend to be distinguished by a lack of fusion or congruence between amount of overt interaction of the given member and his rank on either Idea or Liking criteria. Furthermore, in the Low groups the fusion of status on Ideas and Likes is minimal. The Low groups tend to show a high degree of differentiation in these particular respects. On the other hand there is little evidence of "reintegration" as compared to the High groups. As we have seen in the examination of the interaction between specialists, the evidence of cooperation between members of the top pair is minimal in the Low groups. The differentiation in the Low groups appears not to rest on consensus, but on personality differences among members which impel them in different directions. We are thus led to propose a distinction between *consensual* differentiation and *de facto* differentiation.

If the Low groups are characterized by *de facto* rather than *consensual* differentiation one might hypothesize that they may be composed of members whose tendencies to specialize in particular kinds of behavior may be somewhat chronic, compulsive responses to personality needs rather than flexible responses to the needs of the particular group situation. They may be somewhat "rigid" in their perceptions, and "absolutistic" in their values, as well as compulsive in their behavior.

The relation of personality to role and status in the group constitutes a very large problem area in which there are probably few simple answers. The hypothesis just suggested is obviously highly over-simplified. However, we do have one additional item of information about each individual in the sample which bears upon the hypothesis. All subjects were given the thirty item California F-Scale. High scores on this scale are thought to indicate one kind of rigidity and abso-lutism, associated with the authoritarian personality.[22] (Prob-ably extremely low scores do also, but this is a complication that will be ignored for the present). Table 10 shows the mean

TABLE 10

Mean Scores on 30-item F-Scale for top Men on Five Characteristics and Leader, in High and Low Groups

	High Groups	Low Groups	All Groups
Leader	76.2	85.2	80.7
#1 Guidance	88.7	79.2	83.9
#1 Receiving	83.3	94.2	88.7
#1 Talking	74.9	103.8	89.3
#1 Ideas	82.3	101.2	91.7
#1 Liking	91.1	99.9	95.5

F-scores of the various top men and the chosen leader, in both High and Low groups. In general, top men in High groups have lower F-scores than top men in Low groups. The difference between High and Low groups is particularly clear for the Idea specialist and the top man on Talking.[23] If we compare the Idea men and the best Liked men with each other, we find no difference in the Low groups, but in the High groups the Idea men have a significantly lower mean F-score than the best Liked men.[24] The best Liked men show up as high in F-score.

Analysis of Tables 8 and 9, and the data on attribution of Leadership suggested that certain measures tend toward mini-mum association with each other (Ideas vs. Liking) while others, like Leadership, Guidance, Receiving, tend to "bridge the gap," and to be associated to some extent with both of these. Those that show the greatest tendency toward separation may be said

22. T. W. Adorno, *et al. The Authoritarian Personality* (New York: Harper & Bros., 1950). *Passim.*

23. These differences are significant at the .01 level.

24. Significant at the .05 level.

to be specialized; those that bridge the gap may be called generalized. Table 10 is arranged vertically with the most generalized attributes at the top and the most specialized at the bottom. As we move in the direction of greater specialization, the mean F-scores for High and Low groups combined appear to become progressively higher. Top men on the three most generalized characteristics taken together have in fact significantly lower F-scores than the top men on the three more specialized characteristics (at the .05 level, using a standard t-test).

In general, then, if a relatively high F-score is associated with rigidity, and the relatively lower score with greater flexibility, we can say that the top men tend to be more flexible in High groups than in Low groups,[25] that in High groups the social-emotional specialist is less flexible than the task specialist, and that there is some suggestion that individuals with more specialized characteristics are less flexible than individuals with more generalized characteristics.

Another possible index of "rigidity" may be found in the Like ratings that each individual makes. Some subjects do not make any differentiation in their professed likes toward other members. They say that they like all members equally, and in most cases strongly. Examination of the data indicates that these subjects who do not differentiate their sociometric choices show a significantly (.01 level) higher F-score than those who do differentiate. If we compare the incidence of undifferentiated choices among top men on the five roles, we find that 42% of best Liked men fail to differentiate, as compared with 23% of top men on Talking, 33% of top men on Receiving. 20% of top men on Ideas and 27% of top men on Guidance. The difference between the best Liked men and the other four types is significant at the .06 level, using a Chi-square test.

These best Liked men, then, say in effect, "I like everyone." In connection with their high F-score, this suggests the possibility of a certain rigidity in the attitudes of many best Liked men toward interpersonal relationships. They may "have to be liked" and may achieve prominence in this respect because of the ingratiating skills they have acquired during their lives in bringing this desired situation about. Their avoidance of differ-

25. With the exception of top men on Guidance—an exception for which the hypothesis provides no explanation.

entiation in ratings may be an expression of the compulsive and indiscriminate nature of this striving.[26]

If this interpretation is correct, it provides another possible explanation as to why the best Liked man is so seldom chosen as the Leader of the group. If Leadership, as we have suggested, is implicitly or unconsciously attributed on the basis of several weighted factors, the tendency of the best Liked man toward "rigidity" or overspecialization would tend to lower his rating on the Task Ability and other factors, and so lower his chances of being chosen Leader.

This discussion of "rigidity" in relation to status consensus would lead us to expect that more best Liked men will fail to differentiate in the Low groups than in the High groups. About 62% of the non-differentiating best Liked man are found in Low groups, but the difference is not significant.

In any case, there is a sizeable group of best Liked men who may achieve this position through behavior designed to avoid negative reactions from others. It is interesting to note, in this connection, that the task specialist (operationally defined as the best Idea man) refuses to differentiate less often than any of the other top men. It would seem to be important for the task specialist to be able to face a certain amount of negative feeling toward him without abandoning his role, and his apparent willingness to make differentiated Liking choices may be indicative of at least a minimal ability of this kind. Not to have to like everyone implies an awareness and acceptance of the fact that everyone may not have to like him.

It is interesting now to ask whether the High groups differ from the Low groups in the Liking choices the best Liked man gives the top Idea man. The interaction data reported above on the relation between these two specialists might lead us to expect that in the High groups the best Liked man may more often express liking for the top Idea man than in the Low groups. Examination of the data, however, reveals no differences between High and Low groups. However, pooling High and Low groups, in the 23 relevant cases the average liking given by the best Liked man to the top Idea man was significantly higher (at the .01 level) than the average rating that others gave the

26. For a similar interpretation, see F. Kraüpl Taylor, *op. cit.*

top Idea man in the same session. This is not simply a result of the fact that the best Liked man tends to rate everybody high. The rating he gives to the best Idea man is also significantly higher (at the .01 level) than the rating he gives to others in the group. The fact that this occurs in both High and Low groups, though interaction support is more marked in the High groups, again seems to indicate something over-determined in the Like ratings made by the best Liked man. It appears that regardless of what his interactive relationship with the top Idea man has been, the best Liked man will tend to express positive feeling toward him once the meeting is over.

Other members may exhibit other types of rigidity. One other type, for example, is suggested by the lack of congruence in the Low groups between amount of participation and status on either Ideas or Likes. A reasonable assumption is that the flexible person adjusts his amount of participation according to the esteem and acceptance he receives. The Low groups more often contain persons who persist in very high rates of activity in spite of low acceptance and esteem. Evidence from another study[27] indicates that this type is often "deluded" as to his popularity—he guesses that other persons like him, whereas in fact they do not.

In the Low groups, there is not only a relative lack of consensus as to who stands where in various status orders, but also the lack of consensus appears in conjunction with certain rigidities in perception, value judgments, and overt behavior stemming presumably from personality characteristics of members. It is suggested that the differentiation in the Low groups is more heavily influenced by *de facto* personality differences of members than by consensus on an appropriate division of labor.

Interpretive Summary

Against the background of findings we may now attempt an interpretive summary. The evidence suggests that the degree of consensus on who stands where on various status orders is a critical factor in the structure and development of the group.

---

27. Edgar F. Borgatta, Robert F. Bales, "Sociometric Status Patterns and Characteristics of Interaction." Unpublished manuscript.

Consensus in this respect is probably itself a complicated end result of the social process, but one would suppose that it is affected by the values members hold when they first come together. Measures of values of members were not available for the present sample, but are being attempted for groups at present under observation, and eventually data will be brought to bear on this area of problems.

For the present, we suspect that the groups High on status consensus are those in which, it happens, through original composition, that a fairly high degree of latent consensus in critical values exists. Given this common base, a common interpretation of the nature and importance of the task might reasonably follow, and the result is a high degree of consensus on who is producing the best ideas for task solution. Those so perceived are allowed or encouraged to specialize in the task area, and so build up their total amount of participation.

At the same time, we suppose, even in the High groups, a certain amount of ambivalence tends to center on the task specialist. He tends to be liked because he is satisfying needs in relation to the task area. But he also tends to arouse a certain amount of hostility because his prestige is rising relative to the other members, because he talks a large proportion of the time, and because his suggestions constitute proposed new elements to be added to the common culture, to which all members will be committed if they agree. Whatever readjustments the members have to make in order to feel themselves committed will tend to produce minor frustrations, anxieties, and hostilities. These are centered to some degree on the object most active in provoking the disturbance—the task specialist.

The more the task specialist talks, the more ambivalent the attitudes of other members toward him presumably become, and as a solution, they tend to withdraw some liking from him, and center it on some other person who is less active and may in some way reciprocate their positive affect, or express their negative affect. If some person in the group acts in such a way as to attract positive affect on either or both of these bases, he may become the best Liked man—and in his activity may become a kind of social-emotional specialist.

If the differentiation goes this far, and the evidence indicates that it is fairly typical, even in the High groups, the task specialist can be thought of as "representing" the task values of the members. The social-emotional specialist "represents" other values and attitudes which tend to a certain degree be disturbed, de-emphasized, threatened, or repressed by the requirements of the emerging task solution. The two specialists interact with high frequency in the High groups, and in a generally supportive manner, though probably also with occasional altercations. They constitute a prominent pair within the group, and their complementarity in interaction represents a high degree of closure which might well be referred to as the "inner circle" within the total circle of interaction.

Specialization in the High groups arises in response to a complex of situational demands, the demands of personalities, and the demands of the social system, but it takes place in the context of a fundamental consensus as to how the roles should be performed and how they should complement each other. Inter-specialist interaction and support ensures the maintenance of this consensus and prevents the specialization from taking a rigid or disruptive form.

Leadership and perhaps Guidance are attributed to that member, one of the pair or occasionally a third person, who best symbolizes the weighted combination and integration of the two more specialized functions. The two directions of specialization, though complementary and supporting in the long run, in the short run tend in some degree to conflict with each other in a way that makes it difficult for the same man to be top specialist on both. In the present sample, the stronger probability is that Leadership will be attributed to the task specialist, although the concept of weighted factors implies that if the task specialist is *too* low on Likeability, or if the social-emotional specialist is very high on task ability Leadership may be attributed to the social-emotional specialist. The data suggest that Guidance and Leadership tend to be attributed to the person who accomplishes or symbolizes a higher order integration of the two more specialized task and social-emotional functions.

In the Low groups, we suppose, the low order of consensus as to who stands where is in part a result of an original low degree of similarity in basic values of members. The members differently evaluate the nature and importance of the task, and so lack a common base for arriving at a consensus as to who has the best ideas. Talking and Receiving time are not deter-mined by tacit agreement that participation time should be allocated to any particular persons rather than others. Indi-vidual participation is not regulated by a sensitive adjustment to the response received from others. Individual members may perceive themselves as liked, whereas in fact they are not. Others may believe they like everybody, whereas unconsciously they feel fear and hostility.

Neither the task specialist nor the most active participant in the Low groups is often best Liked, although the latter achieves this position more often than the former. There is a high turnover of personnel in the top ranks of the various status orders. It is difficult for a person who attains top rank in some respect in a given meeting to hold it in the next. Specialization occurs in response to individual needs which are only tangentially related to the demands of the group problem-solving situation. Because the specialized behavior serves the individual who performs it more than it does others, inter-specialist support does not occur systematically. No one individual is able to combine a high activity rate with a high status on both task ability and likeability, and hence adequately to symbolize the balance of functions which leads to the stable attribution of Leadership.

Some Comparisons With the Family

All of the groups in the sample used in this study are single sex groups, with only minor age differences, a minimum of previous contact, a minimum prospective future, and a minimal relation to outside reference groups. The experimenters con-stitute probably the most important outside reference group, and in relation to this reference group, each of the members in the experimental group has a similar status. No one of them initially represents the others, or maintains the relation on which their subsistence and status as a group depends.

In all of these respects the experimental groups are completely different from the typical nuclear family. In the nuclear family there are obvious sex and age differences, a weighty tradition, a deep affective involvement and long time commitment to solidarity, a complex set of outside reference groups, and in particular a relation to the means of subsistence and basic status in the society which usually centers upon a single senior member—the father, in our society. All of these factors help to define the roles of family members vis-à-vis each other.

It is all the more remarkable, then, that small decision making groups, in the absence of any of these "pegs" upon which a differentiation of roles might be hung, nevertheless tend to develop a differentiation of roles. The obvious hypothesis is that the tendency toward differentiation must arise out of factors associated with social interaction over a very broad range of situations. It is probably not dependent upon any gross differences between persons, upon preexisting cultural prescriptions, or upon any particular task demand, although all of these may play their part. The tendency toward differentiation depends basically, we believe, on the fact that all social systems are confronted with several fundamentally differentiated problems, and with a limitation of resources which makes it difficult to keep all of them solved in short time spans.

We have tried to show what we believe to be some of the most important and general of these problems—problems which are confronted in the nuclear family and in our experimental groups alike. One of these problems centers on the difference between overt behavior and the covert manipulation of signs and symbols within the personality system. Learning in the process of socialization to deal with one's world by the covert manipulation of signs and symbols results in a great economy of effort. But when behavior comes to be controlled and guided by a system of symbol manipulation, the system of symbols itself imposes new conditions on behavior. It requires maintenance, reconstruction, extension, generalization, and so on. Overt behavior, and particularly interaction with other persons, is the principal means by which the symbol system is controlled. Behavior at a given moment is guided by the symbol system. But results of that behavior a moment later modify the symbol system. Each feeds back on the other, but the two are not identical with each other, do not necessarily change simultaneously, and not necessarily at the same rate. Both are physical processes in real space and time, but the constrictions of space and time are quite different in the two cases.

The interaction between two or more persons is guided by

the symbol manipulation of each. The result of behavior for each of them is the reaction of the other. The reaction of the other, however, is guided not directly by the behavior of the first, but indirectly through the symbol manipulation the responder goes through before he reacts. Successful behavior for the first then depends upon making his symbol manipulation approximate that of the other, and constantly correcting as the other changes. The result of interaction over time is the construction of a symbol system common to the participants. Each can manipulate certain symbols and behave in ways which give him more or less successful predictions of the way the other will manipulate them, and behave. They now have a common culture. The common culture then acts as a control on behavior, and vice versa, just as in the individual case. But the common culture also requires maintenance, reconstruction, and so on —it requires overt interaction in real space and time, with all the physical constrictions so imposed, in order to be built, and in order to survive and grow.

What is the common culture about? To what do the signs and symbols refer? Some signs and symbols refer to other signs and symbols, of course, and these references must be established by overt interaction. To establish such a system of common symbols and their references to each other is perhaps the most elementary problem of any social system. It is the *sine qua non* of communication and successful control of behavior. But to solve it at a point in time, that is, to arrive at group consensus, or a group decision, is only to pass a point in a never ending series. Overt behavior continues, in real space and time, and is subject to all sorts of other influences, exigencies, and unforeseen consequences.

The problem of guiding behavior successfully in the changing situation then becomes again, at least in part, a problem of extending the common culture. In general, the need is apparent to some member or members before others, or at least, some person speaks of it first. In the nature of the case, there is a time lag between the recognition of a problem, a proposed solution, and consensus on a solution which constitutes an extension of the common culture. The solution adopted is associated in the minds of the members, by the mechanisms of learning, with the member or members who were more active in bringing it about. This association of particular members with particular extensions of the common culture is the beginning of role differentiation.

The directions in which roles become differentiated is a function of the different kinds of problem content which confront the group and which require extensions of the common culture for their solution and control. The degree of detail required to describe the differentiation will grow as the common culture grows. The distinction between the more active innovator and those who react to his lead in the process of reaching a particular decision, is perhaps the most general distinction one can make, and if this begins to happen repeatedly with the same person as the innovator, one is inclined to call him a "leader."

But since there are different classes of problems, one may expect different components of leadership, and there is no compelling reason to suppose that a single person will always combine them in a single leader role. Our results, indeed, indicate a strong tendency toward differentiation among those who are more active into two or more types. If this further differentiation occurs, the specialization seems to appear most clearly between one person who achieves prominence in relation to the task demands made upon the group, and another person upon whom more liking is bestowed who presumably meets more social and emotional needs.

It is probable that further useful distinctions can be made. If one were to extend the logic of "binary division" which is implicit in the notions sketched above, one would look for a further division of each of these types into two sub-types. It may well be that task specialization tends to divide into two types, the more active and single-minded innovator of task suggestions, the "idea" specialist, and the somewhat less active custodian of the common task culture, who controls more indirectly by questions and regulates the passage of innovations into the common culture by his assent or disagreement, the "guidance" specialist. The social-emotional specialization, on the other hand, may tend to subdivide into a type who is well liked because he gives positive emotional responses directly to other members, and symbolizes their optimism and ability to reach a satisfying goal state, and another type who, through his negative reactions and perhaps ambivalent humor, gives indirect gratification to suppressed negative feelings of various sorts.

The way in which these various functions are fused in the role of a particular individual or divided between separate persons is probably a result of many factors. Certainly prominent among these factors in addition to initial personality differences would be the number of members in the group, the permanence of the group, the kinds of tasks, and the amount of positive and negative affect involved. The nuclear family presents important contrasts to the small decision making groups of the laboratory in all these respects, even in the factor of size, though both are "small." From the point of view of the child in the process of socialization, the effective size of the group presumably expands for him as he passes from an exclusive attachment and dependence on the mother to an effective participation with other family members. Nevertheless, there are important similarities as well as contrasts, and one may hope to obtain valuable insights by the comparison.

Especially with regard to the culture building process and the process of role differentiation one can see fundamental similarities. The appearance of a differentiation between a person who symbolizes the demands of task accomplishment and a person who symbolizes the demands of social and emotional needs is implicit in the very existence of a social system responsive to an environment. Any such system has both an "inside" and an "outside" aspect and a need to build a common culture which deals with both. The tendency toward this fundamental differentiation holds whether there are age and sex differences between members or not. In the small decision-making group it appears as the difference between the task specialist and the best liked man, in spite of the absence of differences in age and sex. In the marital couple it appears as the difference between the role of husband and wife, according to the sex difference, with age usually about the same or irrelevant. In the parent-child relation it appears along the age or generation axis, and holds whatever the sex of the parent or child.

Moreover, in none of these contexts is the difference simply one of activity or power. Power is a quite separable variable, and its allocation between specialists often presents a problem of integration of the system, once specialization occurs. The difference is rather one of responsibility for, or vested interest in, maintaining the internal state of affairs of the system in *steady state,* (including existing emotional attachments to persons, objects, modes of gratification, and modes of symbolic control over behavior), versus responsibility for, or vested interest in *change,* usually for the sake of some improved adjustment vis-à-vis the environment. It sometimes happens that the persons reverse roles as time goes on. Indeed this is the typical thing in the nuclear family, as the child becomes emancipated, and the parents change from symbols to him of ever-increasing demands for change toward maturity, to symbols of things as they were.

Not only is the allocation of power an important problem of integration, once specialization occurs. The allocation of positive and negative affect, or in plainer words, love and hate, assumes a particularly crucial importance in a system like the nuclear family, where the degree of emotional involvement is very high, the group small, the relations of long duration, and the transmission of a common culture to the children is a basic function. It is very difficult for one person to produce desired and lasting changes in the behavior of others, or even in himself, without a positive mutual emotional attachment. Lasting changes in behavior require the construction and internalization of a common culture, and the new elements of the common culture have to acquire a certain reward value in themselves. The love attachment can provide an element of immediate reward, whereas the reward that might eventually come from an improved relation to the environment may come entirely too late to produce learning.

It is doubtful whether any learned system of signs and symbols as complicated as that which constitutes the culture of a human social system could ever be constructed without the resource of positive emotional attachment. And conversely, the existence of negative emotional attachment undermines, and sometimes completely reverses, the intended effects of interpersonal influence. It is consequently of the greatest importance for the building of a common culture, and the socialization of new members, that the allocation of power, the role specialization of the system, and the allocation of love and hate should be integrated with each other.

The problem appears in the small decision making group, as well as in the nuclear family. But it has a different complexion, so to speak, because of the radical difference in the quantity and quality of positive (as well as negative) affect present in the two different types. In the small task-oriented group, positive affect is a scarce resource, and the practical problem, usually, is to find enough of it, and keep enough of it centered on the task specialist, either directly, or indirectly through the social leader, so that he does not lose power. In the nuclear family, on the other hand, though essential, positive affect is often present in threatening quantity, and the practical problem may then be to repress enough of it so that it is not all centered on the mother, and enough is made available to preserve the power and authority of the father. Or, similarly, when the mother is in the position of symbolizing task demands made upon the child, love formerly given must be made sufficiently conditional to encourage the child to change his former mode of behavior.

The other side of the problem consists in the disposal of negative affect which to some degree is inevitably generated. In some groups the negative affect is not strong, and may be successfully discharged against some symbolic object external to the group, or fused into the task effort. But the danger is always present that it will be directed against some member of the group who is regarded as deviant in some respect. Unfortunately, the very person who symbolizes the demands of the task, and presses for the extension of the common culture in a previously uncharted direction, is in a sense a deviant—a representative of something that is to some degree foreign and disturbing to the existing culture and set of attachments. There is a certain probability that he will incur some hostility, even though repressed, and the problem is created for the other members of somehow resolving their ambivalence. Centering their positive affect on another person, who in turn supports the task specialist is a possible adjustment, and, we think, a rather common one. The social-emotional specialist, if this is a part of his role, is thus a kind of symbolic transmuter of negative affect into positive affect. His support of the task leader becomes a critical condition of the stability of the group.

In this context, the incest taboo as it appears almost universally the same within the nuclear family, assumes a critical significance. Whatever its other functions, it tends to concentrate the erotic attachment of the marital pair on each other, to preserve their support of each other, though their roles are different and complementary, and to keep the axis of power and authority within the family coincident with the generation difference. It allows the mother to serve as the symbolic focus of love and gratification to the child, and still to make her love conditional as necessary for his socialization. It allows the father to serve as the symbolic focus of negative affect without destroying his authority. Or the symbolic significance may be reversed, particularly perhaps for the female child. Usually, probably, both parents are to some degree symbols of both love and hate, according to context. The important thing is that some leeway should be provided for the resolution of ambivalence by the differentiation of roles according to context.

The incest taboo is one of many mechanisms by which the differentiation of roles in the nuclear family is prevented from becoming ultimately disruptive. The shifting of affect according to context is another. But in general and probably for all sorts of social systems it is the building of a common culture (which justifies the differentiation by linking it with common goals and values) that reintegrates the system, and rescues it from the divisive tendencies that tend to follow in the wake of specialization.

CHAPTER **VI**

Role Differentiation in the Nuclear Family: A Comparative Study

BY MORRIS ZELDITCH, JR.

The analysis of our own nuclear family structure reveals certain patterns of differentiation that we also see in other societies if we clearly distinguish the nuclear family from the extended kinship groupings in which, in a great many societies, they are incorporated. Parsons has pointed out that in this particular instance it is fruitful to begin analysis with the more *highly* differentiated social system of the United States, rather than the so-called "simple" nonliterate societies, because in our society the nuclear family is structurally isolated from extended kin solidarities and functionally differentiated from other systems. But the nuclear family is not something characteristic *only* of our society. Murdock, for instance, has stated flatly that it is a discernible functioning group in all societies entering his sample, and there have been only one or two exceptions reported in the entire anthropological literature.[1]

---

1. Most notably the Nayar. See, for instance, E. K. Gough, "The Traditional Kinship Systems of the Nayars of Malabar," Prepared for the Social Science Research Council Seminar on Kinship. Unpublished. Also, E. K. Gough, "Changing

In our system the marriage pair is given precedence as a solidary unit over any link with the *parents* of either member of the pair. The so-called simple nonliterate societies, on the other hand, often give precedence to solidarities with the family of orientation of one of the pair, or, in more complex forms, strong though differentiated obligations to both parental families. Even in the bilateral cases most closely approaching our own, the isolation of the nuclear family is not the distinguishing structural characteristic; rather a bilateral system generally functions to incorporate the nuclear family in a kin-oriented group, but one in which membership is fluidly structured from generation to generation.

Nevertheless, the nuclear family ordinarily *can* be distinguished, and does function as a significant group. This particular point, in fact, is responsible for a good many of the issues in the interpretation of matrilineal systems, which we will consider later, and a failure to distinguish the nuclear family from other kinship units in which it is incorporated is likely to confuse any sort of analysis of concrete kinship behavior.

The Generic Significance of Nuclear Family Structure

The nuclear family in our society has a particular pattern of roles which we now suggest has a *generic* significance. There is, in other words, an underlying structural uniformity which gives a baseline for the analysis of the range of variation usually noted.

A statement of this sort, of course, can be only hypothetical at this point. It is the purpose of this paper, however, to indicate that it is not *only* hypothetical. On what basis can we argue that this uniformity occurs? A reference to Bales's and Slater's discussion in Chapter V provides at least part of the answer. We argue, for instance, that it is essentially fruitful to consider the nuclear family as a special case of a small group, and that the mode of differentiation observed in small groups has a generic significance which extends to any of its special cases. The fact that Bales's experimental groups are ephemeral compared to nuclear families (even those which are terminated after only a few months of existence) does not imply that the conclusions reached from these groups are ephemeral.

More generally, a nuclear family is a social system, and the peculiar attributes which distinguish it from other systems (its particular age-sex structure and primary function, for instance) should be examined *within* this more general context. All groups are subject to certain imposed *conditions* of existence; not that all groups exist, but that all groups that *do* exist meet these conditions.[2] If we assume the existence of a nuclear family, therefore, we must inquire into the conditions of its existence. And certain of these conditions are common to all groups, appearing in such diverse forms as Bales's experimental groups and the family pattern of peasant Ireland.

Directions of Differentiation in the Nuclear Family

Among the conditions of a system's existence is at least a certain degree of differentiation along lines imposed by the orbits of the system's movement. Consider first the general pattern of differentiation which in broad outline appears from the experimental small group. There is a tendency for a *task leader* and a *sociometric star* to appear. Although there is some problem in clearly isolating the complex factors defining the task leader he seems to be associated with certain *behaviors* (in general terms, "task" behaviors; more specifically in giving suggestions, directions, opinions), and certain *attitudes* (involving, apparently, an inhibition of emotions and the ability to accept hostile reactions from others in the process of pressing a point, etc.). There are also, of course, reciprocal behaviors and attitudes on the part of other system-members towards the task leader. The sociometric star, although the term originally derives from attitudes taken toward ego by alters, also tends to show a certain pattern of behaviors and attitudes; namely, the *expression* of emotions, supportive behavior to others, the desire to please and be liked, and a more generalized liking for other members. The star may,

2. The framework for this analysis is provided in T. Parsons, R. F. Bales, and E. A. Shils, *Working Papers in the Theory of Action* (Glencoe, Ill.: Free Press, 1953), and T. Parsons, *The Social System* (Glencoe, Ill.: Free Press, 1951). A semi-formalized model of the analysis, made as the starting point of the present paper, will be found in Appendix B.

of course, express negative reactions as well as positive supports; typically these are significant in releasing negative reactions (often through humor) of the group as a whole, reducing, in consequence, the general tension level. (The difference between a "leader," here, and one who fails to become a leader may very well lie, in part, in the capacity to express reactions felt by the group as a *whole*.)

From a general theoretical point of view this is *not* a fortuitous pattern of differentiation; it defines, in fact, the two basic conditions of the existence of a social system. In order to clarify and illustrate what we mean by this, we may take the nuclear family as a specific case; and it may be useful at the same time to begin with a differentiation logically prior to role differentiation itself.

Assume a time T_1 in which members of the nuclear family are dispersed somewhere in the external situation involved in devotion to the "task," or what we call "instrumental" activities. By either of these terms we mean here the manipulation of the object-world in order to provide facilities for the achievement of goals defined within the system. In our society, for instance, the husband typically goes to work in the morning, the mother shops or cleans up, the children go to school if they are old enough. In many other societies a similar dispersal, involving a departure of at least the husband-father (out hunting, or farming), often occurs. Now clearly, if there is no second occasion, T_2, during which the members of the system are *reunited*, the system will tend to disappear. It will no longer be identifiable as a system.

There is then, a most primitive level of differentiation here in the simple presence or absence of members on two different occasions. From this it is clear that one imperative of all social systems is integration, a coming together, which of course Durkheim emphasized a considerable time ago.

The other side of the coin, involving here a dispersal of members, introduces a more complex level of analysis. Although dispersal of system members is common during instrumental activities,[3] it is not necessary to define what we are talking about.

---

3. Because resources do not necessarily cluster around the immediate residence of the family, and typically a mother stays near the home partly, we may suppose, to symbolize the latent system.

We merely suggest this as a first point of purchase on the type of analysis involved. Typically, in fact, the mother and children remain at some location symbolically associated with the system's existence—the home is the crucial symbol, of course—and there is always a *latent* existence to the system (*if* it is to reappear). This function of symbols, in giving latent existence to systems, is of obvious importance as a basis for their physical reintegration.

What is significant in the differentiation of these two occasions, however, is not the states of spatial dispersion and integration, physically, but the difference in behavior and attitudes involved. The system may in fact always act in concert from the present point of view, and still show the differentiation we are here concerned with.

Reverting to our time period T_1, then, assume that all members are physically adjacent but devoted to instrumental or task activities. The entire family, say, is out farming in the fields. These instrumental activities involve, in gross terms, the manipulation of objects (plows, or hoes, etc.), and an attitude composed of Parsons' pattern variables "specific, affectively neutral, universalistic, achievement-oriented," or in more gross terms a "rational" attitude towards the external situation, and an *inhibition* of emotions toward other members of the system. *In order for the system to continue as a system,* we now say, there must at some point be a *change* in attitude and behavior to integrative-expressive activities—to laughing, playing, release of inhibited emotions, the expression of affection for each other, a warmth and a symbolization of common membership through supportive, accepting behavior.

If we reverse our assumptions, we arrive at the same basic conclusion, something we were not able to do when we considered only physical presence or absence (we were not, that is, able to show why dispersion *had* to occur). Assume the time period T_2 in which all members are affectionate, responsive, emotionally warm and attached to each other, often symbolized in the meal-time break. The system *cannot* continue in this state forever. It must, at some point, change to the necessary activities—and the associated attitudes—involved in manipulating the facilities of the object world so that the family has the food, shelter, fire, etc., which the external situation can provide.

The family then becomes reinvolved in the *task,* which, no matter how much integrative behavior there was before or will be after—and perhaps also at breaks during the task—must concentrate on *getting the job done.* It must, that is, at least for the time being, devote its attention to instrumenal acts.

A considerable refinement is involved in the further differentiation of the structure of *roles* in the system. One clue, perhaps, is suggested by the earlier peripheral comment that while husband-father is away at work or in the fields, the mother very often stays at home symbolizing the integrative focus of the system (even though her activities may be primarily instrumental during this phase of family activity). The fact that it is the mother who stays home is not, for the present, significant although shortly it will become so. What *is* significant, is that *someone* stayed, and that someone is in fact *more* responsible for integrative-expressive behavior than the person who went off to work.

Why after all, are *two* parents necessary? For one thing, to be a stable focus of integration, the integrative-expressive "leader" can't be off on adaptive-instrumental errands all the time. For another, a stable, secure attitude of members depends, it can be assumed, on a *clear* structure being given to the situation so that an *uncertain* responsibility for emotional warmth, for instance, raises significant problems for the stability of the system. And an uncertain managerial responsibility, an unclear definition of authority for decisions and for getting things done, is also clearly a threat to the stability of the system.

We can say, then, that the system must differentiate behaviors and attitudes in order to continue to exist as a system;[4] and that a further condition of stability is also that some specialization occur in responsibility for the attitudes and behaviors involved.[5]

---

4. There are several implicit assumptions here that are made explicit in the appended formalization of the argument. For instance, that if you are inhibiting emotions in order to perform instrumental tasks, you *cannot* at the same time release them in integrative-expressive behavior. So that it is no solution to the problem to try to do both at once. (Stated in the fourth axiom and its consequent.)

5. This involves an untested assumption derived outside the system of axioms underlying this paper. In the appended formalization, therefore, specialization of roles is postulated rather than derived, because the logic is a trifle loose.

Age and Sex
in the Nuclear Family

We actually want to examine two things in this paper. One is related to the generic significance of a certain pattern of differentiation. The relevant role-system, however, is indeterminate with respect to allocation when taken at this level. It is necessary to consider the nuclear family as a type of group peculiarly structured around age-sex differences in order to arrive at a hypothesis concerning who plays the instrumental and expressive roles.

Now any system, it should be noticed first, has a problem often considered peculiar to families, that is the processing of new recruits. While the "barbarian invasion" may be considered of special significance for the family, and thus to impose special conditions on its existence, the problem is in fact generic to all systems. Thus the family resembles other groups in this respect as well as in the more general terms discussed so far. What differs, and the difference is of crucial structural significance, is the age-sex matrix of the family, and with it the situational reference points for the allocation of *facilities* in the performance of roles. At the grossest level of analysis, for instance, the father is stronger than the son, so that he, rather than the son, is allocated to leadership roles in instrumental activities (with the possible, and amusing, exception of the polyandrous Marquesas).

At least one fundamental feature of the external situation of social systems—here a feature of the physiological organism—is a crucial reference point for differentiation in the family. This lies in the division of organisms into lactating and nonlactating classes. Only in our own society (so far as I know, that is) have we managed to invent successful bottle-feeding, and this is undoubtedly of importance for our social structure. In other societies necessarily—and in our own for structural reasons which have *not* disappeared with the advent of the bottle—the initial core relation of a family with children is the mother-child attachment. And it follows from the principles of learning that the gradient of generalization should establish "mother" as the focus of gratification in a diffuse sense, as the source of "security" and "comfort." She is the focus of warmth and stability. Thus, because of her special initial relation to the child, "mother" is the more likely expressive focus of the system as a whole.

The allocation of the instrumental leadership to the husband-father rests on two aspects of this role. The role involves, first, a manipulation of the external environment, and consequently a good deal of physical mobility. The concentration of the mother on the child precludes a *primacy* of her attention in this direction although she always performs *some* instrumental tasks. In addition to the managerial aspects of the role there are certain discipline and control functions of the father role. Consider, again, why *two* parents are necessary at all. The initial mother-child subsystem can do without the father (except that he provides food, shelter, etc., for this subsystem so that it need not split up to perform many of its own instrumental tasks). But *some* significant member of the nuclear family must "pry the child loose" from the mother-dependency so that it may "grow up" and accept its responsibilities as an "adult." There is necessarily a coalition of father and mother in this, or no stable socialization pattern develops. But the mother, by her special initial relation to the child is relatively more susceptible to *seduction* out of the coalition. We may note, for instance, that one of the pathologies of family dynamics may arise because the father tends to be susceptible to seduction by daughters; and the very fact of his relative power in the coalition makes this *more* of a threat to the family as a system. The problem of the "weak, ineffectual" father is more significant than that of the "weak, ineffectual" mother. (Conversely, of course, and quite as significant, the problem of the "cold, unyielding" mother is more of a problem than the "cold, unyielding" father.) If, therefore, the female is allocated the integrative-supportive role, there must necessarily be an allocation of authority for discipline and relatively "neutral" judgment to the husband-father.

We may summarize the hypothesis we have stated then, in this way. Because the nuclear family is a special case of the more general class of social systems, and because it must meet certain conditions of existence common to all social systems, we suggest that:

1. If the nuclear family constitutes a social system stable over time,

it will differentiate roles such that instrumental leadership and expressive leadership of the system are discriminated.

Because the nuclear family, on the other hand, has certain peculiar features not common to all systems, we are further able to state a certain hypothesis about the *allocation* of these roles to system-members. This peculiar feature is the age-sex matrix of the nuclear family and the differential distribution of facilities for the performance of the fundamental roles. We suggest that:

2. If the nuclear family consists in a defined "normal" complement of the male adult, female adult and their immediate children, the male adult will play the role of instrumental leader and the female adult will play the role of expressive leader.

Choosing a Sample

Two courses are open in making some sort of test of the hypotheses that have been stated. A careful and refined analysis of a few societies, made from the best of the ethnographic reports available, is from many points of view the best approach to take. There is some point, however, in sacrificing both a great deal of information and the more refined aspects of analysis, for a simple replication of cases. In this paper, at any rate, the second approach is taken.

Having made this initial decision, an attempt was made to take a random sample of some sort. This is a particularly difficult procedure with cross-cultural studies. In the first place, the universe one would *like* to use actually falls into two strata, all those societies reported by ethnographers and all those societies not reported. Societies belonging to the second of these strata are immediately excluded, and there is no basis of judging with what confidence inferences can be made from available reports to the entire universe of cases.

The effective universe on which the propositions can be tested, then, is reduced to available reports. In this, as in any case of sampling, significant bias can enter simply by a failure to make an adequate *listing* of the universe from which the sample is chosen. The list for the sample used here was compiled from several sources. G. P. Murdock's bibliography,[6] R. H.

6. *Social Structure* (New York: Macmillan Co., 1949).

Lowie's bibliography,[7] and some additional materials available in the Widener and Peabody Museum libraries at Harvard were the chief listing sources. It is doubtful, of course, that this produced a complete listing.

From this list, nevertheless, about 75 "societies" were selected for examination. From these 75 cases a final sample was chosen according to the following rules:

1. The sample should be random, or failing this, systematic bias should be minimized.
2. Sample units should be independent; i.e., the duplication of cases should be minimized. Because two groups have different names does not mean they are independent cases.
3. If information is incomplete, this will be proper grounds for exclusion from the sample. Information is incomplete where there is insufficient evidence *either for or against* the hypothesis tested.

In the final sample of 56 cases perfect randomness may have failed for two reasons: first, the differential availability of monographs; and, second, the operation of the rule for exclusion. Certain societies were omitted merely because they were more difficult to gather material on than others. These societies failed to get into the list of 75 in the first place. Conversely, certain societies were included in the list of 75 simply because they were readily available. Although these factors, in a certain sense, destroy the original design of the sample, there is no reason to suppose that the bias is systematic; i.e., that only negative cases were excluded, or that more than a proportionate share of negative cases were excluded.

Perfect independence is difficult to achieve because of the problems involved in drawing the lines between cases. This is a serious difficulty, since, having sacrificed refinement, the soundness of the test more or less rests on the numbers involved, and these numbers should not be spurious. Generally, if Murdock included both of two questioned cases in his sample, they were treated as independent; but Murdock's sample is itself open to question on this ground. A check was made with other sources[8];

7. *Social Organization* (New York: Rinehart & Co., 1948).

8. I would like to thank Professor John M. Roberts for some helpful advice on North American cases.

nevertheless judgments are difficult to make. In at least one case of possible duplication both cases were kept because both were negative (Cheyenne and Arapaho).

The cases excluded because of insufficient information were generally patrilineal societies, with strong authority vested in the males, but no clear picture of the role of the "mother." Certain matrilineal societies, in relatively brief reports, show a similar "bias" in reporting; strong authority vested in males of the matrilineage is reported without clear evidence of the role of the "mothers" and "sisters"; or in some cases the role of the females of the matrilineage is discussed, but not in their own nuclear family, violating the boundaries of the specific universe for the test. Thus no clear rating could be made.

It should be noted, finally, that it was taken as a policy decision of some importance, for this paper, that all ethnographic reports would be accepted as accurate. This is not "epistemological realism," it is merely that to question one is to question all. It is for this reason, in fact, that a crude analysis depending for its significance primarily on replication was made at all.

Designation Rules for the Rating of the Cases

Unfortunately, perhaps, the character of the indices used was determined by fortuitous circumstances of the test. The fact that the test was made on already digested material observed by many different investigators using widely varying categories makes a number of indirect indices inevitable, and certain ambiguities unavoidable. The most important operations, of course, should specify the direct designation rules for instrumental and expressive leadership; this is in terms of the patterns of *action* of the role-incumbents. But these can only be interpreted from the *statements* of the ethnographer. It is necessary, therefore, to set up the rules for designation in terms of the statements which will satisfy the theoretical categories involved. These basic categories involve, first, direct responsibility for the solution of group tasks, for the skills and information prerequisite to the role in its adaptive aspects, and for the authority required to make binding managerial decisions; and associated with this "managerial" complex the primary responsibility for discipline and "training" of children. Second, they include responsibility for maintenance of solidarity and management of tensions, for the skills prerequisite to this role, and associated with this "integrative-expressive" complex, the primary responsibility for "care" and emotional support of children.

Ego, therefore, will be considered *instrumental* leader of the nuclear family if the ethnographer's report offers statements of the form:

1. Ego is boss-manager of the farm; leader of the hunt, etc. Ego is the final court of appeals, final judge and executor of punishment, discipline, and control over the children of the family.

Ego will be considered *expressive* leader of the nuclear family if the ethnographer's report offers statements of the form:

2. Ego is the mediator, conciliator, of the family; ego soothes over disputes, resolves hostilities in the family. Ego is affectionate, solicitous, warm, emotional to the children of the family; ego is the "comforter," the "consoler," is relatively indulgent, relatively unpunishing.

The actual performance of the role, however, is often difficult to obtain. It is necessary, therefore, to admit certain indices which are related to the hypotheses by propositions not proved within the test-system itself.[9]

The first set of indirect indices is based on the attitude of *alter* if ego plays the instrumental or expressive roles. If, for instance, ego plays an instrumental role, alter will (it is assumed) displace part of the antagonisms of the action process on ego. In order to preserve the family from disruption, however, alter will (it is assumed) be expected to restrain expression of antagonism, and instead will show "respect." This will be accompanied by a feeling of constraint, reserve, or some form of psychological distance between ego and alter. Or alternatively, one may phrase this as an element of "neutrality" (an inhibition of emotions) in the relation of ego and alter.

Ego will be considered as instrumental leader of the nuclear

---

9. While this is quite normal in any "science," it is nonetheless questionable. The problem of the validity and reliability of the indices is briefly considered in the Note on the Indices at the end of this chapter.

family, therefore, if the ethnographer's report offers statements of the form:

3. Alter shows respect to ego; the relations of ego and alter are con-strained, reserved; alter on occasions indicates hostility toward ego.

If on the other hand, ego plays an expressive role, alter will be more at ease in ego's presence, show attachment, "love," or in general ego will be the "sociometric star" of the family. Alternatively, one may phrase this as an element of "affectivity" in the relation of ego and alter.

Ego, therefore, will be considered *expressive* leader of the nuclear family if the ethnographer's report offers statements of the form:

4. Alter is at ease in ego's presence, emotionally attached to ego, is close and warm in relation to ego.

A second form of indirect index rests on the phenomenon of classificatory "extension" of kinship behavior. On the principle of the solidarity of siblings (which is, of course, not a "law," but one possible structural focus of kin systems) the attitudes to, and behavior of, father's siblings and of mother's siblings constitute extensions of the attitude toward, and behavior of, father and mother.[10] Obviously, where the principle is *not* a structural feature of the system, e.g. in the bilateral case, the index cannot be used. Similarly in matrilineal systems, where mother's brother *is* differentiated in role from mother, the extension index again cannot be used.

Terminological equation is normally taken to indicate classi-ficatory extension of behavior and attitudes; that is, if mother's brother is called "male-mother" the content of the two roles will be assumed equivalent, and similarly if father's sister is called "female-father." If, however, other evidence is available that this type of kinship equation is made, the same assumption of extension will be allowed.

Ego, therefore, will be considered *instrumental* leader of the

---

10. Cf. A. R. Radcliffe-Brown, "Introduction," in *African Systems of Kinship and Marriage*, A. R. Radcliffe-Brown and D. Forde, eds. (Oxford: Oxford University Press, 1950). Also A. R. Radcliffe-Brown, *Structure and Function in Primitive Society* (London: Cohen and West, 1952).

nuclear family if the ethnographer's report offers statements of the form:

5. Ego's siblings are equated in status and role with ego, and play an instrumental role with respect to ego's children; e.g., father's sister is treated with respect, and is called "female-father."

Similarly, ego will be considered *expressive* leader of the nuclear family if the ethnographer's report offers statements of the form:

6. Ego's siblings are equated in status and role with ego and play an expressive role with respect to ego's children; e.g., mother's sister is terminologically a "mother" and is warm, indulgent, close. Or mother's brother is termed "male-mother" and is warm, indulgent, etc.

A General Test for Differentiation

The testing of the hypotheses is broken into two parts. At this point we wish only to test for the general *presence* of differentiation, and for the *directions* of this differentiation. But nothing is implied about the allocation of roles to concrete persons in the family. From the present point of view it makes no difference if a newborn baby is the instrumental leader and his elder sister the expressive leader, the theorems involved will still hold. The first theorem may be stated as follows:

1. If the nuclear family constitutes a social system stable over time, it will differentiate roles such that instrumental leadership and expressive leadership of the system are discriminated.

If we call those cases which are differentiated in the specified directions "D," and those negative for differentiation "not-D," the following results are indicated:[11]

D	not-D
46	10

While these numbers appear reasonably significant, something of interest might be discovered from an analysis of negative cases. We would, certainly, be interested to discover if any systematic principle explains the negative cases.

11. If we assume the sample taken approaches randomness within the limitations of the universe and expect, by the null hypothesis, a chance variation, this difference is significant by a chi square test at better than the 1% level.

The Arapesh and the Mundugomor

In a series of monographs on South Sea Islanders of various sorts, Margaret Mead concerned herself basically with the "innateness" of the characteristics of the female as middle-class America conceived her. Her basic proposition was that sex-typing is responsible for a large part of the differential characteristics of the woman's role. In order to prove the point, she buttressed her argument with certain observations of the following sort:

1. Among the Arapesh, both male and female are "maternally" oriented, undifferentiated and "feminine" from the point of view of middle-class American conceptions of sex-typing.

2. Among the Mundugomor, both male and female are aggressive and prone to high rates of initiation, undifferentiated and "masculine" from the point of view of middle-class American conceptions of sex-typing.

3. Among the Tchambuli, the male and female roles are "reversed" from the point of view of middle-class American conceptions of sex roles.

The third observation need not yet concern us. Now one must be careful not to misinterpret Mead; her categories differ from those of the Parsons-Bales-Shils theory and it may very well be that "temperament" is not a clear index of instrumental-expressive role differentiation. Nevertheless one must gather some residue of negative evidence. Granted the postulates on which the present theorems are based, we should expect any system not differentiated in the stated directions to be under great strain; the Mundugomor family apparently is, but the Arapesh family apparently is not.

Careful analysis of Mead's material is necessary but difficult. She more often states what does *not* appear among the "X" or "Y"—in comparison usually to the American family—than what *does* appear.[12] The system reference continually shifts, which is confusing from the present point of view, if not from her own. And if she had realized what she was saying in certain cases, she

---

12. Particularly in Margaret Mead, *Sex and Temperament* (New York: William Morrow & Co., 1935).

certainly would have looked twice. Such, for instance, is the case for the Arapesh.

The Arapesh are a patrilineal, patrilocal people of the New Guinea mountains. They are a rather passive people in comparison to their beach and plains neighbors. The men are emotionally what Mead refers to as "maternal." Authority over others, and "masculine" prerogatives (as conceived by Margaret Mead's interpretation of American definitions) are treated as necessary evils—onerous and difficult. It is to be noted that, nevertheless, they are assumed (and assumed, furthermore, by males). The men also do the trading which is an important part of the economy and social life. But from the point of view of the usual pattern in patrilineal societies, the most startling observation-statements concern the role of the mother's brother. It is the mother's brothers who are "official executors of punishment."[13] Father is all solicitude; the mother's brother is the instigator of the procedure by which the sister's son is shamed or disgraced for some misdeed. It is also to be noted that father is sponsor of his own child in the ceremonial initiation, whereas in most patrilineal societies this is the role of the mother's brother (for an excellent detailed description, see Gregory Bateson[14]). It is generally in matrilineal societies that father or father's sister is ceremonial sponsor. In other words, the Arapesh system is rather unusual.

From a general sociological point of view Mead's argument has certain interesting consequences. Her fundamental thesis is that male and female are sociologically, not constitutionally, defined. A sociologist would not be disposed to argue with this proposition if it is properly qualified, and yet the *observations* Mead provides in support apparently suggest a sociological dilemma. We must accept the position that the predominant pattern of differentiation is not constitutionally inherent, yet the observations apparently necessary to *prove* this seem to argue that there is *no* basis of differentiation at *all*. A careful review of Mead's material, however, reveals that this paradox occurs *only if system references are not carefully defined.* Mead has stated, for instance, that fathers do not desire to discipline their children nor accept authority. She has also stated that

13. *Ibid,* p. 30.

14. G. Bateson, *Naven* (Cambridge: Cambridge University Press, 1939).

mother's brothers *do* discipline children, and accept at least some authority. We may grant that they do this only reluctantly, nevertheless they do it. Thus clearly *some* differentiation occurs; and the father who is reluctant to discipline in one context must certainly be the mother's brother who instigates punishment in *another* context. It is apparent from this, for one thing, that it is *not* necessary to discover societies in which roles are undifferentiated to prove that such differentiation is not innate in the human constitution. Multiple-memberships are characteristic of *all* societies and always the *situation* ("system-reference") must be specified (i.e., what role is being played) in order to predict the behavior of actors. The *same* man and the *same* woman may play quite different roles in different subsystems of a total kinship system. The father who is the authority figure over his own children may be a joking relative of his sister's son; the warm, loving mother may demand respect, deference, obedience from her brother's son. Thus, clearly, the fact that roles are learned is apparent from their dependence on systems of reference. Having said this, the case of the Arapesh, considered strictly from the point of view of the nuclear family, must be treated as negative. It is certainly, so far as Mead's data go, too equivocal a case, despite the father's "reluctant" assumption of certain instrumental tasks (even in his *own* family, for we cannot count his role as a mother's brother in his sister's nuclear family), to consider positive, in the face of the ethnographer's own clearly-stated interpretation.

The Mundugomor raise a rather different type of problem. To borrow a phrase hallowed by Benedictine anthropology, "they have chosen to emphasize"[15] a pattern of subsystem relations inherent in all cases. The nuclear family is not a simple system; it consists of a set of subsystems each of which may be treated as a system of reference itself. The father-son and mother-daughter systems formed in the normal differentiation of responsibility for task-training of children in many societies would, on the basis of the theory involved here, imply that when the subsystem is taken as a point of reference the mother would be an authority-figure over her daughter, the father over the son; that conversely the focal attachments would be mother-

15. Ruth Benedict, *Patterns of Culture* (New York: Houghton, Mifflin Co., 1934).

son, father-daughter (see Freud, of course, for an alternative "general theory" for this case). Because of the Mundugomor "rope" arrangement, in which alternating generations are linked across sex lines, the father-son hostility and father-daughter affection vs. the mother-daughter hostility and the mother-son affection comes out clearly. (The "rope" need not be the reason for this; quite the opposite would be expected on the basis of general evidence, for father and son are *more* closely attached where they do not belong to the same lineage, in most cases.) Mead's own position is that both mother and father are aggressively hostile, which is true relative to Arapesh but ignores the subtleties of subsystem relationships. Mother's brother, incidentally, is listed as a friend and refuge from the father for the son. Mother's brother, of course, is not in either the son's rope or the father's rope.

The Cheyenne and the Arapaho

There are basic reasons, clearly, for treating parents, from certain points of view, as undifferentiated. The solidarity of the father and mother against the children which is generally necessary to moral training (see Chapter II) leads a number of observers to treat the "parents" as a unit charged jointly with "training" and jointly due "respect"; which from the point of view of the larger kin-group and social system *is* the case. This sort of generalized respect is indeed often owed *all* members of the first ascending generation, but a shift of reference usually shows a differentiation of varying degrees of intimacy and familiarity vs. respect and constraint. In the case of the Cheyenne and Arapaho, Eggan explicitly states, however, the solidarity reference and no differentiation is made.[16] While there is slim evidence that change in reference would reveal the differentiation, these two cases must be treated as negative.

The Cheyenne and Arapaho are bilateral. The father is clearly the instrumental leader; it is not so clear just what the mother's role is. Eggan says, "the parents are responsible for transmitting the social heritage; this transmission involves

16. F. Eggan, "The Cheyenne and Arapaho Kinship Systems," in *Social Anthropology of the North American Indian Tribes,* F. Eggan, ed. (Chicago: University of Chicago Press, 1937).

authority on the part of the parents and obedience and respect on the part of the children."[17] Eggan tends to deal primarily with the instrumental aspect of "training" throughout and more or less ignores any emotional "support" aspect; "the kinship system deals with the conflicts which arise in the elementary family largely by establishing a relation of authority and obedience among its members . . ."[18] But these cases cannot be jettisoned on the ground that the mother is simply not treated, according to the rule for exclusion from the sample. Eggan explicitly states, in the manner of any good structural anthropologist, each role he feels is differentiated. The only discrimination he makes of mother and father is very slight; although "parents are primarily responsible for the care and education of their children . . . ," father is primarily responsible for his son, mother for the daughter. The Cheyenne and Arapaho thus seem to show an incipient Mundugomor pattern. "Children are expected to obey and respect their parents . . . A boy is 'sort of afraid of his father,' while a girl is careful to obey her mother; the relation to a parent of the opposite sex is more affectionate but never one of familiarity."[19]

While it may be failure of the indices more than anything else, there is not sufficient ground here for claiming the Cheyenne and Arapaho as positive, and just barely sufficient for claiming it as negative. The extensions cannot be used as indices, of course, since the cases are bilateral. Both father's sister and mother's brother feel great affection for ego and are "helpful"; they do not punish.

The Nuer and the Problem of Ambivalence

As Freud long ago pointed out, the son abandons his "rivalry" with his father not only because of castration-fears, but also because he loves his father at the same time that he hates him. In the empirical case, that is, both index-attitudes are involved and there is a problem of determining relative primacy. This gets into problems of extreme complexity including time and system reference problems. For instance, in most societies

17. *Ibid.*, p. 76.
18. *Ibid.*, p. 80.
19. *Ibid.*, pp. 49-50.

whether father is later "restrained" in his relations to his child or not, whether he disciplines it or not, the first year or two of infancy is one of indulgence by a father in a *less* equivocally affectionate role than mother. The nuclear family with a one-year-old is quite a different system of roles from the nuclear family with a five-year-old. Again, the solidarity of the mother with the father against the child in the process of training the child in the norms of the group, leaves the mother in an equivocal position, although ordinarily one finds that the child is more able to release its hostility to its mother openly, and thus express itself.[20] The father, on the other hand, is not *all* boss; the necessary basis of identification in object-cathexis precludes an entirely instrumental relation of father and son, and his possibly affectionate relation to his daughter has already been pointed out.

With the Nuer,[21] the problems of the dual components, particularly in the father-son relation, loom significantly large—large enough to make the Nuer a most equivocal case. It is clear that affectionate sentiments focus around the mother and her "byre" and that father is the "unchallenged authority" in the home.[22] But "the father takes an interest in his infant children, and one often sees a man nursing his child while the mother is engaged in the tasks of the home."[23] The fact that this refers to an "infant" suggests the age-grading factor; the Chinese father may also be seen fondling and dandling his infant child.[24] But the general affection of father and child is stressed. Nor is this merely a matter of failure of the indirect indices because the direct designation-rules are more or less fulfilled. "Nuer fathers . . . give much time to (their children), petting and spoiling them . . . and the children are often in the byres with the men. The affection of children for their father is very striking in Nuerland . . . In his first years a child is corrected by his mother and elder brothers and sisters, who may give him a

20. See particularly the Japanese case in Ruth Benedict, *The Chrysanthemum and the Sword* (New York: Houghton, Mifflin Co., 1946).

21. Cf. E. E. Evans-Pritchard, *Kinship and Marriage Among the Nuer* (Oxford: Oxford University Press, 1951).

22. *Ibid.*, p. 133.

23. *Ibid.*, p. 137.

24. Cf. M. Yang, *A Chinese Village* (New York: Columbia University Press, 1945).

few strokes with a grass switch if he is naughy."[25] The instrumental component of the father-child relation appears in the
discussion of paternal vs. maternal ties; e.g., "the paternal ties
are stronger, if there is a touch of hardness in them. The maternal ties are weaker and for this reason are tenderer."[26]

The Nuer are not, in point of fact, more equivocal than the
American middle-class family. But in the latter case a great
deal of information is available and check-observations are ob-
tainable. It would be dangerous to proceed with too much interpretation of the Nuer case, at least if such interpretation is
to suggest the case "fits" the expected pattern. On the other
hand, it must be pointed out that the classificatory extension
of attitudes by the Nuer is suggestive. "The *gwanlen,* particularly the father's half-brother, is portrayed by Nuer as the
wicked uncle and is contrasted with the good uncle, the *nar,*
particularly the mother's uterine brother."[27] The mother's
brother is tender to his sister's children and he is often spoken
of as a "kind of male mother himself."[28] "The mother's sister-
sister's son relationship belongs to the *gaatnyiet* category . . .
Of all Nuer relationships it is the one of the most unadulterated
benevolence."[29] It will be seen that on the basis of the extension
index alone the Nuer enter as a positive case. And it may very
well be that hostile attitudes to father are projected on the
gwanlen. Policy procedure, however, dictates a minimum of
interpretation and the use of direct "action" of father and
mother as indices wherever possible. The Nuer are rather too
equivocal to base any judgment in either direction on them,
but certainly they do not solidly support the hypothesis and a
good deal of information is provided.

Malinowski and the Matrilineal Case

The remaining five cases raise an entirely different problem.
We may suggest the significance of this problem by concentrat-
ing on an analysis, for the moment, of the most famous of these
cases.

25. Evans-Pritchard, *op. cit.,* p. 137.
26. *Ibid.,* p. 139.
27. *Ibid.,* p. 157.
28. *Ibid.,* p. 166.
29. *Ibid.,* p. 168.

The kinship structure of the Trobriand Islands is matrilineal; that is, when a child is born he is assigned to membership in a corporate group to which his mother belongs, and to which his father does not belong. This group is formed on the basis of actual or presumed descent in the female line. It is characteristic of such systems that, where the solidarity with the larger kinship grouping takes precedence over the solidarity of the nuclear family—where, that is, the obligations to members of the matrilineage are presumed to override obligations to members of the nuclear family—some member of the matrilineage has significant rights in authority over the members of the nuclear family. This is ordinarily formulated in the role of the "mother's brother." Entailed in this authority, of course, are also significant responsibilities.

In the Trobriands[30] a significant part of a male's productive activity goes *not* to the maintenance of the nuclear family of which, by definition, he is a member, but rather to the nuclear family of his *sister*. In other words the role entails certain obligations of instrumental support, *not* to the system formed of himself, his wife, and his children, but to members of a "stronger" solidary group. (A more detailed reading of Malinowski might suggest that this is not entirely the case.) The male also assumes the functions of discipline and control over his *sister's* son. With his own child, "father" is a friend and companion. What authority he holds lies in the sentiment-system the child organizes about this affectionate relationship. "The authority over the children is vested in the mother's brother . . . Her children are . . . his only heirs and successors, and he wields over them the direct potestas . . . To the father, therefore, the children look only for loving care and tender companionship. Their mother's brother represents the principle of discipline, authority and executive power within the family."[31]

What Malinowski suggests, therefore (and he suggests this explicitly, with reference primarily to the problem of the Oedipus complex in matrilineal societies), is that there is an entire *class* of cases which do not fit the hypothesis we have

---

30. See particularly, B. Malinowski, *Sex and Repression in Savage Society* (London: Routledge and Kegan Paul, 1927).

31. *Ibid.,* pp. 10-11.

stated; and that furthermore it is a variation in descent grouping which explains these cases.

If this is true, a number of propositions follow. First a significant proportion of our negative cases, Malinowski implies, can be accounted for by the operation of one basic principle. And it is true that half of the negative cases are matrilineal cases.

We might expect also, however, that if we were to partition out all matrilineal cases from our sample the number of proportionate negative cases for Malinowski's hypothesis should be at least no greater than the number of proportionate negative cases for our own hypothesis. (This merely states that we expect all matrilineal cases to show *both* father and mother expressive, but allow a certain "slippage" by comparing this sub-sample with the main sample.)

We may use the same designations, reverse what we take as a positive case, and examine the results for matrilineal cases alone.[32]

Not-D	D
5	14

It is clear that Malinowski's hypothesis does not hold. We must now, however, follow the problem further and ask, just what explains the failure of Malinowski's hypothesis to hold.

The Husband-Father in Matrilineal Systems

The problem of the matrilineal case arises not so much from a failure of our differentiation hypothesis to hold for the nuclear family, but from a problem in the relations of nuclear families to the groups in which they are incorporated. Where the solidarity of the matrilineal descent group takes precedence over the solidarity of the nuclear family a problem arises which makes the matrilineal system particularly difficult to interpret. It is essential to note first that mother and father do not simply exchange roles (as we shall indicate when we test for allocation). The nuclear family in the matrilineage, that is, is not simply a mirror image of the nuclear family in a patrilineage.

32. It may appear that as a matter of fact there is a significant difference here, although reversing Malinowski's hypothesis; but because of the small number of cases there is little significance in this table.

Mother does not take an instrumental role, *either* in matrilineal or patrilineal systems. The problem, rather, is who shall have greater authority and greater responsibility for the mother and children, the father as a member of the nuclear family or the mother's brother representing the matrilineage. A variety of ways of settling this problem are known, depending both on the degree to which the particular culture emphasizes the solidarity of members of the matrilineage and the degree to which mother's brother and father are physically present or absent (these two are, of course, inherently related and the physical presence at the home of the sister or mother may be taken as an index of the solidarity of a male with his matrilineal kin). The basic point is that the problem is one of the relation of the *nuclear family as a system* to the *matrilineage as a system;* so that there is not so much a problem of differentiation in the stated directions within the first system, but rather of the relation of two levels of system reference.

Thus, to cite specific cases the average male in Zuni has been married perhaps three or four times before he settles down. This is an interesting index of the unstable structure of the group of "our bridegrooms" in most matrilineal societies. Yet only among the Nyar does this involve a succession of "lovers" rather than "marriage." While at first the "marriage" is always more or less temporary—on probation—a general pattern is reasonably common; the newly acquired male validates himself, with the passage of time, through hard work and abundant procreation. And as a "father" or "grandfather" of the group his authority in the *household* is often great. The older males of the domestic group are ordinarily stable; more significantly, they are the most important instrumental figures in the *household* group taken as a distinct system. A breakdown of the instrumental role into "provision" and "socialization" functions is particularly illuminating at this point. For the case of the Trobriands is almost as unique as the Nyar. Of 19 matrilineal cases *only* in the Trobriands does the husband-father "provide" regularly for his *sister's* family; even there this is not entirely the case. In other words, in *both* the matrilineal case and the supposedly more patripotestal patrilineal case, the husband-father is generally held responsible for the support of his *own* wife and children.

A further breakdown of the relative instrumental authority of father and mother's brother in the socialization context is also revealing. We may distinguish the *jural* significance of the father's authority and the *de facto* significance of the father's authority. This, in a sense, distinguishes the status of the husband during the probation period from the status he gradually acquires as he validates himself in his role. An examination of this table gives a clue, I think, to the factors operating in the matrilineal case.[33]

	Provision				Jural		
	Fa	Mobro			Fa	Mobro	
S o c i a l i z a t i o n	15	1	mobro		0	5	D e F a c t o
	3	0	fa		4	10	

We may ask first, I think, what discriminates the cases in which *father* holds both jural and de facto authority over his children from those in which mother's brother holds both jural and de facto authority over his sister's children. The Kaska, for instance, in which father holds jural authority over his children as well as de facto authority, *approach bilateral symmetry* by attenuating the extension of kin obligations. The Crow similarly effect a symmetry, not by attenuating kinship obligations so much as by emphasizing the importance of the patrikin. The Haida, in which the mother's brother has both jural and strong de facto authority, on the other hand, strongly emphasize the avunculate and hence the exclusive solidarity of the matrilineage. And in general the father plays the least part as an authority

---

33. The number of cases, of course, is too small for statistical significance, even if we assumed a random sample.

figure where the solidarity of the matrilineage is most heavily emphasized.[34]

The cases in which the mother's brother holds jural authority and father de facto authority actually vary along a range depending on the degree to which the instrumental male (either fa or mobro) is incorporated into the functioning household group. The system of matrilocal residence operates to detach the mother's brother from effective participation in his sister's nuclear family unless he can return to it often (any other residence rule accomplishes the same end, of course, except in the Nayar.) If this is the case, clearly (if our hypothesis is correct) some more immediately present participant of the group would be expected to take a significant instrumental role. Thus the father takes over the problems not only of provision but also of de facto discipline and control of the child, in the absence of the jural authority figure, the mother's brother. The father's *jural* significance (or insignificance) rests on essentially the same principle, applied in reverse; he approaches the core of the matrilineage as a stranger, he is only tentatively incorporated into the family at first. He cannot be officially responsible for the smooth functioning of a group from which he may soon part. And he is never a member of the corporate group to which his children belong by birth. As time passes, however, a dual authority pattern apparently emerges.

The crux of this pattern is a relation between *two systems,* the household group and the descent group; it is *not* a question of who, *in the nuclear family,* will play the instrumental role. The mother's brother holds the position of authority in the descent group, but the father controls the domestic household. The relative distribution of instrumental responsibilities of the two from case to case may be expected to vary with the relative degree of incorporation of each in the household group on the one hand, the matrilineage on the other. Avunculocal residence particularly should materially reinforce the mother's brother's control; if residence is matrilocal, the more often the mother's brother can be present in his sister's household, the more important in fact will be his control by definition; if the

34. Culminating in the unique case of the Nayar, where the matrilineage is emphasized at the expense of the entire conception of the father as a role in continuous relation to either mother or children. See Gough: 1952, 1954.

father is away at the home of *his* sister more often than not, this too, of course, affects the distribution of authority and control. But clearly, the problem rests on the relation of nuclear families to more extensive systems in which they are incorporated. In most societies, although a unilineal kin group is not necessarily found, a much stronger solidarity is formed with one or both families of orientation of a conjugal pair, than we normally expect in our own society. It may be that only one of these families has rights or duties in relation to the pair, or that both have rights and duties of various sorts. Ordinarily the issue is the membership of the children born to the pair in one, or both, or neither of the descent groups from which the parents come. It is the rights over the children, that is, who are members of one or another extended kin grouping that focus the relations of nuclear families to larger kin groupings. Having rights over the children, the descent group has rights over the nuclear family; and in matrilineal systems the mother's brother represents the descent group in its relation with his sister's children.

The mother's brother, however, is not a constituent member of the nuclear family. And the father generally, *relative to the wife-mother,* plays a distinctly instrumental role in almost all cases. Where the nuclear family is subordinate to the matrilineage, the father is, clearly, subordinate in authority over his wife and children to the mother's brother as representative of the matrilineage. And the more significant the role of the mother's brother as an authority figure, the more the father is freed from any restraint and inhibition in his relation to his own children. But relative to his wife, and *more* significantly to the degree that the mother's brother is *less* significant, the father plays the role both of provider for the family and of authority in socialization.

The Allocation of Roles in the Nuclear Family

Although a great deal has been said about the role of mother and father in the discussion of matrilineal systems, in point of fact only the *presence* of differentiation, and not the allocation of roles to system members, was at stake up to this point. It could quite easily have turned out that mother took the instrumental role, on the basis of her position as a representative of the matrilineage, and the hypothesis being tested would still have held. As a matter of fact, digressing for a moment, this would have provided a much clearer picture of the problems in the relation of the nuclear family to the matrilineage as a corporate group. It would, that is, have been more obvious that *two levels* of authority were involved in the discussion of the relation of the authority of the mother's brother to instrumental leadership *within* the nuclear family as a system, since it would have been a question of the relative primacy of two members of the same unilineal corporate group. This would have been more clearly a matter, then, of the relative solidarity of the descent group as against the nuclear family, and the relative precedence of obligations to each.

The "matriarch" of a matrilineal system, however, is *not* primarily an instrumental figure. In most matrilineal societies women have high status; and in many they have great influence. We may compare, however the "Virgin Mary" in patrilineal imagery, and the "behind the scenes" influence of the woman who "really runs things" or "really holds the family together" in the "patripotestal" case. One is as likely to find an "old matriarch" in the one case as in the other. In both matrilineal and patrilineal societies, the "influence" of women seems to rest on their role as integrative focus of the family rather than on instrumental control. The exceptions reported are not generally explained by matrilineal bias; only the Tullushi of South Africa,[35] characterized by dual descent but with much conflict between patrilineal and matrilineal sentiments, seem to show "dominant" women on this basis. It is often the case, as among the Hano,[36] that within the reference system of the larger kingroup, the "mother's mother" or some other senior "mother" is respected highly for her place in lineage councils; she is often also responsible for the allocation of household labor among the subordinate "mothers" and orders younger household members around. It is apparently not the case that her husband or brother "obey" her; her position does not, in fact, differ materially from

35. Cf. S. F. Nadel, "Double Descent in the Nuba Hills," in A. R. Radcliffe-Brown and D. Forde, *op. cit.*

36. Cf. F. Eggan, *Social Organization of the Western Pueblos* (Chicago: University of Chicago Press, 1950).

the role of the "mother-in-law" in strongly patripotestal China.[37] A test for the instrumental leadership of mother in matrilineal cases, independent of the test for mother's brother or father, indicates the following, where "E" designates expressive leadership and "I" instrumental leadership in the nuclear family:

E	I
19	0

Clearly, the effect of focus on mother's descent group does *not* reverse the allocation of roles in the nuclear family. The entire problem of interpreting the allocation of instrumental leadership in matrilineal societies, therefore, rests in the relation of father and mother's brother, as we have already shown; and the crux of *this* problem is the relation of two systems (the nuclear family and the descent group) to each other and their relative solidarity.

If we are to look for cases which are negative for the allocation of roles according to the hypothesis we have stated, it is apparent that we must investigate not the matrilineal, but the patrilineal, bilateral, and dual descent cases in the remaining portion of our sample. Any new negative cases that might be added will be found in this portion of the sample, since, in effect, we have already treated allocation in the matrilineal case.

The sample includes 37 patrilineal, bilateral, and dual descent cases. In patrilineal societies we would expect that the father would take the instrumental role, *either* on the basis of the hypothesis we first stated, or on the basis of his role as representative of the descent group to which both he and his children belong. There is, as usual, a definite problem of distinguishing levels of authority and system reference here but, since both focus on the same person, there is no consequent problem in interpretation of concrete systems. Nevertheless, in bilateral systems it is much more clear that the results obtained are due to the hypothesis that factors inherent in the situation of nuclear families account for the allocation of the instrumental and expressive roles. There is no "bias" of the system in the direction of father as a representative of the superordinate system to which the family belongs since the family belongs to a much

37. Yang, *op. cit.* See also, M. J. Levy, *Family Revolution in Modern China* (Cambridge, Mass.: Harvard University Press, 1949).

more loosely structured bilateral kindred. The father should, we expect, play the role of instrumental leader in the nuclear family simply because of the character of the nuclear family as a system. Clearly, we assume that the mother plays the role of expressive leader on grounds already stated. If we use the designations "A" and "not-A", the "patripotestal" sample divides as follows:[38]

A	not-A
29	8

Of the eight negative cases, five are accounted for by the Arapesh, Mundugomor, Cheyenne, Arapaho, and Nuer, which have already been discussed. Of the remaining three, two are reported by Margaret Mead.

Tchambuli and the Manus

The Tchambuli[39] and the Manus[40] seem to present another problem of almost but not quite. It is almost certain that in the case of the Tchambuli it is merely the categories which confuse the issue. While from the point of view of Mead the men act like women, from other points of view the Tchambuli are a regular patrilineal society. There is a strong respect relation between father and son. While the women do all the trading and fishing, they are nevertheless the solidary focus of the whole society. ". . . the women remain . . . a solid group upon whom (the male) depends for support, for food, for affection."[41] From Mead's point of view the men play at life while the women contribute the solid work which sustains them. This is a common Meadian theme, of course. It also resembles a common picture of the Irish urban family—of the drunken lower-class father besotted in the local pub while the mother slaves to hold the family together; but this is closer to the role of "integrative focus" than "instrumental provision." The Tchambuli men "are theoretically dominant, but . . . play an emotionally sub-

38. Assuming, again, a random model, this difference would be significant at better than the 1% level.

39. M. Mead, *op. cit.*

40. Margaret Mead, *Growing Up in New Guinea* (William Morrow & Co., 1930).

41. M. Mead, *op. cit.*, p. 173.

servient role, dependent upon the security given them by women."[42] This is not a contradiction of the hypothesis. But it is also the women who "control the economy"; it is the women who "initiate action." The marketing which the men are "allowed" to do, they turn into an expressive activity, or a "gala occasion" as Mead states it. It might be sound to argue that given the task definition of the Tchambuli, the men are responsible for its accomplishment, or that had Mead arrived four years earlier—before the British stopped cannibalism—she might have observed a somewhat different pattern; and certainly the attitude and extension indices (mother's brother is expressive, father's relatives are respected, one is uneasy in their presence) indicate a paradigmatic case. Nevertheless, on the "not quite" argument, Tchambuli is treated as negative.

A briefer discussion should suffice for Manus. Here the distinction of task-functions is again necessary. In the task of provision, the male is instrumental leader. But in socialization he is expressive—affectionate and "preferred" by his children to the mother. One is not quite certain what the female is, except unhappy. Father holds the authority in the family, but it is through the mother evidently that he disciplines the child— that is, he disciplines the mother and she is responsible for the child's behavior. This enters as a negative case on the grounds that there is not adequate evidence of roles clearly allocated in the direction expected and explicit statement of the contrary pattern in a least one task-function.

The Marquesas

Among the polyandrous Marquesans,[43] the wife is explicitly an expressive leader for the husbands of the family. The leading husband is the instrumental leader, "an organizer." For the system formed of wife, head husband, and secondary husbands the hypothesis holds, and the allocation is in the direction expected. But there is a good deal of evidence that for the children of the family the secondary husbands are the expressive foci. Certainly the mother is not. "The child is not breast-fed

---

42. *Ibid.*, p. 182.

43. Cf. A. Kardiner, ed., *The Individual and His Society* (New York: Columbia University Press, 1939). See Chapters 5 and 6.

and the feeding procedure . . . is rather harsh according to our standards. . . . These facts cannot in themselves be of any great significance as regards permanent effects on the child's development. They are, however, characteristic of the attitude of mother to child. Maternal care is a secondary interest to the women, the basic one being that of courtesan to the men."[44] On the other hand, "The real protectors of the child are the secondary husbands. . . . The mother as a protectress and caretaker suffers by comparison . . . .[45] The attitude indices support this interpretation. "In this society the male, as child or adult, shows the inability to trust, or to feel that the woman is devoted to him."[46] While "Children were respectful but indifferent toward their mothers, they seemed much more interested in the males of the household."[47]

Since there is no instinctive reason for the "normal" sex allocation, *some* variation which is valid should be expected. That most of the cases cited by Mead appear on analysis rather as if they might not be negative from the present point of view, does *not* mean that negative cases should be regarded as impossible, at least for the allocation theorems.

Summary and Conclusions

While rather significant conclusions can be drawn, the crudeness of the method of verifying them makes them rather difficult to evaluate. This should be carefully considered in accepting the conclusions of the tests. In at least half of the cases, for instance, if "respect" and "affection" do not in fact indicate instrumental and expressive leadership (i.e., as defined in terms of actions of ego), then the hypotheses cannot be legitimately considered "proved" *or* "disproved." This chance was taken on the grounds that, having sacrificed the method of intensive analysis in the original conditions of the design, extensive replication was necessary. This demands numbers; and the number of monographs which provide evidence on the basis of direct designation rules is limited. Differences in rating might also

---

44. *Ibid.*, p. 205.
45. *Ibid.*, p. 213.
46. *Ibid.*, p. 215.
47. *Ibid.*, p. 159.

be considered; although it may fairly be said for the differentiation hypothesis, at least, that the number of negative cases could have been increased by the equivocal cases finally judged positive and the hypothesis would still have held. The chief equivocal cases were the Lozi and the American middle-class family, which some raters might have treated as negative.

We may, as a matter of fact, consider the American middle-class case in reviewing the definitions we have given to instrumental and expressive leadership. From certain points of view the American middle-class family approaches most clearly to equal allocation (or "no allocation") of instrumental and expressive activities. The universalistic value schema (in which women are "just as good as" men) coupled with the general attitude toward the explicit expression of authority ("I'm agin it") apparently constitutes the limiting case of no differentiation at all. Underlying this broad value-schema, however, a rather clear differentiation occurs.

In the distribution of instrumental tasks, the American family maintains a more flexible pattern than most societies. Father helps mother with the dishes. He sets the table. He makes formula for the baby. Mother can supplement the income of the family by working outside. Nevertheless, the American male, by definition, *must* "provide" for his family. He is *responsible* for the support of his wife and children. His primary area of performance is the occupational role, in which his status fundamentally inheres; and his *primary* function in the family is to supply an "income," to be the "breadwinner." There is simply something wrong with the American adult male who doesn't have a "job." American women, on the other hand, tend to hold jobs *before* they are married and to quit when "the day" comes; or to continue in jobs of a lower status than their husbands.[48] And not only is the mother the focus of emotional support for the American middle-class child, but much more exclusively so than in most societies (as Margaret Mead has pointed out in her treatment of adolescent problems). The cult of the warm, giving "Mom" stands in contrast to the "capable," "competent," "go-getting" male. The more expressive type of male, as a matter of fact, is regarded as "effeminate," and has too much fat on the inner side of his thigh.

48. See Chapter I.

The distribution of authority is legitimized on a different basis in the "democratic" family than in the so-called "traditional" one; but the father is "supposed" to remain the primary executive member. The image of the "henpecked" husband makes sense only on this premise. His "commands" are validated on the basis of "good judgment," rather than *general* obedience due a person in authority. But when the mother's efforts at "disciplining" fail, she traditionally tells the errant child, "Wait till daddy gets home."

In generalizing this pattern, of instrumental leadership focussed on the achievement of tasks and expressive leadership focussed on emotionally-supportive behaviors, the most difficult problem of interpretation lies in clearly distinguishing the nuclear family from the descent groups which in some cases took precedence as solidarities over them. This may be discussed in terms of two rather unique cases. The Nayar (who do not appear in this sample) so completely incorporate the mother-child system in the matrilineage that no husband-father status *exists* in the sense usually given to this term. The males of the matrilineage take over the husband-father's functions, and to all inents and purposes *no nuclear family exists*. This is the limiting case in the incorporation of nuclear families in larger descent groups. It is, in a sense, the mirror opposite of the American isolated conjugal family; the same principle, applied in different ways is at stake. The question is simply the relative solidarity of two cross-cutting systems. In our society the nuclear family is clearly a stronger solidarity than any other kinship based group and no *corporate* descent group exists. Among the Nayar, the matrilineage was the clearly dominant solidarity to the unusual extent of destroying the nuclear family as a continuously functioning group entirely. Somewhere in between these poles lie most of the cases known. The Trobriands approach the uniqueness of the Nayar, however, in giving the mother's brother more extensive obligations to and responsibility over the nuclear family of his sister than is common even in matrilineal societies. (It may some day turn out that many of these obligations are primarily symbolic and do not in fact take up as much of the mother's brother's productive activity as has been supposed.) The effect of this is to reduce the husband-father's role in the nuclear family, since he is a mother's brother in someone else's nuclear family and is occupied in task-functions *outside* his own nuclear family. Again, the basis of this is clearly the relative emphasis on the *lineage* as a solidarity.

Ordinarily, however, the solidarity of the lineage does not completely obscure the husband-father's instrumental role in his own nuclear family. The Trobriands, that is, is *not* the paradigmatic matrilineal case, any more than the Nayar is. And where the husband-father spends any time at all in his own nuclear family even in the matrilineal case he takes on significant de facto instrumental authority. To the extent, that is, that the nuclear family *does* function as a system, it differentiates in the direction expected.

In dealing with the allocation problem, it is apparent that the initial relation of mother and child is sufficiently important so that the mother's expressive role in the family is largely *not* problematical. It is particularly important to note that apparently no *systematic* principle, such as the impingement of descent groupings, tends to reverse her role, unless the Mundugomor can be taken as an instance. (It is likely that the problems of the Mundugomor arise because of the cross-cutting solidarities within the household group, and that it can best be described, *not* from the point of view of aggressive, dominant roles *defined* for the mother and father, but rather as a system subject to great tensions which are revealed in mutual hostilities.)

The allocation of instrumental leadership to the father, on the other hand, is only problematic in the sense that the interrelation of the nuclear family and the descent group may, in one class of cases, obscure the husband-father's role. And this we have already discussed. In the patrilineal cases, in which this particular problem raises fewer interpretative issues in concrete systems (except that, of course, there *are* important problems in the relation of a husband-father to *his* father) the role is reasonably clear. This is true also for bilateral systems.

On the whole, therefore, when the nuclear family can be clearly distinguished from incorporating solidarities, it differentiates in the direction expected and allocates the relevant roles to the persons expected. And the problems which are raised in interpreting the data do not arise so much from whether or not this is true, but rather from what effect the precedence of obligations to corporate descent groups may have. This becomes, stated in a general form, a problem of the relative authority of the husband-father compared to that of some person in the superordinate descent group; where this descent group is matrilineal, the problem is one of the relative authority of father vs. mother's brother. The effect on patrilineal systems is to confine the difficulties in this relationship *within* the corporate descent group; and eventually the husband-father achieves a role of dominance in the descent group as well as the nuclear family. The effect in matrilineal systems is different, since the father can never become a member of the matrilineage. He must validate his position through his contribution to the everyday life of the household group, and his position is much less stable. In a great many cases, nevertheless, he *does* become the significant instrumental figure in the household group; and *always,* relative to *mother* this is the case. From the point of view of his legal status in the system, he is at the same time freed from certain obligations to his own family and denied certain rights in control of his own family; from the point of view of the general conditions for the existence of social systems as systems, however, he *must* accept some of these obligations and be allowed certain of these rights.

A Note on the Indices

1. The Validity of the Indices.

1.1. The extension index appears to be valid on the basis of internal evidence of the monographs. Although in strict form the propositions on which the index rests cannot be treated here, the process of extension is neatly indicated for North Malaita: "A close personal relations exists from the beginning between an infant and its parents, but from the fourth month onwards it comes in contact with several other persons. It soon becomes friendly with those it sees most often and makes no objection when they take it in their arms. It always sleeps with its mother, however, and as she alone suckles it, it is far more at ease by her side. The first words learnt are the terms for mother and father, and these are applied not only to the real parents but also to the other persons whom the child knows. At this early age a baby cannot realize, of course, that a specific relationship is implied ... The terms acquire their true significance with the family, for though other persons may share some of the responsibilities for the child's up-bringing, the main obligation rests on the parents, and they are its most constant companions. At the same time, little difference is to be observed between its behavior towards its parents and towards these others. It looks to all the women ... to provide protection and food, and obeys all the men." The child is encouraged to extend these attitudes to the proper relatives as he grows up. "Thus maternal tenderness is displayed by the women called mother in the expectation that they in return will be shown filial devotion. Behavior considered proper between a son and his real father has also to be carried over to the men classed with him, and so forth ..."[49] For the Nuer, on the other hand, the extension fails to indicate the equivocal status of the nuclear system.[50]

1.2. There is some question as to whether we are measuring what we intend to measure in using the attitude index. Where both direct designation and attitude index are present some comparison is possible. It is significant that in the Marquesas the child is indifferent to the women, does not trust them, and prefers the men of the household; in view of the direct determination of the roles in Marquesas, the attitude varies in the expected direction. Since this is a negative case for allocation, the correlation of the two methods of determination is particularly important and indicative. Among the Tallensi, however, reverse English is applied to the indices. "There is a familiarity, almost a camaraderie, between parent and child that makes the observer wonder how the authority of the parent can be as effective, and the respect and obedience of the child as sincere as the evidence of custom and belief show them to be ... There is ... more restraint in the manner in which a person speaks to his mother ... (although) her love for her children is subject to no limits or laws. ..."[51] The social image of the parents in Tale society fits closely the patrilineal paradigm: "The mother is thought of as the foodgiver. ... Her relations with them are based on love tempered with authority. The father is thought of as the source of discipline, the guardian of good conduct. He is strict without being harsh or tyrannous. ... His relations with his children are based on his authority over them, his responsibility for them, and justice tempered with love."[52] Fortes' explanation of these attitudes: "The liberty to address his father by name is a reassurance, to the child, of the love and solicitude that lie behind the authority his father exercises over

49. Hogbin, *Experiments in Civilization* (London: G. Routledge, 1939), pp. 29-30.

50. Evans-Pritchard, *op. cit.*

51. M. Fortes, *The Web of Kinship Among the Tallensi* (Oxford: Oxford University Press, 1949), p. 196.

52. *Ibid.*, pp. 196-198.

him. . . . And the greater deference in his behavior towards his mother than towards his father is a sign that he recognizes her control, though she seems to have only love and devotion for him. . . . The greater overt freedom with father compensates for the greater emphasis on respect and dependence in the child's relations with him; the franker signs of deference towards the mother compensate for the greater emphasis on her love for the child against her authority over him."[53]

It is apparent that if this sort of reversal holds for any significant number of cases and direct designation is not available, the basis of the tests is materially weakened.

2. The Reliability of the Indices.

2.1. Because the extensions usually are less ambivalent than the attitude to or behavior of the father and mother, they are peculiarly suited to being reliable indices: two or more raters are quite likely to make the same judgment concerning them.

2.2. The attitudes, on the other hand, are if anything peculiarly unreliable. The problem centers on the meaning of the term "respect." A statement of the form: "Son respects father" is taken as an index of the instrumental leadership of father. But the term respect is by no means univocal. A statement of the form "Son respects mother" may or may not mean the same as "Son respects father." The solidarity of the parental generation may operate here; it is much more likely that the second statement means merely "Son does not express contempt for mother." The mixture of "respect and affection" is common but "respect" in this case may mean merely that the person in question is "thought highly of." This is not what one intends by the usage "respect relation," however. A good deal of third hand guess work goes into the decision in such cases and the use of the index is restricted as much as possible. The decision in each case to class "owing respect" as an index of the attitude to "instrumental activity" is based on whatever evidence obtains that this refers to "distance, or constraint" vs. "closeness or ease."

3. Paradigm of the Patripotestal Nuclear Family: The Irish Peasant.[54]

3.1. The role of the Father: "On the normal farm there is an adult male farmer who is husband, father, and owner of the farm. Within the group he has the controlling role, subject to conventional restric-

---

53. *Ibid.*, p. 198.

54. C. Arensberg and S. T. Kimball, *Family and Community in Ireland* (Cambridge, Mass.: Harvard University Press, 1948), pp. 47-59.

tions on his authority. In farm work . . . he directs the activity of the family as it works in concert. . . . In his special province he looks after and cares for the cattle . . . disposes of income they bring in. But all this he is obliged to do in the interests of his wife and children.

"It goes without saying that the farther exercises his control over the whole activity of the boy. . . . Indeed the father is the court of last resort, which dispenses punishment for deviations from the norm of conduct in all spheres. Within the bounds of custom and law he has full power to exercise discipline.

"This fact colors greatly the relationship of father and son as far as affective content goes. There is none of the close companionship and intimate sympathy (which characterizes the relationship to the mother). In its place there is developed, necessarily perhaps, a marked respect. . . ."

3.2. The role of the Mother: "The relationship (to mother) is the first and earliest into which a child enters. It is very close, intimate and all-embracing for the first years of life: only gradually does the experience of the child expand to include brothers, sisters, and last, the older male members of the household.

"Until seven, the child of either sex is the constant companion of its mother. If the family is numerous an elder child may take over much of the mother's role, but the mother is always near by. As the woman works in the house or fields, the child is kept by her side. . . . It learns its speech from its mother, amid a flood of constant endearments, admonitions, and encouragements. The woman's work never separates her from the child. Custom imposes no restraints or interruptions in her solicitude. She looks after its comforts, gives it food, dresses it, etc. . . .

"The (constant) controls she exercises are of a different kind from those of the father. She is both guide and companion. Her authority most often makes itself felt through praise, persuasion and endearment. Only when a grave breach of discipline demands a restraining power greater than hers, or when an appeal to ultimate authority is needed, does father begin to play his role. . . .

" (The Son) becomes confirmed, it is true, in a masculine scorn for feminine interests and pursuits, but he can and must still look for protection to his mother against a too-arbitrary exercise of his father's power. In family disputes the mother takes a diplomatic, conciliatory role.

"Throughout the years of the son's full activity in the farm economy under the father's leadership, the mother still remains the source of comfort and the preparer of food and is still infinitely solicitous of his welfare . . . If the child must leave the farm for other walks of life, the closest possible relationship is still maintained. When one goes home, it is to see one's mother . . . In exile, the bond lingers as a profound sentimental nostalgia."[55]

4. Paradigm of the matrilineal case: The Hopi Pueblo.

4.1. The role of the Mother's Brother: "The relation of a mother's brother to his sister's children is . . . one of the most important in the Hopi kinship structure. As head of his sister's lineage and household, his position is one of authority and control; he is the chief disciplinarian and is both respected and obeyed. . . . To make him a good Hopi, he may get his nephew up early to run around the mesa and bathe in cold water; if he is lazy, he will pour water on him. In return a nephew is frequently afraid of his uncle, particularly where punishment is administered, but an uncle usually has his nephew's interests at heart. . . ."[56]

4.2. The role of the Mother: "From the first day of his life the baby was surrounded by constant care and attention, . . . from his mother (and also) from his mother's mother and her siblings as well."[57] "Hopi mothers are notoriously over-indulgent towards their children. . . . Mothers often scold and threaten punishment but only rarely do they make good their threats. . . . Despite occasional quarrels; a good deal of affection is usually involved in the relationships of mother and daughter."[58]

4.3. The role of the Father: "A husband has the economic obligation of helping to support not only his wife but the whole household. . . ."[59] ". . . A child belongs to the mother's lineage and clan but is a 'child' of the father's clan; although both are recognized as kin, the two parental groups are rather sharply differentiated in attitudes, behavior, and residence. The father . . . is mainly responsible for preparing (his sons) to make a living. . . . The position of a father in relationship to his son is something like that of an older comrade and teacher. There is affection but little in the way of punishment, and while a boy respects his father, he does not ordinarily fear him. . . ."[60]

55. *Ibid.*, pp. 59-60.
56. F. Eggan, *op. cit.*, p. 37.
57. *Ibid.*, p. 224.
58. Cf. M. Titiev, *Old Oraibi*. Papers of the Peabody Museum. Vol. 22, No. 1, 1944, pp. 20-21.
59. F. Eggan, *op. cit.*, p. 34.
60. *Ibid.*, pp. 31-32.

Rating of Cases in Sample for Differentiation and Allocation*

PATRILINEAL CASES

Case	Fa Role	Mo Role	Rating on Diff.	Rating on Alloc.
1. Arapesh	e	E	neg	neg
2. BaThonga	I	E	pos	pos
3. China	I	E	pos	pos
4. Fr. Canadian	I	E	pos	pos
5. German	I	E	pos	pos
6. Iatmul	I	E	pos	pos
7. India	I	E	pos	pos
8. Irish	I	E	pos	pos
9. Japan	I	E	pos	pos
10. Malaita	I	E	pos	pos
11. Manus	Ei	Ie	pos	neg
12. Marquesas	Ie	ie	neg	neg
13. Nama	I	E	pos	pos
14. Nuer	IE	EI	neg	neg
15. Nyakyusa	I	E	pos	pos
16. Papago	I	E	pos	pos
17. Piliga	I	E	pos	pos
18. Polish	I	E	pos	pos
19. Sp. American	I	E	pos	pos
20. Swazi	I	E	pos	pos
21. Tallensi	I	E	pos	pos
22. Tanala	I	E	pos	pos
23. Tikopia	I	E	pos	pos
24. Tswana	I	E	pos	pos
25. Tchambuli	E	Ie	pos	neg
26. Zulu	I	E	pos	pos

BILATERAL CASES

Case	Fa Role	Mo Role	Rating on Diff.	Rating on Alloc.
1. Arapaho	I	I	neg	neg
2. Cheyenne	I	I	neg	neg
3. Chiricahua	I	E	pos	pos
4. Comanche	I	E	pos	pos
5. Dakota	I	E	pos	pos
6. Kiowa Apache	I	E	pos	pos
7. Lozi	Ie	E	pos	pos
8. Samoa	I	E	pos	pos
9. U.S. (M-class)	I	Ei	pos	pos

*Roles are indicated according to the following key: I for instrumental leader; E for expressive leader; IE or EI for equivocal cases, with possibly more dominant characteristic recorded in initial position; i for subordinate instrumental, e for subordinate expressive; i or e in combination with a capital in initial position indicates a strong sub-component of role. In the matrilineal sample "i" or "ie" is used for father role where mother's brother has clear rights of authority over nuclear family of father but father has significant de facto authority; "i" alone indicates a relatively strong instrument role; "I," indicates that mother's brother has few rights over sister's children, the father holding jural authority.

Rating of Cases in Sample for Differentiation and Allocation (contd.)

MATRILINEAL CASES

Case	Fa Role	Mo Role	Rating on Diff.	Rating on Alloc.
1. Acoma	ie	E	pos	pos
2. Ashanti	ie	E	pos	pos
3. Bemba	i	E	pos	pos
4. Buka	e	E	neg	neg
5. Crow	l	E	pos	pos
6. Haida	e	E	neg	neg
7. Hano	e	E	neg	neg
8. Ila	i	E	pos	pos
9. Kaska	l	E	pos	pos
10. Laguna	e	E	neg	neg
11. Hopi	ie	E	pos	pos
12. Mandan	i	E	pos	pos
13. Navaho	ie	E	pos	pos
14. Trobriands	e	E	neg	neg
15. Truck	i	E	pos	pos
16. Ulithi	i	E	pos	pos
17. W. K. Shoshone	l	E	pos	pos
18. W. M. Apache	l	E	pos	pos
19. Zuni	ie	E	pos	pos

CASES OF DOUBLE DESCENT

Case	Fa Role	Mo Role	Rating on Diff.	Rating on Alloc.
1. Mundugomor	l	l	neg	neg
2. Yako	l	E	pos	pos

Case List: Sources*

Acoma: F. Eggan, 1950 (11)
Arapaho: F. Eggan, 1937 (9)
Arapesh: Mead, 1935 (50)
Ashanti: Fortes, 1950 (17)
BaThonga: Radcliffe-Brown, 1952 (66)
Bemba: Richards, 1939 (68); 1950 (65)

Buka: Blackwood, 1935 (6)
Cheyenne: F. Eggan, 1937 (9)
China: Levy, 1949 (40); Yang, 1945 (74)
Chiricahua: Opler, 1941 (55)
Comanche: Hoebel, 1939 (28)
Crow: Lowie, 1935 (42); Lowie, 1948 (43)

---

*The number in parenthesis refers to the particular volume in the Bibliography which contains case histories pertinent to the tribes in question.

Dakota: Hassrick, 1946 (25); Erikson, 1945 (12)

French Canada: Miner, 1939 (51)

Fox: Tax, 1947 (71)

Germany: Becker, 1946 (4); Erikson, 1942 (12); Lowie, 1948 (43); Parsons, 1942 (1), (58)

Haida: Murdock, 1934 (57)

Hano: F. Eggan, 1950 (11)

Hopi: D. Eggan, 1943 (9); F. Eggan, 1950 (11); Goldfrank, 1945 (20); Aberle, 1952 (1); Titiev, 1944 (72)

Iatmul: Bateson, 1939 (3)

Ila: Richards, 1950 (67)

India: Mandelbaum, 1948 (46)

Ireland: Arensberg and Kimball, 1948 (2)

Japan: Benedict, 1946 (5)

Kaska: Honigman, 1946 (31)

Kiowa Apache: McAllister, 1937 (47)

Laguna: F. Eggan, 1950 (11)

Lozi: Gluckman, 1950 (19)

Malaita: Hogbin, 1939 (29)

Mandan: Bowers, 1940 (7)

Manus: Mead, 1930 (49)

Marquesas: Kardiner (Linton), 1939, Chs. 5-6 (33)

Mayombe: Richards, 1950 (67)

Mundugomor: Mead, 1935 (50)

Nama (Hottentot) Radcliffe-Brown, 1952 (66)

Navaho: Kluckhohn & Leighton, 1951 (35); Kluckhohn, 1945 (34)

Nuer: Evans-Pritchard, 1951 (13)

Nyakyusa: Wilson, 1950 (73)

Papago: Joseph, 1949 (32)

Samoa: Mead, 1928 (48)

Sp. American: Edmundson, 1952 (8); Kluckhohn, 1951 (35)

Swazi: Kuper, 1950 (37)

Tallensi: Fortes, 1949 (16)

Tanala: Kardiner (Linton), 1939, Chs. 7-8 (33)

Tikopia: Firth, 1936 (14)

Toca: Herskevits & Herskevits, 1947 (27)

Tchambuli: Mead, 1935 (50)

Truck: Gladwin & Sarason, 1953 (18)

Tswana: Shapera, 1950 (69)

Trobriands: Malinowski, 1926 (44); Malinowski, 1927 (45)

Tullushi: Nadel, 1950 (54)

Ulithi: Lessa, 1950 (39)

U.S. Mid. Cl.: Parsons, 1942 (58); Parsons, 1950 (61); Stouffer, 1952 (6)

White Knife Shoshone: Harris, 1940 (24)

Wte. Mtn. Apache: Goodwin, 1942 (21)

Yako: Forde, 1950 (15)

Zulu: Gluckman, 1950 (19)

Zuni: F. Eggan, 1950 (11); Goldfrank, 1945 (20)

J. Roberts: unpublished field material.

BIBLIOGRAPHY

1. Aberle, D., "A Psycho-Social Analysis of a Hopi Life History," *Comparative Psychology Monographs*, Vol. 21, No. 1, University of California Press, 1951.

2. Arensberg, C., and Kimball, S. T., *Family and Community in Ireland,* Harvard University Press, 1948.

3. Bateson, G., *Naven*, Cambridge University Press, 1939.

4. Becker, H., *German Youth,* Oxford University Press, 1946.

5. Benedict, R., *The Chrysanthemum and the Sword,* Houghton Mifflin, 1946.

6. Blackwood, B., *Both Sides of Buka Passage,* Oxford University Press, 1935.

7. Bowers, A. W., *Mandan Social and Ceremonial Organization,* University of Chicago Press, 1940.

8. Edmundson, M. S., *Los Manitos,* unpublished Ph.D Thesis, Harvard University, 1952.

9. Eggan, D., "The General Problem of Hopi Adjustment," 1943. Reprinted in Kluckhohn, C. and Murray, H., 1949 and 1953.

10. Eggan, F., "The Cheyenne and Arapaho Kinship Systems," in Eggan (ed.) *Social Anthropology of the North American Indian Tribes,* University of Chicago Press, 1937.

11. ———, *Social Organization of the Western Pueblos,* University of Chicago Press, 1950.

12. Erikson, E. H., "Hitler's Imagery and German Youth," 1942. Reprinted in Kluckhohn and Murray, 1949.

13. ———, "Childhood and Tradition in Two American Indian Tribes," 1945. Reprinted in Kluckhohn and Murray, 1949.

14. Evans-Pritchard, E. E., *Kinship and Marriage Among the Nuer,* Oxford University Press, 1951.

15. Firth, R., *We The Tikopia,* G. Allen Unwin, 1936.

16. Forde, D., "Double Descent Among the Yako," in Radcliffe-Brown and Forde, 1950.

17. Fortes, M., *The Web of Kinship Among the Tallensi,* Oxford University Press, 1949.

18. ———, "Kinship and Marriage among the Ashanti," in Radcliffe-Brown and Forde, 1950.

19. Gladwin, T., and Sarason, S. B., *Truk: Man in Paradise,* Viking Fund Publications in Anthropology #20, 1953.

20. Gluckman, M., "Kinship and Marriage among the Lozi of Northern Rhodesia and the Zulu of Natal," in Radcliffe-Brown and Forde, 1950.

21. Goldfrank, E., "Socialization, Personality, and The Structure of Pueblo Society," *American Anthropogolist* 47: 516-539, 1945.

22. Goodwin, G., *Social Organization of the Western Apache,* University of Chicago Press, 1942.

23. Gough, E. K., "The Traditional Kinship System of the Nayars of Malabar," prepared for the Social Science Research Council Seminar on Kinship, Harvard University, 1954, unpublished.

24. ———, "Changing Kinship Usages in the Setting of Political and Economic Change Among the Nayars of Malabar," *Journal of the Royal Anthropological Institute,* LXXXXII, 1952.

25. Harris, J. S., "White Knife Shoshone of Nevada," in Linton, 1940.

26. Hassrick, R. B., "Teton Dakota Kinship System," *American Anthropologist* 46: 338-347, 1946.

27. Henry, J., and Henry, Z., "Doll Play of Pilaga Indian Children," 1944. Reprinted in Kluckhohn and Murray, 1949.

28. Herskovits, M., and Herskovits, F., *Trinidad Village,* A. Knopf, 1947.

29. Hoebel, E. A., "Comanche and Hekandika Shoshone Kinship Systems," *American Anthropologist* 41: 440-457, 1939.

30. Hogbin, I., *Experiments in Civilization,* G. Routledge, 1939.

31. Homans, G., *The Human Group,* Harcourt, Brace, 1950.

32. Honigman, J., *Culture and*

Ethos of Kaska Society, Yale Publications in Anthropology No. 40, 1946.

33. Joseph, A., Spicer, R., and Chesky, J., *The Desert People,* University of Chicago Press, 1949.

34. Kardiner, A., *The Individual and His Society,* Columbia University Press, 1939: Chapter 5 (Linton, R.) and 6; and Chapter 7 (Linton, R.) and 8.

35. Kluckhohn, C., "A Brief Paretian Analysis of a Navaho Personal Document," *Southwestern Journal of Anthropology* 1: 260-283, 1945.

36. Kluckhohn, C., and Murray, H., *Personality in Nature, Society and Culture,* Knopf, 1949 and (with David M. Schneider ed.) 1953.

37. _____, and Leighton, D., *The Navaho,* Harvard University Press, 1951.

38. Kluckhohn, F., *Los Atarquenos,* unpublished Ph.D. Thesis, Radcliffe, 1941.

39. Kuper, H., "Kinship among The Swazi," in Radcliffe-Brown and Forde, 1950.

40. Leighton, D., and Kluckhohn, C., *Children of the People,* Harvard University Press, 1948.

41. Lessa, W. A., *The Ethnography of Ulithi Atoll,* Pacific Science Board, Washington, D.C., 1950.

42. Levy, M. J., *Family Revolution in Modern China,* Harvard University Press, 1949

43. Linton, R., *Study of Man,* Appleton-Century, 1936.

44. _____, (ed.) *Acculturation in Seven Indian Tribes,* Appleton-Century, 1940.

45. Lowie, R., *The Crow Indians,* Farrar and Rinehart, 1935.

46. _____, *Social Organization,* Rinehart, 1948.

47. Malinowski, B., *Crime and Custom in Savage Society,* Routledge and Kegan Paul, 1926.

48. _____, *Sex and Repression in Savage Society,* Routledge and Kegan Paul, 1927.

49. McAllister, J. G., "Kiowa Apache Social Organization," in Eggan, 1937.

50. Mandelbaum, D. G., "The Family in India," *Southwestern Journal of Anthropology* 4: 123-139, 1948.

51. Mead, M., *Coming of Age in Samoa,* William Morrow, 1928.

52. _____, *Growing Up in New Guinea,* William Morrow, 1930.

53. _____, *Sex and Temperament,* William Morrow, 1935.

54. Miner, H., *St. Denis,* University of Chicago Press, 1939.

55. Murdock, G. P., "Kinship and Social Behavior Among the Haida," *American Anthropologist* 36:355-85.

56. _____, *Social Structure,* Macmillan, 1949.

57. Nadel, S. F., "Double Descent in the Nuba Hills," in Radcliffe-Brown and Forde, 1950.

58. Opler, M. E., *An Apache Life Way,* University of Chicago Press, 1941.

59. Parsons, T., "Democracy and Social Structure in Pre-Nazi Germany," 1942 (1). Reprinted in Parsons *Essays,* 1954.

60. _____, "Age and Sex in the Social Structure of the United States," 1942 (2). Reprinted in Parsons *Essays,* 1949 and 1954.

61. _____, "The Kinship System of the Contemporary United States," 1943. Reprinted in Parsons *Essays,* 1949 and 1954.

62. _____, *Essays in Sociological Theory,* The Free Press, 1949.

63. _____, "Theoretical Problems in the Study of Social Mobility," Section on the American Middle-

class Family, mimeographed, 1950.

64. _____, *The Social System*, The Free Press, 1951 (1).

65. _____, and Shils, E. A., (eds.) *Toward a General Theory of Action*, Harvard University Press, 1951 (2).

66. _____, Bales, R. F., and Shils, E. A., *Working Papers in the Theory of Action*, The Free Press, 1953 (1).

67. _____, "Psychoanalysis and Social Science with Special Reference to the Oedipus Complex," in Alexander, F., & Ross, H. (eds.), *Twenty Years of Psychoanalysis*, W. W. Norton & Co., 1953 (2).

68. _____, "The Father Symbol," in *Symbols & Values: an Initial Study*, 13th Symposium of the Conference on Science, Philosophy and Religion, Harper & Bros., 1954. (1).

69. _____, *Essays in Sociological Theory* (revised edition), The Free Press, 1954 (2).

70. Radcliffe-Brown, A. R., & Forde, D. (eds.) *African Systems of Kinship and Marriage*, Oxford University Press, 1950.

71. _____, "Introduction," in Radcliffe-Brown and Forde, 1950.

72. _____, *Structure and Function in Primitive Society*, Cohen and West, 1952.

73. Richards, A. I., *Land, Labor, and Diet in Northern Rhodesia*, Oxford University Press, 1939.

74. _____, "Some Types of Family Structure among the Central Bantu," in Radcliffe-Brown and Forde, 1950.

75. Shapera, I., "Kinship and Marriage Among the Tswana," in Radcliffe-Brown and Forde, 1950.

76. Stouffer, S., "Why our Occupational Sex Ratios?," unpublished mimeo, 1952.

77. Tax, S., "The Social Organization of the Fox Indians," in Eggan, 1937.

78. Titiev, M., *Old Oraibi*, Papers of the Peabody Museum, Harvard University, Vol. 22, #1, 1944.

79. Wilson, M., "Nyakyusa Kinship," in Radcliffe-Brown and Forde, 1950.

80. Yang, M., *A Chinese Village*, Columbia University Press, 1945.

VII

Conclusion: Levels of Cultural Generality and the Process of Differentiation

BY TALCOTT PARSONS
AND ROBERT F. BALES

In this concluding chapter we should like first briefly to summarize the empirical aspects of our study; and to state tentatively some hypotheses suggested by the empirical data. Secondly, we should like to take up the threads of theoretical analysis mentioned in the first chapter and discuss the two principal problems we there called attention to, in the light of the material of the intervening chapters. These, the reader will remember, were the relations of personality, social system and culture, and the process of differentiation.

We began with an attempt to assess the nature and significance of recent trends of development in the American family system. We took the position that the familiar phenomena of reduction of family size, "loss of function," and even high divorce rates, could reasonably be interpreted as phases of a general process of further structural differentiation and the attendant strain which has been going on in the society as a whole, rather than as a process of radical disorganization. The family has, in this process, been coming to be more sharply differentiated from other units and agencies of the society, and hence coming to be more specialized in its functions than has been true of the family in our own past and in other known societies.

In its structural aspect, this process of differentiation has resulted in accentuation of the isolation of the nuclear family from other kinship units. Concomitant with this has come the primacy of dependence of the family unit on the occupational earnings of its members, independent of proprietary interests which follow kinship lines. Thus "independent" sources of income, independent residence and independent basis of position in the community have come to be the rule. Also, the break between status as child in the family of orientation and as adult spouse-parent in the family of procreation is sharper than in other kinship systems.

In its functional aspect the effect of the process of differentiation is a sharp concentration on the two functional areas we have indicated as articulating personalities with the social system; namely, the socialization of children and the "pattern maintenance and tension management" functions in relation to adults. The performance of these functions is, essentially, a matter of providing mechanisms which meet some of the essential *psychological* conditions of continuity and stability of the society.

Because the modern American, especially the urban, family is such a highly differentiated unit in the social structure, we feel that it has presented a particularly favorable empirical case for the analysis of certain fundamental problems of the relations between personality, culture and social structure. These relations are to be seen in the process of socialization in the family and in the relation of the outcome of the process to certain fundamental features of the adult personality. The relations are clarified because this modern family is "stripped down" to what apparently approaches certain minimal structural and functional essentials. The fusions with wider kinship groups on a structural level which we find in so many other societies are not present to any large extent in our own society. Similarly, many of the "auxiliary" functions, such as those of economic production which are common in kinship units, are here reduced to a minimum.

The nuclear family, as we see it in these terms, has a distinctive structure as a social system. It is a small group, sharing characteristics found to be common to small groups of about the same size which are of a quite different character in other respects, as in personnel composition and in function. The characteristics in which we are most interested, concern the universal presence of two axes of differentiation, namely an hierarchical axis of relative power and an instrumental-expressive axis. More specifically, the hierarchically uppermost part of the structure, the "leadership" part, involves *both* predominantly instrumental and predominantly expressive roles; it has a dual character.

Not only does this basic pattern of social structure, which is clearly characteristic of the American nuclear family, correspond in the critical respects with that found in a certain class of experimental small groups in our own society, but Zelditch's material, as reviewed in Chapter VI, makes it clear that in a broad sense it may be held that this type of pattern is characteristic of nuclear families on a very broad cross-cultural basis. Without any question this holds for the overwhelming majority of cases in his sample. Furthermore, though with appropriate scientific caution he classes as negative certain cases which were not beyond any possible doubt positive, his detailed discussion of the problematical cases makes it clear that there is not a single one of which it can be said that there is decisive evidence, either that there is no significant differentiation along the instrumental-expressive axis in the leadership structure, or that what we regard as the "normal" allocation of the roles by sex is reversed. Furthermore, he found no evidence of any general *type* of family structure which was variant from his "normal" one in these crucial respects. Where, as in the Nayar case, its maintenance became impossible, the family itself gave way; it did not change to another structural type. We regard this combination of evidence from the study of small groups and from cross-cultural sources as strong indications that the broad structural outlines of the American nuclear family, as we have delineated it, are not "fortuitous" in the sense of being bound to a particular, highly specific social situation, but are of generic significance with respect to the structure and functions of the family in all societies. Furthermore this evidence is reinforced by two other sets of considerations; namely, the facts we have brought forward with respect to the high level of differentiation of the family from *other structures* in American society, and the facts concerned with the universality of the incest taboo, which have been reviewed in the foregoing chapters and elsewhere.

Finally, we may regard the evidence as clear on still another major empirical point. This is that the family, which is essentially a four-role-type structure everywhere, stands midway in complexity between its universally present mother-child subsystem and a more complex set of structures in which every individual must learn to participate before he can become an adult in any society. In many societies some, if not most, of these other structures are primarily organized on a kinship basis. But it is a crucial fact that they are not identical structurally or functionally with ego's own nuclear family, and the roles he must learn to play in them are different from those in his nuclear family. This point has been clearly brought out in Zelditch's analysis. Indeed, the cases which raise questions about the two hypotheses on the nuclear family which Zelditch tests, can *all* be said to constitute cases where roles in these extrafamilial kinship groups impinge on the nuclear family. Thus, in the classical matrilineal case the mother's brother exercises, vis-à-vis his sister's family, a position of authority as a representative of the matrilineage. The important point is that the matrilineage, though a kinship group, is *not* a nuclear family, and has quite different functions in the society from those of the nuclear family.

Indeed, in this volume and elsewhere, we have argued consistently that the nuclear family not only *is* not, but *cannot* be, an independent society, but is always a differentiated subsystem of the society. The structure into which it fits varies greatly over the range of social types, but there are certain things these structures have in common. They articulate with the nuclear family mainly through the nonfamilial roles of the adult members of the family and they constitute more highly differentiated structures than *any* nuclear family. Furthermore, our evidence suggests the near if not complete universality of the proposition that the extrafamilial participations of the masculine role are, in any given society, both more complex and weigh more heavily in the personality structure than is the case with the feminine personality in the same society.

These are, in the broadest outline, the facts of the social structure of the family, and the structures with which it articulates most directly, which are most crucial to our account of the process of socialization and its bearing on the nature of human personality and its development. This view of personality development holds, it will be remembered, that, after a first major stage in which the "mother-child identity," the first internalized social object, has become established, with oral dependency-gratification as its goal, the process is one of differentiation through binary fission of the social object-system which had been internalized at the preceding stage and then the reintegration of the differentiated, hence more complex system.

At each stage this process of differentiation takes place through the impact on the personality system of the social object-system at the level of complication next higher to that into which the personality had previously been integrated. Thus, after the oral dependency stage, the decisive structure is the two-member mother-child love-attachment system, then the four-role nuclear family and so on. Each cycle of the process results in the internalization, not just of *one* new social object, but of a new and more complex *system* of objects. This system must in the nature of the case be an authentic and functioning social system, a subsystem of the larger society. The personality is in this respect, as we have put it, a kind of "mirror-image" of the succession of social systems into which it has been integrated, organized in depth over the requisite series of stages.

Personalities and social systems are, according to the implications of this view, not directly homologous; they are differently organized about different foci of integration and have different relations to the sources of motivational energy. But they are more than merely "analogous," they are literally "made of the same stuff"; as we have so often put it, they are not merely interdependent, they *interpenetrate*. Above all, it is important that the *focus of organization* of both types of system lies in certain aspects of the revelant culture patterns, namely the value-systems which have been institutionalized in the social system, internalized in the personality system. Moreover, these are not merely the "same kind" of cultural values, they are literally *the same* values, looked at and analyzed in terms of different system-references. Neither of these system-references is the "right" or the "real" system reference, both are equally real and stand on the same ontological level. This in essence is what Durkheim meant by his famous aphorism that "society exists only within the minds of individuals." The converse also applies; Freud or Mead might have said, though they did not in these exact words, that a *human* person exists only in so far as he has taken "society" into himself.

But neither a personality nor a social system is merely a "realization" of these values in the sense of emanation; it is an *organization* of action or behavior which is based on *commitment* to these values, but which must face the complex exigencies to which a system of action is subject in the real world; adaptation to its situation, adjustment to scarce and uncertain opportunities for goal-gratification, integration of its own sub-units, and maintenance, as a *realistic* process, of the integrity of the value-pattern itself over time, including management of the motivational tensions which threaten to disrupt it.

The fundamental facts here are that both personalities and social systems are *organized about* systems of internalized-institutionalized values, which are the same values for both, and that these are realistic systems of action, not merely values "expressing themselves." But in addition to these, the most important implications of the facts about family and personality we have reviewed concern the problems of the intricate set of inter-relations between systems and subsystems which result from the situation we are discussing. Besides the fundamental fact of interpenetration we have just noted, there are two other fundamental aspects of these interrelations. The first is the fact that, in a variety of vital respects, any given system, A, within a network of social-personal systems of action, serves as a critical part of the situation within which system B must function, to which it must adapt. A leading example of this is the way in which the behavior of a socializing agent introduces changes into the situation in which the socializee has to act. This general order of relation is of the first importance as between social systems at various levels, between personalities and social systems, and even, we suspect, between different subsystems of the same personality system, though this is more difficult, in the light of common sense, to grasp.

The second aspect concerns the fact that systems in the field of action, as in other fields, are organized on a hierarchical basis in relation to each other. The mother-child system must be regarded as a subsystem of the nuclear family, the family in turn as a subsystem (from the latency-child's point of view) of the "community" which comprises school and peer group as well, and this "latency-child's society" in turn must be regarded as a subsystem of the society in which his parents and adults participate. Thus the earliest system into which the child is socialized, that comprising his "identity" with his mother, is the most specialized, from the point of view of the society, of all those in which he participates.

There is a similar hierarchical structure in the relations of the subsystems of the personality to each other. The original single-unit personality, we hold, differentiates into two, four, eight, and so on, need-disposition types or units. At each successive level a single type is more highly differentiated than any from which it has been derived, hence is more specialized in its functions in the total personality as a system. But as we have repeatedly noted, the superordinate motive systems, the "genetically prior objects" do not cease to exist, but remain, in transformed ways, operative as genuine systems in the personality itself.

Levels of Cultural Generality in Group Performance and in Socialization

This hierarchical ordering of systems and subsystems in all complex systems of action, both social systems and personalities, involves, we believe, a most important aspect of the structure of the cultural systems which have come to be institutionalized or internalized as the case may be in action systems. Our analysis gives us, we believe, not merely a general insight into this fact, but a basis on which we can work out an hypothesis of a specific pattern of this structure and its relation to the processes of differentiation. The pattern appears most clearly perhaps in the cases where we have carried analysis of the processes of action to the more microscopic levels; in Bales's and Slater's analysis of interaction in the small group, and in Parsons's and Olds's analysis of

the single cycle of the socialization process in an attempt to identify the psychological mechanisms at work. When these two cases
are juxtaposed with each other, it appears that the two basic
axes of differentiation with which we have been concerned, that
on the basis of power and that on instrumental-expressive lines,
are most intimately related to the processes of culture-building
and culture-internalization respectively.

According to our present views, the most fundamental point
of reference for the analysis of differentiation is the state of the
common culture of a social interaction system at a point in time.
The extension of the common culture takes place by the construction, from some point in time, of symbolic objects recognized as
new or different, which are in one respect derived from, but also
then require to be fitted into, the existing system of symbolic
objects. The extension of the common culture, a piece at a time,
is simultaneously a process of its own differentiation, of differentiation of the roles of the group members, and of differentiation
of the personality of each. The process by which new symbolic
objects are created in common, is the overt interaction of members, which is, by its nature, time-bound. The process is forced
to take place a "piece at a time."

Recent developments in the attempt to understand the relative
frequencies of different types of interaction in groups working
on Bales' standard task, have considerably clarified the sense in
which interaction may be conceptualized in one principal aspect
as a "cultural building" process.[1]

"Early in the research it was noted that the rates of giving
suggestion, giving information, and giving opinion frequently
came out in a ratio very close to 1:2:4 [as may be seen in Chapter V]. It was known that the uniformity held especially well for
the standard task, though natural groups engaged on similar tasks
showed similar ratios. But in the standard task a special effort
had been made to insure that the members faced three problems
of about equal urgency: the problems of mobilizing the information that had been distributed separately among them, extending
it by inference and evaluating it, and suggesting a concrete solu-

---

1. Reported by R. F. Bales in "How People Interact in Conferences," *Scientific
American*, March, 1955. The portion quoted here is from an earlier draft of the
published article.

tion. Why, then, should the rates of information, opinion, and suggestion be so unequal?

"A plausible theory was recently suggested by an attempt[2] to compare what was known about the interaction process with some features of an air defense network—a more or less typical large scale communication and control system. Separate sections of the organization performed the functions of surveillance of the air picture, identifying the observed tracks as friendly or unknown, and controlling fighters sent out to intercept unknown planes. There is some similarity, on an abstract level, between these three problems and the three problems we had tried to make about equally urgent in the standard interaction task. But in the operation of such a defense network the process of gathering facts, making inferences, and gathering further facts to check the inferences in order to arrive at an identification is especially obvious. It appeared that the stepwise operations involved in the total network, as well as in various component sections, could be tolerably well described as an interlocking series of some seven types of information processing operations. These seven types are shown in Figure 1.

"For a simple application to the air defense problem, "x" might be defined as a plotted track from the radar, "O" might be the class of objects "Unknown," "y" could be the fact that no flight plan matched "x," the link of "O" with "W" could consist of a rule "All Unknown planes should be intercepted," and "w" would be the order to intercept.

"The steps, or elements, of course, are very general, and can be applied to many kinds of content at many levels of abstraction. Not all of the elements are primarily logical in character. They involve perceptual elements in the observation of primary and check facts, elements of memory, association, and perhaps creative insight in the tentative induction, and certainly an element of "confidence' of some kind in making the various non-logical inductive leaps required for movement from step 1 to 2, step 4 to 5, and step 6 to 7. But they do "make sense" as a set of symbol transformations which could guide the specific output of a behavioral system in relation to specific event inputs from the

---

2. In collaboration with John Kennedy of the Systems Research Laboratory at the Rand Corporation.

FIGURE 1

Seven Types of Component Acts in Building a Group Decision

Interaction Form of Message Sent to Other Components

Logical Structure of Cultural Object

1. *States primary observation:*

"I observe a particular event, x."

2. *Makes tentative induction:*

"This particular event, x, *may* belong to the general class of objects, O."

3. *Deduces conditional prediction:*

"*If* this particular event, x, does belong to the general class, O, *then* it should be found associated with another particular event, y."

4. *States observation of check fact:*

"I observe the predicted particular event, y."

5. *Identifies object as member of a class:*

"I therefore identify x-y as an object which is a member of the predicted general class of objects, O."

6. *States major premise relating classes of objects:*

"All members of the general class of objects, O, should be treated by ways of the general class, W."

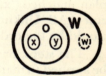

7. *Proposes specific action:*

"This particular object, x-y, should therefore be treated in a particular way, w."

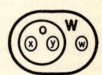

system environment. Finally, it will be noted that the seven steps explicitly include an error-checking sequence in steps 2, 3, and 4. The similarity to many descriptions of the scientific method will be obvious.

"The whole process may be thought of as one of "culture

building." By successive steps, the group members relate one specific event to another through symbolic manipulation to obtain a more complex symbolic structure which hangs together sufficiently well to control further stages of behavior. This kind of interrelated symbolic structure we usually call a "decision." When the error-checking process has included not only factual inputs from the environment, as in steps 1 and 4, but also deductive inputs from the major premises of a common culture, and social inputs from the agreement and disagreement of group members, we speak of a "group decision," or "consensus."

"It may now be noted that in the idealized seven-step outline there is *one* final step, 7, which has the interaction form of "giving suggestion." There are *two* early steps, 1 and 4, which have the interaction form of "giving information," and *four* intermediate steps, 2, 3, 5, and 6, which have the interaction form of "giving opinion." If groups performing on the standard interaction task actually went through the process of building a series of group decisions, and if each chain did indeed take one each of the seven steps in order to reach a kind of "critical mass" adequate to support joint action, then we would expect the observed ratio of 1:2:4 in the categories of giving suggestion, giving information, and giving opinion.

"It further follows that in groups where the ratios are 1:2:4 we might also expect to find, on the average, about equal numbers of each of the seven-step elements. Although this kind of analysis has not yet been carried far, preliminary trials indicate that problem-solving attempts in written transcripts of interaction on the standard task can be reclassified reasonably into the finer breakdown of seven types, and that something like equal numbers of each type are found.

"Of course, complete and contiguous chains, with each step in the indicated time order are seldom found. Strings of facts, or inferences, or suggestions are frequently found, which suggest that it is quite as important psychologically to tie bundles of chains together as it is to fill in the missing links in chains. And in any real interaction an interlocking structure of chains is found, not just a series. A more or less complete chain may be required to establish a single step in another chain. And so on, to many degrees of complication.

"But it is definitely possible to reconstruct, from a written transcription, many complete chains ending in suggestion that were adopted, from elements that were separated in time in the original interaction. If there is a kind of elementary seven-step structure which tends to give rise to the observed frequencies, it should be thought of as a kind of "latent structure," or felt necessity in the minds of the members, which is realized more or less imperfectly, depending upon many kinds of conditions. . . .

"In the social-emotional area, as well as in the task and common value area, a process of "culture building" apparently goes on, though perhaps not so obviously. Here again, the key process seems to be generalization [this time of cathexis]. Specific events —acts of the members—are generalized into more and more complex objects, and these objects are related in turn to generalized ways of feeling about them and acting toward them. Feelings of liking or disliking for particular persons are apparently built up in this way, and tend toward constancy, but change gradually, with a time lag, if the quality of overt interaction with the person is changed and held at a new level by some other factor. For example, persons who like each other may quarrel periodically because of task demands without losing their liking, but if they quarrel persistently, their feelings of liking are apt to decrease. Conversely, persons who do not like each other may agree periodically because of task demands, without changing their basic feelings about each other much, but if they agree persistently, their feelings of liking are apt to increase."

Bales and Slater have further called attention to the striking difference between the qualitative profiles produced by what they call "proactive" and "reactive" behavior respectively in the process of group interaction. They suggest that the concentration of proactive behavior in the categories of giving information, opinion, and suggestion has to do with the requirement of continuity and logical connectedness in the extensions of the common culture by the construction of new symbolic objects, whereas "reaction" or the administration of sanctions, does not require the same order of continuity. This difference may be considered to be an index of characteristics which indicate the growing point of differentiation in both its hierarchical and its qualitative aspects. Thus, we may say that if continuity and a larger share of facilities are required for effective extension of the common culture, there will tend to be a larger share of "power" granted to the part or member of the system with greatest effectiveness in this area, so long as his action is in accord with the latent value system. At the same time, however, such differentiation involves qualitative discrimination between problems faced by the group, in that it is not focussed equally on all the functions of the group as a system, but in one area. From the perspective of the already existing common culture, any problem singled out around which new attitudes must be built, acquires a "task" or instrumental character, even though its content from a later perspective, may be social, emotional, or normative.

The process in the small group as just analyzed is primarily one of task-performance. In analyzing it we assume that the main structure of the common culture is already present. It is the culture which the members of the group bring with them into the experimental situation. The fact that it is a common culture derives from their common membership in the same society and their broad similarity of status within it as male college students. The basic categories of this culture are thus not internalized in the course of the experimental group process, but these general categories are "particularized" to meet the facts and exigencies of the specific task-situation. What is being created is a new subculture which is particular to this small group, and which is differentiated from the wider culture with reference to this task situation and to these personalities interacting to constitute this particular social system. Because the experimental system is evanescent in time, and does not deeply engage the constituent personalities, i.e., requires only slight commitments from them, it is a "minor" subculture from the point of view both of the society and of the personalities. But it is none the less authentically a culture, and processes both of institutionalization in the group and of the internalization in the personality, are present in the processes we have just outlined.

It will be noted that in the task-performance process just reviewed, three hierarchical levels of generality of cultural structure of the object system were involved: first, the particularized events, x and y; second, the category, O, which comprised them both; and third, the general norm or "major premise," W, which comprised both the class of objects O and the specific way of doing things, or treating the objects belonging in O, w. We have noted above that the value pattern of a system of action defines the main framework of the structure of the system itself. From the point of view of the units of the system these patterns of structure appear as norms. Hence we may conclude that the normative pattern W belongs in a system of an order of generality at the next level above that involved in O.

Furthermore, when we see the pattern of the seven steps thus reviewed in this light, the four acts classified as giving opinion may be interpreted in such a way that two of them constitute taking the step from a particular instance or subclass to the superordinate class of which it is an instance (2,6) and two of them relate two instances within a class to each other (3,5). We may then say that the first type involves acts of generalization, the second of discrimination.

The involvement of three levels of generality, the highest of which is treated as normative in character, combined with the involvement of four logical operations, two each of the generalizing and two of the relational or discriminating character, constitute the elements of pattern which are *common* to the task-performance as just reviewed, and to the cycle of the socialization process, which we now take up.

In order to describe the latter in relatively comprehensible terms we have chosen the first step of differentiation of the initially undifferentiated "mother-child identity" for purposes of illustration. On the analytical level we will refer throughout to the account of a socialization cycle presented by Parsons and Olds in Chapter IV. Figure 2 shows the steps involved in schematic and graphic form.[3]

We assume then that Ego at the start of a cycle is, on the relevant level, an undifferentiated actor-object. There are, however,

---

3. The parallel between Figures 1 and 2 we are presenting here has been quite recently developed. We have not attempted to present the two cases in such a way as to be sure they are on exactly the same level of generality. We are sure only that the above group decision case is clearly one of performance, while that of socialization is one of learning. Moreover, our socialization case is stated from the perspective of the personality of the child as a system-reference while the group decision case referred to a social system. We include this rather crude statement of the parallel here because of its clear relevance to the general problem of differentiation and integration in the action field, and the light it throws on the social and cultural structures involved in it. We fully expect that there will be a series of further refinements and elaborations and that on a later occasion we can present a more adequate analysis.

within this object, performances and qualities which can be localized in either the behavior of the child-organism or that of the mother-organism. There is initially a "matching" of certain accustomed performances or acts localized in the child-organism and certain others, which can be interpreted from Ego's point of view as sanctions to these performances, localized in the mother-organism. We can then in Step 1 speak of such a performance w_1 at a given time encountering, not the familiar and gratifying sanction, x, but an unfamiliar and frustrating result, differing from x, which we can call y. This is simply a schematic description of what we called the initial phase of a perception of error and relative deprivation in the more extended analysis of Chapter IV.

We then presume that, after the structure of the object O_1, which is the initial ego-actor-object, has been shaken up and partially disorganized by the frustrating experience, y, there will, in the cognitive aspect of the process, in Step 2, be a tentative generalization to the effect that O_1 is a more complex object than had previously been supposed and may prove to be a *class* concept, O_2 (in Olds's sense of the term concept) which includes y as well as x and w_1.[4] It will be remembered that in Chapter IV we presume that Ego's motivation to this generalization has something to do with the beginning of an input of support from the concrete mother in the interaction process.

The generalization that O_2 may be a class which is wider than O_1 may then lead to certain implications. If O_2 includes y, then it may also include other previously unknown intentional performances of Ego, located in the child-organism, and also other sanctioning acts localized in the mother-organism which are different from x in that they are previously unknown, but also different from y in that they are gratifying instead of frustrating to Ego; they hence belong to a class z of previously unknown positive sanctions. It might appear that the most obvious and in a sense natural line along which the components of the redefined class O_2 could be subclassified is the distinction between

4. It may be remembered that any true *social object,* which we assume O_1 to be, has been interpreted always to be a *complex object* which is inherently capable of being broken down into components. We interpret w_1, x, and possibly y and others, to be such components. See T. Parsons, R. F. Bales, and E. A. Shils, *Working Papers in the Theory of Action* (Glencoe, Ill.: The Free Press, 1953), Chapter II. Hereinafter referred to as *Working Papers.*

the previously familiar items and the previously unfamiliar ones; this would place w_1 and x together as familiar, y, w_2 and z together as unfamiliar as shown under Step 3, Figure 2. It will be remembered that in the group decision case of Figure 1, there were only two events distinguished and observed, of which one was unfamiliar, x, the other familiar, y; so this was the line of discrimination followed in the performance case, in so far as discrimination was relevant.

There is, however, in the present case another possibility, which we interpret to be perceived in Step 4. This is the use of location relative to the two organisms involved as the points of

FIGURE 2

Seven Types of Component Acts in Building an Internalized Norm

Mode of Change of State of Ego as Personality in Relation to Alter   Logical Structure of Internalized Object System

1. *Primary perception of error and relative deprivation:*

A given way of acting, w_1, which previously had been cognitively located within an undifferentiated Ego-actor-object, O_1, is followed at some critical point by a perceived discrepancy between a familiar and gratifying result, x, also part of O_1, and a new and frustrating result, y.

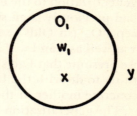

2. *Tentative generalization of cognition of objects:*

It is tentatively hypothesized that the previously undifferentiated object, O_1, may be a *class* of objects, O_2, which includes y as well as x, and is not just a single object.

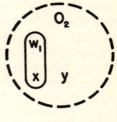

3. *Conditional discrimination of new ways of acting:*

It is conditionally deduced that *if* the unexpected result, y, does belong to a *class* of objects, O_2, *then* there must be other ways of acting, w_2, which will be associated with other results, z.

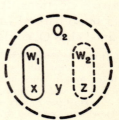

FIGURE 2 (cont.)

Seven Types of Component Acts in Building an Internalized Norm

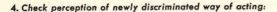

Mode of Change of State of Ego as Personality in Relation to Alter | *Logical Structure of Internalized Object System*

4. *Check perception of newly discriminated way of acting:*

By experimenting, Ego finds a new way of acting, w_2, which leads to a gratifying experience, z, in relation to Alter. But it is also observed that w_1 and w_2 are *both* ways Ego can act, by intention, whereas x, y, and z are all results associated with the intentions of the same concrete cognitive object (Alter), and not produced directly by Ego's volition.

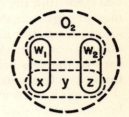

5. *Objects differentiated (fission), and identified as members of restructured class:*

Ego concludes that O_2 is a real class of interdependent acts and events, w_1, x, y, w_2, and z. But ways of acting w_1 and w_2 are associated in a volitional sub-class identified by Ego as an object called IS (internalized self). Conversely, x, y, and z, are associated in an independently volitional sub-class identified by Ego as an internalized object called IM (internalized mother). IS and IM together constitute an interdependent class O_2, identified by Ego as his new personality, P.

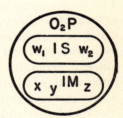

6. *Tentative generalization of new acts and results into a class of norms applying to members of restructured class of objects:*

The new way of acting, w_2, and the new gratifying result, z, are hypothesized to be particular cases of a class of norms, W_2Z, which should govern the behavior of IS and IM as together constituting P.

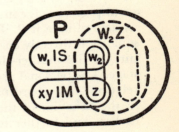

7. *Action based on new normative premises:*

As Ego continues to act in new particular ways, w_3, that are instances of the class W_2, and receives gratifying results, z_2, which are instances of the class Z, he internalizes or becomes committed to the norms W_2Z which govern the behavior of IS and IM as one of its sub-systems. (Ordinarily W_2Z are the norms of a superordinate system of objects, in the present case, the nuclear family as a whole.)

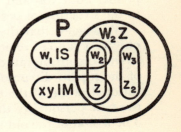

reference for discrimination. Then Ego, we suggest, classifies w_1 and w_2, which refer to the child-organism, together as acts attributable to his own intention or volition to constitute one sub-object of O_2, while x, y and z are classified together as belonging to the other sub-object because they are associated with, i.e., constitute the consequences for Ego of, the behavior of the mother-organism, thus expressing her volition or intention. Then Ego's personality may be said to begin to divide into two sub-objects, one internalized about the reference point provided by each of the two behaving organisms which together constitute the interactive system, Ego-Alter.

In Step 5, then we conceive this newly emerging structure to become established in that O_2, from a tentative generalization becomes an established object, the redefined personality of Ego. The components which are comprised in it are further grouped to form two sub-objects, the internalized autonomous self-object, which acts intentionally in relation to mother and the internalized mother-object which, by taking the role of mother toward himself, generalizes mother's sanctioning behavior toward Ego into a mode of his own action relative to the rest of his personality. These two sub-objects of O_2 may from now on be called IS (internalized self) and IM (internalized mother) respectively. The newly defined total O_2 then is the personality to which the personal pronoun, I, can properly be applied for the first time; let us denominate it P. This newly emergent structure of the personality is directly cognate with the more complex social structure of the mother-child subsystem of the family at this new stage. The personal pronoun, I, becomes meaningful through its relations to a coordinate "you" and to the source of sanctions in the behavior of the mother-object, now defined as external to Ego, and further to a "we" which is the social system comprising both you and I. But what of "they" and their relation to the structure of personality?

We suggest that the simultaneous establishment of two sub-objects organized relative to the discrimination between the behaving organisms rather than to the familiar-unfamiliar axis, and of the superordinate object P, do not complete either the institutionalization of the new social system, or the consolidation of the new personality through the full internalization of values. The fission of the old undifferentiated object, its differentiation into two, has, to be sure, as we interpret it, occurred in Step 5. But it is not yet possible for the new structure to function autonomously, either in its social system or its personality aspect, without outside support. We suggest that this becomes possible only through two further steps, which result in the institutionalization and internalization of a set of norms which regulate the behavior of this system in its relation to a system of higher order in the social structure, namely the nuclear family.

The first of these two steps, No. 6 in our list in Figure 2, is a case of generalization. The autonomously discovered way of acting, w_2, has been experienced to produce gratification by what is interpreted to be the *intentional* action of mother in imposing a positive sanction. What is satisfactory to mother, who occupies a superior status in the mother-child interaction system which is expressed in the fact that Ego is dependent on her, is felt to be "right." The experience that there are particular acts of which Ego is spontaneously capable, which are "approved" by mother and rewarded, is generalized to the notion that there is a *class* of such acts, W_2, which is in the first instance defined empirically by the fact that they produce a corresponding *class* of positive, gratifying sanction-experiences, Z.

The final step, then, we interpret to be the confirmation of this generalization through reinforcement in the ordinary psychological sense. For its completion the process must proceed to the point where Ego comes to be committed to act, in the relevant situations, in ways defined as members of the class W_2, even though on particular occasions his particular act w_3 or w_4 may fail to bring about the corresponding positive sanction, z_3 or z_4. When Ego's commitment to act in accordance with the generalized normative pattern W_2 has reached this stage of independence of specific particularized positive sanctions or rewards, we can speak of the *internalization* of the normative pattern. Of course this does not imply that the absence, over a long period, of rewards of the general class Z for any performances in the class W_2 would not disturb the internalization of the norm; what is essential for our purposes is only a *relative* independence from experience of particular rewards for each particular act. When this has happened there has occurred motivational generalization of cathexis which matches the cognitive generalization of Step 6.

We may attempt to interpret the meaning of these last two steps in the process as follows: By Step 5, we assume the bare structure of the new personality system, as an object O_2 with two sub-objects, IS, and IM, has been determined. Above all it is important that the two new sub-objects came to be organized about the reference-points of the two behaving organisms of child and mother rather than about what, from a performance point of view, was the "more natural" axis of the familiar and the unfamiliar. But *how* this new personality system, having this outline of structure, is to behave, is not yet determined. This determination, the stabilization of a pattern of behavior, depends not merely on the *fact that* mother has matched Ego's new way of acting, w_2, with *a* positive sanction, z, but on the *kind* of positive sanctions she administers, and the ways in which the different sanctions for different acts, including their selectivity, namely the refusal of reward for some acts (denial of reciprocity) and positive reward for others, are organized to constitute a *system* of sanctions. It is this system of sanctions which provides the stimuli of the situation in which an incipient pattern of Ego's behavior can be consolidated by reinforcement.

But the patterning of this system of sanctions cannot be derived from interaction of Ego and mother on Ego's level alone, even as a newly differentiated personality system. Relative to Ego's tendencies of behavior there is an element of "rigidity" in mother's reactions, there is a class of acts w_2, w_3, ... which she rewards, but another class of acts w'_2, w'_3, ... which she does not reward. Her capacity to introduce and enforce this selective pattern in her interaction with Ego derives from two sources. The first is the superior power position she occupies in the mother-child interaction system, by virtue of which Ego has become "dependent" on her. This is one fundamental axis of asymmetry of the system. The second is the fact that her total personality includes roles in the superordinate familial system; the norms of that system are internalized in her personality. She is, therefore, constrained, in her interaction with Ego, both by the internalization of these norms, and by the fact that she is dependent on sanctions from other members of the family which would be jeopardized by violation of the norms. Her membership in the superordinate family and her representative role vis-à-vis Ego on behalf of that system are therefore

essential conditions of her acting as an effective agent of socialization in the final stages of the cycle. This second basis of
asymmetry can be alternatively stated by saying that the mother
performs the more instrumental role in the system, the child
the more expressive one.

We pointed out above that in the group decision case, the
category O and the major normative premise W were already
present in the culture of the group; what was necessary was
to particularize them so they would serve to organize and
control the particular events x and y and the ways of acting
in relation to them, w. In the socializing case, from the point
of view of Ego, the category O_2, which admits of two sub-objects
on the relevant level, and the generalized norm W_2, do not
exist at the beginning of the process. It is true, these categories
exist in the culture of the family and are internalized in the
concrete mother's personality, but not yet in that of the child.
We suggest that it is this difference which accounts for certain
fundamental differences between the processes schematically
depicted in Figure 1 and in Figure 2, which stand out in contrast to the striking similarity of pattern in other respects which
we have followed through.

There is, we feel, already one essential difference at Step 1.
The observation of a "new" event is always in some sense a
disturbance of equilibrium; what we mean by "action" on a
common-sense level is the series of reactions set in motion by
such a disturbance. We can however suggest that there is first
a quantitative difference between the two cases; the frustrating
experience y in Figure 2 must create a considerable disturbance
to be effective. But more important, y is defined in terms of its
discrepancy from a familiar and expected result, x, of a way
of acting, w_1; in the other case x "just happens"; it does not in
the same sense result from a way of acting on Ego's part.

Then, at Step 2, in the decision case the act of generalization
consists in the *search for* the relevant general category under
which to subsume x. In the socialization case, on the other hand,
it constitutes the beginning of the *redefinition* of the category
O_2, which we have assumed to be present already; it is the first
stage of defining a previously unknown category, O_2.

With the emergence, at Steps 3 and 4, of w_2 as a new way of
acting, and its linking with the experience of z, we seem to have

the beginning of a parallel classification under O_2 on the axis of the distinction between the familiar and the unfamiliar. But we suggest that this tendency is counteracted by a fundamental set of psychological forces which come fully into operation at Step 4. These consist in the fact that w_2 is associated with an *experience of gratification,* combined with the fact that the gratification is imputed to an *intentional* act located with reference to the mother organism. We feel it legitimate to assume that sensitivity to mother's intentions has been established prior to this stage of the socialization process; oral dependency as a precondition of the present stage meant precisely this.[5] Thus the combination of gratificatory significance and *common agency* are the basis on which x and z come to be classified together. Correspondingly the combination of acts on ego's part which *result* in gratification, with common agency in terms of organism-reference in this case also, constitute the basis on which w_1 and w_2 are classified together. It is then the "intentional" input of gratification or reward, for which there is no analogue in the bare performance cycle, which is the decisive factor in determining the axis on which the fission of O_1 occurs. In the strict performance case there need be no fission; two events are merely classed together preliminary to a decision as to how the unfamiliar event can be controlled.

This brings out with striking clarity the basis of the importance of *interaction* on the social levels for the type of learning involved in personality development. Our hypothesis is that there are two necessary conditions of learning which must be present in order to bring about the structural conditions necessary to internalize a new norm; namely, 1) the establishment of sensitivity to the *intentions* of a significant alter and 2) the linking of a familiar and an unfamiliar, previously unlearned way of acting with gratificatory experiences, *both* of which are interpreted to be intentional sanctions on the part of the sanctioning agent. (Incidentally it is probably only in this way that the disturbing effect of the frustrating experience, y, can be overcome and w_1 can be suppressed or repressed.)

The combination of disturbances and the two factors just stated are, we suggest, if properly timed and on the requisite

---

5. See Chapter II, and *Working Papers,* Chap. II.

levels of intensity, adequate to produce the fission of an earlier personality structure; the construction of an O_2 with sub-objects organized about the points of reference provided by the inter-action system, i.e. the agents of performance and sanction respectively. But these factors are not alone sufficient to establish a pattern of stable orientation for the new personality system; for this to happen there must be in addition a *selectively ordered* system of sanctions for new ways of acting, applied over a sufficient period of time. For this again, which is taken account of in steps 6 and 7 of the socialization case, there is no parallel in the group decision case. This is because the norm W is assumed to be present initially in the personalities of all members of the group. What is necessary is only that it should be "applied" to the case in hand, that is a *particular* way of acting w, must be found which is appropriate to the situation x, y, and is a special case of the general norm, W.

But in the socialization case the norm W_2 is not present in the personality of Ego either in the O_1 or in the O_2 stages. Strictly it is not part of the initial interaction system of Ego and mother until the 6-7 stage. But W_2 is present in the *concrete* situation in which Ego acts, specifically in the familial system of which child-mother constitute a subsystem, and in the personality of mother in her representative role in that system vis-à-vis Ego. Once the requisite new structure O_2 has been established, then this norm can be "transferred" from the family system to the personality of Ego through the personality of mother in her role as socializing agent. In general then, it is the fact that Ego does *not* initially possess the cultural structure of the family system on both of two essential levels, that of O_2 and W_2, which accounts for the essential differences between the paradigm of group decision and that of socialization which we have reviewed. A third condition (3) of pattern-learning, then, is the imposition of O_2 from *outside* by an interacting agent of a *selective pattern of sanctions* in conformity with the norm of a superordinate system.

These differences, important as they are, do not, however, obscure the immense importance of the parallel between the group decision and socialization cases. This is not, we are sure, a mere analogy, but is deeply grounded in the processes of action. We suggest that the seven steps state some highly general conditions of successful transition from one state of equilibrium of a system of action to a new one. These conditions involve not only a given number of steps of given qualitative types, but also probably some requirement as to their occurrence in a definite temporal order. There must, in Bales's terminology, be inputs of information or orientation at two points in the process, at the beginning and at Step 4; there must be evaluations (by opinion) of two types following each input of information, Steps 2 and 3, and 5 and 6. Finally there must be a commitment to a pattern of action in terms of a norm (suggestion) at Step 7. Furthermore, within each pair of evaluative actions, there must be one act which is primarily an act of generalization to a superordinate class and one which is primarily an act of discrimination within a class, but at the two stages in the cycle they occur in reverse order; in the earlier stage the generalization comes first, in the later stage the discrimination comes first. First it is necessary to generalize *from* the event which is the source of the initial disturbance of equilibrium, while later it is necessary to generalize *to* the norm, the use of which makes stabilization of the system at the new state of equilibrium possible.

This pattern clearly highlights the significance of the *three* levels of generality in the hierarchical structure of a cultural object-system, to which we called attention at the beginning of this discussion. At several points we have called attention to the significance of the problems of control in systems of action. Indeed, relative to the situation in which it operates, we suggest that a system of action is in effect a system by which various components of that situation are brought within an orbit of control. This happens through the discrimination between the elements which are treated as part of the "external" situation, and those which are brought into the system itself and thereby subjected to a particular and more rigorous type of control.

In the context of the structure of hierarchies of action systems we suggest, that as looked at from a logical point of view this involves a series of inclusion-exclusion relations. In the group decision case discussed above, x could be controlled because in the first instance it was brought within the category O and thus classed together with the known event y. Once having classed these two events together, it was then possible to bring them jointly into a meaningful relation to the norm W through the particular operational procedure, w. Only by establishing the hierarchy (x,y), O, W could control over x be established. Essentially this seems to be a matter of recognizing and implementing a pattern of *order* which spans the three levels.

In the case of socialization it is not, as we have already pointed out, a matter of "recognizing and implementing," but of learning and internalizing a corresponding pattern of order which also involves at least three hierarchical levels. It is a matter, from the initial starting point, of abandoning the commitment to the initial O, treating its components as a set of prototypical instances; then of generalizing to the category which could include both the members of this category w_1, x, and the unfamiliar experiences, y, w_2, z, and bringing both sets together under O_2. Finally, O_2 had to be subsumed through the relation between w_2 and z, under the normative category W_2-Z. Only when this had been worked out could the category O_2, as the structure of a system of action, be stabilized.

In socialization terms Ego's experience in this respect may be likened to a man climbing a ladder. As he reaches up with his hands to rungs not previously within his experience, he does not immediately let go of the lower rungs on which his feet have rested. The process is rather something like this: he reaches up to a new rung, grasps it tentatively and only when he is rather sure of its location and solidity does he venture to pull himself up and let the lower foot finally leave the lowest rung on which he has been supporting himself. We suggest that the series of interactions with systems in which the socialization process operates is analogous to the ladder. The mother, by offering solid and gratifying experience as linked to conformity with the norms operative in the next higher system, makes it possible to overcome the anxiety inherent in taking leave of the lowest rung on which the climber has heretofore been resting his weight. Essentially we are saying that such a process is not possible if the climber is in touch only with two adjacent rungs of the ladder; there must be at least three; otherwise the uncertainties inherent in securing his grip on the unfamiliar top one of the series will not allow him to let go of the bottom one; he must have a "middle" basis of security on which he feels he can rely.

Before leaving this topic we may point out one further implication of the analysis for the process of socialization. It is clear that, as was noted above, the element of intentional agency is, combined with the experience of gratification, the decisive basis for the fission of the personality system on the axis determined by the behaving-organisms of child and mother respectively, i.e., the *role*-structure of the system of social interaction which performs the socializing function. By extension of this argument it is clear that the corresponding function at the next, the oedipal stage, is performed by the differentiation of the familial system on the basis of sex. It is categorization by sex which provides the polarity of reference points at this stage which corresponds to the two behaving organisms at the previous stage. Because of the enormous discrepancy of facilities inherent in the relations of these two organisms (an adult and a small child) it is reasonable, we have argued, to identify the first polarity with that of the power axis of the structure of interaction systems. We have then consistently argued that the sex dichotomy, as built into the structure of the nuclear family, is a special case of the instrumental-expressive axis of the differentiation of small groups. We can then regard the analysis of the process of binary fission in the above detailed terms as confirming our general impression of the fundamental importance of these two axes in the differentiation of systems of action.

If this is correct it raises the question: what are the reference-points which operate at the next, the first postoedipal stage of development. We suggest that in this case membership in the family, the group to which Ego *belongs* par excellence, provides one of them, that around which the particularistic patterns crystallize. The other, the universalistic point of reference is, we suggest, in our society provided mainly in the structure of the school situation, where the child is, independent of his family membership, held to universalistic standards of performance and judged accordingly. The peer group seems to stand in an intermediate position in this respect, hence to function as a kind of "shock-absorber" for the tensions generated on both sides, and to mediate between them.

Some Similarities and Differences of Personalities and Social Systems with Respect to the Process of Differentiation

The above considerations give us certain starting points for approaching the question of the relations between the processes of differentiation in social systems and in personality systems respectively. It is clear from the discussion of Bales and Slater, that the imposition of a task on a previously undifferentiated group tends to lead to a process of differentiation of roles among the members of the group, which is worked out in the course of the process of task-solution itself. The initiative in starting out this process of differentiation rests with the individual member or members who take the largest share of responsibility in the task-solution or instrumental functions of the group; then the resulting deficit in the area of social-emotional or expressive function creates an opportunity for the differentiation of a complementary role (or roles) which specialize in the expressive direction.

It is a clear inference from the treatment of the socialization process by Parsons and Olds in Chapter IV that this also should, from the point of view of the evolving personality system as the system of reference, be treated as a task-oriented process. By their imposition of new adaptive demands on the child, the socializing agents, like the small group experimenter, set him a task. But the similarity extends even farther. They not only set a task, but they make available new facilities for its effective performance—the basic initial input into the system is that of new information. Furthermore, the new elements in the personality structure which come to be differentiated off from the old are always relatively *more instrumental* in function than the ones from which they were differentiated; this is true of the "autonomy" motive system relative to that of "dependency" and of the adequacy and conformity systems relative to those of nurturance and acceptance; and similarly for later stages. It seems to us reasonable to interpret the Bales and Slater findings as directly parallel to these; the role of the "best liked" man is the residual role from which the more instrumental roles tend to become differentiated off as a result of the system facing the adaptive exigencies of the task situation.

For purposes of working out this parallel, it is a fortunate circumstance that Bales's program of small group research has dealt with groups which were initially undifferentiated as to role; such personality differences as there were having been randomized. Then in both cases, the nature of the task is such as first to put a premium on the use of certain new facilities, and to make such facilities available in limited amount. This new situation is presented to a system which in the relevant respects is initially undifferentiated. The new situation is initially disturbing, but as the immediate effects of the disturbance are absorbed, there develops a differential tendency within the system to utilize the "opportunity" offered. Some of the component elements take advantage of the opportunity more fully than do others, and assume both leadership and instrumental functions. But as differentiation proceeds, other elements assume roles which are complementary to those of these units. The opportunity presented to them, so far as they do not "compete" in the instrumental context, lies in the integrative-tension-management direction of function.

We may therefore hazard the tentative generalization that the impetus for a step in differentiation in systems of action always comes from an attempt to extend the existing structure of symbols, viewed from a present point in time as a "task" i.e. in an instrumental direction. The new symbolic object, however, may be relevant to any of the problems of the system, and may later not appear to have an "instrumental" character. The line of differentiation at the time of development of the new cultural objects comes to be drawn between those elements of the old system which are more "enterprising" in seizing the opportunity offered by the task itself and by the availability of facilities for its performance, and those which are less enterprising in this respect. But if the system is to achieve a relatively high level of integration on the new basis, then competition for the instrumental-leadership roles must not be too long-drawn-out and chronic, and the residual roles must assume positive functions in the system on the new basis which are complementary to those of the newly differentiated ones. Bales's and Slater's high consensus groups may be considered broadly as cases where the differentiation has been accompanied by complementarity and reintegration, the low consensus groups are those in which it has remained competitive.

Broadly, then, we may say that the "spearhead" or growing point of a process of differentiation lies in an urgency to attain a system goal. But given the tension involved in this urgency it is the adaptive exigencies of the situation, not only in the sense of conditions which must be met, but of their significance as the source of facilities which can be utilized, which then constitute the source of the pressure for *structural* change within the system. But this pressure is in some way always balanced by a complementary pressure, to meet the internal, integrative exigencies of the system which are *increased* by the goal-oriented-adaptive effort. Both sets of exigencies can be more effectively met if there is a differentiation, a division of labor among the elements of the system than if the tendency is for all the elements to try to perform an equal share of all the functions.

We may restate this proposition in the more technical terms of our action-system paradigm. The initial pressure is to change the state of the system by a strong movement along the goal-attainment dimension. But an appreciable movement of the whole system in that direction creates strains in relation to situational exigencies. There must, therefore, be a "spread" of interest and activity, a lessening of "single-minded" devotion to the goal, in favor of more careful attention to the necessary conditions and means of attaining it. But this spread in turn has two kinds of effects; first where this attention is unevenly distributed in the system, it puts larger facilities and hence power and rewards into the hands of those who take the lead in these respects, and secondly it postpones the consummatory state and creates or maintains tension among the units which are highly motivated to its attainment. Both these orders of effect heighten the urgency of the integrative problem and hence create the opportunity for complementary specialization in the integrative direction as well. We might perhaps use the metaphor of a ship driving at high speed through the sea. Not only does the ship make progress through the water in the direction of its goal, but this process creates new structures in the body of water, i.e. "waves" on *both* sides of the bow. Because of the piling up of water in these waves the pressure against the sides of the ship is greater than it would be were it standing still and this is true on both sides of the initial source of disturbance. Our suggestion is that a system of action cannot "drive" toward a goal without creating increased pressure both in the adaptive context and in the integrative. Without such pressure toward a goal there would be no differentiation. But the distinction between adaptive and integrative exigencies of the system forms the basic axis on which differentiation takes place when it occurs.

The point at which our metaphor breaks down is in the fact that it provides no analogy for the "skewing" toward the adaptive side which a process of goal-attainment of an action system initially sets in motion. The basis of this asymmetry lies in the fact that differentiation is always the result of a learning process and that in a learning process, given "drive," i.e., impetus toward the attainment of a goal, it is the adaptive exigencies which are always the *initial* focus of strain in the process. The heightening of the urgency of integrative exigencies then comes as a consequence of the changes of the system which result from the process of attempting to meet the adaptive exigencies.

There is a further parallel which is suggestive. We have many times insisted that differentiation is a process which takes place within systems of action which have already reached certain levels of integration. This means the institutionalization or internalization of a common value system. Bales and Slater suggest that it is a characteristic of their low status consensus groups that the initial level of integration about a common value system is lower than in the case of the high status consensus groups. The low consensus groups fail to develop a reintegration which makes the de facto differentiation of roles into a cooperative rather than a competitive constellation.

Is there not a parallel here to the suggestions made by Parsons in Chapters II and III that the degree to which the initial process of internalization of a social object creating the mother-child identity succeeds has important bearing on the conditions for the subsequent process of differentiation and integration of the personality system? It was further suggested in Chapter IV that the psychopathic personality reflected under-integration at this stage. Differentiation is one aspect of organization; is it not possible that there is a parallel between the relatively imperfect integration of the low consensus groups and that of the psychopath? Unfortunately Bales and Slater do not have any data as to what would constitute an "over-integrated" group which might be parallel to the compulsive personality type.

All this, we believe, is common to the process of differentiation in personality systems and in social systems; indeed the parallel in these respects is one of the strongest confirmations we have of our view of the importance of the factors *common* to all types of systems of action. What then can we say of the fundamental differences in these respects, between the two types of system?

Let us start by noting that by our theory the critical distinction between the two does not rest on a difference in basic mode of relation between motivation and the normative control of action. In one respect it rests rather in a difference of modes of participation in the total of the cultural system of a society. The essential restriction is that on the *initial* value system of the personality as related to that of the society; it must be *differentiated variant* of the total value system of the society which has one particularly crucial set of properties, namely those which enable it to serve as the common value-system of the mother-child collectivity in its earliest phase. Or, put a little differently, it must constitute the value-component of the mother role in its early phase as mother-of-infant. Seen in terms of its relations to the known variety of value-systems and their subsystems this is a highly specialized type of value system, corresponding to the specialization of type of the mother-infant relationship, as differentiated from others in the society.

Relative to a society and its system of values, this level of specification can only be reached by a *series* of steps of differentiation. We do not know exactly what the number of such steps is or has to be. But some clue is given by the place of the nuclear family in the nesting series of social interaction systems involved in socialization, namely the fact that in all societies it stands somewhere in the middle. The nuclear family is, if we have interpreted it aright, basically a four-role-type social system, removed by two steps of increasing complexity from the mother-infant system. Then the initial value system of the child must be specialized by two steps of differentiation relative to that of the family.

But we have also argued that it is intrinsically impossible for the nuclear family as we know it ever to constitute a society.

If this is true the value system which is common to the members of the family as a subsystem must be in turn a differentiated subsystem of that of the society. Even in societies where all or almost all social organization is couched in kinship terms, the "extended" kin groups are not nuclear families and have different value systems from those of nuclear families. Above all they have to bear the brunt of the economic and political functions of the society. On grounds put forward in Chapter IV we may at least suspect that at least two steps in differentiation beyond the nuclear family are necessary to meet the minimum functional exigencies of a complete society. Then the initial value system of a personality must be removed by at least four steps of differentiation from that of a society; hence be "specialized" to that extent. Pari-passu an individual must undergo at least four major steps of differentiation of his personality system, learning to participate, i.e. assume roles, in the corresponding succession of collectivities, before he can be an "adult" personality in *any* society. But in so doing the combination of roles played by any one individual must come to be differentiated from that of other classes of individuals in the same society. There must, in any society, be not one but several types of adult "basic personality." We have suggested that the most elementary of these types are based on the differentiations by sex and by class.

With respect to their value-system content, that is the most critical part of the internalized-institutionalized culture, personalities and social systems thus differ in that they embody obverse modes of organization with respect to differentiated subsystems of the total cultural system of the society. The initial point of reference for the differentiation of the societal value system relative to its subsystems, which are collectivities and the roles of individuals, is one which comprises all the roles and all the basic personality types in the society. But the initial point of reference for differentiation of the personality is, though a true value system, a relatively very specialized subtype of this paramount societal value-system.

As the personality system becomes progressively more highly differentiated, the individual participates in an increasingly larger proportion of the roles and hence values of the society. The full adult is a participant in the total society as a collectivity, but never in all of its possible roles. The multiplicity of roles performed by the same individual constitutes one of the cardinal facts of social organization and thus of the relation between society and personality, but it is an equally cardinal fact that in no society does the same individual play all the critically important types of role in the society. The convergence of the two processes of differentiation, therefore, is complete only with respect to the collective value-system of the society as a collectivity; never with respect to the actual role-commitment of the individual. It is his participation in a role-system composed of adults which involves functions on behalf of the total society as a system which constitutes full maturity for the individual.

In formulating this focus of the difference between personality and social system, we have deliberately ignored the considerations which have figured most prominently in psychological thought, namely those having to do with the exigencies imposed by the structure of the human organism. We have done this because we feel that it is the *internalized culture* of the personality in its relation to the structure of the social object-system, as it has impinged on the individual over time which is the main source of the structure of the personality itself as a system of action. But once this set of relationships has been adequately analyzed and can be kept clearly in mind, we feel it is then possible and profitable to come back to the problems of the relation of personality to the organism.

It is, we feel, in this direction that the explanation of the fundamental fact to which we have just called attention, that in no society does the same person perform all *types* of roles, is to be found. This conclusion does not, in our opinion, rest mainly in the postulation of a genetic disposition, for instance, of male and female organisms to assume masculine and feminine roles. It is rather that a society is a type of system which requires a higher order of role-differentiation than the normal personality is capable of achieving, and that this limitation on capacity goes back to the exigencies imposed on personality development and functioning by its connections with and organization relative to the organism.

In our opinion the best approach to this question lies in consideration of the nature of the process of growth or development as we have outlined it. This is, in the personality case, a process of the orderly differentiation of an internalized object-structure, and the corresponding processes of reintegration of the system on each of the new levels. One essential set of conditions of the process concerns the presentation of the "information" with respect to the cultural content which is to be internalized, and the proper ordering of conditions for its internalization through the behavior of the socializing agents. A second equally essential set of conditions concerns the motivational states of the organism and the ways in which these bear on the control of bodily processes in the interest of the personality.

Motivation, we have held[6] should be regarded for personality theory as "initially" undifferentiated. As we see it now, this should be taken to mean that the first phase of the socialization process produces an *organization* of the components of organic motivation, of "primary drives" if you will, which is capable of functioning as a system. This we presume takes place through the processes of "conditioning." But unlike most behavior psychologists we focus our attention, not on what happens to any one specific drive, but on the nature of the whole *system* comprised by an organized plurality of conditioned drives.

For our present purposes the most important property of this system lies in the fact that, *as a system,* it may be held to have acquired a *single* new system-goal which as such is not constitutionally given, but learned; at the first step this is the goal of maximizing "oral gratification." At the same time, because this rudimentary personality is a system in the action sense, it is subject to integrative exigencies in processes pursuant to that goal. From this point of reference the process of differentiation takes place.

The ultimate source of motivation is, we postulate, organic, so the organism must somehow continue to provide motivation in ways which the personality can use. Furthermore the body itself provides the most important single set of facilities for processes of action of the personality and many of its rewards; and the body must thus be integrated in and with the system of action. The ways in which cathexes of the body and its parts become established, and instrumental controls over it set up,

---

6. *Working Papers,* Chap. V, Sec. vi.

constitutes a critically important aspect of the developmental process which we have not been able to follow out in this volume.

We believe sex to constitute in a developmental sense the most "primitive" of the differentiations of generic personality type to which we have referred. The cathexis of the characteristics of the body which are differentiated by sex can therefore serve as a prototypical illustration for this phase of the problem. The outcome of this cathexis constitutes an institutionalized and internalized system of *meanings of situational objects* which thus become symbols. These differentiated meanings become the major focus of orientation of the individual for his own role-categorization and of course for alter in orienting to him. Motivationally it means the acceptance of the set of goals ascribed to one's own sex-role, and correspondingly renunciation of those ascribed to the other.

We thus believe that the basic limitation on all persons playing all roles which are necessary for the functioning of a society goes back to the exigencies involved in putting together and balancing on the one hand the development of a personality organized about a system of internalized cultural values, and on the other hand meeting the needs of the human organism. This in turn goes back to the characteristics of the family as the special kind of small group which can undertake the earlier phases of the socialization function, and to the exigencies of guiding and organizing motivation for the assumption of social roles. All children, regardless of sex, start with an undifferentiated internalized value system inculcated in the family. For it to be possible to take the critical steps necessary to step outside the family group and assume other roles, it is necessary that certain lines of differentiation be introduced into the internal structure of the socialization system, i.e. the family, itself.

We may put this a little differently. The universality of families as a feature of the structure of societies involves a certain special "skewing" of the pattern of organization of the society, if the latter is viewed from the perspective of the ways in which value-systems can be implemented in organized social structures. We believe that this skewing results from the fact that it is concrete human organisms which have to be socialized for the performance of social roles, not just a mathematician's abstractly conceived unit of a social system. The role of the family in society therefore can constitute on one level a measure of the impact of biological factors on society.

The difference between this way of looking at the problem and that generally current lies in the fact that we take the society as an established fact and a going concern and inquire how certain features of it must be accounted for by factors which in strict theoretical sense are extraneous to it. The other view essentially says, man is an organism, and asks what special features of this organism account for the fact that he forms culture-level societies? Both perspectives are legitimate and fruitful, but we feel that ours can illuminate neglected aspects of this critical relationship.

The Gradients of Symbols and Generalization

Let us now return for a moment to the more general relations between personality and social structure to take note of one particular problem area in which we feel that much further work is needed. This is the problem area concerning the gradients on which various kinds of symbolic generalization take place. A particular aspect of this area which is of great theoretical significance concerns the relations between what, in any given structure, are subordinate and superordinate objects. Our analysis leads us to the discrimination of three different sets of structural relations in this field.

The best known of these concerns what may be called the "regression series" as this is treated in personality psychology. Every internalized object system which constitutes part of a personality structure involves, in one aspect, differentiated sub-objects relative to what we have called "genetically prior objects." Thus the internalized mother and autonomous self as objects are differentiated from the earlier internalized mother-object of the mother-child identity stage; the internalized father and mother, from the love-attachment mother, the masculine and feminine selves from the first autonomous self, etc. We have repeatedly argued, in accord with established psychological views, that under certain pressures the tendency is to regress from the more differentiated to the less differentiated object, to revive orientations which were appropriate to the earlier and less differentiated stage of development. This occurs, on the one hand because these earlier objects, though transformed, do not lose their positive functions in the personality system, and on the other because motivational elements which are inappropriate for later stages are not completely extinguished.

We may, then, think of two obverse aspects of generalization, in both cognitive and cathectic respects relative to this series. One is the process of generalization we analyzed as occurring in the developmental process itself by which the new object-systems are built up. The other is the "regressive" generalization whereby from "higher" in the sense of more differentiated, structures and from situational sources, there is generalization "back" to the genetically prior structures. It is well known that the operation of the mechanisms of defense in pathological syndromes is dominated by this type of symbolic generalization. It is in this sense that we speak of father and mother symbols in reference to extra-familial contexts, and of anal and oral symbolism in the phantasy-production of adults.

It is a ready inference from our analysis that there is a directly analogous structure of symbolic generalization gradients for societies and other social systems. This set of gradients connects current structures of the social system with the genetically prior structures out of which the current ones have differentiated. On the societal level we suggest that the various "romantic" nostalgias which connect with nationalism and other "fundamentalist" orientations and ideologies, constitute in this sense regressive generalizations which are analogous to the regressive symbolizations of personality. Under certain types of social pressure this type of preoccupation may be expected to appear. The same would of course, with different specific content, be true of partial social systems. These would, in common with the regressive generalizations of the personality, have a reference to a genetically prior stage in the actual history of the social system in question.

But these two structural series do not exhaust the field. There is in addition the set of relationships which are involved in the *current* interpenetration of personality and social structure, of which we have made so much in connection with the internalization of social value systems. As we have put it, every role-expectation is a meeting-point, a node of integration, of several subsystems of the social value-system and of several need-disposition components of the personality at the same time. These integrations all function on a level of symbolic meaning. A disturbance, therefore, will be propagated through such a system along the appropriate gradients of symbolic meaning, that is the gradients of meaningful relations of the component internalized-institutionalized objects to each other. Therefore we suggest that generalization occurs not only "up" and "down" each of the two "regression gradients" we have distinguished, but also "across" in three senses. First there will be an "across" generalization in the sense of generalization from one social structure to another; second from one need-disposition to another, and third from social structure to need-disposition and vice versa.

We may illustrate these points developmentally as follows. With the development of the modern type of occupational structure in industrialized societies, there must also be a change in family structure if only because the same person, e.g. the husband-father, plays crucially important roles in both structures, and because children must be socialized for roles in both. This leads us back to the integrative imperatives of the social system. In the personality case, then, the first stage of the assumption of a masculine role through identification with the father in the oedipal phase cannot leave the boy's other main need-dispositions untouched. Not only is the rank order of importance of these need-dispositions different from that in his sister's personality, but the internalized mother in his must be different from that in hers. This type of generalization thus relates to the integrative imperatives of the personality system. Finally, the third type results, in psychological terms, from the interplay of the mechanisms of defense and those of adjustment. Seen in one perspective it is this generalization which makes socialization itself possible since what originally are situational demands posing an adaptive problem eventually become internalized. Conversely the latent value-structure of the personality can, as Bales and Slater have indicated, within limits impose itself on the structure of the social situation.

We suggest that these distinctions are of the first importance for the problem of the interpretation of symbolic behavior whether it be in the symptomatology of personality disorders, in ritual or in other fields. In principle we feel that every significant symbol in an action system should have "meanings" in *all* of these contexts. Which of them is most important will be a function in the first instance of the problem under consideration, and secondly of the system references which are defined in relation to it. Thus a political authority-figure associated with a disturbance of social equilibrium may, like McCarthy, be to many individuals as personalities an incarnation of the "archaic" superego, a "father figure" who arouses primitive unresolved guilt-reactions. But *at the same time* for the society as a system he may have a relation to the social regression-scale, symbolizing the nostalgic sentiment that, if only these disturbing "communists" were exorcised, it might be possible to enjoy the benefits of a primitive "Americanism." Yet again, however, there are references to strains in the current internal role-structure of the society as is evidenced by the selectivity of internal scapegoats such as presumptively disloyal Democrats or professors or Eastern upper-class people, and within the personalities of political adherents and sympathizers.[7] Thus according to our view there is no such thing as the one "real" meaning of an expressive symbol if by this is meant that it has one and only one meaning which is scientifically important. Multiplicity of meanings is in the nature of the role of symbols in action. But this is not a random multiplicity which defies analysis. It is ordered and structured. We suggest that the discrimination of three main types of context in which this meaning can be interpreted as outlined above should be helpful in developing our understanding in this very important field to a higher scientific level.

The Classification of Personality Types

There is one final theoretical problem on which we feel that our material justifies a few words. This is the much vexed problem of the classification of types of systems in action. The present volume is not directly concerned with the broader problems of comparative sociology, so we will not attempt to discuss the problem in its social system aspects but only that of personality systems.

7. See T. Parsons "McCarthyism and American Social Tensions," *Yale Review,* (Winter, 1954-5).

We feel it justified to conclude from our material that workable classifications of personality types should be derivable from two fundamental points of reference. The first of these is the classification of value-systems themselves in the relevant respects, the second, the classification of pathological syndromes, as we attempted it in extremely tentative fashion in Chapter IV. Furthermore we feel it is one of the most important inferences from our analysis that these two bases of classification should be treated as fundamentally independent of each other.

If the theoretical premises on which the whole of our analysis in this volume is built are acceptable, it is clearly a necessary inference that there should be a determinate range of possible value systems which are internalized in personalities and institutionalized in social systems. This range is defined in the first instance in terms of the relative predominance or rank order of importance of the four fundamental types of norm in the total composition of the system of values which we have so often discussed. Or, we may put it a little differently, what we call the value system is, we hold, a description of the location of a system in action-space. Relative to a given point of reference, then, the position of a given system is defined in terms of the four coordinates of the space, by the relative distances on these coordinates from the "point of origin" which is chosen.

There are two critically important qualifications of this general proposition which must be clearly kept in mind in interpreting it. The first is implied in the statement of it which has just been made. This is the *relativity* of any classification to a point of reference and to comparative judgments as seen from this point of reference. It is thus not proper to say in absolute terms, that American Society is characterized by a "universalistic-achievement" value system in general without specification of the point of reference and the implicit if not explicit comparisons—e.g., within modern Western society as a superordinate system. Similarly it is not possible to say in absolute terms that Jones is a universalistic-achievement oriented person, except when the point of reference—i.e., in his society—is specified, and there is at least implicit comparison with other personalities within the same "universe." In other words if he uses our sorts of terms, a person who talks about types of personality as defined by their internalized values, but does not specify his system reference or the comparisons he is making within that system reference should be called immediately to account. Endless confusion will arise if these qualifications are not scrupulously kept in mind.

The second field of qualification concerns the relation of a value-system to the situational and integrative exigencies of a personality system. In the social system case we have just been discussing the fact that the family and its relation to the socialization of children "skew" the structures and distribution of value-pattern types of societies. This skewing we account for by the double facts that it is human personalities which must play roles in social systems and the human personality is a system of the behavior of organisms of a particular species, hence bound to the exigencies inherent in the organism as a biological system.

Similarly, the exigencies of its relation to the organism impose certain constraints on the variability of personality types, which are independent of the variability of value-systems. But with reference to that aspect of the concrete personality which is a system of action, we maintain emphatically that the strategically critical focus for classification is not the type of organism in a biological sense but the type of value-system by virtue of which the personality is articulated with the society of which it is a part. The *organism* or one of its needs is not a unit of a society for the simple reason that they are two different orders of system. In the same sense a carbohydrate molecule is not a "cell" in the sense in which the latter is a unit of the structure of an organism.

But taking the internalized value system as the focus for the classification of personality types does not imply that no other criteria are to be treated as relevant. It only means that these other criteria are to be evaluated in the frame of reference in which value-systems are crucial, that their significance is a function of the ways in which they modify or reinforce the organization relative to values.

We have suggested above that our analysis leads us to the con-clusion that the classification of pathological syndromes should be treated as theoretically independent of the classification of "normal" personality types which uses the internalized value-system as the paramount point of reference. First, we may note that this view is parallel to that put forward by Parsons[8] that in social system terms, the analysis and determinants of the directions of deviance could be treated as independent of variability in the structure of the institutionalized role-pattern system. This, we feel, is another critically important respect in which the problems of personality systems and social systems parallel one another.

If it is correct that pathological types are independent of the variability of normal structures, this fact should have a most important set of implications for the empirical application of our theory. It should, for example, imply that "cultural" differences would not mean that there were pathological syndromes specific to particular cultures, that for example to speak of a Chinese schizophrenic was a contradiction in terms, since schizophrenia must necessarily be a "culture-bound" phenomenon peculiar to the modern Western world.

If our view is correct all the main pathological syndromes should be found in all human populations. Their relative incidence, however, would be expected to vary substantially. Furthermore, many special features of the phenomena found should be a function of the particular social structures and situations in which they are found. But the generic features on the one hand of personality systems on the other hand of societies should be sufficiently important so that the basic classificatory scheme is independent of the variability of societies. This should prove to be a testable claim.

---

8. *The Social System* (Glencoe, Ill.: Free Press, 1951), Chapter VII.

APPENDIX A

A Note on Some Biological Analogies

BY TALCOTT PARSONS

The material which has been reviewed in the last three main chapters of this volume will have suggested to a reader familiar with biological theory that there were a number of rather striking analogies between the type of theoretical constructs we have developed here and certain ideas which are current in biological thinking. Our argument for our theoretical constructs in the socio-psychological field does not rest either logically or empirically on these analogies; it stands on its own feet. But the biological analogies have had some suggestive influence on their development. In any case they are of considerable interest and may possibly turn out to be important. It has hence seemed worth while to call the reader's attention to them in this appended note.

The first of the analogies will probably have struck many readers independently. This is that involving the conception we presented in Chapter II of the process of personality development as first establishing a single internalized object-motive system, which then underwent a process of differentiation and integration by binary fission. The biological model which corresponds to this is of course the conception that the first step in development is fertilization, only then to be followed by division of the fertilized ovum, a process which then follows the binary pattern. One may speak of the two elements which correspond analogically to the female and the male germ cells (ovum and spermatozoön) respectively as the "organism" of the neonate on the one hand, the set of cultural norms or values on the other hand. Only when a certain *organization,* combining as we have put it motivational elements and cultural elements, has been set up, does the process of development in our sense get under way. Then again in both cases this development goes by relatively *discontinuous* stages as in the case of the earliest embryological stages; a two-cell, four-cell, eight-cell etc. stage. This of course comprises only the very early embryological stages of complex organisms but the similarity of pattern is unmistakable.

It seems to us probable that this pattern of binary fission is of very general significance in the world of nature. Recent developments in linguistics (Wallon, Jacobsen, Lévi-Strauss) have laid great stress on it. Similarly, it is well known that a similar pattern, in the form of the concept of the "bit," plays a central part in the theory of communication in the physical-engineering sense. It is suggested that with respect to any system, binary division presents the most "economical" way of taking any given step from relative simplicity to a higher level of complexity. We suggest that a similar idea is likely to be fruitful in the analysis of evolution of social structures.

The second suggestive analogy is that between the role of the gene, as the unit of heredity in biological systems, and the units of cultural inheritance through internalization and institutionalization. In a very broad way of course this has been a commonplace, theorists of culture having often spoken of the "social heritage." But the kind of analysis we have given of the process of internalization of social object systems makes it possible to carry the analogy considerably farther than has been customary in the field. The cultural aspect of an internalized object is what we have called a "symbol-meaning" complex. Culture from this point of view, in its impact on the developing personality, is not continuous, but is "fed in" in relatively discrete organized units, which in turn are parts of more extensive systems, especially through what, in Chapter IV we have called the mechanisms of "induction" and "identification." Is not, possibly, such a unit fairly closely analogous to a gene? It also is now held by biologists that the gene is not a "monolithic" entity but is a boundary-maintaining system, which under certain circumstances undergoes processes of change. Furthermore, there are not genes on just one microscopic-macroscopic level, but on many such levels; the choice of unit, that is to say, may be relative to the problem in hand. Clearly all these properties are shared by the cultural element of the internalized object as an organized subsystem of the culture which can be transmitted with minimal change from one personality to another, and in an analogous way from one social system to another. The whole view of socialization we have presented in this volume gives substance to the idea that we have here a complex of mechanisms of transmission which are essential to the stability and development of socio-cultural systems.[1]

The third analogy we have in mind is that between sexual reproduction as a biological process, and the transmission of culture through families the composition of which is regulated by exogamy and incest taboos. This is essentially an extension of the analogy between gene and cultural symbol-complex. Through sexual reproduction, which of course is universal among the higher organisms, it is insured that the hereditary constitutions of all new organisms will derive from *two* relatively independent reservoirs of genes, not just from one. The great biological importance of this apparently has largely to do with variation; it is a mechanism which continually produces *new* combinations. On the other hand the fact that distinct species do not interbreed sets a limit to this variation which has something to do with preventing its becoming too drastically disorganizing. It is, therefore, a controlled variation. Though change in the germ plasm is slow, the presumption is that without the variation introduced by sexual reproduction it would be far slower, and hence the process of evolution greatly inhibited. It is further emphasized on biological grounds that the functional advantage of sexual reproduction cannot possibly rest in its superior efficiency as a reproductive mechanism. Its functional significance is to the species as a system, not to the immediate parent-offspring continuity.

The action-theory analogy is a sociological one. The incest taboo insures that no newly socialized child receives his cultural heritage from only one line of descent. His parents have been socialized in *two* independent nuclear families and the internalized culture of his own personality will, with respect to the foundations laid down in his family of orientation, be a resultant of combining these two partially independent heritages. There is, in such a situation, far greater potentiality of *cultural* variation than there would be if the mixing of the cultures of families were not forced by the incest taboo. But at the same time the fact that the individual is socialized in a family which has its own imperatives of integration as a system, insures that there will in the interest of stability be limits set to the variation. If the

---

1. For insight into this analogy and its possible importance, and the one next to be discussed between sexual reproduction in the biological sense and exogamy and the incest taboo in the social, I am particularly indebted to Professor Alfred Emerson of the University of Chicago (oral communication).

marriage pair—and wider kinship groups in which they are integrated —do not have sufficient common culture to constitute a stable family type, they will not contribute greatly to the future culture of the society. Furthermore there is reason to believe that a poorly integrated family tends to produce more than its share of psychopathologically burdened offspring, who are not, relatively speaking socioculturally viable; they are less likely to leave cultural descendants than others.

Again, similarly to the biological case, it does not seem possible to explain the incest taboo on grounds of its functional utility to the particular nuclear family. In going societies it is built into the family structure so that incest would in general be disorganizing to individual families as we know them, but this is probably a resultant phenomenon. The taboo roots in the importance of transcending the nuclear family by a wider social organization.

There is still a fourth suggestive field of analogy. Throughout our discussions a certain feature of the conception of systems of action with which we have been working stands out. This is the separation of the "latency cell" of our tables out from the other three. It is in this aspect or part of the system that we put the internalized or institutionalized "pattern-system." It is held to be relatively stable compared to the rest of the system, and not in the same sense involved in direct input-output interchanges over the boundaries of the system; in this sense it is "inside" the system, "surrounded" by the other parts or subsystems. Its relative stability is also related to the processes of transmission of culture; it changes mostly in the "radical" learning processes of which socialization is a prototype.

It is not a very drastic leap to see in this an analogy with the biological structure of the cell, the division between nucleus and cytoplasm. Biologically it is clear that the genes are carried in the nucleus. Only in the processes of cell division presumably do radical changes in the nucleus take place; it is certainly less involved than the cytoplasm in the ordinary physiological interchanges with the environment of the cell; it is relatively insulated from them. Similar analogies can certainly be seen with differentiation of the complex organism; the sensory and motor systems, the respiratory and alimentary systems are directly involved in adjustments to the environment; the skeleton, the main structure of the central nervous system etc. are insulated from such influences. But we will not attempt to push the analogies farther here. The simpler nucleus-cytoplasm case is probably more apposite.

A fifth analogy may, even more tentatively, be finally suggested. This is between the family in a highly differentiated society and the germ plasm of the higher organisms. If our suggestions about the analogy between gene and cultural symbol-complex have anything in them, it is quite clear sociologically that the family is universally in all societies the primary organ for the transmission of the fundamentals of the patterns of culture. In very primitive societies the whole social structure is organized about kinship—though *never* the nuclear family alone. But in highly differentiated societies like those of the modern Western world, the family has become a rather "specialized" agency and participates as such little in the macroscopic structures of the society—though of course its members do so in non-familial roles. It, and, in other for present purposes less fundamental respects, agencies of formal education, have similar functions. But with biological evolution the perpetuation of the genetic basis of the species ceases to be a function of the organism as a whole and comes to be specialized in a particular, rather specially protected, part of it. Is not this also a trend which accompanies the differentiation of social systems?

We do not wish on this occasion to attempt to assess the possible significance of these analogies. Only one suggestion will be made. By and large the biological and socio-psychological points of view from which they are suggested are relatively recent. It seems possible that the conflict between the two fields which marked what might be called the "war of independence" of the sciences of action to emancipate themselves from the biological sciences of fifty years ago, was bound to a particular stage in the development of both fields. It seems altogether possible that as both reach higher levels it will become increasingly clear that a common conceptual scheme underlies theory in both of them. This is logical if we assume, as I think we must, that human personality and society are best conceived as in the broadest sense "in nature" as not as set "over against" nature. Biology is our nearest neighbor in the community of sciences and such substantive relationships should be expected. We are both part of the same larger "community" of human knowledge.

APPENDIX B

A Note on the Analysis
of Equilibrium Systems

BY MORRIS ZELDITCH, JR.

1.1. The Bounded System.

A semi-formalized version is presented in this section of the theoretical model stated by T. Parsons, R. F. Bales, and E. A. Shils in the *Working Papers in the Theory of Action* (Glencoe, Ill.: The Free Press, 1953), Chapter V.

The general propositions concerning the tendency of all social systems to structural differentiation and the frame of reference for describing the direction of such differentiation derive essentially from the conception of a hypothetical "boundary-maintaining" system, any act of which may be referred to its effect on the oscillation of the system in and out of a "stable state" and across or within the boundaries. The scale of the system may range from a plurality of need-dispositions to a plurality of collectivities, though we shall here deal with a plurality of actors (for definition of such notions as "actor," "interaction," etc., here undefined, v. Parsons and Shils 1952 and/or Parsons 1951). It is necessary always, however, to distinguish that which is taken as a "unit" and that which is treated as a "system."

D.1. A unit=df that which is treated as an elementary particle.

It is to be understood that this implies a "volition" of the observer, not a statement concerning the ontological reality of the object so treated.

D.2. A system=df two or more units, $x_1, x_2, \ldots x_n$, related such that a change in state of any x_i will be followed by a change of state in the remaining $x_j, \ldots x_n$ which is in turn followed by a change in the state of x_i, etc.

Two or more units in the relation specified in D.2. are said to be interdependent.

A unit might in a different context be treated as a system. It is conceivable that units could be in relations other than interdependent. The basic assumption on which analysis is predicated, however, treats *"interacting"* units as interdependent; this could be made to follow from the definition of interaction, but is here simply stated as axiom 1.

A.1. Two or more units in interaction with each other form a system.

This may be sharpened by consideration of the fact that any actor interacts at different times in a number of systems, so that strictly speaking an "actor" cannot be treated as the unit of social system. The unit in this case is customarily referred to as a role, and the axiom would link two or more *roles* as a system (v. Parsons 1951).

A system as defined in D.2. could conceivably oscillate indefinitely, but Parsons, Bales, and Shils take it as axiomatic that systems "seek equilibrium." Again one might easily *define* systems as equilibrium-seeking; the mode of procedure chosen here is arbitrary.

D.3. Equilibrium=df a state of a system such that there is zero change of state of the units of the system relative to each other.

D.3.1. A system seeks equilibrium=df a change of state of x_i is followed by a change of state of $x_j, \ldots x_n$ such that no further change of state occurs in the system.

It should be emphasized that zero changes of state does not refer to zero *movement* of the system. An atom, for instance, may be regarded as a stable system because the position of neutrons, electrons, and positrons, though continually moving, retain essentially the same relation to each other, i.e. the same structural *form*. This may be informally referred to as the "stable state" of an "on-going" system.

A.2. Initial change of state of a system is followed by attempts to seek an equilibrium.

Social systems, however, have a further property which is not characteristic of all systems. In physics and chemistry one generally deals with systems which have indefinite extensions, and to use Willard Gibb's phrase, "change phase" rather than disappear altogether. In

biology and social science, the systems dealt with are said to be
"boundary-maintaining." The notion of extension is taken as a primitive idea in defining this conception of boundary-maintenance.

D.4. A system has a boundary=df the state of the system is limited in extension and the state-description of the system may be discriminated from
the state-description of that which is non-system.

D.4.1. The environment=df that which is discriminated as non-system.

D.4.2. A system is boundary-maintaining=df the reaction to initial change of
state is such that the system retains its boundaries relative to its environment.

D.4.3. A system is dissolved=df the reaction to initial change of state is such
that the system does not remain discriminated from the environment.

A.3. Let the interaction of two or more actors be termed a "social" system.
Initial change of state of a social system is followed by attempts to maintain the boundaries of the system.

It is to be noted that it does *not* follow from A.3. that all social systems
do in fact preserve themselves from dissolution or assimilation.

1.2. The Coordinates of Action Space.

From these principles Parsons, Bales, and Shils develop a scheme
for "placing" acts in the interaction process, and propositions concerning the conditions and directions of action.

It is possible from this conception of a boundary-maintaining system and its interchange with the environment (both physical and
social) in which it is embedded, to derive a coordinate system for the
description of any act in the system. Essentially any act is categorized
in terms of how it affects the state of the system relative to its equilibrium and its discrimination from the environment, how, that is,
it *moves* the system towards or away from the hypothetical ideal state
of bounded equilibrium. It is inherent in this conception that movement too far from equilibrium should be treated as a "strain" on the
system and action process should be seen as the process of developing such strains and the attempts of the system to "re-equilibrate" in
the face of such strains. The system is never empirically at "rest"
because of continual inputs from motivational and situational factors
"outside" the system—but we shall not treat formally the input-output
problem.

The directional focus of such system-process is goal-attainment and
the consummatory gratification of the member-units. But this involves
exigencies of "adaptation" to the situation, of manipulation of the
object world so that it will provide this gratification. At the same
time, preservation of the boundaries of the system involves the inte-

gration of member-units in a solidary system and the reduction of intra-unit tensions developed during the adaptive process.

D.5-8. The following four coördinates are defined:

D.5. Goal-attainment=df the gratification of the units of the system.

D.5.1. An act may be treated as an increment or decrement in the gratification of the member-units.

D.6. Adaptation=df the manipulation of the environment in the interests of goal-attainment.

D.6.1. An act may be treated as an increment or decrement in adaptation to the environment.

D.7. Integration=df the attachment of member-units to each other in their distinction from that which is non-system.

D.7.1. An act may be treated as an increment or decrement in the integration of member-units.

D.8. Tension=df the malintegration of member-units seen as themselves systems.

D.8.1. An act may be treated as an increment or decrement in the tension of member-units.

For the purposes of the crude indices with which this particular project works, the four coordinates may be reduced to two on the basis of the broad discrimination of interchange with the environment and preservation of the boundaries defining the internal state of the system.

D.9-10. Reduction of the coördinate system.

D.9. Instrumental activity=df the goal-attainment and adaptation aspects of the coordinate system.

D.10. Expressive activity=df the integrative and tension aspects of the coordinate system.

D.11-15. The following location terms and temporal discriminations are defined.

D.11. A point in action space=df the intersection of the coordinates defining the place of an act.

It is possible to state O-points in a coordinate so that an act has *no* relevance on one or more; this is empirically unlikely.

D.12. An area in action space=df a mass of points.

An area or point may be elliptically characterized by the coördinate it maximizes; thus an "expressive" area is one of *relative* preponderance of acts along the expressive coordinate.

D.13. Maximization along a coördinate=df the primacy of one coördinate relative to the other three in the state-description of the act or system.

D.14. Motion in action space=df change of system state from one point to another in successive units of time.

D.15. A phase=df a temporal slice of action process during which there is maximization of points in one area in the given time span.

In this usage, the system goes through an "adaptive" phase if, relative to the other three coordinates, the system is at the time primarily manipulating situational objects. It is important to distinguish phases and coordinates which may be referred to under the same term.

P.1:1-4. The following propositions are asserted as postulates.

P.1. It is a condition of a steady state of the system that it meet the exigencies of action along all four coordinates of action space.

P.1.1. If the member-units of a system are to maintain the boundaries of the system relative to its environment, the system must provide an optimum of gratification for the several member-units.

P.1.2. If the member-units of the system are to achieve goal-gratification there must be some diversion of motivational energy to the adaptive problems of relation of the system to its environment.

P.1.3. If the member-units are to maintain the boundaries of the system relative to its environment there must be some diversion of motivational energy to the integrative problems of their mutual solidarity.

P.1.4. If the member-units are to maintain the boundaries of the system relative to its environment, there must be some diversion of motivational energy to the expressive problems of their several tension-states.

It will be noted that underlying these postulates is a conception of the unidirectional expenditure of energy such that it must be "diverted"; it cannot, it is assumed, be both stored and expended at the same point in time. Therefore, the following axiom is necessary:

A.4. The expenditure of motivational energy is unidirectional.

A.4.1. Action cannot be maximized along all coordinates, nor along any two coördinates, at the same point in time.

1.3. Structural Differentiation in Action Space.

The conceptions of point and motion in action space can be used to define differentiation in the space. Differentiation works out in two ways, structurally and temporally, both considered as reducing strain on the system. Structural differentiation, further, has both qualitative and quantitative aspects. From the propositions that action cannot be maximized along more than one coördinate at any time point in time and that prolonged action along any one places a strain on the system, differentiation into phases is easily derived as a necessary condition of the existence of the system. Structural differentiation, with which this section is concerned, involves further the proposition that *within* any one phase, or at any one point in time, the various units of the system are at different points in the space, and describe different paths through the space.

By structural differentiation of the system we mean that the several units of the system have different "orbits" during the cycle of action.

D.16. An orbit=df a pattern of temporal succession of unit phases.

D.16.1. Two member-units of a system are structurally differentiated=df they have different orbit-patterns.

An orbit-pattern of a member-unit does not go through all possible points and does not pass through all phases at the same rate. That the orbits will be repeated patterns follows from the assumption that the system seeks a stable-state. In each system-phase the units are, relative to each other, in different phases, areas, or points. That the direction of differentiation is along the coördinates of action space follows from P.1; any other course leads to dissolution of the system. That differentiation *must* occur at all is rather less certain. Assume, therefore, a system which is originally undifferentiated; the grounds for this are laid down as sociologically axiomatic.

A.5. Constitutional and temperamental equipments of actors vary at random with respect to the solution of system problems.

Since the direction of system-process is goal-gratificatory, in the initial undifferentiated state we therefore assume that all members of the group are acting along the goal-attainment coördinate. By postulate 1.2 the members must devote some energy to the adaptive problems of the system and by axiom 4.1 the members cannot maximize action along both the adaptive and goal-gratification coördinates at the same time. Assume therefore that the system is in an adaptive stage. As yet undifferentiated, all members are now competing for the facilities necessary to achieve along this coördinate. Granting that facilities are scarce relative to the demand for them (just as rewards in the goal-gratification coordinate are scarce relative to the demands for them) one has grounds for the proposition that:

Maximization of the action of all actors along the adaptive coordinate is followed by increments in the tension state of the system and constitutes a threat to the maintenance of the boundaries of the system.

This procedure merely exhibits the "argument from the condition of strain"; it can be reexhibited for action maximized along any other coordinate—with perhaps some slight variation. Since the argument is not water-tight, however, its general form must be taken as a postulate:

P.2. If all members of the system maximize action along the same coordinate at the same period in time, then the increments of strain in the system will threaten the dissolution of the system.

That differentiation entails some degree of specialization can also be stated. Since no one is initially responsible for action along any particular coordinate, it is a matter of some choice as to who shall be initially singled out for which role. But it follows from the conditions stated that the system will approach stability in this respect, and that there will be normative regulation of the action process so as to ensure that *someone,* and moreover *some particular person,* is responsible for the various solutions.

The argument, therefore, implies the following theorems, assuming always the "if" condition of boundary-maintenance:

T.1. System exigencies impose a set of differentiated orbit-patterns on any social system.

T.2. The differentiation of orbit-patterns is in the direction of system problems.

T.3. The members of the system tend to specialize in the imposed orbit-patterns.

FIGURES 1-3:

Designation of General Terms

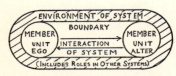

Figure 1: Unit, System, and Environment

The point of reference is always the system, which is made up of two or more units or members who interact with each other. The system is embedded in an environing situation; this includes other actors and roles. The units move the system, but their own location is specified with regard to their effect on system movement. The unit is treated as undifferentiated, as a "particle"; however, it may itself be treated as a system, in which case the "reference point" is shifted. This same problem arises with respect to time spans.

[continued on next page]

FIGURES 1-3: (contd.)

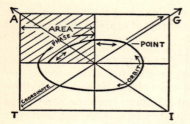

Figure 2: Point, Area, Phase,
Orbit, and the Coordinates

The coordinates are derived from the conception of a boundary-maintaining system and its interchange with the environment. The directional focus of process is goal-attainment (G); this involves exigencies of adaptation to the situation (A); preservation of the boundaries at the same time, however, involves the integration of member-units as a solidary system (I) and the reduction of tensions engendered in the member-units during the adaptation process (T). Every act is categorized in terms of its contribution to one of these four system problems and process in the system may be seen as the provision of solutions for these four problems.

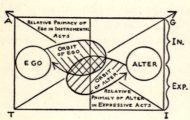

Figure 3: Orbit Differentiation
and Relative Primacies

Movement from point to point describes a regular path termed an orbit. A temporally discriminated part of the orbit is termed a phase. A unit-phase may be distinguished from a system-phase. A unit-orbit may be distinguished from a system-orbit. Two unit-orbits may differ in the points through which they pass and/or in the rate of movement. This, by definition, is structural differentiation. Two differentiated orbits may be summarily characterized by the maximization of points in one of the areas relative to the other three. The terms "instrumental" and "expressive" refer respectively to maximization in adaptive-goal-attainment directions, and maximization in integrative-tension-reducing directions.

Bibliography

The following bibliography is intended primarily as a collection of the items referred to in the body of the text. It is not a complete coverage of any of the fields involved. References in Chapter VI are not included (see bibliography to Chapter VI).

Adorno, T. W., *et al., The Authoritarian Personality,* New York: Harper & Bros., 1950.

Allport, G. W., *Personality: A Psychological Interpretation,* New York: Henry Holt & Co., 1937.

Bakke, E. W., *The Unemployed Man,* New York: E. P. Dutton & Co., 1934.

Bales, R. F., *Interaction Process Analysis, A Method for the Study of Small Groups,* Cambridge, Mass.: Addison-Wesley Press, 1950.

————, "A Set of Categories for the Analysis of Small Group Interaction," *American Sociological Review* 15:257-263, 1950.

————, "Some Statistical Problems of Small Group Research," *Journal of the American Statistical Association,* 46:311-322, 1951.

————, "The Equilibrium Problem in Small Groups," Chapter IV in T. Parsons, R. F. Bales, and E. A. Shils, *Working Papers in the Theory of Action,* Glencoe, Ill.: Free Press, 1953.

————, "How People Interact in Conferences," *Scientific American,* March 1955.

————, and Strodtbeck, F. L., "Phases in Group Problem Solving," *Journal of Abnormal and Social Psychology* 46:485-495, 1951.

————, Strodtbeck, F. L., Mills, T. M., Roseborough, M., "Channels of Communication in Small Groups," *American Sociological Review,* 16:461-468, 1951.

Barnes, H. E., and Ruedi, O. M., *The American Way of Life,* New York: Prentice Hall, Inc., 1951.

Borgatta, E. F., and Bales, R. F., "Sociometric Status Patterns and Characteristics of Interaction," Unpublished MS.

Braithwaite, L., "Social Stratification in Trinidad," *Social and Economic Studies,* Oct., 1953.

Burgess, E. W., and Locke, H. J., *The Family,* New York: American Book Co., 1950.

Carter, L. F., "Leadership and Small Group Behavior," in Sherif, M., and Wilson, M. O., *Group Relations at the Cross-Roads,* New York: Harper & Bros., 1953.

Carver, T. N., *Essays in Social Justice,* Cambridge, Mass: Harvard University Press, 1915.

Erikson, E. H., "Hitler's Imagery and German Youth," in Kluckhohn, C., and Murray, H. A., *Personality in Nature, Society, and Culture,* New York: Alfred A. Knopf, Inc., 1948.

————, *Childhood and Society,* New York: W. W. Norton & Co., 1950.

Frazier, E. F., *Negro Family in the United States,* Chicago: University of Chicago Press, 1939.

Freud, S., *The Problem of Anxiety,* Trans. by Bunker, H. A., New York: The Psychoanalytic Quarterly Press and W. W. Norton & Co., 1936.

—————, *The Ego and the Id,* London: The Hogarth Press, 1927.

—————, *Group Psychology and the Analysis of the Ego,* Trans. by Strachey, J., London and Vienna: International Psychoanalytic Press, 1922.

Glick, P. C., "The Family Cycle," *American Sociological Review,* 12: No. 2, April 1947.

Heinicke, C. M., and Bales, R. F., "Developmental Trends in the Structure of Small Groups," *Sociometry,* 16:7-38, 1953.

Henriques, F., *Family and Color in Jamaica,* 1953.

Holt, L. P., *Psychoanalysis and Social Process,* Doctoral Dissertation, Radcliffe College, 1949.

Kendall, M. G., *Rank Correlation Methods,* London: 1948.

Kluckhohn, C., Murray, H. A., and Schneider, D. M. (eds.), *Personality in Nature, Society, and Culture,* New York: Alfred A. Knopf, Inc., 1953.

Maier, N. R. F., *Frustration,* New York: McGraw Hill, 1949.

Malinowski, B., "Introduction" to Hogbin, H. I., *Law and Order in Polynesia,* London: Christophers, 1934.

Mann, R., *The Relation of Informal Status to Role Behavior in Small Discussion Groups,* Unpublished Honors Thesis, Harvard College, 1954.

Mead, G. H., *Mind, Self, and Society,* Chicago: University of Chicago Press, 1936.

Merton, R. K., and Kitt, A., "Contributions to the Theory of Reference Group Behavior," in Merton, R. K., and Lazarsfeld, P. (eds.) *Continuities in Social Research,* Glencoe, Ill.: Free Press, 1950.

Murdock, G. P., *Social Structure,* New York: Macmillan Co., 1949.

Murray, H. A., *Explorations in Personality,* New York: Oxford University Press, 1938.

National Office of Vital Statistics, "Abridged Life Tables, U. S., 1951," *Vital Statistics—Special Reports, National Summaries,* Vol. 38, No. 5, 1954.

—————, "Summary of Marriage and Divorce Statistics, U. S., 1951," *Vital Statistics—Special Reports, National Summaries,* Vol. 38, No. 5, 1954.

Office of Population Research, Princeton University, and Population Association of America, Inc., *Population Index,* 1954.

Ogburn, W. F., "The Family and its Functions," *Recent Social Trends in the United States,* Report of the President's Research Committee on Social Trends, 1933.

Olds, J., *The Growth and Structure of Motives,* Glencoe, Ill.: Free Press, 1955.

Parsons, T., *The Social System,* Glencoe, Ill.: Free Press, 1951.

—————, "Illness and the Role of the Physician," in Kluckhohn, C., Murray, H. A., and Schneider, D. M., (eds.), *Personality in Nature, Society, and Culture,* New York: Alfred A. Knopf, Inc., 1953.

————, "The Incest Taboo in Relation to Social Structure and the Social-ization of the Child," *British Journal of Sociology*, June, 1954.

————, "The Father Symbol," in *Symbols and Values: an Initial Study*, Finkelstein, *et al.* (eds.), New York: Harper & Bros., 1954.

————, "Psychology and Sociology," in *For a Science of Social Man*, J. Gillin (ed.), New York: Macmillan Co., 1954.

————, "The Kinship System of the Contemporary United States," in *Essays in Sociological Theory*, Parsons, T., Glencoe, Ill.: Free Press, (revised edition), 1954.

————, "Consciousness and Symbolic Processes," in *Problems of Consciousness*, H. A. Abramson (ed.), New York: Josiah Macy Foundation, 1954.

————, "McCarthyism and American Social Tensions," *Yale Review*, Winter, 1954-1955.

————, and Fox, R., "Illness, Therapy, and the Modern American Urban Family," *Journal of Social Issues*, Vol. VIII, No. 4, 1952.

————, and Shils, E. A., "Values, Motives, and Systems of Action," in *Toward a General Theory of Action*, Parsons, T., and Shils, E. A. (eds.), Cambridge, Mass.: Harvard University Press, 1952.

————, Bales, R. F., and Shils, E. A., *Working Papers in the Theory of Action*, Glencoe, Ill.: Free Press, 1953.

Piaget, J., *Language and Thought of the Child*, London: Routledge and Kegan Paul, Ltd., 1926.

————, *The Moral Judgment of the Child*, New York: Harcourt, Brace & Co., 1932.

Riesman, D., *The Lonely Crowd*, New Haven, Conn.: Yale University Press, 1950.

Sears, R. R., and Whiting, J. W. M., *et al., Patterns of Child Rearing*, MS in preparation.

Smith, T. F., *The Rural Negro Family in British Guiana*, Doctoral Dissertation, University of Cambridge, 1954.

Solomon, R. L., and Wynne, L.C., "Traumatic Avoidance Learning: the Principles of Anxiety, Conservation, and Partial Irreversibility," *Psychological Review*, Nov. 1954.

Taylor, F. Kraüpl, "Quantitative Evaluation of Psycho-Social Phenomena in Small Groups," *Journal of Mental Science*, 97:690-717, 1951.

U. S. Bureau of Labor Statistics, *Fact Book on Manpower*, 1951.

————, *New Construction Expenditures, 1915-1951, Labor Requirements, 1939-1951*, 1953.

Waller, W., "The Rating and Dating Complex," in Wilson, L., and Kolb, W. L., (eds.), *Sociological Analysis*, New York: Harcourt, Brace & Co., 1949.

Wallon, H., *Les Origines de la Pensée Chez l'Enfant*, Paris: Boivin & Cie, 1934.

White, R. W., *The Abnormal Personality*, New York: Ronald Press, 1948.

Williams, R. M., *American Society*, New York: Alfred A. Knopf, Inc., 1951.

Index

BOOKS PUBLISHED BY

The Free Press

Lord Acton, *Essays on Freedom and Power* $6.00

Franz Alexander, M.D. and Hugo Staub, *The Criminal, The Judge, and the Public,* revised and enlarged ed. 4.00

Aristides, *To Rome* 1.00

Aristotle, *Constitution of the Athenians* OP

Raymond Aron, *German Sociology* 4.00

Mikhail Bakunin, *The Political Philosophy of Bakunin* 6.00

Edward C. Banfield, *Government Project* 3.50

Bernard Barber, *Science and the Social Order* 4.50

Salo Baron, Ernest Nagel and Koppel S. Pinson, eds., *Freedom and Reason: Studies in Philosophy and Jewish Culture in Memory of Morris Raphael Cohen* 5.00

Karl Bednarik, *The Young Worker of Today* 3.00

Reinhard Bendix and Seymour M. Lipset, eds., *Class, Status and Power: A Reader in Social Stratification* 7.50

Bernard Berelson, *Content Analysis in Communications Research* 4.00

Bernard Berelson and Morris Janowitz, eds., *Reader in Public Opinion and Communication,* revised and enlarged ed. 6.00

Bruno Bettelheim, *Love Is Not Enough: The Treatment of Emotionally Disturbed Children* 4.50

Bruno Bettelheim, *Symbolic Wounds: Puberty Rites and the Envious Male* 5.00

Bruno Bettelheim, *Truants from Life: The Rehabilitation of Emotionally Disturbed Children* 6.00

Robert Blood, *Anticipating Your Marriage* 5.00

Eugene Burdick and Arthur J. Brodbeck, eds., *American Voting Behavior* 6.00

Herbert Butterfield and others, *The History of Science* OP

Richard Christie and Marie Jahoda, eds., *Studies in the Scope and Method of "The Authoritarian Personality"* 4.50

Albert Cohen, *Delinquent Boys* 3.50

Morris R. Cohen, *American Thought: A Critical Sketch* 5.00

Morris R. Cohen, *A Dreamer's Journey: An Autobiography* 4.50

Morris R. Cohen, *King Saul's Daughter* 3.00

Morris R. Cohen, *Reason and Law* 4.00

Morris R. Cohen, *Reason and Nature,* revised ed. 6.00

Morris R. Cohen, *Reflections of a Wondering Jew* 2.75

Commission on Educational Reconstruction, *Organizing the Teaching Profession* 4.50

Charles Horton Cooley, *The Two Major Works of Charles H. Cooley: Human Nature and the Social Order* and *Social Organization,* 2 vols. bound in one 7.50

Lewis Coser, *The Functions of Social Conflict* 3.50

Donald R. Cressey, *Other People's Money: The Social Psychology of Embezzlement* 3.00

Herbert Dinerstein and Leon Gouré, *Two Studies in Soviet Controls: Communism and the Russian Peasant* and *Moscow in Crisis* 4.50

Emile Durkheim, *The Division of Labor in Society* 5.00

Emil Durkheim, *Education and Sociology* 3.50

Emile Durkheim, *Elementary Forms of the Religious Life* 5.00

Emile Durkheim, *Rules of the Sociological Method* 3.00

Emile Durkheim, *Sociology and Philosophy* 3.00

Emile Durkheim, *Suicide: A Study in Sociology* 5.00

W. J. H. Sprott, *Science and Social Action* ... 3.50

Chalmers Stacey and Manfred DeMartino, eds., *Counseling and Psychotherapy with the Mentally Retarded: A Book of Readings* ... 7.50

Alfred Stanton and Stewart Perry, eds., *Personality and Political Crisis* ... 3.75

George Stern, Morris Stein and Benjamin Bloom, *Methods in Personality Assessment* ... 6.00

Eric Strauss, *Sir William Petty: Portrait of a Genuis* ... 5.00

Leo Strauss, *On Tyranny* ... 2.50

Leo Strauss, *Persecution and the Art of Writing* ... 4.00

Adolf Sturmthal, *Unity and Diversity in European Labor* ... 3.75

Sol Tax and others, *Heritage of Conquest: The Ethnology of Middle America* ... 5.00

Dinko Tomasic, *The Impact of Russian Culture on Soviet Communism* ... 4.50

Ernst Troeltsch, *The Social Teachings of the Christian Churches*, 2 vols. ... OP

Jacob Viner, *International Economics* ... 5.00

Jacob Viner, *International Trade and Economic Development* ... 2.75

W. Allen Wallis and Harry V. Roberts, *Statistics: A New Approach* ... 6.00

Max Weber, *Ancient Judaism* ... 6.00

Max Weber, *General Economic History* ... 4.50

Max Weber, *The Methodology of the Social Sciences* ... 3.50

Max Weber, *The Religion of China* ... 4.50

Henry N. Wieman, *The Directive in History* ... 2.50

Harold Wilensky, *Intellectuals in Labor Unions* ... 6.00

W. M. Williams, *Gosforth: The Sociology of an English Village* ... 5.00

Martha Wolfenstein, *Children's Humor: A Psychological Analysis* ... 3.75

Martha Wolfenstein and Nathan Leites, *Movies: A Psychological Study* ... 4.00